LIBRARY OF RELIGIOUS BIOGRAPHY

Edited by Mark A. Noll, Nathan O. Hatch,
and Allen C. Guelzo

The LIBRARY OF RELIGIOUS BIOGRAPHY is a series of original biographies on important religious figures throughout American and British history.

The authors are well-known historians, each a recognized authority in the period of religious history in which his or her subject lived and worked. Grounded in solid research of both published and archival sources, these volumes link the lives of their subjects -- not always thought of as "religious" persons — to the broader cultural contexts and religious issues that surrounded them. Each volume includes a bibliographical essay and an index to serve the needs of students, teachers, and researchers.

Marked by careful scholarship yet free of footnotes and academic jargon, the books in this series are well-written narratives meant to be *read* and *enjoyed* as well as studied.

LIBRARY OF RELIGIOUS BIOGRAPHY

Her Heart Can See

The Life and Hymns of Fanny J. Crosby

Edith L. Blumhofer

William B. Eerdmans Publishing Company
Grand Rapids, Michigan / Cambridge, U.K.

Wm. B. Eerdmans Publishing Co.
255 Jefferson Ave. S.E., Grand Rapids, Michigan 49503 /
P.O. Box 163, Cambridge CB3 9PU U.K.

Printed in the United States of America

10 09 08 07 06 05   7 6 5 4 3 2 1

Library of Congress Cataloging-in-Publication Data

Blumhofer, Edith L.
    Her heart can see: the life and hymns of Fanny J. Crosby / Edith L. Blumhofer.
        p.   cm.   — (Library of religious biography)
    Includes bibliographical references and index.
    ISBN 0-8028-4253-4 (pbk.: alk. paper)
        1. Crosby, Fanny, 1820-1915.   2. Hymn writers — United States — Biography.
    3. Poets, American — 19th century — Biography.   4. Blind — United States —
    Biography.   5. Gospel music — History and criticism.   I. Title.   II. Series.

    BV330.C76B58   2005
    264'.23'092 — dc22
    [B]

                                              2005040487

www.eerdmans.com

Contents

Introduction

Frances Jane Crosby was born in Southeast, New York, 24 March 1820. She died in Bridgeport, Connecticut, 12 February 1915, ninety-four years, ten months, and nineteen days later. Her lifetime overlapped those of every president from John Adams to Dwight D. Eisenhower. During her life the country's population swelled from 5 million to 100 million, and the number of stars on the flag increased from twenty-three to forty-eight. In 1820 James Monroe sat in the White House; in 1915 Woodrow Wilson led a nation poised at the brink of World War I. In 1820 the population included millions of slaves, and the *Mayflower of Liberia* sailed from New York to return eighty-six blacks to Africa; in 1915 millions of recently arrived southern and eastern Europeans challenged Americans to adapt to greater religious and ethnic pluralism. The young Crosby rode about in horse-drawn carts. The year she died, railroads crisscrossed the United States and the Ford Motor Company produced its millionth automobile.

Sweeping cultural change, then, was the most constant reality in Crosby's life. For the most part, she looked forward rather than backward, embracing change as progress. She yearned in old age for a recovery of cultural reverence for the Bible, found distressing an apparent breakdown in the stable family life she thought befitted a God-fearing society, and retained an outmoded style of dress that became her trademark. Otherwise, Crosby cultivated young people and entered into their hopes with an avidity that endeared her to Christian Endeavor youth, YMCA men, and Epworth Leaguers as well as to Sunday school scholars around the country. Crosby manifested a sort of primal nineteenth-century evangelicalism that, until clarified in twentieth-century conflicts (intellectual and otherwise), was fluid, imprecise, and evocative — inchoate rather than rigid.

By any standard, Crosby deserves study. She produced thousands of hymns and thus left her mark on Protestant devotion. A contemporary newspaper tribute by Annie Willis observed of Crosby: "The writer of favorite hymns is one of the great powers that influence the world." Certainly her contemporaries deemed Crosby worthy of notice. Crosby's blindness and her involvement in New York State's pioneering efforts in blind education make her story part of the larger fabric of the Protestant-inspired benevolence that launched efforts to uplift the physically challenged. Crosby's adult embrace of Methodism and her affinity for the Holiness movement bound her to two of the era's vibrant populist religious movements and influenced her later views on church and society, while they also brought her into a circle of activist women intent on using organized benevolence to wield cultural influence. One such person was Margaret Bottome, founder in 1886 of the King's Daughters, a female service guild with "In His Name" as its motto; another was Crosby's wealthy benefactor, Phoebe Palmer Knapp. The ease with which Crosby rhymed text made natural her relationship to the burgeoning music publishing business that promoted music conventions, normal institutes, music education in public schools, and children's hymns for Sunday schools. This, in turn, put her in place for association with evangelist D. L. Moody and his songster, Ira D. Sankey. Meanwhile, her involvement with New York City's rescue missions manifested her concern for Christian outreach in a venue historically hospitable to women's voices. She shared a birth year with Susan B. Anthony and lived through a rising tide of feminist assertiveness. She responded to urban poverty by finding a niche in Manhattan's rescue missions. Crosby's life story, then, illuminates almost a century of Protestant New York. A white woman who traced her ancestry to the Plymouth and Massachusetts Bay colonies, Crosby came of an extended family that boasted some wealthy Manhattan businessmen and clergy. A "country cousin" of these Crosbys of means who inhabited her Manhattan world, she found in words the venue for the public usefulness the extended Crosby clan valued.

Music ran in the family. Jonathan Crosby, one of the extended clan, conducted singing schools for the early Mormons. Another, a contemporary of Fanny's named Thomas V. Crosby, published scores of popular songs. The most famous of the clan's musicians, crooner Bing Crosby, like Fanny a direct descendant of Simon Crosby's son Thomas, was one of the clan of seafaring Crosbys who forsook Cape Cod for pioneer life near Tacoma, Washington. Already in Fanny's childhood the North American branch of the family stretched from Canada to Georgia, while others had moved west. They had long since lost track of one another. The Puritan faith of their forebears had often yielded, through marriage, proximity to other options, or mobility, to other affiliations or none. Fanny Crosby knew only a handful of those who bore her name, though she followed from a distance the accomplishments of more of them.

Despite obvious reasons for learning about Fanny Crosby, writing her biography presents significant challenges. As a blind person, she did not leave the range of personal papers on which biographers usually depend. Most writing about her relies heavily on the autobiography she dictated late in life, *Memories of Eighty Years*, published in 1906. The Fine Arts Library of the New York Public Library at Lincoln Center holds a scrapbook with odds and ends her friends collected during her later years. The reminiscences of some of her cohorts amplify the narrative a bit, but the paucity of family resources precludes a full biography in any traditional sense. The lack of such materials has not discouraged a bevy of writers from marketing Crosby biographies strong on inspiration but light on interpretation and context. Only Bernard Ruffin, a Yale Divinity School–trained Lutheran pastor rather than a professional historian, offers something more (*Fanny Crosby*, 1979). One cluster of studies by hymnologists examines Crosby's story through a different lens. Within the limits presented by sources, they address an audience with more focused interests.

The chapters that follow respond to the state of the sources by drawing on the basic narrative of Crosby's life to explore aspects of Protestant New York in the nineteenth century — especially Protestant impulses, Sunday schools, rescue missions, revival, and music publishing. This text now becomes part of a Crosby literature riddled with contradiction over basic elements in her story. Some contradictions derive from reliance on oral tradition and the tendency to privilege as more accurate the incidents recalled by particular people. For example, the Putnam County Historian's Office (Crosby was born in what is now Putnam County, New York) has on file an accepted local rendering of Crosby's early history that disputes just when her family moved to New York. According to the local lore, her parents moved from Cape Cod and her grandparents, Sylvanus and Eunice Crosby, came to New York from Boston only after she became blind. Locals also place Crosby in Southeast for vacations long after her 1858 marriage to Alexander van Alstine. No documentation exists; in fact, proofs for another rendering abound. Yet this version of her beginnings persists, legitimated by its being endorsed in her hometown.

Other discrepancies result from subtle additions to the sources — inferring more than they say, or imposing on the past generalizations rooted in the present. As one author cites another, misrepresentations grow. A third source of confusion resides in the religious uses to which Crosby's life story — one might say, rather, the uses to which the myth of Crosby — has been put. Some inspirational authors find what they want to find and draw spiritual applications that go beyond the sources or use history to make a point.

Muddled details of Crosby's life began appearing as soon as she died. The two leading newspapers in her home city, Bridgeport, Connecticut, offered contradictory obituary narratives, and the author of the least-accurate tribute professed to have interviewed Crosby recently. It is little wonder, then, that renderings of her life differ. Building their sketches on such sources, borrowing heavily from one another, or relying entirely on Crosby's spotty episodic reminiscences published late in her life, some Crosby biographers have perpetuated false information. Part of the problem, then, is the state of the sources, and newspapers are not the only culprits. Memoirs of some of her cohorts, constructed, like Crosby's, late in life, may give approximate rather than accurate dates or places. In this regard, the opening lines of the *Reminiscences* of Crosby's famous contemporary Lyman Abbott are instructive: "These papers are reminiscences, not history," he warned. "They lay no claim to accuracy." Abbott probably did not need the disclaimer; those who did often failed to give it.

It is frustrating to search the many contemporary newspaper and magazine stories about Crosby only to discover that most repeat the same trite information. And they fail to address the most intriguing questions, in part because certain literary conventions governed the proprieties of interviewing and publishing. As a result, the researcher discovers little about the largely separate lives of Crosby and her husband, Alexander van Alstine. The Crosby presented by contemporary writers was inevitably cheerful, supremely confident, and sublimely unselfish. Relying on such accounts, later writers usually gushed over her as a "Protestant saint." She had no warts and pressed confidently through every problem. Getting behind such descriptions to discover the texture of her emotional and spiritual life is almost impossible. At best, one can surface occasional admissions of vulnerability or find hints in her poems of "dark nights of the soul."

Perpetuating the image of Crosby the cheerful saint, entrepreneurs maintain flourishing enterprises offering impersonations of her. For decades these have drawn audiences to large and small venues around the country. In 1977 the *Guinness Book of World Records* listed Crosby as history's most prolific hymnist. In 2003 Gateway Films released a new Crosby movie on video and DVD. One can purchase a Crosby collectible doll or view on the Web a gentle prize-winning llama named Fanny J. Crosby. She still fascinates the public, and the reason seems to reside in the combination of her prolific output, her blindness, and a carefully nurtured myth of her sanctity handed down through an array of inspirational biographies whose text becomes script for impersonators.

As a nineteenth-century woman, Crosby manifested unusual independence, the more striking because she was blind. Since conventional schooling was not an option, other women — especially her mother, grandmother, and Ridgefield, Connecticut, landlady — trained her mind to recall instructive texts like long passages of the Bible and the classics of English poetry. (She memorized by listening and repeating.) They stirred her imagination with books that increased her vocabulary and perception of a world she could not see. In short, they trained her to the best of their ability to be independent. Adept with her needle (she did intricate fancywork by learning the stitches and then counting) and alert to the practical knowledge that enabled day-to-day existence in and around the home, she was not spoiled or pampered because of her handicap. This training stood her in good stead when, at the age of fifteen, she left rural upstate New York for Manhattan and the New York Institution for the Blind. At an age when many young women married, then, Crosby began formal schooling. She conformed to the school's strict regimen, but she also expanded her skills, learning marketable crafts. Her remarkable memory and her winsomeness opened to her the opportunity to teach. From her youth, then, Crosby manifested independence, and her talent with words gave her opportunities to address formal audiences, governmental and other, always as a blind person, never as a woman. Her blindness served to excuse any infelicity and magnify any accomplishment. Life in Manhattan shaped her worldview, and she enjoyed relative independence navigating city streets, asking people for help along the way.

Crosby made no reference in her autobiographies to the Seneca Falls Convention or to the personalities associated with the women's rights movement. Aspects of her life, though, suggest certain sympathies with those who struggled to gain public recognition of the full humanity of women. In 1858 Crosby entered a marriage in which she and her spouse, Alexander van Alstine, apparently soon thereafter opted for utterly separate lives. She retained her maiden name (she said at his insistence), and for many years they had separate addresses. She was not with him during his last illness; others tended him. She provided no marker for his grave in a Queens, New York, cemetery. She is buried in Connecticut. These realities hint at marital circumstances that defy the image of family in Victorian America. Both Crosby and van Alstine had careers, another unusual circumstance at the time. Crosby's career included empowering congregations to express faith, entreating the lost to "come home," and teaching the basics of the nineteenth-century evangelical mix of God and country to the nation's youth. She spoke to large conventions and preached Sunday morning and weekday sermons with no sense of impropriety. Her blindness eased her way into some male spheres — the circle of hymn-tune writers at her New York publishers, for example. It made possible her close working relationships with married male tunesmiths.

The rescue mission circuit, on the other hand, easily promoted women's speech, and Crosby was often one of a handful of women exhorters well known among Manhattan's downtrodden. Her Methodist leanings brought her into a circle of influential outspoken and socially concerned women in the tradition of Phoebe Palmer, Phoebe Palmer Knapp, and Margaret Bottome. She shared the platform with the intractable Maggie van Cott, the first Methodist woman to achieve ordination (though the General Conference refused to seat her), and helped the holiness teacher Sarah Lankford Palmer however she could. Such women devoted their prodigious energies to a mix of religion and social action, and her contacts with them nurtured Crosby's awareness of social ills she could not see. These women also encouraged her to take opportunities for public speech. Crosby applauded such socially aware Protestant women, endorsed the many-faceted endeavors associated with Frances Willard and the Women's Christian Temperance Union, and in other ways manifested her solidarity with women who expressed their convictions in public and private venues. She spent her last years in the female world constructed by her sisters and their daughters in Bridgeport. For Crosby, home and family focused almost entirely on women while her poetry and hymn writing drew her into a predominantly masculine world.

There the sheer volume of Crosby's output apparently combined with her blindness to make her an exception to gender rules. We do not know how — or if — she wrestled with the realities that made feminists of some of her contemporaries, but we do know that she did not face all the obstacles to public expression that sometimes hampered women. Independent and self-assured, Crosby had been trained from childhood to be self-sufficient. Her blindness made her exceptional, in part by blurring boundaries in the gendered world of nineteenth-century northeastern Protestants.

While her opinions about the feminist agenda cannot be recovered, one can reconstruct her use of female experience in crafting some of her enduring hymns. Crosby often related what she called "incidents" of her hymns, and the "incident" that rehearsed the circumstances behind her famous hymn "Rescue the Perishing" offers a case in point. Crosby already had the general topic in mind, but an experience in a Manhattan rescue mission (ca. 1869) framed the text, and the text exudes her own gentle, motherly approach to errant people. Convinced that some "mother's boy" in attendance needed to commit his life to his mother's God, Crosby rose and offered to pray with anyone who had wandered from his mother's teaching. A young man approached her, prayed with her, and left her with the assurance, "Now I can meet my mother in heaven; for I have found her God." That night, with this experience in mind, Crosby composed the hymn. Her words often tended to privilege "mother's teaching," but her childhood as well as her gender may help account for that. Crosby's own upbringing came almost exclusively from women.

Feminist scholars have suggested as well that emphases in her hymns both revealed and accelerated the feminizing of American evangelicalism. Ann Douglas argued (in *The Feminization of American Culture*) that "nineteenth-century American women were oppressed and damaged" and that, therefore, "the influence they exerted . . . on their society was not altogether beneficial." Working from a myth of female powerlessness, Douglas and others have maintained that female authors emasculated American religion and participated unwittingly in a shift from rigorous Calvinism (with its privileging of strength and tenacity) to an anti-intellectual and sentimental mass culture that had profound negative impact on American religion. Crosby was one of a host of emerging female writers, and her lyrics often brim with sentiment and nostalgia. But gender offers an incomplete explanation: among other factors, audience and purpose must be taken into account. Sunday schools addressed juveniles, and nineteenth-century Sunday school hymns were part of an emerging mass culture aimed at children and shaped by the children's novels of Jacob Abbott as well as by Crosby's lyrics. Nostalgia and sentiment had a prominent place in gospel hymns because their purpose was, in part, to recall the erring to childhood faith. Sentimental discourse aimed at hearts and feelings rather than at minds, and its nineteenth-century American expressions relied heavily on eighteenth-century antecedents. "The idea that social benevolence had to come from the heart rather than the head," Mary Lenard maintains in *Preaching Pity*, was "a carry-over from the eighteenth-century 'cult of sensibility'" to which John and Charles Wesley were indebted. Continental Pietists, too, contributed to the religious discourse on the affections. Though by the end of the eighteenth century British literary critics had begun to identify the word "sentiment" with "indulgence in superficial emotions," such qualities of sentimentalism as sympathy and compassion empowered women to engage social and political issues and to promote social reform. These qualities also energized women for religious work of many kinds.

Drawing on Douglas's basic notions and noting especially Crosby's many references to the suffering and the nurturing Christ, June Hadden Hobbs argued that Crosby and others highlighted his feminine characteristics and that the submissive believer they idealized adopts a gendered position, too (see Hobbs's *"I Sing for I Cannot Be Silent"* [the title is a line from Crosby's "Redeemed, How I Love to Proclaim It"]). Such observations relate directly to only one chapter of my book — chapter 10, on Crosby and gospel hymns. Hobbs's interdisciplinary study of gospel hymnody maintains that female hymn writers of the late nineteenth century undermined male power by "centering religion in home rather than in church; locating God within themselves, separating intimacy from sexual submission, and emphasizing service over conquest." Women like Crosby introduced a nonlinear sense of time and used hymnody to create community, she argues, "undermining patriarchal religion" for at least fifty years so successfully that men embraced a feminized faith. Hobbs sets out to prove her assumptions rather than to derive conclusions from hymns, and so she uses hymns to prove rather than to construct her thesis. I am uneasy with her conclusions. It is easy to find in Crosby's thousands of texts those that justify preconceived ideas. It is much more difficult to analyze the corpus and derive from the texts generalizations supporting Hobbs that take into full account Crosby's lived religion and the popularity of the wider corpus of gospel hymns among men and women. One must recognize as well the constraints under which Crosby often produced. As often as not, she composed on demand to specifications that came from tune writers and assigned topics. It is also problematic to argue that late nineteenth-century Protestant women sought empowerment by strategizing a fundamental shift in meaningful Protestant metaphors. The particular imagery late nineteenth-century evangelicals found relevant was part of a larger community of discourse and must be understood within the broad cultural context and the social world that made gospel hymns an ongoing feature of the popular religious landscape. The hymns packed emotion and sentiment into simple tunes and text on the assumption — alive and well in American Protestantism at least since the eighteenth century — that stirred sentiment could be a powerful instrument for change. Right feelings would lead to right action and thus benefit the individual and society. Hobbs and others do not offer a methodology for demonstrating the power of "ordinary" women, nor do they move beyond disparaging the influence of sentimentalist discourse in American Protestantism.

The most helpful study for situating Crosby's hymns in the social context of post–Civil War revivals remains Sandra Sizer Frankiel's *Gospel Hymns and Social Religion* (1979). A revision of Sizer's University of Chicago doctoral dissertation, the book examines the place of sentiment and emotion in gospel hymns and explores the "community of feeling" that gospel hymns structured. Sizer's concern is much broader than Crosby, and Crosby's texts do not uniformly support Sizer's observations, but the questions Sizer asks of the gospel hymns illuminate how such texts might be used to examine broader questions about American religion. Some of Sizer's work informs my chapter 10 on Crosby's evangelical message. Crosby's proclivity for holiness language and experience, however, sets her apart in important ways from Sizer's work. Crosby's story suggests the wide appeal of such language in evangelical imaginings of spirituality, if not in formal evangelical theology.

Crosby's long life is important for more than the hymns she composed. She honed her abilities during her late teens as a student at the pioneering New York Institution for the Blind. She knew the city's first supporters of this cause, and her story offers glimpses of how such education proceeded. She stayed at the Institution until she had passed her thirty-eighth birthday, moving from pupil to teacher and publishing several collections of prose and poetry as fund-raisers for the school. Her compositions and frequent public recitations, presented as proof that the blind could learn and excel, gave her name recognition. The philanthropic culture that nurtured the Institution, meanwhile, brought her access to some of the era's best-known people — Hamilton Murray, Anson Phelps, Henry Clay, Winfield Scott, James Polk, Jenny Lind.

The Institution became as well Crosby's connection to the world of music. Its music department secured distinguished vocal and instrumental instructors, and Crosby took advantage of their presence by learning to play the piano, organ, harp, and guitar. Her way with words drew the attention of the voice master, George F. Root, a young and rising protégé of Boston music educator Lowell Mason. Root invited Crosby to provide text for his tunes for popular music, singing school collections, normal musical institutes, and other venues. These cantatas and songs carried her words to the expanding national market that nurtured music education. Root's musical world included as well Peter Stryker, the Dutch Reformed pastor who introduced Crosby to William Bradbury, another Mason protégé, and W. C. Van Meter, the man through whom she met her frequent collaborator, William Doane. Dense overlapping northeastern Protestant networks reached into the Institution for the Blind and set the stage for Crosby's life beyond its halls.

The Institution also became Crosby's entry point for a wide exposure to northeastern Protestantism. An array of pastors from different denominations supplied the Institution's chapel, but Crosby visited local churches, too. Her first sustained exposure to the Methodism she later embraced came when she agreed to play the piano for a weekly class meeting at the Institution. In such small venues she polished her ability to speak of her religious experiences and bare her soul before others. This practice stood her in good stead when fifteen years later she first tried her hand at gospel hymns destined to shape much larger "communities of feeling." Crosby's religious world included as well her participation in Manhattan's annual May Anniversary Week when Protestants assembled to consider the progress of the voluntary associations central to their hopes for a Christian America. On behalf of the Institution, Crosby stood annually before assembled thousands to recite original compositions.

If the Institution stretched her intellectual and spiritual prowess, it also expanded her social horizons, allowing interaction with a wide variety of people as well as travel to then-faraway places like Toronto and Washington, D.C. In its confines, too, she came to know — first as pupil, then as colleague — Alexander van Alstine, the man she married in 1858 when she was thirty-eight and he was just twenty-seven.

The Institution for the Blind molded Crosby's initial adult religious and social experience of New York, expanding her exposure to some of the people whose abilities and ideas made them icons of the day. From her marriage in 1858 forward, she extended her commitment in some of the networks to which she had been exposed at the Institution. William Bradbury and others greatly expanded but also narrowed her opportunities in hymn composition. Instead of writing for the broader world of normal institutes, music conventions, and popular culture, after 1864 she directed her attention to clusters of activities around Protestant churches — Sunday schools, revivals, youth movements, temperance activities, rescue missions, YMCA. Instead of experimenting widely with many churches, she now based herself formally in one denomination, although she was still an occasional visitor at Brooklyn and Manhattan churches of different communions. Instead of delivering annual original compositions on behalf of education for the blind, she now stood before assembled thousands to recite hymns and their "incidents," interspersed with personal testimony and exhortation. The Institution for the Blind had provided formal and informal preparation for her first career as a teacher and poet. By introducing her into the overlapping networks that shaped, served, and profited from popular evangelicalism, the Institution eased her into her second career in evangelical hymnody. No other scholar in the Institution's history even approached the fame that followed.

Crosby herself thought she had two careers. In one sense, one can argue that, despite her age, she did not really grow up until she left the Institution. She manifested restlessness there and could not feel settled about her life. She wanted to be married, a desire she uttered forthrightly in her poetry: her marriage in 1858 was, then, a watershed. Before it her life revolved around the Institution; after 1858 her life played out on the ever-larger stage of evangelical Protestantism. Late in life she seemed to devalue the work she did before her marriage, claiming that she only found her vocation when she associated in 1864 with Bradbury to write hymns. Perhaps her marriage offers an instructive insight. After marriage — even one that clearly failed to measure up to her earlier romantic yearnings — she had no option but to keep busy and go on. Past forty, she no longer lived in the artificial environment of a juvenile institution where all her needs were provided. School was over, and the responsibilities of her adult world offered no other viable release from restlessness than focused work. Divorce was beyond imagination; loneliness was not.

Since Crosby reveled in belonging everywhere and to everyone, I concluded early that I would never be able to retrace all her steps or read every local newspaper article that described her public addresses. She crossed paths with so many people, and so many wanted to share their impressions, that one keeps discovering more mentions of her name. These tend, however, to offer "more of the same" rather than new insights, and I am satisfied that what follows is full enough to assess her life fairly.

A note about the spelling of her name is in order. In 1858 Crosby married Alexander van Alstine. I have followed this spelling, the rendering of the name the van Alstine family historian prefers. Some of the family opted for Alstyne, while on other occasions the same people may be listed under Alstein or Alsteine. One finds Crosby and Van, as she called him, making use of all the above spellings — or at least being introduced at different times under each.

Unattributed text at the head of the following chapters is by Crosby.

I am indebted to many libraries, local church historians, pastors, town and county historians, and archivists for assistance with sources. Especially the staffs of the New York Historical Society; the New York State Library (Albany); the Putnam County, New York, Historian's Office; the Regenstein Library of the University of Chicago; the American Baptist History Center at Colgate Rochester Divinity School; David Himrod, retired expert on the Methodist Collection at Garrett-Evangelical Divinity School; the Music Division of the Fine Arts Library of the New York Public Library; the Brooklyn Historical Society; the Newberry Library (Chicago); Moody Bible Institute; the Billy Graham Center Archives; and Wheaton College gave invaluable guidance and access to resources. Graduate students at the University of Chicago and Wheaton College helped immeasurably along the way — Elizabeth Alvarez, Jonathan Ebel, Paula Gallito, Jeremy Cunningham, Blake Killingsworth. Two assistants — Mary Noll Venables at the Public Religion Project (University of Chicago) and Katri Delac at the Public Religion Project and, later, at the Institute for the Study of American Evangelicals (ISAE, Wheaton College) — provided office and research support. Despite her undergraduate concentration in other areas, Katri Delac manifests a flair for historical research that has helped me immensely and made her an invaluable associate in my work.

In the course of my research, the ISAE received a generous grant from the Lilly Endowment, Inc., to support a three-year study of the history of American hymnody and its relationship to the larger landscape of American Christianity. I am grateful for the support the grant provided for my work on Fanny Crosby and for the impetus the grant offered for networking through the ISAE with others interested in what studies of hymnody can teach us about American religious history. Mark Noll (McManis Professor of Christian Thought at Wheaton

College) and Stephen Marini (Professor of Religion, Wellesley College) shared with me responsibility for overseeing the grant and editing the books it produced. Their work on hymnody and evangelicalism encouraged and improved mine. Grant Wacker and Mark Noll read my manuscript-in-progress, and it is stronger as a result.

Of the many people Lilly Endowment funding brought together, one — Mary Louise Van Dyke — stands out especially for her knowledge, generosity, and eagerness to assist with anything related to hymnody. Tucked away in the stacks of the Oberlin College library is a small office overflowing with hymnals in which Mary Louise Van Dyke works on the enormous hymn database project of the Hymn Society of the United States and Canada. I am grateful to her for access to the database, for sharing her wealth of knowledge, and for her generous spirit.

Preparing this book demanded flexibility from my family. Time spent in research and writing is time apart from other responsibilities, and the cooperation of my husband, Edwin, sons Jonathan and Christopher, and daughter, Judy, helped us all not only survive but thrive.

I grew up in a music-loving family of Swiss-German heritage and in a nondenominational German-speaking church. I cannot recall a time when I did not know Fanny Crosby's name, nor do I remember when I did not know a Crosby hymn or two. It was not that the church was especially devoted to Crosby texts; rather, our Sunday morning services were in German, and we sang many staples of Lutheran and Pietist hymnody. But Crosby supplemented this legacy. In the 1890s Walter Rauschenbusch, the German Baptist prophet of the Social Gospel, coordinated the translation of Ira Sankey's gospel hymns, including Crosby texts, into German. Crosby entered my awareness many years before it occurred to me to inquire into her larger significance in the evangelical story.

My early memories came flooding back in the summer of 2001 when I walked onto the Hamanskraal campus of the University of Pretoria, South Africa, just in time to hear the chorus of a familiar gospel hymn sounding from the chapel. The hardy souls gathered for devotions before a rigorous academic program came from all parts of the globe and represented many native tongues. As I stood outside and listened, it was immediately apparent from the enthusiastic singing that "Blessed Assurance" was part of their common language. Like several other hymns provided in multiple languages for use by the assembled historians of world Christianity, the words came from the pen of Fanny Crosby.

A few weeks later in a Hallmark store in Wheaton, Illinois, I noticed a Precious Moments figurine called "Safe in the Arms of Jesus," a reference to another Crosby favorite. A few weeks after that, a friend invited me to her church to watch a Crosby impersonator, and my father wrote from Germany about a traveling German quartet whose entire repertoire was Fanny Crosby. Clearly this diminutive woman still has appeal. The following pages explore why.

Many of my childhood memories cluster around music making at home and in church with members of my family. No family gathering was complete without hymn singing, and so it seems appropriate to dedicate this story of one of the American makers of sacred song to my parents, Edwin and Edith Waldvogel, whose lives rendered a song of faith as lovely as the hymns they sang with all their hearts.

Her heart can see, her heart can see!
Well may she sing so joyously!
For the King Himself, in His tender grace,
Hath shown her the brightness of His face.

Frances Ridley Havergal (1872)

1 Family (1635-1835)

My forefathers were America in the making. . . .
Every drop of blood in me holds a heritage of patriotism!
I am proud of my past. I am an American!

Elias Lieberman

My ancestors were Puritans; my family tree rooted around
Plymouth Rock; all my predecessors of lineage died at a good
old age.

Fanny Crosby, 1903

Sixty miles north of New York City, the Croton River and its tributaries
water the rugged hills of a narrow strip of land in eastern Putnam
County, near the Connecticut border. Here Frances Jane Crosby,
"America's sweet singer in Israel," was born 24 March 1820 in a small
clapboard house built in 1758 and standing just back from Foggintown
Road. Locals called the winding street "the sequestered valley road,"
suggesting the tall trees, thick underbrush, and stone fences that the
occasional passerby noticed more readily than the handful of homes

1

that dotted the way. The road traversed a section of Southeast, New York, a designation that denoted a township rather than a village.

The only child of John and Mercy Crosby, Fanny Crosby was born into a humble home crowded with extended family. They boasted few worldly goods, but they cherished a rich family lore. The adult Crosby liked nothing more than an excuse to recite her "granite stock" pedigree. Animated by nostalgic pride in her forebears and uncomplicated devotion to liberty and democracy, she carried a small American flag wherever she went. She boasted a family line that valued the "stuff" of fabled Yankee pride — independence, sobriety, thrift, morality, hard work, public service, family loyalty, unashamed patriotism, and above all, devotion to duty. To her, words like "English" and "Protestant" described not only her lineage but also — she hoped — a certain essence of character. The Crosby family saga shaped Fanny Crosby's sense of self and country. It also offers glimpses into the lives of some of the nameless people whose choices have woven the fabric of the American dream.

OLD AND NEW ENGLAND

As Fanny Crosby told it, the family saga began in Great Britain, where at least eight ancient sites bear the Crosby name. Crosby means "town of the cross," and the first occurrence of Crosby as a family name is probably a reference found in 1204, the sixth year of the reign of the ill-fated King John of Magna Carta fame. In those days a Crosby was constable in Tickhill in Yorkshire, near the border with Nottinghamshire. Over the years the family name described a handful of distinguished sons among a long roster of ordinary citizens. In 1466 one John Crosby, a wealthy London merchant, built Crosby Hall on Bishop's Gate Street in London (later the residence of Richard III and referenced in Shakespeare's play; Thomas More lived in the house for seven years, and there he wrote his *Utopia*). During the reign of Henry VIII, a Richard Crosby collected rent at the Monastery of St. John in Yorkshire. Records list Julianus Crosby as rector of Leke in Nottinghamshire; Edmundus Crosby as cantor of St. John's, Doncaster; John Crosby as presbyter and cantor in Lincoln cathedral, on the royal payroll. One branch of the family moved to Ireland, but Fanny Crosby's story zooms in on the Yorkshire Crosbys, specifically on those who lived in Holme-on-Spalding Moor near the shire's southwest boundary. From All Saints, the ancient parish church atop a small oval-shaped hill, on a clear day one could glimpse the spires of York Cathedral fifteen miles to the northwest.

In Yorkshire, then, the New World Crosby story begins, most directly with Simon and Ann Brigham Crosby, a young couple beckoned by "far away places . . . far away over the sea" (as their descendant Bing Crosby put it) most likely because they felt driven from home. In the seventeenth century Holme-on-Spalding Moor was a hotbed of Puritanism. Sir William Constable, lord of the manor and estate, would march in the 1640s with Oliver Cromwell and sit as a Commissioner of the High Court that tried Charles I. Constable signed the king's death warrant. By then, financial pressures had forced him to sell parts of the manor of Holme. Simon and Ann Crosby came of age on former manor lands, part of two extended families of landowning yeomanry in the sparsely populated parish where agriculture and grazing provided much of the livelihood. Married in April 1634, Simon and Ann sailed from London in spring 1635 for Massachusetts Bay with their infant son, Thomas. Ann's older brother, Thomas, traveled with them. Simon had with him his share of his father's substantial estate.

The *Susan and Ellen,* a ship that regularly traveled between New and Old England, brought the Crosbys to Boston harbor in the summer of 1635 with a shipload of other hardy souls, most under forty and eager to help carve a holy experiment in the wilderness of North America. Among their shipmates were the saintly Peter Bulkeley and his family, soon to take up residence in the parsonage at Concord. The men of the ship's company carried certificates assuring that they were not "subsidy men" and that they were "conformable to the order and discipline of the Church of England." A bevy of new settlers arrived in 1635, so the Crosbys had many cohorts also settling in. (In the spring, six ships docked in six weeks; by the end of 1635 nineteen passenger ships from London had swelled the colony's population. The *Susan and Ellen* alone made three voyages from London to Boston in 1635.)

Simon's father, Thomas (then aged sixty-five), followed Simon and Ann to New England a few years later with his wife, Jane Sotheron Crosby, and Anthony, the young orphaned son of Simon's brother William. This Thomas's eldest son, another Thomas (Simon's brother), remained in England on the extensive family holdings. The younger Thomas's two daughters married into families of the "armorial landed gentry," and the line continued, though the Crosby name died out at Holme-on-Spalding Moor.

English Puritans had planted Boston in 1630, and by 1635 several thousand English settlers had come through the port. The Crosbys were typical of the larger lot. They came with resources and with staunch religious convictions. The vast majority stayed in New England, many in Boston, the growing hub of this Puritan commonwealth. The Crosbys opted to cross the Charles River and put down their roots in Cambridge (then Newtown), where another new arrival with Yorkshire ties, the saintly pastor Thomas Shepard, would soon take up residence and safeguard proper Puritan practice in church and civic affairs. Thomas and Jane Crosby, noted in one record as "owld Crosby," first joined Simon and Ann in Cambridge. They later moved on to Rowley on Boston's north shore to sit under the preaching of another onetime Yorkshire divine, the Reverend Ezekiel Rogers.

Both Rogers and Shepard had won the Crosbys' loyalty in Old England. Fired by the fervent faith of these giants of the Puritan pulpit, the first American Crosbys were, from the start, part of a community defined by religious convictions and molded by common experiences in the turmoil of Stuart England. Rogers had preached twelve miles to the southeast of Holme-on-Spalding Moor. Shepard preached in 1631 and 1632 at Buttercrambe, twelve miles to the northwest, and apparently brought Simon Crosby to a decisive religious commitment. The two were close in age, and under Shepard's tutelage Simon embraced the strong convictions that animated Puritan pilgrims. The party of settlers Simon and Ann joined comprised some of Shepard's following from his contacts in Essex, Yorkshire, and Northumberland. Their common experiences in Old England and their devotion to Shepard provided the foundation for their lives in Massachusetts Bay.

The Crosbys disembarked at Boston at a particularly tumultuous moment in the colony's brief history. The popular minister in Newtown (Cambridge), the Reverend Thomas Hooker, was actively planning to leave the Massachusetts Bay Colony to plant a settlement in Connecticut. Much of the congregation of the town's First Church signaled their decision to go with him, creating an opportunity unusual in so new a colony: developed houses and land for sale. These were ideal — if still somewhat crude — properties, for Hooker's followers had roofed their homes with slate or shingle instead of thatch and had conformed to a uniform plan by setting all homes six feet back from the streets. In 1633 one William Wood praised the town as "one of the neatest and best compacted Towns in New England, having many faire structures, with many handsome contrived streets." Neatness and prosperity befitted the town that Governor John Winthrop hoped would be the capital of Massachusetts Bay. In 1635 the town register listed some sixty families. In 1636 the town paid the largest tax of any Massachusetts Bay town, manifesting its relative wealth and population (a standing it soon lost as outlying regions attracted new arrivals).

After first trying to dissuade those planning to depart, magistrates grudgingly authorized the Hooker party's exodus. Town records reveal that only eleven families of Newtown's earliest settlers stayed; most of the rest followed Hooker. Thanks to the pace of arrivals in 1635, though, the small community stood to replenish its population without missing a beat. Abandoned houses and properties would not be empty long. And a new pastor whose popularity in both Englands rivaled Hooker's considerable fame, Thomas Shepard, stood in the wings with a following of his own to reconstitute a covenanted community at the heart of this Puritan settlement.

In 1635 the colony's chief architect, John Winthrop, still envisioned Massachusetts Bay as "a city on a hill." If, as Winthrop fondly hoped, "the eyes of the world" had happened to glance toward New England in 1635, however, they would have looked on a troubled scene. Implementing "a due form of government civil and ecclesiastical" within the legal parameters of the colony's corporate charter provoked unexpected discord in civil and religious affairs. Between 1634 and 1636, the colony's General Court elected three different men to the governor's office. The turnover reflected in part unhappiness with the colony's civil mastermind — Winthrop himself. Religious unrest complicated civil discontent, and the survival of this Puritan experiment seemed jeopardized on several fronts. Indian raids, internal disagreements, and English ecclesial designs boded ill for God's outpost in New England.

Religious unrest centered around two figures whose names live on in American lore: Roger Williams and Anne Hutchinson. Williams, later celebrated as the champion of religious liberty and founder of Rhode Island, stubbornly and publicly differed with Winthrop's most basic views and openly criticized the particular blend of the civil and religious that was emerging as the New England Way. He rejected the Bay Colony's church order and denied the validity of the colonial charter. Convinced that magistrates had no right to enforce laws that governed one's relationship to God, Williams would neither conform to the religious and legal blend required by the colony's General Court nor embrace the colony's official stance toward the Church of England. At length, his persistent willfulness "provoked the Lord to move the Court" to banish Williams, a man with many friends on Boston's north shore. The Crosbys arrived toward the end of this protracted unhappiness.

The devout had no time for a sigh of relief, since as Williams left, new problems mounted, this time centered in the claims of Mistress Anne Hutchinson. She had arrived in 1634 and soon opened her home for prayer meetings and sermon discussions. Before long she bristled under the reigning assumption that moral uprightness suggested spiritual health. Believing that the Holy Spirit "illumined the hearts" of true believers, she accused colonial leaders of being under a "covenant of works" rather than a "covenant of grace." In effect, she challenged the carefully nuanced framework on which the fabric of colonial life rested. If direct action by the Holy Spirit on the hearts of the devout could supersede the written law of Scripture, how could the colony guard itself against anarchy? Known as antinomians or familists, Hutchinson's followers seriously divided the churches of the Massachusetts Bay Colony. Young arrivals and merchantmen as well as a handful of disenchanted Puritan stalwarts rallied to support Hutchinson in her mounting disagreement with entrenched leadership. In 1636 a young Hutchinson admirer, Henry Vane (like the Crosbys, a 1635 arrival), won election to the governor's office. Only by careful maneuvering and the narrowest of margins did John Winthrop regain office in 1637. With office came the opportunity to dismantle Hutchinson's power base. It took Winthrop until 1638 to manage her banishment from the colony.

If the New World setting to which they came offered little immediate tranquillity, the England Simon and Ann Crosby left was in the throes of even more fundamental upheaval. At the ruthless hand of

Archbishop William Laud, English Puritans suffered sustained persecution. Intent on purging the Puritan virus from the Anglican Church,
Laud initiated a vigorous reform movement that frustrated Puritans at
every turn. Statistics manifested Laud's effectiveness. When Charles I
appointed Laud archbishop of Canterbury in 1633, 700 Puritans (double the number that had migrated in each of the preceding two years)
promptly left for the New World. Some of the Massachusetts Bay Colony's leading lights — Thomas Shepard, John Cotton, Thomas Hooker,
Richard Mather — were "harried from the land" by Laud. Pressures at
this time on the Puritans in the vicinity of Holme-on-Spalding Moor
likely contributed to the Crosbys' decision to leave.

Laud did not let these émigrés go in peace. Instead, he hoped to
dismantle the Massachusetts Bay Colony by calling in its charter. But
the wily Puritans had taken their charter with them, and in the end
Laud had no real power over them. Nonetheless, threatening rumbles
echoed across the Atlantic from Old to New England. The structure
through which Laud schemed was known as the Commission for Reg-
ulating Plantations, created by King Charles I in 1634, and headed by
Laud. Massachusetts Bay leaders responded by agonizing over the
sins that had brought this evident divine wrath upon them, openly re-
nouncing such finery as beaver hats and lace and prohibiting the public use of tobacco. And the government called the colonists to a day of
fasting, repentance, and prayer.

Winthrop absolutely refused to relinquish the colonial charter,
and his cohorts talked boldly of armed resistance — or at least resolute
civil disobedience — if the mother country threatened their shores
with either royal governor or soldiers. In the end, Puritans in England
left the king and Laud little time or taste for the Puritans in Massachusetts Bay. Laud's schemes against the colony failed, even as new colonists poured in — some three thousand in 1638 alone. And so the tu-
mult of the 1630s passed, and Massachusetts Bay survived with
Winthrop, for the moment, at its helm.

Against this backdrop, Simon and Ann Crosby purchased several parcels of land and acquired from one William Spencer a three-
acre homestead with a house and cultivated garden in the part of
Newtown known as Westend. (Fanny Crosby liked to boast that Harvard College was built on some of the acres once owned by Simon.
Over time an embellished rendering made Simon "one the founders of

Harvard College." Some of his land did pass indirectly in 1707 to the Reverend William Brattle, and Harvard's Brattle House now stands on it, close to the site on which Simon's house once stood.) The Crosbys had arrived with cash and the ability to access what meager comforts the fledgling colony afforded. Simon Crosby and Thomas Shepard became freemen on the same day — 3 March 1636 — and later that year Simon was one of seven residents selected "to order the towne Affayres for this yeare following." The freeman's oath bound him to submit to the colony's rulers and laws and to "advance the peace and welfare" of Massachusetts Bay. In the next few years he added to his landholdings and served a term as surveyor of highways.

Early in 1636 (after the first part of Hooker's group had left for Connecticut but before the majority did), Shepard sought permission to gather a congregation in Newtown to replace the one being dissolved. John Winthrop's *Journal* records that a large crowd assembled on the appointed day (the date was 1 February 1635, rendered in the seventeenth century — when New Year's Day was celebrated on 25 March — as 1 February 1635-1636), and a small group among them "made confession of their faith and declared what work of grace the Lord had wrought in them." These next assented "in a solemn and orderly manner" to the church covenant and heard addresses from Shepard and John Cotton. Many of the new settlers in Cambridge, the Crosbys among them, were Shepard partisans, as devoted as ever any of Hooker's following had been. Sometimes described as "Mr. Shepard's party," they were amenable to his leadership and eager for his preaching. Certainly Simon and Ann Crosby were among the early members of his congregation. As members they testified to evidence of God's work in their souls, attended the meetinghouse at the corner of Mt. Auburn and Dunster Streets, and voted on church matters, partook of communion, and presented their children for baptism. In Newtown the Crosbys had two more sons — Simon, born in August 1637, and Joseph, born in February 1639.

As the young family grew, so did the town. Plans to establish a college nearby accelerated in 1636. Shepard boasted much later that Newtown became the site for Harvard College because he had successfully excluded Anne Hutchinson's insidious views. (As Cotton Mather put it, the vigilant Shepard had preserved his flock from "the *Rot* of these Opinions.") Shepard's enduring reputation as New England's "most powerful evangelical preacher" apparently justified the confidence colonial leaders placed in his potential to influence Harvard College men and, through them, the posterity about whom the Bay Colony's founders worried. Situating Harvard in Shepard's parish perhaps compensated as well for abandoning the idea of Newtown as the fortified colonial capital. And, as Harvard historian Samuel Eliot Morison noticed, it was also a likely attempt to "stop the leake to Connecticut" that so drastically diminished the town's population in June 1636. Newtown, with the Charles River meandering nearby, stirred colonial founders' memories of bygone days in the English university town of Cambridge, and so on 2 May 1638 the legislature ordered: "Newtown shall henceforward be called Cambridge."

Beyond the troubles of the moment, then, a brightening future beckoned. Prospects dimmed for the Crosbys, however, when Simon died at the age of thirty-one in September 1639. After his death his parents and his young nephew left Cambridge for Rowley, a place to which the preaching of Ezekiel Rogers drew them. In Rowley was another Crosby family headed by Constance, sister of Ann Crosby and young widow of Robert Crosby of Holme-on-Spalding Moor. Constance and her three daughters had come with the party that accompanied Rogers in the fall of 1638. The Rowley branch of the family was prosperous and devoutly Puritan. (Eventually all of Ann's siblings — Constance, Jane, Mary, and Hannah — migrated from Holme-on-Spalding Moor to Rowley.)

In 1645 Ann married the widowed Rev. William Tompson, since 1639 the "learned, solid, sound Divine" who had replaced John Wheelwright, Anne Hutchinson's banished brother-in-law, as pastor of the church at Braintree (now Quincy). Tompson, a native of Lancashire and graduate of Oxford, had been a noted Puritan preacher in England. After a brief stint as a missionary from Massachusetts to Virginia (some Virginia settlers had requested Puritan preachers), Tompson settled for the rest of his life in Braintree, south of Boston, where his sprawling parish encompassed present-day Braintree, Quincy, Randolph, and Holbrook. With Tompson's consent, Ann settled Simon's estate, dividing most of his property (reckoned at more than 450 pounds) among their sons. The marriage made Tompson the head of a blended family numbering seven sons and two daughters until the birth of Hannah in 1648 added another. Tompson died in 1666 following a long bout with depression: "He fell into the bath of the devil, a black melancholy," recorded Cotton Mather, but at length the devil fled and "the end of that man was peace." Ann died in October 1675 at the age of sixty-eight.

In the late 1640s Tompson prepared two sons of this Braintree household — Thomas Crosby and William Tompson — for Harvard. They graduated in the class of 1653 (along with Thomas Shepard, son of the Cambridge pastor) with a B.A. earned in three years of study. When Second Church in Boston called John Mayo, pastor at Eastham in Cape Cod, to its pulpit in 1655, the Eastham church chose Thomas Crosby to succeed him, charging him "to conduct public service on Lord's days" at a salary of fifty pounds per year. His ministry in Eastham continued until 1670, apparently without his ever becoming ordained. Eastham, settled in 1644 by Pilgrims dissatisfied with their land grants in the Plymouth Colony, dominated a narrow strip of land dotted with marshes, ponds, bogs, and forest. The Atlantic Ocean stretched unbroken to the east, and on the west was Cape Cod Bay. Not surprisingly, whaling, fishing, and saltworks rather than agriculture fueled the growth of this picturesque town. Here Thomas and his wife, Sarah, raised a family. Five of their twelve children died in infancy, but the surviving seven flourished on Cape Cod. Records testify that Thomas found other sources of income to supplement his preaching. His residence was listed among the places where one might procure liquor, powder, and shot.

In 1670, for unknown reasons, Thomas relinquished the pulpit for the life of a merchant in Harwich (in a section of Cape Cod that is now Brewster), an unincorporated hub for Cape Cod fishing and farming. After the town's incorporation in 1694, he took his place among those who covenanted to form a church. He died in 1702 while in Boston on business. That year also saw the publication of his book *The Work of a Christian: An Important Case of Practical Religion; or, Directions how to make religion ones business.* Thomas Crosby's son and namesake, also an active layman, became a Harwich deacon. All of the elder Thomas's descendants eventually forsook Eastham to pursue better prospects in Harwich or Yarmouth. His "posterity on the Cape was both numerous and respectable," a local chronicler assured.

Simon and Ann's second son, Simon, settled north and west of Cambridge in Billerica, where he and his wife, Rachel Brackett, kept the first inn. A three-term representative to the General Court, he died in 1725. The youngest Crosby, Joseph, also filled a term as representative and helped to lay out 6,000 acres of local land in 1673. He and his wife, Sarah Brackett (sister to his brother Simon's wife), raised a family in Braintree, where Joseph died in 1695.

This first American generation of Crosbys established three separate branches of the Crosby family (while a fourth derived from their cousin Anthony Crosby, a physician in Rowley who inherited his grandfather Thomas's full estate in Old and New England, and a fifth from their widowed aunt, Constance) and manifested several enduring family traits. They cherished community, civil, religious, and social; they engaged in public service; they identified prominently with the church, having been steeped from childhood in the New England Way by several of its most revered advocates — Thomas Shepard, William Tompson, and Ezekiel Rogers. They scattered beyond Boston's immediate environs, though they apparently did not stray far from its Puritan values. On Cape Cod Thomas's descendants intermarried with at least two families of the famous 1620 Pilgrims, that of the colony's longtime leader, Elder William Brewster, and that of its three-time governor, Edward Winslow. These connections later allowed Fanny Crosby — to whom such things mattered deeply — the delight of membership in the exclusive circle of the Daughters of the Mayflower.

NEW YORK

In the eighteenth century some of Thomas Crosby's seafaring grandchildren ventured ever farther from the Cape Cod shores. They purchased trading vessels and engaged in a widening circle of enterprises that took them in the next century to China. (Some of these Crosby merchants — crooner Bing Crosby's forebears among them — eventually helped establish settlements in the state of Washington, a more convenient location from which to exploit the Oriental trade.)

Still others of the Crosby clan preferred to depend on the land and looked westward for new opportunities. Members of the family, led by several of Thomas's grandsons (among them four with the biblical names favored by the family — Thomas, David, Joshua, and

Eleazar), made their way in the mid–eighteenth century from Cape Cod across southern Connecticut and over the hilly border country into Dutchess (now Putnam) County, then a remote corner of upstate New York. Soon Crosbys could be found in all the old settlements just west of what is now Danbury, Connecticut, and, for good measure, some farmed the land between. Along with others they knew from Cape Cod, they settled mainly on a long two-mile-wide tract of land known as the Oblong that ran along the border with Connecticut (which had ceded the land to New York in 1731). In 1788 New York divided its counties into towns. Town boundaries, settled in 1795, created Southeast by combining the southern half of the Oblong with another area known as Frederickstown. Here one branch of this transplanted Crosby clan thrived. Thomas's grandsons fathered large families. The Crosbys were remembered locally as early and principal settlers who showed public spirit and religious devotion.

Crosby lore assigns to the family a variety of patriotic exploits during the Revolutionary War. When General Warren fell at Bunker Hill, Crosbys insisted that a Crosby picked up the flag that fell from his hands. Even more thrilling was the tale of Enoch Crosby, born in 1750 in Harwich on Cape Cod, a great-grandson of the Thomas Crosby who had first moved the family there. Part of the Crosby clan that trekked west to New York in the 1740s, Enoch volunteered in 1775 to serve in the Continental Army. While en route to join the troops at White Plains, New York, he learned of a Tory design against the patriots. He passed his information to John Jay, who gave him troops and sent him to foil the plot. Jay then enlisted him as a spy, and Putnam County preserves the records of his service in the form of his deposition to qualify for a veteran's pension. The Crosby clan venerated Enoch as the prototype for Harvey Birch, the protagonist in James Fenimore Cooper's famous novel *The Spy,* a book about the Revolutionary War years in the so-called Neutral Ground of New York's Westchester and Dutchess Counties. In the nineteenth century the merits of the claim fueled sharp debates among literary critics, but in the New York counties that border on Connecticut Enoch Crosby loomed larger than life. (It did not hurt that Phineas T. Barnum devoted his considerable promotional skills to assuring Enoch's place in history.)

Fanny Crosby undoubtedly took less pride in another part of the Crosby clan. Some of her Cape Cod forebears forsook Massachusetts in the 1770s because their Loyalist sympathies made the colony an inhospitable place. They established a branch of Simon Crosby's family in Nova Scotia. Although their stance distanced them from the Yankee fervor of their cousins in New York, their choice accents Fanny's story as a fundamentally American saga. Revolutionary loyalties divided many New England families, while painful choices scattered colonial clans and helped build Canada.

Fanny was a great-granddaughter of this American Revolutionary generation of Crosbys. Pride in her neighbors' and her family's contributions to the war effort animated the patriotism that nurtured her all her life. Her great-grandfather, Isaac Crosby (son of the Joshua who moved from Cape Cod to Southeast), fought in the Revolution. He and his wife, Elizabeth, had nineteen children. Their son Sylvanus married Eunice Paddock, whose family farmed six miles away in North Salem, Westchester County. The couple had five sons and daughters: Mercy, Theda, Joseph, Paddock, Polly (Mary). Paddock's name disappears from the record. Mercy Crosby, born in 1799, was Fanny's mother.

Intermarriage was common in the extended families that sprawled across the sparsely settled region. Mercy married John Crosby, a widower and distant relative, and set up housekeeping (most likely with her parents) in Putnam County. Mercy's family home stood among tall maples in the midst of hilly stone-fenced fields along a narrow winding road, about a mile and a half from the hilltop meetinghouse at which the family worshiped. This section of Southeast was then known as Gayville for the family that had first settled the area. Southeast's more densely populated sections had neighborhood names but were not towns in any conventional sense. At Fanny's birth in 1820, sprawling Southeast was home to 916 white males, 926 white females, and 62 black slaves. The meetinghouse rose above a section called Doanesburg (named for Elnathan Doane, who — like the Crosbys — came from Cape Cod in the 1740s), its tall narrow steeple visible from the hillside on which the Crosby house stood. Old Southeast Meeting-house was the first constructed within the limits of the county, and its scant surviving records testify to Crosby participation in a wide range of its activities. The winding road in front of the Crosby homestead led as well toward the West Church (now Gilead Presbyterian Church in Carmel, New York), a smaller congregation related to Southeast's, which Fanny's grandmother, Eunice Paddock Crosby, joined in 1809.

Most early settlers of Southeast came, like the Crosbys, during the 1740s from Massachusetts and Connecticut, attracted by the promise of rich land along the Croton River. They soon learned that the grassy hills offered good grazing rather than prime farmland. The hills yielded iron, too, presenting another economic possibility. In the end, though, the Croton River and the streams that fed it became the county's most valuable resource: in 1835 Manhattan officials settled on the Croton River as the source for New York City's water.

A decade before Manhattan tapped Southeast's principal resource, Fanny Crosby played among the shallow streams that fed the Croton River. She spent her first years in an extended family clan among early Southeast settlers, but in old age she recalled a childhood shaped almost entirely by her immediate family. Nothing is known of her father, John Crosby. She had a much older half sister, John's daughter by a prior marriage, who played little apparent role in her life. Her life focused on her mother and her grandparents. Mercy's youngest sister, born just two years before Fanny, filled the role of playmate.

In old age Fanny recalled her grandmother, Eunice Paddock Crosby, as the most significant influence in her childhood. The Paddocks had a family line that resembled the Crosbys'. They, too, boasted ties to the first Pilgrims, with whom they had intermarried in colonial times. They, too, settled on Cape Cod at about the same time the Crosbys did. On both her Crosby grandparents' sides, then, Fanny descended from Massachusetts Bay Puritans and *Mayflower* Pilgrims. Just a few years before the Crosbys, in 1740, the Paddocks moved from Cape Cod to the land that would become Southeast, while others of the Paddock clan settled a few miles away in Salem, Westchester County. The Southeast Paddocks, too, lived near what was known as the Presbyterian Meeting-house and took an active role in its affairs. Crosby took pride in her kinship with the several Paddocks who fought in the Continental Army.

The only specific record of Fanny's childhood home life comes from the reminiscences she dictated in adulthood. Tempered by time, her memories featured sentimental attachment to people and places whose imperfections had faded with the years. Her story proper begins with the oft-repeated tale of the simple tragedy that her family believed made her blind. Her impaired sight defined her, set her apart in ways that transformed her opportunities, and played a role in her later wide appeal. Had she not been blind, she might have had little recoverable past.

Crosby rendered the story so often that it became common knowledge. Before she was two months old, in the absence of the family's physician, her family allowed a stranger who claimed medical know-how to treat an eye inflammation. The cure included the application of hot poultices (one of Crosby's renderings says "mustard poultices") that destroyed her sight, though she could perceive the presence and absence of light. Common wisdom held that when this tragedy became known, the man disappeared without trace, leaving the Crosbys with a circumstance that occupied them in one way or another for the next ninety-five years.

As an elderly woman, Crosby insisted that she had never felt resentment toward the man she believed impaired her sight. Instead, her Christian faith provided her with the assurance that he had been an instrument in God's hands to "consecrate" her to her life's work. Only one of her several autobiographies admits youthful discouragement over her handicap. Whether or not her determined cheerfulness was always as firm as the elderly Crosby was wont to claim, one thing is certain: Crosby's blindness soon opened for her opportunities that were most unlikely for a nineteenth-century female in Southeast, New York. In one tragic moment, Crosby intimated, a nameless man shaped an infant's destiny.

This most basic piece of Crosby lore may plausibly be questioned and even rejected. Did her blindness result from the application of hot poultices? Modern physicians suggest that it is much more likely that her blindness was congenital. Heat by itself, they say, would have caused intolerable pain to the eyelids before affecting the eyes. While a poultice might have included ingredients that caused a chemical burn, this, too, would have resulted in excruciating pain to the eyelids, though even a momentary chemical burn to the eye itself would result in permanent damage. Since this incident occurred when Crosby was only six weeks old, it is impossible to know that her sight was normal to begin with. But the chance treatment by an unknown practitioner offered a scapegoat as well as an explanation on which the family seized for what comfort it afforded.

Late in life Crosby recalled her mother's early comments on her blindness. Mercy Crosby observed that two of the world's greatest poets (Homer and Milton) were blind. She also instilled in her daughter the view "that sometimes Providence deprived persons of some physical faculty in order that the spiritual insight might more fully awake[n]." Fanny Crosby also remembered her mother's periodic discouragement and anxiety for her blind daughter's future. It fell to Eunice Crosby to encourage both her daughter and her granddaughter and to improvise ways to cope.

The new opportunities the Crosbys now discovered began at home and gave them opportunity to manifest some of the Yankee ingenuity Crosby claimed as her heritage. An abiding Christian faith sustained Crosby's childhood home life, and so a brief look at the elements of that faith as taught in both of the nearby Presbyterian meetinghouses with which the family had connections offers a logical place to begin a consideration of the ethos of her childhood.

Only fragments remain to provide clues into the religious aspects of Crosby's family heritage, but they yield a surprisingly suggestive portrait. At its center stands the Bible in the classic rendering of the Authorized Version. Crosby frequently admitted its centrality in her childhood home, where the family altar found a regular place. Although she could not read for herself, she memorized Scripture under the patient tutelage of her grandmother. Evidence suggests that this Crosby family pegged its understanding of duty, community, and family to the biblical text. Shaped by the Calvinist reading of Scripture that years before had prompted the family's migration to the New World, the Crosbys of Southeast understood that God had a purpose for whatever happened; they clung to the certainty that God was in control. They knew God as the source of true pleasure and believed that all they had — meager or abundant — came from God's hand. They took time from hard lives to enjoy the wonders of nature, and they imbued young Fanny with an appreciation for beauties she could not see. As lived out at home — at least in Crosby's recollections — the Calvinism of these sons and daughters of Massachusetts Bay was serious without being dour, joyous without being frivolous. It refreshed the soul while sustaining the body, and so it seemed particularly suited to those who, like the Crosbys, eked out hard, meager livings from the land.

It made room for literature too. Intimately familiar with the poetry of Milton, the plays of Shakespeare, the progress of John Bunyan's pilgrim, and the hymns of Isaac Watts, young Crosby also roamed Nottingham Forest with Robin Hood and traversed the Spanish countryside with Don Quixote. Such literary classics, like the Bible, fired her imagination and supplied secondhand a rich vocabulary of color and form.

Her home church setting was apparently a different matter. The family worshiped most often at the Presbyterian meetinghouse that stood prominently atop a nearby hill. The Fairfield County East Association of Connecticut had supplied the adjoining New York communities with their first settled pastors, sending Elisha Kent in 1742 to preach at two stations on a regular basis. Southeast, or the Eastern Society of Philipse Precinct, was organized first, with the West Church of Christ in Philipse Patent following the next year. After a few years the West Church called its own pastor, the Reverend James Davenport of Great Awakening notoriety. Davenport had "come to his senses" and disavowed the fanaticism that in the throes of the Great Awakening had tarnished his reputation. His earnest orthodoxy helped the West Church flourish. It was this congregation that Fanny's grandmother, Eunice, joined in 1809. From their front door the Crosbys could easily ride or walk in either direction to worship at the East or the West Church.

Local lore, though, associates them more directly with the Southeast (or East) Church, the original meetinghouse on the Philipse Patent. In 1762 Kent, onetime preacher for both congregations but since 1750 full-time pastor in Southeast, took the initiative in establishing the first New York presbytery outside of New York City. This Dutchess County Presbytery brought three area congregations under a church judicatory. Kent died in 1776. The church called as its next pastor the Reverend Ichabod Lewis. Lewis took another organizational stride by drawing up a covenant signed by eighty-seven men who pledged to worship "agreeably [according] to the rules and doctrines of the Gospel as explained by the Kirk of Scotland." In addition to assuring proper Calvinist doctrine and order, this choice guaranteed unaccompanied congregational singing and suggests that the congregation preferred the Psalter to the hymnal.

During the 1790s the congregation moved from its log meetinghouse to a more commodious building, painted on the outside and "properly pewed" within. It called a new pastor, the Reverend Jehu Minor, beloved for "preaching the Gospel in its purity, with fervor and fidelity." Minor died in 1808, and a succession of pastors supplied the pulpit until 1827. Only one of them, the Reverend Joshua Spaulding (pastor when Fanny Crosby was born), left any printed legacy. The congregation took pride in his accomplishments: he compiled a small hymnal, one of the first available in the area, though it apparently was intended for devotional use rather than for the noninstrumental psalm-singing church; and he published a volume of lectures on the second coming as well as a two-volume work, *The Divine Theory*.

With the arrival of Abraham Stansbury in May 1827, the church found a greater degree of stability. For a time it had removed from Presbyterian jurisdiction and functioned as a Congregational society, apparently still conducting its affairs under the Kirk of Scotland's Second Book of Order. Stansbury brought it back to its Presbyterian affiliation. (Crosby would recall the congregation's style as "primitive Presbyterian.") An Englishman, he offered the unlikely combination of eloquent preaching, inventive genius (he owned several patents), and a passion for mineralogy. Like most of his predecessors, he died young. His successor, the Reverend Robert McLeod, whose loyalty to Scottish church order seemed assured by firm family ties to the old country, arrived in Southeast in 1829 and served the church until his death in 1856. Before the end of this long pastorate, all but one of Crosby's closest family had left the area permanently.

Had the Crosbys remained on Cape Cod, these years of regularizing the relationships and doctrines of Southeast's church would likely have proceeded differently. Radiating from the Bay Colony's oldest and most prestigious pulpits, Unitarianism reconfigured the religious landscape and the church affiliations of some of Crosby's distant cousins who had not joined the westward exodus of the 1740s. No hint of a religion of reason or a challenge to the orthodoxy of the Kirk of Scotland appeared in the more isolated environs of Southeast. Rain or shine, the people climbed the steep hill to their place of worship. Long sermons and tedious music, "deaconed out" in the absence of printed Psalters and tunes, occupied the hours in the austere sanctuary. Crosby had no taste for the singing in her family's church, but she found in its teaching the pattern for her life.

Her youthful exposure to Southeast's version of Scottish Presbyterianism gave her a firm foundation that stressed duty, purpose, diligence, and thrift. It assured her that a holy God ruled the events of history and the details of her life. The adult Crosby reminisced that it neither instilled a love for church music nor offered a "felt" assurance of salvation. These came later and elsewhere, for Crosby's horizons were about to expand.

Her first experience of life beyond Southeast contrasted dramatically with anything she had known before. In 1825 Mercy Crosby took her five-year-old daughter to New York City to consult one of the best-known surgeons of the day, Valentine Mott. Mercy had researched the possibilities and resolved to have her child evaluated by the most qualified doctor she could locate. The son of a physician, Mott was an 1806 graduate of the Medical School of Columbia College (now University) and a pioneer of arterial surgery. He continued his studies in London and Scotland and opened a practice in New York City in 1809 (while also a professor of surgery at Columbia College). When the Crosbys visited, Mott was Chair of Principles and Practice of Surgery at the College of Physicians and Surgeons. A pioneer of complicated surgeries, he enjoyed a reputation unsurpassed by any of his contemporaries. An influential teacher, he was also a devout member of the Episcopal Church. Mercy found in him America's premier physician, a man his colleagues hailed as "Dr. Mott the GOOD."

The Crosbys' journey to New York was an adventure that accents the concept of distance measured in time rather than miles. A seven-hour wagon ride brought mother and daughter to the wharf on the Hudson River at Sing Sing, where they boarded a sailing sloop bound for Manhattan. Hudson River sloops plied the river, carrying passengers and cargo, depending on a fore-and-aft rigged single mast with one or two headsails. They might carry as many as ninety people. A cow on board provided fresh milk, and passengers cooked their food, sang and conversed as the sails caught the breeze for a voyage of uncertain duration. In Manhattan a family acquaintance named Jacob Smith offered the hospitality of his home at 10 Roosevelt Street on the island's southern tip, and Crosby clung to her mother as, bewildered by the bustle of the unfamiliar metropolis, she made her first foray into the city she would later know as home.

But even the famous physician could offer no help. His examination brought the dreaded verdict that Crosby would never regain sight. He consulted with Dr. Edward Delafield, an up-and-coming younger colleague educated in the most modern European under-standings of ophthalmology, but the verdict stood: nothing could be done. Mother and daughter soon retraced their steps to the familiar surroundings of Putnam County. As Crosby recalled the return trip, her mother was far more distraught than she. She now found in her grandmother "more than I can ever express by word or pen." Eunice Crosby began describing nature — shapes, colors, birdcalls, flowers — so vividly that Fanny learned to distinguish among them. On long walks Eunice described the trees and their leaves and taught the child shapes and fragrances that helped her learn their names. Despite the family's involvement in church, Crosby always insisted: "It was Grandma who brought the Bible to me, and me to the Bible. The stories of the Holy Book came from her lips and entered my heart and took deep root there." At Eunice's knee, Fanny learned to kneel and say her prayers.

Fanny's next experiences beyond Southeast came when her mother took employment in nearby towns. Crosby particularly re-membered lengthy stays in North Salem, New York, and Ridgefield, Connecticut (where her mother worked for several years). A glance at a map reveals that these towns are not far apart, but in 1830 tiresome journeys separated them and forced Mercy Crosby and her child to board out. The child sometimes spent prolonged periods with her grandparents, but during her times away from Southeast she readily made new friends, too. In North Salem, a community in northern Westchester County bounded on the west by the familiar Croton River and just six miles from Southeast, Mercy worked in the home in which the two boarded. Mercy had relatives on her mother's side in North Salem, where the Paddocks and the Cranes had put down roots. There Fanny first came to know members of the Society of Friends.

Quakers had been in the area for a century already and had grad-ually earned local respect. Early Quaker settlers had roused an irate Anglican rector's wife to complain that they "swarmed" to meetings and "spared no pains to infect their neighborhood." By the late 1820s they had found their niche, mostly in the central part of Westchester County. New Englanders had followed Indian trails to the land just over the Connecticut line, the Dutch lived along the Hudson River, and local wags noted that the animosity between them left expanses of relatively empty land for the Quakers to fill. Crosby thought the Quakers enchanting. They had clung for a century to the "plain speech" that had long set their community apart, and the child adopted their idiom and learned their ways.

North Salem was a sizable though sleepy town for rural northern Westchester County, and during Crosby's childhood the town as well as the surrounding parts of the county changed considerably. Construction in northern Westchester County of the famous Sing Sing State Penitentiary as well as of a state almshouse expanded job prospects. There was serious talk of a railroad in the future, and the population of Westchester County grew apace. Yet, despite its proximity to New York City, the area seemed in many ways remote, with sailing sloops along the Hudson River offering the most direct passage downstate. Robert Fulton's steamboat, the *Clermont,* made its debut around the time the Crosbys lived in North Salem. Its thirty-two-hour voyage from New York Harbor to Albany astounded skeptical New Yorkers, thousands of whom lined the banks of the Hudson along the ship's entire route, cheering the ship some had once derided as "Fulton's Folly." Steamboats did not immediately change the way people traveled, but the voyage betokened a gradual transformation of the area — especially the sleepy town of Peekskill, destined to become the depot of choice for farmers in Westchester and Putnam Counties as well as in far western Connecticut to ship produce and cattle to New York City. Northern Westchester County had the additional advantage for the Crosbys of proximity to Southeast that permitted Eunice Crosby to make an occasional visit.

If progress beckoned North Salem and other inland Westchester towns to anticipate great things ahead, nothing seemed likely to upset the rhythms of life in the next place Mercy and Fanny Crosby moved. Life in Ridgefield, Connecticut, was staid, even tranquil, and its citizens liked it that way. The town's name described its features: it was, wrote one early settler, "a collection of hills rolled into one general and commanding elevation." Ridgefield's population was decidedly homogeneous. One Ridgefield native who came home from New York City for the holidays in the 1830s noticed approvingly that not even an Irish servant challenged the "pure English extraction" of Ridgefield's 2,300 citizens.

A busy village on the main road to Boston, Ridgefield was a stop on the Danbury–New York stage. The town received mail twice weekly from New York, and the stage stop made the tavern (which boasted a British cannonball embedded in its wall) the center for news and gossip. Shoemakers, harness makers, silversmiths, tanners, candlemakers, coopers, carpet weavers, and even a lawyer hung their shingles downtown, but "the great geographical monument" was the Ridgefield meetinghouse. Despite its simple clapboards and shingles, the meetinghouse served the community as the point of reckoning for this life and the next. First Church was Congregational, though a few years before the Crosbys arrived the congregation briefly came under the Westchester Presbytery. In 1831 it reunited with the consociation of the Western District of Fairfield County. (This explains the confusion in some sources about the Crosbys' Presbyterian involvement in Ridgefield.) Crosby apparently knew two pastors — the Presbyterian Samuel Phelps and the Congregationalist Charles Grandison Selleck (Yale College, 1827). Membership grew rapidly during the few years of Selleck's tenure. Between 1831 and 1833, he added 180 members to the rolls.

In Ridgefield the Crosbys boarded with a Mrs. Hawley, a widow who had married into the clan of Hawleys in the region. Mercy Crosby hired out to work by the day. The journal of one of Ridgefield's sons describes such servants who made themselves indispensable to Ridgefield life. His words, penned late in life, suggest some of the circumstances that irked him elsewhere. In the 1820s he noted approvingly that Ridgefield servants were "not Irish" and had "not as yet imbibed the plebeian envy of those above them." Rather, servants tended to be — like Mercy Crosby — the daughters of local farmers and mechanics whose devotion to the interests of the families they served assured that they were treated as friends. Household service implied neither degradation nor reproach. In this congenial, hardworking environment, Mercy Crosby found her niche. Boarding in the spacious Hawley home put her and her daughter squarely at the heart of Ridgefield life among one of the community's most prominent families.

The Reverend Thomas Hawley, a graduate of Harvard College and progenitor of all the Ridgefield Hawleys, had been the first pastor of Ridgefield's meetinghouse (established 1712). As an incentive to settle in Ridgefield, Hawley had been granted a twenty-ninth share of the town's land, property that passed down through his family. A century later a host of Hawleys had descended from the "illustrious able divine," Thomas. Fanny Crosby's Mrs. Hawley was a devout church member. Her home stood just across the green from the sanctuary, making Crosby's attendance at the meetinghouse a simple matter. Mrs. Hawley took a kindly interest in the child. She nurtured her interest in the Bible and challenged the child to memorize its words. This project, of course, entailed reading passages over and over, a task Mrs. Hawley apparently patiently performed. She also instilled in the child a love for poetry. In a day when the lines between Congregationalists and Presbyterians sometimes blurred, Crosby remembered Mrs. Hawley as a staunch Puritan Presbyterian whose biblical literalism did not preclude a rich imaginative bent. In addition to the first four books of the Old and New Testaments, Mrs. Hawley soon had Crosby reciting many psalms, the book of Ruth, the Song of Solomon, and innumerable poems. (Crosby later cited Deuteronomy 32 and 33 as her favorite Old Testament chapters.) The neighborhood abounded with children, and Crosby enjoyed regular evening frolics on the common with more than a dozen cohorts. Some of these childhood friendships stood her in good stead much later in her life.

In Ridgefield Crosby took an active part in several of the era's innovative opportunities. She regularly attended both Sunday school (where her competitive nature made her anxious to prove that a blind child could memorize Scripture as well as anyone else) and the twice-weekly evening singing schools at the meetinghouse that helped Ridgefield residents, like those of other New England towns, while away long winter evenings. However inept the instructor or ungifted the pupils, singing masters across New England in the 1830s made a case for music as a popular pastime and set ordinary people to singing in harmony. Their usual text in Crosby's experience was the acclaimed *Handel and Haydn Collection,* first published in 1822, and frequently revised and expanded by its chief compiler, Lowell Mason. Though his text steadily gained an increasing share of the market, Mason did not create the vast popular interest in music that marked early nineteenth-century America. Rather, vocal music was an enduring part of American culture, helped along early in the eighteenth century by a score of New England divines who endorsed the first singing schools as a way to improve congregational singing. Mason's endeavors were part of another burst of interest in "better music," and his efforts instilled a new sense of purpose and direction into an existing groundswell of popular song.

The records of the Presbyterian Society in Ridgefield (like the Southeast church, this congregation moved between Presbyterian and Congregational affiliation) contain a contract signed 27 December 1827 by one Harvey Betts that describes a typical contemporary singing master's arrangement to conduct a school: "This may certify that I the subscriber am willing to teach singing in the Presbyterian Society in Ridgefield, and sing as often as may be judged necessary by the Committee from 3 to 6 months in the year and on Sabbath evenings at one Dollar per evening including the Sabbath, and also to attend regularly on the Sabbath at all other times throughout the year (sickness &c. excepted) for twenty-five cts per day for taking the lead in singing."

Under such a tutor, then, Crosby was introduced to Lowell Mason's name and to choral singing. Like Crosby, Mason traced his ancestry to the early English settlers of Massachusetts Bay and was steeped in the New England Way that had defined colonial New England culture. A generation later Crosby would join the aging Mason's circle. But during her childhood Mason was just beginning to build his reputation as music educator and hymn-tune writer and arranger. Crosby knew only his first published book. Its precepts and tunes began to hone her considerable musical skills.

Crosby's musical exposure beyond the singing schools did not always fire her enthusiasm for choral numbers. Singing school helped people pass dreary winter evenings and could be embraced for that purpose if for no other. In the meetinghouses, though, songs tended to be tediously lined out for the congregation, a practice subsequently abandoned by some congregations in favor of choirs that contemporaries accused of "bawling" tunes. The Ridgefield meetinghouse had opted for a choir and taken the novel approach of "distributing" the choir into four parts and placing each part in a different section of the gallery. The saintly Deacon Hawley, the village cabinetmaker, led the tenor voices. (The town boasted of this deacon: "He was a cabinet maker by trade, a chorister by choice, a deacon by the vote of the church, a Christian by the grace of God.") A pitch pipe gave the key, and Mear, Old Hundredth, Aylesbury, and Montgomery — tunes "full of piety and pathos in which the whole congregation simultaneously joined" — carried vocal praise in "hearty echo from the bosom of the assembly."

While in Ridgefield, Fanny learned firsthand about other forms of congregational song than those the heirs of the Puritans she knew best embraced. She met a Methodist tailor who introduced her to the immense corpus of sacred song that welled from Methodist hearts. In 1832 she attended her first Methodist meeting, where she encountered a new idiom of religious language for congregational use. She knew Watts and Newton and had heard the congregation of Ridgefield's First Church struggle through "homegrown" hymns written weekly by deacons and elders, but nothing in her meager experience had intimated the possibilities of hymn singing demonstrated by the Methodists. The varieties of tune and text rather than the excellence of the singing won Crosby's admiration.

Ridgefield boasted the third-oldest Methodist class meeting in New England. A generation earlier the first Methodist circuit rider in the area, Jesse Lee, had expected and found "many oppositions" to his labors in southern New England. Citizens seemed intent on refusing him permission to preach anywhere, but persistence had paid off. Methodists planted themselves in several towns neighboring Ridgefield and soon had enough people to hold camp meetings. When Dr. Baker, a respected Ridgefield physician, "became imbued with the rising spirit," the followers of Jesse Lee gained a toehold in the town. From four members gathered around the Bakers' kitchen table, the Ridgefield Methodist class meeting had grown to nearly 100 strong in Crosby's childhood. Nurtured by revivals and zealous itinerant preachers intent on routing the Deist scourge from New England, Methodists proudly built their first sanctuary in the mid-1820s, and there Crosby heard their songs. By midcentury the Methodist Episcopal Church boasted the highest attendance of any meetinghouse in town. Some of these faithful had strayed from the fold of First Church to become "spoil of the enemy," but others had once been classed among "the idle, dissipated and irreligious," and the town applauded their transformation into "trophies of grace." In this motley assembly, Crosby gained a different sense of the power of congregational song.

To be sure, Crosby had long recognized the influence of hymn texts as poetry. In old age she still recalled her grandmother's reassuring the family with the final stanza of the confident hymn "Jehovah-Jireh! The Lord Will Provide" that John Newton (Anglican cleric and author of "Amazing Grace") had written for his 1779 *Olney Hymns:*

Though troubles assail and dangers affright,
Though friends should all fail and foes all unite;
Yet one thing assures us, whatever betide,
The Scripture assures us the Lord will provide.

Crosby's dawning conviction of the power of such hymns as aids to corporate worship began in Ridgefield. It took decades to flower, but she carried from her brief exposure to Methodists memories that later stood her in good stead.

Despite these occasional moves within the general area, Crosby's childhood life was stable, anchored in Calvinist faith and guided by her grandmother's wisdom reinforced by Mrs. Hawley's patient teaching. Determined that her granddaughter should live as much like sighted children as possible, Eunice Crosby urged her to try what other children did. The biggest obstacle, of course, was obtaining a formal education. As an adult, Crosby recalled occasionally trailing off to school after her friends. But she could not follow the lessons and did not formally enroll. Instead, she imbibed learning from every available source, however eclectic. Outgoing and winsome, she conversed with adults as readily as she played with children. Especially from her grandmother and Mrs. Hawley, she learned to discipline her mind to retain information. These kindly women filled her imagination with descriptions of the natural beauty she could not see, and she reveled in the power of words and senses to bring to life what was denied forever to her sight.

While Crosby was still a young child, she showed unusual capacity to express her thoughts in verse. She lived in an age in which poetry was common: every newspaper and magazine filled random space with rhymed text of greater or lesser merit, and children dutifully memorized lines from the great poets of the past and present. In Crosby's Ridgefield experience, deacons or elders weekly composed poems to be sung. Her attempts to mimic such efforts are hardly surprising, and her family and friends saw to it that she cultivated the ability. One of her earliest efforts survives (she later dated it 1828 or 1829 and offered it as evidence of the "optimism and thankfulness" that pervaded her childhood):

Oh, what a happy soul I am,
Although I cannot see,

I am resolved that in this world
Contented I will be.

How many blessings I enjoy
That other people don't!
To weep and sigh because I'm blind
I cannot nor I won't.

Those childish lines aptly capture the values her family instilled: happiness, contentment, thankfulness, determination. All depended on her; disposition was entirely optional, a matter of the will quite independent of outward circumstances. The record suggests that she learned this lesson well. Mercy Crosby and Mrs. Hawley mailed specimens of Crosby's rhymes to Southeast, and Sylvanus Crosby promptly became the first in a long line of enthusiastic boosters of her poetic efforts.

Eunice Crosby died about 1831 at the age of fifty-three, worn out by work and disease. She lived on in her granddaughter's vivid sightless world of memory and imagination, where the beloved rocking chair in which the two spent happy and productive hours became a focus for fond reminiscence.

There are forms that flit before me,
There are tones I yet recall;
But the voice of gentle grandma
I remember best of all.

In her loving arms she held me,
And beneath her patient care
I was borne away to dreamland
In her dear old rocking chair.

Eunice and Mercy Crosby, widow Hawley and the other women of Fanny Crosby's childhood modeled for Crosby a construction of femininity that became foundational for the child's life. Neither they nor she enjoyed a privileged position on a pedestal. Home connoted shelter and community; Victorian notions of domesticity did not intrude. The women Crosby knew were hardworking, not pampered.

They strove to be useful, and they modeled for Crosby both the importance and the meaning of usefulness. Eunice and Mercy worked as hard as any men, Mercy outside the home in order to support her child. They relished tales of Mercy's grandmother, Elizabeth Crosby, who several times mounted her horse and set off alone "across the wilds of Connecticut" to visit relatives back on Cape Cod. Evidently no one suggested to Crosby that gender might preclude travel or education; in that regard, blindness seemed a much bigger obstacle than sex. The women in her life were not advantaged, but they knew the classics of English literature and had a rich store of homespun wisdom. Crosby remembered them as her primary teachers, as people who valued literature and practical learning as much as careful discipline. To be sure, Crosby also mastered particular household tasks and became adept at needlework (which she grasped by learning a stitch and then counting), but she fed her mind on the same ideas and activities that the men of the household enjoyed — books, newspapers, sermons. Adults encouraged her to develop her natural facility for language. She frolicked with boys and girls and spent a good deal of time outdoors. The large lot on which the Crosby house still stands is hilly, studded with trees, crisscrossed by water and rugged with natural beauty. She had room there to explore as well as to exercise, to encounter the natural world in great detail under the tutelage of her grandmother. She easily identified flowers, shrubs, trees, and birdcalls. Crosby looked forward to a life of hard work in the middle of whatever was happening, surviving by doing whatever life demanded, seizing any opportunities it afforded.

Crosby women did not speak in the meetinghouse, but they knew their Bibles and translated stern Calvinist sermons into a lived religion of confidence, duty, self-sacrifice, and love. If early influences suggest future probabilities, her childhood made it likely that Crosby would become a self-reliant woman little fazed by the emerging notion of a separate, hallowed woman's sphere. In her world certain responsibilities differed by gender, but gender offered no respite from the endless toil necessary for survival. Men and women faced the troubles of life together, as they did life's pleasures. Crosby's experience of what it meant to be female in the 1820s and 1830s in the then-remote hills of southeastern Putnam County suggests that the notion of a separate woman's sphere with its hallowing of "ladylike" domesticity would simply not have rung true.

By modeling the integration of faith with life and considerable but informal learning, the women of Southeast and Ridgefield prepared young Fanny Crosby to fend for herself, a valuable lesson that readied her for an astonishing next step. In 1834 Mercy Crosby learned that the New York state legislature had passed an act to provide stipends to enable blind students to enroll at the new Institution for the Blind in Manhattan. She seized on this unanticipated possibility, and only occasional worries about homesickness tempered Fanny's excitement as her mother attended to the details of application and enrollment. Education beckoned at last, and Crosby made up her mind to follow even though it meant life among strangers in the confusing exhilaration of New York City. Just sixty miles away, Manhattan was now only a day's journey but still a world apart from the haunts of Fanny Crosby's childhood.

2 Education (1835-1845)

Touched with compassion for their woes,
A philanthropic few arose,
Resolved to educate the blind,
And throw some light on darkened mind.

On 3 March 1835 Fanny Crosby set out for her new life in New York City, reconciled to the unknown by the unexpected opportunity for schooling. In old age she recalled her youthful eagerness for education as something palpable, and it was the only reason she ever admitted to regretting her blindness. "I had long been contented to bear the burden of blindness," she told her friend, poet Will Carleton, in 1903. "But my education — my education — how was I to get it?" Now, a few weeks before her fifteenth birthday, she stood on "the very tiptoe of expectation," with mixed emotions. For the first time she would be without her supportive coterie of family and friends, but the chance of a lifetime diminished her worries.

Despite her youth, Crosby must have marked the decided contrast to the inconveniences of her first trip to Manhattan a decade earlier. This time, instead of a tedious, bumpy seven-hour wagon journey westward, she took the regular morning stagecoach east from Ridge-field, bound for Norwalk, Connecticut, and an easy steamship cross-ing of Long Island Sound. She reached Manhattan in the late afternoon of the same day. She later quipped that in 1825 she had journeyed to Manhattan in an unsuccessful quest for physical "light." In 1835 she pursued "light" for her mind and knew she would not fail.

The city had changed dramatically since her first visit, and over time the ever expanding metropolis would shape Crosby's worldview. She came to love Manhattan and ultimately to find her calling in its most crowded neighborhoods among its immigrants and poor. Be-tween 1820 and 1830 the population of Manhattan and its immediate environs grew by 59 percent. An ever increasing percentage — more than 20 percent already in 1830 — was foreign-born. In the 1820s packet boats had driven down the price of the passage from Liverpool, and they quickly became the transportation of choice for the poor. Catholics from southern Ireland soon poured in, joining earlier Protestant Scotch-Irish settlers in ever growing numbers. The destitute among them crowded the slum known as the Five Points on Man-hattan's lower east side. In this "great central ulcer of wretchedness" they mingled with the poorest of the city's growing free black popula-tion, some 14,000 strong in 1830.

Manhattan was a mix of poverty and wealth, of working-class wards and so-called Yankee-Knickerbocker prosperity, though the "Knickerbocker" component was fading quickly. When Crosby ar-rived, a mere 4 percent of the population controlled some half of its wealth. Until 1830 Manhattan's most prestigious addresses stood on the crooked narrow streets of its lower west side. (Of these winding thoroughfares Washington Irving quipped: "The sage council not be-ing able to determine upon any plan for the building of their city, the cows, in a laudable fit of patriotism, took it under their peculiar charge and established paths, on each side of which the good folks built their houses.") But in the 1830s a trickle of the well-to-do headed north to find living space beyond the bursting neighborhoods of lower Manhattan. In time the center of the city wended northward, too, ab-sorbing along the way the country estates of the rich. Contemporaries began charting "the uptown movement" with care. They planned for it, too. A survey in 1811 laid out wide, straight streets — 100-foot-wide avenues running north and south, and 60-foot-wide numbered streets crossing the avenues at right angles. The northward thrust demanded expanded transportation networks to unite the growing metropolis. In 1834 three days of mob violence during city elections accented as well the need for new ways to preserve public order in a growing city. One thing stimulated another — new streets, transportation systems, urban services — and the city embarked on a century of unprecedented expansion that turned upward when it could no longer move outward. Crosby arrived at an exhilarating moment when stable, ordered ways of life seemed vulnerable to the onward march of progress. She would be challenged at first to feel at home in a city undergoing the throes of relentless change.

In 1831 New York City incorporated the first street railway in the world. Known as the New York and Harlem, its prospects generated such popular furor that the general rush to buy subscriptions resulted in overcapitalization. People complained that streetcars were crowded, dirty, and supervised by rude conductors, and those who could afford them preferred the handsome coaches known as stages that seated twelve people lengthwise. The masses walked. Crosby later claimed that, by their readiness to offer a helping hand, these walking masses facilitated her determination to get to know the city on her own.

The bustling city was home to the nation's best-known writers. The poet William Cullen Bryant edited the *Evening Post*. The irascible James Fenimore Cooper resided at Broadway and Prince Street, and Edgar Allan Poe lived on Sixth Avenue near Waverly Place (where he wrote "The Fall of the House of Usher"). Literary New York often welcomed Washington Irving, too. The University of New York (later New York University), established in 1831, capitalized on the city's reputation as a cultural center. Manhattan, bursting with energy and rich in untried promise, clearly offered something for everyone's tastes. A Quaker wag aptly described the bustling metropolis: "New York is not prone to get into the stillness to express any of her emotions." Crosby enjoyed the excitement, and the Institution occasionally welcomed one or another of the city's literary giants to speak to the pupils. Crosby greeted them with poems and thrilled to the chance to speak personally with editors and writers.

In teenaged Fanny Crosby's New York, then, immigrants and Yankees jostled one another on the streets and in the polling places.

Democrats claimed the immigrants, and the not-yet-notorious Tammany Hall lured them to social and benevolent clubs throughout the city. Crosby enjoyed political news and fancied herself an active supporter of an array of local and national office seekers. She loved the excitement generated by politics although she did not dwell deeply on political issues. Manhattan's underside was readily evident in soaring crime reports, and the seamy lives of some of its citizens could not be avoided in the neighborhood known as Five Points, "the very rotting Skeleton of Civilization," of which it was said that "nearly every house and cellar is a groggery below and a brothel above." The Five Points slum, known technically as the Fourth Ward, reminded Protestants of human degradation and sparked a burst of religious benevolence in which Crosby would later participate.

A growing number of daily newspapers titillated public imagination with stories of the licentious side of urban life. Historians of New York note that these papers cultivated the large and varied "public" that *was* New York readership and so offered citizens "the technical and textual means to grasp their city's growing miscellaneity." With offices within a stone's throw of each other in the vicinity of Park Row, popular reporters and writers crafted newspaper paragraphs rich with anecdotes, personal tidbits, dialogues, and generous illustrations from the everyday life they watched from their windows. Their buildings stood hard by City Hall and the city's commercial and political core, and they never lacked copy. Despite the constraints of small type and crowded pages, the day's popular publications dutifully sketched the city's varied character. Their style influenced early guidebooks to the city, giving New York a public face that cleverly featured both its bleak and its bright sides and helped make New York "the most closely watched city in the world." As a student at the New York Institution for the Blind, Crosby regularly heard readings from these daily papers; they framed her first sense of the issues of the day.

Among the bleak realities that worried Protestant observers of the city's bewildering growth was the apparent failure of the city's established churches to find effective means to absorb the influx of new arrivals. Stalwart Protestants firmly believed that the churching of immigrants was a necessary part of their Americanization. Troubled by "the peril of immigration" as well as exhilarated by its promise, the faithful pondered how to cope with change of rapid and staggering proportions. The city's best-known Protestant churches typically rented their pews, a practice that generally excluded the poor. A few years before Crosby arrived, the Association of Gentlemen, composed of some of the city's up-and-coming merchants, bankers, and other men of influence, approached the best-known evangelist of the day, Charles Grandison Finney. Imploring him to bring his gospel energy to their "Stupid, Poluted, and Perishing City," they pledged to under-write a free church that welcomed the poor.

Finney obliged, and his hosts provided him with a succession of commodious buildings, the last of which they called the Broadway Tabernacle and built to his specifications (a place Crosby would come to know well). It stood on Worth Street, near New York Hospital and Columbia College, at a busy crossroads that attended to the minds and bodies and now to the souls of New Yorkers. The Tabernacle audito-rium quickly proved a magnet for gatherings of all kinds. One of its historians hailed it as "a veritable tribune of the people." The list of those whose voices thundered from its pulpit included the era's most eminent preachers and most earnest reformers. The famous Hutchin-son Family Singers poured their usual passion and pathos into songs about freedom; the new Philharmonic Society thrilled vast crowds; temperance orators moved people to laughter and tears as they begged for signatures on pledge cards. Old-timers fondly insisted that there was no place in New York quite like the old Broadway Taberna-cle. Occasionally Crosby would recite poetry from its platform or sit in its pews to hear a famous orator.

The Tabernacle soon began replicating its religious side. By 1840 eleven new free churches acknowledging Finney as their model dot-ted the city. Some regretted that women rather than working-class men seemed most conspicuous among the evangelist's followers. Those who thought they could measure Finney's success in numbers of converted souls showed disappointment when he suddenly left Manhattan to take up a new post at the fledgling Oberlin College near Cleveland, Ohio. But anyone looking for immediate numerical results missed Finney's most enduring contribution to Manhattan's religious culture. With hindsight, as New York historians Edwin Burrows and Mike Wallace suggest, the most significant result of Finney's Man-hattan preaching was his rousing a host of the evangelical faithful to action.

Finney invigorated men and women whose dreams for America included a "benevolent empire," a nondenominational interrelated cluster of voluntary societies drawing impetus from Protestant teaching and united by the determination to give public expression to personal Christian commitment. Outlets for evangelical moral zeal, such voluntary associations arose alongside popular denominations as significant institutional forms of evangelicalism. By firing the enthusiasm of the converted and encouraging them to unite in societies that "lived evangelical religion" in public ways, Finney helped set in motion in Manhattan an era of remarkable Christian activity. New York City's Protestants embarked on a generation of institution building that had global ramifications.

The evangelical impulse in its most basic form pervaded much of Manhattan Protestantism. Evangelicals believed that Christian life began with a personal conversion experience that led naturally to a life marked by uprightness and moral endeavor. The largest popular national denominations — Baptists, Presbyterians, Methodists — were evangelical, as were other groups spawned by revivals from the Great Awakening forward. Some Episcopalians manifested evangelical sympathies as well. The evangelical bond transcended denomination, governed the goals of voluntary societies, and found expression in the nation's common school textbooks. It nurtured (as President John Tyler said in 1843) a "union of feeling" and a broad consensus about the nation's purpose as well as concerted common action. In this forward-looking evangelical ethos, Crosby came to view Christian service as national service. Summoned by the visions of activists in the benevolent empire, Crosby would first applaud, then embrace, the cause.

Education for the blind was one of many efforts that profited from this devotion to institution building grounded in Christian intention. Influenced by impulses rooted in the Second Great Awakening on the eastern seaboard, New Yorkers found in their work among juvenile delinquents, orphans, or the deaf, dumb, and the blind opportunities to do their Christian duty, improve the society, and act on their professions of faith. Supporters of New York Protestants' efforts on behalf of the needy set aside a week each May for public recognition of their accomplishments. Known as Anniversary Week, its series of meetings in the city's largest halls drew a cross section of Manhattan's hardworking Protestants for self-congratulation and recommitment to the cause. The press dutifully made the proceedings available to those unable to attend. Over time, annual assessments invited participants to reflect on the impact of the efforts and the tasks still to be accomplished.

Among the larger concerns of the day were some that defied the straightforward approach of the causes celebrated during Anniversary Week. In particular, temperance, immigration, and slavery loomed with urgency and seemed to many to pose especially ominous threats to realizing a Christian America. Demon rum, available in inexpensive, potent, even deadly varieties, flowed freely in places evangelical Christians considered "playgrounds of all the evil passions." Their crusade to improve matters lasted the entire century, but it already stirred the populace in 1835. Finney's devotees stood in its front ranks. One hatter tucked a temperance tract into each hat he sold. Others formed raiding parties that stormed into saloons. Christian spies, organized by Finney's friend, the zealous merchant Lewis Tappan, sought out and reported violations of the city's liquor ordinance. The New York Temperance Society, formed in 1829, published its own newspaper, the *Genius of Temperance*. By 1835 the Society had chapters in each of the city's wards, plus forty-five church-based chapters as well as evangelistic temperance outreaches targeting sailors and workers in specific trades. African Americans carried out a temperance program through their churches under the banner of their own Society for Temperance. By the mid-1830s more than 50,000 members of these societies marched to the beat of the temperance drum. The boundary between this temperance advocacy and Protestant evangelism often blurred until it disappeared. The urban environment made temperance a pressing issue, and Crosby was a convert to the cause.

Many temperance advocates also supported the city's antislavery societies. One of the most visible was the wealthy merchant Arthur Tappan, who worked at the delicate task of forming in the city a racially integrated antislavery society. In 1833 he launched a newspaper to advocate abolition. At Tappan's expense this *Emancipator* reached thousands of Protestant clergy in the Northeast. Late in 1833 New Yorkers — black and white, in a remarkable, risky demonstration of cross-racial middle-class solidarity — organized the American Anti-Slavery Society. Members worked hard — and with mixed results at best — to convince the city's growing labor class that its own interests mandated "right thinking" on the slavery question. Race riots erupted in the city in 1834, accenting the urgency of the issues at stake. New York had abolished slavery in 1827, but merchants and traders, thinking of the cotton market, often favored continuing slavery in the South. It was at once dangerous and thrilling to advocate abolition, even within the New York Protestant fold. (Disagreements over slavery already rumbled in the churches, and in 1844 began tearing apart the national denominational fabric.) The *New York Herald*, for one, urged the city's 150 churches (Presbyterians led with 39 Manhattan congregations) to curb the impulses Finney fueled: "There is some trouble yet in some of the Baptist, Presbyterian and Methodist churches in our city with reference to the abolitionists. We say in the spirit of all kindness, pitch out such, head and heels. What right have a few fanatics to disturb the peace and order of a whole church? The members must rid themselves at once of such enthusiasts."

The *Herald's* outspoken anti-abolitionist editor, James Gordon Bennett, also fumed about Lewis Tappan's "exhibition of the Amistad niggers throughout the United States," an enterprise he estimated would net Tappan some $30,000. In a case that galvanized the nation, the Supreme Court declared in March 1841 that the blacks aboard the *Amistad* (a slave ship seized off Long Island in 1839) had been kidnapped and enslaved illegally and were therefore free. According to Bennett, after using them to support his abolitionist views, Tappan would, in accordance with his Christian principles, return them to Africa. In fact, Tappan exhibited them, beginning at the Broadway Tabernacle where he charged fifty cents for admission, to raise money for their expenses and build public support for his pet scheme of a Christian mission among the Mende people in Africa. Bennett's powerful Protestant voice opposed evangelical abolitionists with considerable effect at every turn. Tappan's exhibitions were, Bennett charged, "better business than selling dry goods in Pearl Street or abolitionist books and pictures in Nassau Street."

Like all public matters, the slavery debate within and among the city's Protestant churches played itself out against the backdrop of immigration. In the 1830s New York's population became more varied than ever. Irish laborers poured in and the ranks of Catholics swelled, raising divisive questions that bore especially on the character of public education and the frenzy of politics. In 1841 New York Protestants, responding to what they perceived as actions to secularize the public schools, created the American Protestant Union in part to oppose "the subjugation of our country to the control of the Pope of Rome and his adherents." In the opinion of Protestant stalwarts, immigrants also tended to feed the ranks and coffers of the Democratic Party, flaunt the temperance societies, and violate the Sabbath mores cherished by the descendants of Yankee Puritans and Dutch patroons. Occasional glimmers of progress in the temperance cause — in May 1841 some four thousand Brooklyn Catholics signed the pledge, eliciting the assurance from the acerbic Bennett that "the Virgin Mary was always a teetotaller" — barely impacted the population. The more embattled Protestants thought they were, the louder they cried for blue laws and excise taxes. In 1835 Irish immigrants arrived in the greatest numbers. By 1850 Germans and Jews poured in after the latest round of failed liberal revolutions in Europe. Protestants worried aloud about German "infidels" and "Hebrews with no conscience in regard to the Christian Sabbath." The city's ever changing, always swelling population made room as well for large numbers of native-born Americans — especially young men — who moved from the country and inhabited boardinghouses. Protestants worried that the absence of family and small-town social constraints made such boardinghouses seedbeds of vice. Against this backdrop Crosby honed her antislavery convictions (slavery had been part of her early childhood; New York State abolished slavery only in 1827) and her devotion to the dispossessed.

In the late 1830s the Democrats temporarily lost their political supremacy, and Whigs rode the Panic of 1837 to city and state office. Despite the economic woes people blamed on Andrew Jackson and Martin Van Buren, Crosby was an ardent Democrat, and she expressed her political sympathy with fervor that bordered on the religious. She gave no clue why she was a Democrat — she seldom even hinted about her views on political issues — but certainly some political personalities held her interest and loyalty without regard to party. The Democrats' emphasis on local autonomy and the "common man" together with their opposition to monopoly and privilege coincided with her democratic sympathies. Crosby's politics were not consistent, though her devotion to heroic figures was. But New York's Protestants had no political consensus. Some favored the Whig Party, which considered itself the conservator of "order, morals and religion," three principles dear to the hearts of the Protestant cultural elite who orchestrated the activities of the city's benevolent empire.

The Manhattan setting provided more than a forum for public issues. It also exuded a sense that all things were possible. Entrepreneurs attempted grand schemes, and often failed grandly, too. But ingenuity and persistence brought people a long way. One could see, do, and attempt more in New York than in any other American city. Theater and music vied with lectures and entertainments for people's spare time. Plans for a great "central park" were already in the offing, none too soon since open land was quickly disappearing. European visitors, scholars, medical scientists, and performers passed through the Port of New York with the tens of thousands of immigrants who came to stay. The city had a cosmopolitan flavor that lured Americans to visit as well as to work. Already a center for higher education and medical care, New York offered the blend of high and popular culture that gave the feel of something for everyone. On the other hand, New York's seamy side seemed more hopeless every year. Benevolent Protestants and beleaguered civil servants simply could not keep pace with the massive social needs of the growing metropolis.

When Crosby first arrived, she knew only the promise of education. The pulsating tempo, enormous problems, and uncharted possibilities of city life dawned on her only gradually. After a few days visiting family friends, she composed herself for her new life. On Saturday, 7 March 1835, she was driven for the first time up to the door of the New York Institution for the Blind, where Superintendent John Russ offered a cordial welcome. She had made up her mind that she was now ready to do whatever it took to realize her life's dream of formal education. "Behold me, now, Miss Fanny Crosby, full-fledged student, in a city school!" she beckoned in retrospect in 1903. "I assure you, it seemed a great step forward — and upward — to me."

On Manhattan's far west side, just beyond the northern edge of the developed part of the city, the Institution boasted (for the sighted) unbroken views of the Hudson River and the New Jersey shore beyond. Several acres of trees from many places — a catalpa from Japan, an ailanthus from China, a European linden (donated at considerable cost by a benevolent citizen) — shaded walkways, while the front yard, laid out with graveled walks, boasted circular beds of flowers and shrubs. The location's natural beauty could not appeal to Crosby's sightless eyes, and even the kindness of those who welcomed her could not assuage the loneliness that gripped her as she thought about loved ones far away. But with the first day those feelings passed, and Crosby came to love the place that would be her home for more than twenty years. Within its walls she found stability amid the clamor of progress and protest that defined New York.

The world Crosby embraced that week was in reality farther from Southeast, New York, than mere distance suggested. The city resonated with the hopes and dreams of some quarter-million people. The Institution itself was the focus of the attention of wealthy benefactors, state legislators, and earnest church members. Still in its infancy, it was beginning to feel its way forward. Leaders and prospects were largely untried, but anticipated resources promised to create possibilities beyond the imagination of most ordinary citizens in Crosby's more circumscribed upstate world. Conveniences like indoor plumbing and gas lighting; entertainments; excursions; access to famous places and people — such things stood just beyond the threshold. The setting pulsated with promise. Crosby never turned back.

THE NEW YORK INSTITUTION FOR THE BLIND

When Crosby arrived in 1835, the New York Institution for the Blind occupied large premises that suggested the optimism of its sponsors. Chartered in 1831 and opened in 1832 with a class of three that met in a rented room, the Institution was part of a much larger scheme promoted by New York activists to provide services for those with impaired sight. The school also had a place in the commitment of New York State's energetic new governor, William Marcy, to improve public education. When Marcy took office in 1833, some 500,000 pupils were enrolled in the state's 9,600 public schools, and Marcy made a priority of both teacher training and "the education of all classes and conditions of our future citizens as should qualify them for usefulness and virtue."

The New York state legislature responded by voting scholarship funds sufficient for the expenses for one blind child from each New York county to enroll at the Institution. This action was part of a broader though modest legislative program directed toward assisting the blind. In 1822 New York State had chartered the New York Eye and Ear Infirmary, a hospital Governor Marcy's administration continued to support with modest grants. Like the education of the blind, the Eye and Ear Infirmary took its cue from Europe. There Edward Delafield and John Rodgers, two graduates from the College of Physicians and Surgeons of New York City, had studied recent advances in treatments for the blind. Lectures at the London Eye Infirmary (established in 1804) introduced them to aspects of blindness and eye disease of which they realized Americans — even the most advanced physicians — were ignorant. Upon their return to New York in 1818, the two established an infirmary. From modest beginnings they raised subscriptions and proceeded to build a pioneer American institution.

During the same years, in a remarkable convergence of awareness and interest, other Americans specifically addressed the plight of those whose impaired sight left them without the training necessary for gainful employment. Some of the milestones in the resulting programs of education for the blind came from the same intellectual sources that had shaped the views of the Founding Fathers: the writings of French Enlightenment philosophers. Denis Diderot, for example, published a famous "Letter on the Blind" and an "Addition to the Letter on the Blind" in which he made the case that blind persons had the capacity to lead normal lives. He urged contemporaries to converse with the blind (rather than to make assumptions about them) and described his own interviews with three blind contemporaries. Diderot encouraged; he did not offer practical suggestions. His young disciple, Jean-Jacques Rousseau, went on to sound the humanitarian challenge: "What can we do to alleviate the lot of this class of sufferers, and how shall we apply to their education the results of metaphysics?"

In Paris in 1784 Valentin Haüy, a young devotee of Rousseau's, ventured a practical answer and opened the first school for blind children. Haüy had been appalled when he saw Parisians insulting the blind. He acknowledged as well the influence of Maria Theresa von Paradis, a blind pianist and vocalist from Vienna who was the sensation of the 1784 Paris season. Her voice had enchanted the Austrian empress Maria Theresa (at whose court the blind girl's father served), and the empress arranged for a music teacher and a stipend to support her education.

Having observed in the singer the capacities of the blind, he searched Paris for a promising blind youth to tutor. He found Francois Lesueur begging at the Church of St. Germain and persuaded him to relinquish his profitable spot on the church steps for an experiment in education. In six months Haüy taught his pupil to write and to read embossed type. His next step was a public demonstration before the Royal Academy of Sciences. With the Academy members' approval, Haüy next enrolled as pupils fourteen blind children who were in the care of the Philanthropic Society. His school, known as L'Institution Nationale des Jeunes Aveugles, was the first formal school for blind children. Haüy saw to it that the children learned history, geography, music, science, and languages as well as reading. He solved the obstacle of teaching reading by creating a book with embossed letters mass-produced for blind education. Within a generation Germans, Danes, and Austrians had produced their own embossed books. Over time, with significant modifications, their combined effort complemented the work of the Frenchman, Louis Braille, who devised the alphabet and printing method that bear his name. (Braille graduated from a school Haüy established.) This mounting interest also greatly stimulated discussion of the manner and means for educating the blind. Before Haüy's death in 1822, schools for the blind had been established in sixteen countries of Europe. Those who carried his work forward realized his limitations, but Samuel Gridley Howe, the premier United States educator of the blind, acknowledged his pioneering genius: "Hauy merits the endearing title 'father of the blind'; a reward richer than a crown; a title more truly glorious than that of conqueror."

Haüy's work plus contact with several schools for the blind in Britain, then, prompted some Americans to envision similar attempts at home. After long years of neglecting the blind, Americans in three northeastern cities in quick succession adapted European models. Soon the country boasted three schools devoted to the education of the blind and their preparation for employment. A growing cadre of physicians who specialized in diseases of the eye shared the passion of the first educators of the blind.

The New England Asylum (renamed Perkins School for the Blind after its first major benefactor, Col. Thomas Perkins) opened in Boston in 1832. Incorporated in 1829, it was technically the oldest of the schools, and under the guidance of its longtime superintendent, Samuel Gridley Howe (husband of poet Julia Ward Howe, author of the

"Battle Hymn of the Republic"), who visited most of the European schools to observe their methods, it gained a reputation for excellence. A Brown University graduate, Howe attended lectures at the Harvard Medical School and clinics at the Massachusetts General Hospital before seeking more specialized training in Europe (and participating in the Greek struggle for independence). In time the Perkins School's work with two women who were both blind and deaf — Laura Bridgman and Helen Keller — gave it wide publicity, and Howe's crusading efforts bore fruit far beyond Boston. Oliver Wendell Holmes eulogized Howe as the ambitious herald in the United States of the conviction that those with impaired vision had something valuable to contribute to their society:

> He touched the eyelids of the blind,
> And lo! The veil withdrawn,
> As o'er the midnight of the mind
> He led the light of dawn.

Despite the earlier mobilization of Boston supporters of education for the blind, the New York Institution for the Blind, chartered in 1831, was the first of the American schools to open its doors. Quakers sponsored a third school in Philadelphia in 1833. Each of these early ventures valued models implemented in Edinburgh and London. Europeans were the pioneers, Americans followed in their footsteps. Within two generations of Diderot's pathbreaking writings, his views had inaugurated British and American attempts to address the needs of the sight-impaired.

The specific story of the New York Institution for the Blind began on 15 March 1832, almost exactly three years before Fanny Crosby's arrival, when a widow living on Canal Street, a busy lower Manhattan crosstown thoroughfare, opened her home to John Denison Russ, an earnest young teacher, for the instruction of three blind children from the city Alms House. Russ soon enlisted three more children. In May the pupils moved to other premises at 47 Mercer Street and slowly built a promising track record. Russ experimented freely, relying on general principles supplied by James Gall, president of the Edinburgh (Scotland) School for the Blind. Then, in the summer of 1832, over three thousand New Yorkers succumbed to a severe epidemic of "that terrible scourge, the Asiatic cholera." It claimed the life of one of Russ's pupils, but he refused to be deterred. To solicit funds to keep the school open, Russ organized a public program to demonstrate the attainments of his remaining pupils and his methods of instruction. An event on 13 December 1832 raised both public awareness and the funds necessary to assure the continuity of the school.

An 1823 graduate of Yale College, Russ had pursued medical studies in Boston and New Haven before leaving for Europe where he, like Howe, participated in the Greek struggle for independence (and made the acquaintance of Lord Byron) before continuing his studies at Paris, London, Edinburgh, and Dublin. Already before his departure for Europe, Russ had manifested a deep personal interest in improving opportunities for blind Americans. When he returned to New York, his evident dedication brought him to the attention of others who shared his sense of urgency for the task. Two of these, Samuel Akerly, a physician and tireless advocate of the Institution for the Deaf and Dumb, and Samuel Wood, a well-known benevolent Quaker bookseller and former teacher, enlisted him as superintendent when they moved in 1831 to incorporate a New York Institution for the Blind.

With Akerly as the first president of the Institution's Board of Managers (a group of twenty men), the fledgling institution authorized Russ's small experimental efforts, which he carried forward without salary. By the beginning of 1833 the enterprise had paid its bills and put money in the bank, and the future seemed brighter. Still, the first benefactors met sharp public disbelief about the possibility and worth of education for the blind. And so the realities of survival demanded that the inner circle make the case repeatedly that the school deserved support. Creative and dedicated, Russ himself provided much of the genius that assured the early success of the school. He personally learned basket weaving, mat making, and carpet weaving so that he could teach these marketable skills to his pupils. He invented a phonetic alphabet, a new process for mapmaking, and a simplified mathematical system. His scheme became his mission, and he devoted himself to it so entirely that his health gave way and forced him to resign. But he proved first that the blind could learn productive skills as well as information; he implemented for them a new and creative process of education; and he tirelessly promoted their interests. Others now had a legacy to follow.

In the fall of 1833 the Institution's Board of Managers took a ten-year lease on property in a section of Strawberry Hill, a site that ran between Eighth and Eleventh Avenues and Twenty-ninth and Thirty-ninth Streets. A large house of Sing Sing marble, buttressed and turreted, offered ample living space in a section deemed "one of the pleasantest situations on Manhattan." A spacious attic made an ideal workshop, and two stone kitchens stood apart from the house near a two-acre garden. The city had not yet opened and paved the streets, the property lacked city water and sewers, and gas lines came later. But that did not dim the excitement of those for whom the property represented the fulfillment of a dream. (Amid the severe financial woes of the Panic of 1837, James Boorman, the wealthy merchant who owned the property, parted with it at $10,000 below market value. State grants and generous donations enabled remodeling and expansion.)

In October 1833 William Murray arrived from Edinburgh, Scotland, to undertake teaching the pupils to produce willow baskets, mats, and mattresses. Blind himself, Murray exhibited skilled craftsmanship and instructed the older pupils in making manila mats, hair mattresses, and woven rugs. He taught younger children to braid palm leaves. A December exhibition at the City Hotel attracted a crowd of the well-to-do who enjoyed an afternoon of displays of remarkable facility in choral and instrumental music, arithmetic, and geography as well as the opportunity to purchase the expanding line of goods Murray's pupils offered. By 1834 the school had 26 pupils, 10 of whom received funds from the state. (By 1850 state funds supported 128 pupils, and others paid $130 per year.) Enthusiastic New Yorkers underwrote the remaining costs with donations.

When Fanny Crosby enrolled in 1835, the school boasted 41 scholars, 28 of whom were state supported. The days when a single instructor could handle the school had long passed. Crosby found a superintendent, a matron, two assistant teachers, a music master, a basket maker, a weaver, a gardener, and house servants. In 1835 the small-scale public holiday fund-raisers of past years gave way to a three-day event between Christmas and New Year's Day billed as a Ladies' Fair. Run by a group of "active and benevolent" women, the programs and goods raised well over $2,000.

In these early years the school organized its educational program under three departments, each entrusted with cultivating a particular skill. Together they instilled Christian morals that valued hard work, patriotic feeling, and responsible citizenship — all on the assumption that public virtue had deep roots in evangelical religion. The intellectual department offered instruction in reading, writing, mathematics, geography, history, grammar, and literature. Instructors used maps and globes designed by Russ, distinguished by raised lines, grooves, and "prominences." To teach writing they placed paper on grooved pasteboard and gave students pencils.

Instructors taught reading with embossed letters and after 1835 procured books from Boston where the enterprising Samuel Howe had established a suitable press. Public and private demonstrations proved every year that students at the New York Institution for the Blind could equal if not surpass sighted students in any school in grammar and geography. In old age Crosby recalled the demanding "pandect" of a grammar text that drilled her English usage. It was new in 1835 and soon to be a standard of the era, Goold Brown's *The Institutes of English Grammar Methodically Arranged*. Crosby delighted in its details and mastered the exercises that accompanied the lessons. She learned rules for versification, in which she had a natural gift, and her instructors insisted that she apply the discipline of her new learning to the composition of poems. She also studied the poetry of Henry Wadsworth Longfellow; Alfred, Lord Tennyson; John Greenleaf Whittier; James Montgomery; Thomas Moore; William Cullen Bryant. (Bryant visited the Institution, read and critiqued some Crosby poetry, and encouraged her to persist.) She once wrote a poem on these poets who fired her imagination:

> You from whose garners I have gleaned
> Such precious fruit, the task has seemed
> So pleasant that my humble pen
> Would fain resume its work again;
> In your bright realms 'twere bliss to stay;
> But time forbids, and I obey.

The mechanical department assured that students learned a marketable skill. The music department offered instruction on musical instruments as well as choral opportunities. The Institution owned several pianos and an organ in addition to many portable instruments, and soon concerts added to the revenue.

Late in life Crosby recalled her single-minded interest in poetry. To some extent the Institution exploited her ability to express herself in meter, often presenting her publicly to prove the worth of educating the blind. The ease with which rhyming words tumbled from her lips made her a natural choice to welcome visiting dignitaries at a moment's notice. But her mentors also disciplined her by insisting she refrain at times from verse and devote herself also to her other studies.

If she delighted in words, Crosby abhorred numbers. She remembered arithmetic as "a great monster" approached with the help of a metal slate punched with holes to help with counting. She subdued neither that monster nor the mysteries of Braille. The elderly Crosby blamed her discomfort with Braille on the other uses to which she preferred to put her sensitive fingers — knitting, fancy sewing, and playing musical instruments. Much later her friend Hubert Main admitted as well Crosby's poor penmanship: "She has attempted to write her name but once to my knowledge, and you would not know the result from a pile of spider's legs. She has an idea of how capital letters look, also such letters as are in the Bible for the blind, but nothing else."

Crosby learned quickly that discipline extended to all areas of the students' lives. They rose at the sound of a bell at 5:30 or 6:00 A.M. (depending on the season), tidied their (shared) rooms, and proceeded every morning into a regimented day. A second bell summoned them to 8:00 chapel worship led by the superintendent or a male teacher. Breakfast followed, and in this gendered setting students stood behind their regular seats until a male pupil took his place between the girls' and boys' dining rooms and asked a blessing. School hours ran from 9:00 A.M. to noon and from 1:30 to 4:30 P.M. At 7:00 P.M. pupils assembled to hear reading from daily newspapers. At 8:00 the school proceeded to the chapel for worship. After prayers, pupils might while away an hour in conversation, games, or songs in one of the school's commodious parlors. Older students headed for their rooms by 9:45, said their prayers and went to bed. The rules required "entire separation of the sexes" for most of the day, except in the classroom. Male students spent their time in the northern half of the buildings and grounds, while females passed the day in the southern half. Sleeping rooms were off-limits to all between breakfast and bedtime. During free hours students practiced being model ladies and gentlemen, conversing politely in the drawing room or walking in the garden. Occasional playtimes and outings varied the daily routine, but the school sought to instill a firm sense of duty and order. The system curtailed but could not suppress the students' irrepressible delight in practical jokes. They raided the garden, hid the postman's logbook, and Crosby composed her share of jingles poking fun at people and events.

Surviving records acknowledge few negative traits in the young Fanny Crosby. A few lines in her autobiographical musings, though, hint that her instructors detected unlovely pride in her response to the flattery her poems elicited — pride expressed, as she put it, in "an air or two." Crosby recalled that one superintendent, Silas Jones, summoned her to his office and dealt with her kindly but firmly. Throughout her life she remembered his two observations ("bombshells," she thought them at the time): she knew very little; and God, not self, was the source of any small abilities she manifested. Taken together, Crosby's multiple autobiographies suggest that she recognized periodic inner turmoil over the egotism Jones detected. Everywhere people remarked on her unassuming ways; Jones first surfaced for Crosby the contours of a lifelong struggle with pride.

During her first year in New York, an enormous fire that began in Maiden Lane and swept through lower Manhattan changed the face of the city forever. The blaze consumed some 600 buildings and property worth at least $20 million. It also eradicated a way of life. Stunned New Yorkers watched helplessly as the intense cold of a December night hampered efforts to quell the blaze. The flames quickly became unmanageable, and the "apathy of despair" gripped the firefighters as well as the assembled crowd. It also brought into view the city's underside. "Miserable wretches" drunkenly plundered the ruins, wrote former New York mayor Philip Hone in his diary, and "a gang of low Irishmen" inaugurated a run on city banks. (Accusations about the unruly Irish framed much political comment in Crosby's Manhattan.)

The fire destroyed Knickerbocker New York, obliterating most remaining traces of the old Dutch city. Lower Manhattan was rebuilt in granite and marble, with brown freestone used on the fronts of some of the more expensive new residences (the first brownstones). Only the opening of the Erie Canal in 1825 had worked comparable change on

Manhattan. The canal had made New York America's commercial center, sent the population soaring and for more than a generation poured generous revenues into state coffers. Now from the ashes of the great fire rose a modern city. For the moment, Yankee flavor predominated.

Crosby's day-to-day life in New York proceeded against an ever changing backdrop of "revelations" and agitations over personalities, religion, politics, or immigration. Topics or people seized public imagination at least weekly, if not daily, only to be abandoned for the next absorbing excitement. But orderly life continued, too. Institution students followed an array of compelling current concerns, some promising to alter the lives of ordinary people. Every night they listened to the reading of the day's newspaper. But causes of the moment, while they influenced the Institution's visitors list, did not vary the Institution's routine.

The school's 1837 roster introduced fifty pupils by name, eighteen females and thirty-two males. Donors supporting Institution programs now included such famous names as John Jacob Astor, reputedly the wealthiest of all Americans, and multimillionaire industrialist Anson G. Phelps (vice president, then president, of the Board of Managers).

Two Crosbys sat on the Institution's early board: William and John. Like Fanny, they descended from Thomas Crosby, but unlike her, these two sons of William Bedloe Crosby had been born to wealth and privilege. After the premature deaths of William's parents, he had been reared by his maternal grandmother's brother, the irascible, wealthy bachelor Colonel Henry Rutgers. On Rutgers's death, William inherited well over a million dollars as well as the substantial Rutgers mansion (occupying an entire square city block). William's twelve sons and daughters embraced the same Calvinist heritage Fanny cherished, and their consequent commitments to duty and good works made them prominent on New York's benevolent scene. John Crosby, son-in-law of Martin Van Buren's attorney general, Benjamin Butler, practiced law in New York for the firm of Crosby, Hoffman and Crosby and was "largely engaged" in the business of religious and benevolent societies. A trustee of the Presbytery of New York and of the College of Physicians and Surgeons, he was also a manager of the Institution. His brother, William Henry Crosby, was equally prominent in New York's Presbyterian and corporate circles. At the Institution, then, Fanny met these fellow descendants of Thomas Crosby from Holme-on-Spalding Moor. While life's circumstances had dealt differently with them, they had in common the Calvinist religious faith and strong devotion to duty that stood at the core of their common Puritan heritage.

New Yorkers of all classes felt the pain of the economic crisis of the late 1830s. Stalwarts of the city's Protestant elite faced financial ruin. In 1840 the young George Templeton Strong, well on his way to becoming a wealthy lawyer and leading citizen, recorded in his diary: "Manhattan Bank stock is at seventy and Arthur Tappan has exploded, and everybody and everything is going, going, going to the devil. The history of New York for the last three years is comparable to nothing but the explosion of a pack of crackers — pop, pop, pop — one after another they go off, and all their substance vanishes in fumes."

January 1838 brought to the Institution a new pupil and to Crosby a roommate named Alice Holmes, a resident of Jersey City, New Jersey. Born in Norfolk, England, Holmes had lost her sight when she came down with smallpox on the family's voyage to New York. Nine years old, she had begun school in England, and her family placed her in a private school near their new home in Jersey City. She soon exhausted its resources. A painful eye inflammation brought Holmes to the New York Eye Infirmary, and a physician told the family about the Institution for the Blind. Just a year younger than Crosby, Holmes became a lifelong friend. Holmes's description (in *Lost Vision*, 1888) of their first evening together offers a rare glimpse of the eighteen-year-old Crosby:

> At a quarter before ten, Miss Crosby announced that she would take charge of the new pupil from New Jersey, as I was to room with her, and at once, with a kind good-night to all, taking me by the hand, she started off at a pace which rendered me rather timid, every step being new and strange to my "unfrequented feet," which, observing, she told me not to be afraid as she would not let me break my neck; and after crossing one of the main halls and reaching the third door beyond a long flight of stairs, she remarked, "Here we are; this is our room." We entered, and closing the door she said, "Now Dollie (which was one of her pet names), this is a square room facing Eighth Avenue, and right here on this side is your bed, and here is your trunk, and here is a place to hang

your clothes"; in short, she "tended me like a welcome guest." Before saying our prayers, however, she inquired into my religious views, and I at once declared myself an Episcopalian, to which she humorously replied, "Oh, then you are a churchman," and made a rhyme which ran something like this: Oh! How it grieves my poor old bones/To sleep so near this Alice Holmes/I will inform good Mr. Jones/I cannot room with a Churchman. Then she hoped I would not be offended or feel hurt, as she was only in fun; and with a warm good night retired to her side of our apartment.

Awakened by a bell and "a pleasant morning salutation from Miss Crosby," Holmes started her new schedule — breakfast, with the proviso that any who failed to arrive within five minutes of the bell could not enter; study time; morning prayers at 8:00; a lecture on phrenology for the entire school. Only then did the regular school day begin.

The plenary lecture on phrenology showed the Institution's participation in a fad that provided distraction in the midst of the economic downturn between 1838 and 1840. A newly popular "science" that read personality by analyzing the contours of the skull, phrenology had excited enormous curiosity and become a popular diversion. New York and the entire Northeast buzzed with talk of the visiting George Combe, a British phrenologist acclaimed as one of the fathers of the science. Combe's reputation (he had published extensively on the subject) combined with amateur interest to prompt people to buy advance tickets for his lectures and practical demonstrations. Combe sailed into New York harbor on 25 September 1838, spent three busy days planning his schedule, and embarked for Boston. Along the way, throngs turned out to greet him as his stage rolled across the countryside. In Massachusetts he conversed at length on education with the governor, Edward Everett, and Horace Mann, state secretary of education (with whom he began a lifelong correspondence). His views intrigued such leading citizens as George Bancroft, William Ellery Channing, Daniel Webster, and George Ticknor. Fascinated by educational theory, Combe captivated these Americans with his unusual claims about the human temperament. "My eyes never rested on such a collection of excellent brains," Combe wrote of one Boston audience. He meant more than intellectual capacity; he looked as well to the form of the skull itself. His "demonstrations" offered "scientific" con-

clusions about individual inclination and character derived from precise measurements and analysis of the skeletal structure. From these,
Combe distinguished what he called "temperaments." "The state of
the organs," he insisted, manifested "the mental powers and dispositions." (In his *Memoirs* Combe included his measurements and intriguing analysis of the estimable Boston Unitarian preacher William Ellery
Channing.)

A series of lectures in Manhattan followed Combe's triumphs in
Boston. Again he fascinated prominent citizens — medical men,
judges, lawyers, legislators. He devoted two to three hours every
morning to "practical demonstrations" and one day visited the Institution for the express purpose of "examining the craniums" of the blind.
Those who manifested unusual abilities, among them Fanny Crosby,
were chosen to submit to his analysis. Much later Crosby remembered
that Combe had endorsed her interest in poetry: "Here is a poetess,"
she reported he said. "Give her every possible advantage. Read the
best books to her, and teach her to appreciate the best poetry." For the
next few years lectures on phrenology were incorporated into the institute's curriculum. To Crosby's delight, Combe's verdict led Institution
personnel to redouble efforts to encourage her facility for words. She
regarded herself, with some justification, as the unofficial "poet laureate" of the Institution. A poem she wrote in 1848 — perhaps in deference to the long obsession around her with one's skull — recorded her
musings as she held a skull and placed a watch inside it. "Time Chronicled in a Skull" began:

> Why should I fear it? Once the pulse of life
> Throbbed in these temples, pale and bloodless now.
> Here reason sat enthroned, its empire held
> O'er infant thought and thought to action grown.

For more than a year, Combe lectured up and down the East
Coast. He dissected brains with medical students and held audiences
spellbound with his demonstrations, but by 1840 he concluded that
American interest ran no deeper than a passing fancy. Disappointed,
he returned to Scotland, and New Yorkers moved on to other pastimes. But Crosby never forgot him, and his "reading" of her ability
found an enduring place in the Crosby myth.

In 1839 (the same year iceboxes made their appearance in New York City markets and New York theaters produced wildly popular stage versions of new works by Charles Dickens), the expanded premises of the Institution were ready for occupancy. The cornerstone had been laid in 1837. The ceremony — attended by the mayor and city council — included words by Crosby set to a march tune composed by Anthony Reiff, the Institution's new instrumental music instructor:

> This day may every bosom feel
> A thrill of pleasure and delight;
> Its scenes will in our memories dwell
> When Time shall wing his rapid flight.
>
> May the great Being who surveys
> The countless acts by mortals done,
> Behold with an approving eye
> The structure that is now begun.

In June 1841 the Institution dedicated a long-awaited chapel. Unequivocally Protestant but free of denominational control, the chapel would soon expose Crosby to a menu of religious ideas and styles that influenced her perceptions of American Protestantism. For the dedicatory service, she composed a sacred text:

> Oh, Thou omniscient, omnipresent Lord!
> Invisible, eternal God of all!
> The vast creation trembles at Thy word,
> And at Thy footstool nations prostrate fall.
>
> Thy throne is fixed above the starry frame;
> Yet Thou in earthly temples lov'st to dwell;
> The humble spirit thou wilt not disdain,
> The wounded heart Thy balm divine dost heal.
>
> Father, we humbly supplicate Thy grace,
> May Thy benignant smile on us be given,
> Thy blessing rest upon this sacred place,
> Thine earthly house, we trust, the gate of heaven.

Here will we listen to Thy holy word;
Light on our path, thus, may its precepts be;
Here shall the voice of praise and prayer be heard —
Ourselves, our all, we dedicate to Thee.

Pupils provided much of the choral and instrumental music for the dedication, while three New York pastors read, preached, and prayed their way through the momentous occasion. Students had all along met for daily morning and evening prayers. Now they anticipated regular Sunday services featuring "some of the prominent clergy of our city from different denominations." The school required that all students attend morning and afternoon Sunday services on site unless they gained permission to be present at church elsewhere. Crosby, the self-styled "primitive Presbyterian" whose brief exposure to Quakers and Methodists had first beckoned her beyond her childhood limits, would now sit under the sermons of Dutch Reformed, Methodist, and Episcopalian divines as well as under the more familiar ministrations of the occasional Presbyterian or Congregationalist.

The Institution's 1841 report indicated some difficulty in identifying twenty "intelligent and benevolent gentlemen" for the Board of Managers. Despite its progress, the school had not won the full sympathy of Manhattan citizens. In 1845 its leaders still found it necessary to make the case for the school's goal of helping the blind lead useful lives against rumors that it existed primarily for "the indigent blind" whom it sought to feed and clothe "at the lowest possible expenditure." It is no wonder that official delegations of state and city legislators called frequently to keep abreast of progress, nor that the Institution seized opportunities to use Crosby and other pupils as examples of the worth of the endeavor.

While renovation and construction improved their immediate surroundings, Institution pupils had been caught up in the city's excitement over the 1840 election. The Panic of 1837 and its aftermath doomed Martin Van Buren's chance for a second term as president and paved the way for months of extraordinary political excitement. A "sound money" man, Van Buren stood for the absolute divorce of the government from the business of banking. To oppose him in 1840 the Whigs nominated William Henry Harrison. Not even Harrison's detractors blamed him for the mayhem that followed. William Allen Butler, a prominent Manhattan lawyer and Van Buren stalwart, confided to his diary that the campaign was "unparalleled for the gross and demoralizing methods by which it pandered to the cravings of the people for a change of administration." Manhattanites, ever ready for a thrill, threw themselves into "monster mass meetings" complete with the log cabins, raccoons, and hard cider that symbolized the Harrison/ John Tyler ticket. New Yorkers gave the Whig campaign a local hub by constructing a log cabin in a vacant lot at the corner of Broadway and Prince Street. They turned the long weeks of the campaign into an enormous popular frolic complete with processions, picnics, and shouts of "Van, Van is a used up man." Crosby heartily supported Harrison (though she later came to know and admire Van Buren). New Yorkers who did not tended to agree with the disenchanted William Butler: "Had I not been an eye-witness of these performances, I could hardly believe that a civilized people, the founders and promoters of free government on the western hemisphere, could have exhibited such a travesty on the serious business of electing a president."

Crosby apparently allowed herself to be moved by the national excitement that gave the election to Harrison. She still thought of herself as a Democrat, but she held war heroes in the highest esteem. Her happiness over Harrison's election gave way a few weeks later to mourning his untimely death, an event marked publicly in the city, which paused for a day in honor of the hero of the Battle of Tippecanoe. Crosby vented her private grief in a poem of lament:

He's gone; in death's cold arms he sleeps.
Our President, our hero brave,
While fair Columbia o'er him weeps,
And chants a requiem at his grave;
Her sanguine hopes are blighted now
And weeds of sorrow veil her brow.

Ah, Indiana, where is he,
Who once thy sons to battle led?
The red man quailed beneath his eye,
And from his camp disheartened fled.
With steady hand he bent the bow
And laid the warlike savage low.

The forest with his praises rung,
His fame was echoed far and wide,
With loud hurrah his name was sung,
Columbia's hero and her pride.
The tuneful harp is now unstrung
And on the drooping willow hung.

When the new president, John Tyler, visited Manhattan, Crosby
recited a poem of welcome for him including the lines:

And the glad song of our nation shall be,
Hurrah for John Tyler and liberty tree.

The Protestant ritual of Anniversary Week in May 1842 involved
as usual the public recital of the annual accomplishments of the city's
Protestant-based endeavors for the common good. This time the self-
congratulatory crowds appointed an hour to note the progress of the
Institution for the Blind. After paying the requisite admission fee, the
assembled thousands heard Crosby celebrate the knowledge that was
beginning to make a difference to her prospects in life.

The smile that decks the human face,
The brilliant eye, the joyous brow
Are beauties we may never trace;
A rayless midnight shrouds us now
But why, O why the falling tear?
Why heaves the sad, unbidden sigh?
The lamp of knowledge, bright and clear,
Pours luster on our mental eye.

References to education as light pervade the poems Crosby composed at the Institution to welcome dignitaries and demonstrate the capacities of the blind. Another put it this way: "May we not hope the
scene you now behold/will prove to every mind/Instruction hath a ray
to cheer the blind." In this connection, it is helpful to remember that
Crosby could perceive light, though she could not distinguish objects.

The Institution's 1842 report to the New York state legislature for
the first time appended a section titled "Specimens of the Composi-

tions of the Pupils." Among the poems and essays were two Fanny Crosby contributions, both poems: "The Blind Girl's Lament" and "They're Gone." Future reports contained other samples of Fanny's work: "To the Memory of the Honorable Hugh S. Legare, of South Carolina, Late Secretary of State" or "Address to Board of Managers of the New York Institution for the Blind."

The words Crosby addressed to the memory of Legaré, John Tyler's cabinet officer, highlight the efforts of the Institution to inculcate civic pride. Pupils knew the news, followed legislative developments, and understood the process of government. In a day when newspapers often published detailed daily accounts of legislative sessions, teachers easily kept the students abreast of current events. A bevy of prominent people paraded through the Institution. For some public figures, it was an obligatory stop when visiting New York, and the mayor and city aldermen frequently accompanied distinguished visitors to the city. In this way Crosby met people in the news — the "sensations" of the day as well as a succession of New York mayors and legislators; Johann Tellkamp, the personable professor of German at Columbia College; the famous Whig editor Horace Greeley (who published a few of her poems); Mexican War hero General Winfield Scott; the "Great Compromiser," Henry Clay; the "Swedish Nightingale," Jenny Lind; poet and editor William Cullen Bryant. She listened attentively to the famous Irish temperance activist, Father Theobald Mathew, who enlisted millions of men and women in a mass movement for social reform. She submitted to examination by Dr. Combe. Much later Crosby recalled the attention important people had paid her; as her fame grew, she, too, took time for those who sought her out.

New group experiences filled these busy student years, expanding Crosby's social world as well as her intellectual opportunities. In August 1842, in the school's most ambitious publicity effort to date, twenty selected students and staff, including Crosby, sailed the "great highway" of the waterways of the Erie Canal. They navigated its shallow waters (nowhere more than four feet deep) in a canal boat towed by mule team, served by a crew of captain, driver, and maid. Covered, with a spacious salon and a kitchen on board, the canal boat made slow progress through the many locks along the way, sometimes traveling no more than three miles per hour. While they waited for the locks to fill or empty, students got their daily exercise by running ahead on the towpath accompanied by a sighted teacher. The group stopped to perform — sing, declaim, demonstrate their mathematical skills — in canal boomtowns and tiny hamlets, generating expanded awareness of the Institution's presence and purpose, recruiting students, and learning about the history and topography of New York State. Along the way they sometimes shared the canal boat with other passengers (although much of their journey was on a chartered boat), and they met the mayors and prominent citizens of the state's larger cities. The trip culminated in a visit to Niagara Falls, where the students heard the roaring water, felt its spray, and listened as other visitors described the view.

For the stops on this voyage, Crosby again wove the image of light into the lines she delivered at the end of the oft-repeated students' program:

But there's a lamp within whose sacred light,
Burns with a luster ever pure and bright —
'Tis education we have shown to you
What by its rays illumed, the blind can do.

Without it, life a dreary waste would be,
With nought to break its long monotony —
No sunny beams to light our cheerless way —
Our vacant thoughts, ah! Whither would they stray?

But thanks to God, his sovereign care we own,
He hath not left us friendless and alone.
His pitying eye beheld the helpless blind
And reared us friends affectionate and kind.

For a child of Southeast, New York, transplanted to Manhattan, the mammoth public excitement in the fall of 1842 must have had special significance: Crosby's hometown Croton River water flowed into the pipes that supplied New York City. A multiyear project had dammed the Croton River near Southeast in 1837 to create Croton Lake, covering 400 acres that in Crosby's childhood had been farmland. Slowly construction moved south. Contemporaries marveled at the massive stone, brick, and cement aqueduct, arched above and below and standing 7.5 feet wide and 8.5 feet high, through which water flowed to Manhattan, some forty miles to the south. This engineering marvel crossed the Harlem River via a magnificent stone bridge 1,450 feet long, resting atop fourteen immense piers 114 feet high. A receiving reservoir stood at the corner of Eighty-sixth Street and Sixth Avenue in Manhattan (a site later absorbed by Central Park), where a lake covering 35 acres held 150 million gallons of water.

Earlier in 1842 festivities to mark the opening of the reservoir had been incorporated into the city's annual lavish celebration of the Fourth of July. Excitement mounted until the completion of the project in the fall. City officials declared 14 October a holiday, and a daylong celebration interweaving religious fervor and American pride brought Manhattan residents into the streets to mark the completion of the water project. At 10 A.M. citizens thronged the streets to cheer along a seven-mile-long civic and military procession that moved uptown from the Battery canopied by flags and stepping to lively music. Careful timing allowed authorities to turn on the grand new fountains (that justly became the pride of New Yorkers) precisely as dignitaries stepped up to one square and park after another. Manhattan leaders exuded satisfaction with their system: "As an instance of the liberality and enterprise of a free people it stands preeminent," they announced, insisting that only ancient Roman engineers had approached — though they had not equaled — the magnitude of New York's accomplishment. The festivities culminated late in the day with speeches followed by the New York Sacred Music Society's rendering of a song commissioned for the occasion:

Water shouts a glad hosanna,
Bubbles up to Earth to bless,
Cheers it like the precious manna
In the barren wilderness.
Here we, wondering, gaze, assembled
Like the grateful Hebrew band
When the hidden fountain trembled
And obeyed the Prophet's wand.

From October 1842, a distribution reservoir between Fortieth and Forty-second Streets (the site of the New York Public Library) covered four acres and rose forty feet above the city streets. From there, underground iron pipes conducted the water to every part of New York City. The famous radical abolitionist and journalist Lydia Maria Child in 1844 reminisced about the day: "Oh, who that has not been shut up in the great prison cell of a city and made to drink of its brackish springs can estimate the blessings of the Croton Aqueduct? Clean, sweet, abundant water! Well might they bring it thirty miles under-ground and usher it into the city with roaring cannon, sonorous bells, waving flags, floral canopies, and a loud chorus of song!"

In the winter of 1842, Crosby — now twenty-two years old — continued her studies but also started teaching younger pupils, and explored the city's growing array of churches. In the spring the Institution's directors began planning another foray into upstate New York.

But first the Institution welcomed the entire New York State Senate. Their arrival on 22 June 1843 lived on in Crosby's memory as a thrilling event that followed long preparations. Crosby addressed them:

> Yon glorious orb that gilds the azure skies
> Sheds not a ray to cheer these sightless eyes;
> The dewy lawn, mild nature's sylvan bowers —
> To trace these lovely scenes must ne'er be ours;
> But education's pure refulgent light
> Illumes our souls, dispels our mental night;
> Joy on each brow a smiling garland weaves;
> Here, too, her magic strain soft music breathes.

In late summer selected students and staff embarked on a trip that proved far more grueling than the previous year's adventure on the Erie Canal. Instead of living on a "floating hotel," the scholars and their chaperones rode uncomfortable wagons over rough upstate roads, often to out-of-the-way places. For several weeks they roamed from one small interior New York town to another, answering the awkward questions of curious well-wishers who did not know what to say to blind students and doing their best to exhibit their accomplishments. The aged Crosby liked to recall lines from the invitation she composed:

Is there no tender parent here,
Who oft in sorrow weeps alone,
For the sweet child he holds so dear,
O'er whom a rayless night is thrown?

Then place amid our youthful band
That loved one cherished long by thee;
There will her intellect expand
And her young heart beat light and free.

There will her fingers learn to trace
The page by inspiration given;
The page of sacred truth and grace —
The star that guides her soul to heaven.

The program advertised for Oswego, New York, offers a glimpse of what these summer exhibitions were like. On Wednesday, 6 September 1843, the *Oswego Palladium* announced an exhibition for Friday, 22 September, for Oswego and the next day at nearby Fulton. Admission was twelve and a half cents. Two managers, the superintendent, the matron, a teacher, and fourteen pupils composed the traveling group that promised an address, examinations, and vocal and band music as well as sales of goods made at the Institution. The editor urged friends of the county's nine blind people to bring them to the program.

A severe storm delayed the arrival of the *Oneida*, the Lake Ontario vessel on which the Institution travelers sailed from their prior engagement, and forced a late start and an abbreviated program at the Oswego Methodist church. The audience nonetheless filled the church for a program that "exhibited capacity for mental, moral and religious improvement" that "could not but affect the benevolent." By the time they stood before the Oswego crowd, the group had rehearsed its program in all the major towns between Albany and Buffalo to appreciative audiences. Among the crowd that heeded advice to bring Oswego County's blind to the program was Mary Dowd van Alstine, whose son, Alexander, was legally blind. In 1858 van Alstine and Crosby would be married. Crosby liked to say that she had delivered the invitation to the Institution that his mother heeded, thus bringing the two together.

The pupils gave their program as well in Utica, a city eighty-five miles south of Oswego. With the hope of persuading at least a few of the forty-seven blind residents of Oneida County to enroll at the Institution, eleven male and four female students told the audience "of the wonderful blessings conferred by this development of Christian enterprise and love." Of Crosby's recitation, a Utica reporter wrote: "There was a touching piece of poetry, the composition of one of the sightless young ladies, and recited by herself in a modest and yet distinct manner, that could not have failed to reach all but marble hearts."

The party reached Manhattan late in September to resume the rhythm of life at the Institution. That fall (1843) brought to Manhattan General Count Henri-Gratien Bertrand, Napoleon's famous field marshal and companion in exile on Saint Helena. With Bertrand's arrival the city turned from its preoccupation with the visit of the famous English tragedian William Macready, manager of London's Drury Lane Theatre, to devote its resources to feting the venerable Bertrand and waxing sentimental about Napoleon. "Extraordinary civilities, public and private" honored this veteran of European upheavals. Among them was a ceremony at the Institution where Crosby, of course, offered an emotion-packed tribute composed in the general's honor:

When by those he loved deserted,
Thine was still a faithful heart;
Thou wert proud to share the exile
Of the hapless Bonaparte.

The same year New Yorkers followed the experiments run by Samuel F. B. Morse, who had recently received permission to string a telegraph line between New York and Baltimore. He had publicly exhibited his invention at the University of New York in 1837, and city residents watched the progress of yet another sign of the future. The Manhattan of Crosby's youth hummed with hopeful excitement about progress, and pupils at the Institution followed its course.

The year 1844 began with a journey Crosby always remembered as a highlight of her life. On Wednesday evening, 24 January, sixteen selected students from the Institution gave a program in the Assembly Hall of the House of Representatives at the capitol in Washington, D.C. The goal was a practical demonstration for the benefit of members of the House and Senate, of the educability of the blind. Sitting among the audience were some of the decade's most famous Americans — past and future presidents and eminent legislators: John Quincy Adams, then a Massachusetts representative; Andrew Johnson, senator from Tennessee; James Buchanan of Pennsylvania; Stephen Douglas of Illinois; Thomas Hart Benton of Missouri; Jefferson Davis, future president of the Confederate States of America; Georgia's Alexander Stephens (later vice president of the Confederate States of America); Hannibal Hamlin, later Lincoln's vice president. Crosby's part in the program, a thirteen-stanza "poetical address," drew calls for an encore.

What though these orbs in rayless darkness roll?
Instruction pours its radiance o'er the soul,
And fancy pictures to the mental eye
The glittering hosts that 'lume the midnight sky.
O ye who here from every State convene,
Illustrious band! May we not hope the scene
You now behold will prove to every mind
Instruction hath a ray to cheer the blind.

For her encore Crosby chose the words she had dedicated a few months before to honor the memory of Hugh Legare, Tyler's cabinet member who, on Daniel Webster's resignation, became interim secretary of state. Legare's death of a heart attack in 1843 while laying the cornerstone at the Bunker Hill Monument in Boston had shocked the nation and prompted an outpouring of patriotic grief. Crosby's poem moved the audience, crowded with Legare's colleagues, to tears, and she was rewarded by a handshake from John Quincy Adams and a ring from Legare's sister. During a visit to Congress, Crosby heard the aging Adams argue on behalf of the Smithsonian Institution. She cherished the memory for the rest of her life.

On the return trip the twenty students detoured to Trenton, where on 29 January 1844 they offered "An Exhibition" before the New Jersey governor, council, and assembly. Crosby urged their attention to the matter of education:

We — honored legislative band
With glowing hearts before you stand; —

We plead for those bereft of sight,
Who sigh for education's light.

The March 1844 edition of the *Columbian Magazine* introduced its readers to Miss Frances Jane Crosby as the author of a long poem, partly autobiographical, entitled "The Blind Girl." Under the heading "Eyes to the Blind," the editors remarked on Crosby's "abundant exhibition" of the ability of the blind to form mental images of objects. Extolling her descriptions as "invariably true," her comparisons as "faithful," and her epithets as "appropriate," they wondered if the blind possessed a batlike faculty that supplied "to a great extent the vision of which they are deprived." The poem traced Crosby's move from sightless ignorance to illumined mind:

How changed that sightless orphan now!
No longer clouded is her brow,
Her buoyant step is light and free,
And none more happy is than she,
For education's glorious light
Hath chased away her mental night.

Later in the spring of 1844, this poem became the title number of Crosby's first book of poetry. A fund-raising ploy for the Institution rather than a personal endeavor, *The Blind Girl and Other Poems* collected verse she had prepared for public moments over her years at the Institution. The prominent New York banker and Institution benefactor Hamilton Murray wrote a preface presenting Crosby's work as evidence of what a blind person could accomplish rather than offering the poems first and foremost as poetry. Their quality varied widely but compared favorably to the early work of contemporaries like Bryant or the ever popular Bayard Taylor. Her verses often gained popularity not because they were extraordinary but because their language and sentiments struck familiar chords, and because she was blind. A review in a New York weekly, the *New Mirror*, though, enthused that the book justified "great modification of our pity for the blind," for "eyes could scarce do more!" The reader would never suspect the author's blindness, the reviewer insisted: "She seems to forget it herself. She talks of 'crimson tints' and 'purple west' and 'stars of mildest hue' with quite the familiarity of those who see." The 160-page collection, published by the well-known firm of Wiley and Putnam, sold widely enough to raise funds for the Institution, and it also introduced Crosby's name to a wider public. Crosby later remarked that her first three hymns appeared in this 1844 book. She identified them as "Evening Hymn," a meditation on Psalm 4:8 ("I will both lay me down in peace and sleep; for thou, Lord, only, makest me to dwell in safety"), "Easter Sunday," and "Christmas Hymn."

At the end of the 1844 school year, Crosby's roommate Alice Holmes graduated and returned to Jersey City. Years later she addressed a poem "to my friend and classmate, Miss Frances J. Crosby," in which she offered a glimpse of life at the Institution:

> Yes! Frances, dear, when I recall
> To mind those bygone, happy days,
> When we with youthful ardor sought
> The golden light of learning's rays,
> And shared each other's joy and grief,
> And daily worshiped at one shrine,
> And in our leisure moments sought
> Fresh budding wreaths of love to twine,
> And oft at twilight's rosy hour,
> Some favorite strain from thy guitar,
> An echo found in many a heart,
> As zephyrs bore its tones afar,
> And when beneath the willow's shade,
> Thou wouldst repeat enchanting lays,
> Thus newly by thy muse inspired,
> 'Twas pleasure sweet to give thee praise.
> And e'en in sadder, darker hours,
> When grief or pain oppressed my heart,
> Thy tender care, thy counsels sweet
> Would to my soul new joys impart.
> And though those days fled fast away,
> Of them bright visions oft return;
> And cherished sparks of friendship still,
> For thee on my heart's altar burn.
> And Frances, dear, may I not hope,

> In all thy life, through good and ill,
> That she who treasures sweet thy name
> May sometimes be remembered still?

As the 1844 presidential election approached, Henry Clay, the "Great Compromiser" from Kentucky, won the Whig Party's nomination. "Clay balls" were all the rage in New York that year, and during Clay's campaign visit to New York Crosby warmed to his personality though she still clung to her preference for Democratic politics. By mid-1844, though, worn out by the round of recent excitements — travel, book preparation, teaching, and the pressures of her busy life — Crosby seemed on the verge of physical collapse. She spent the summer recuperating at her mother's Bridgeport, Connecticut, home, and in September returned to her routine refreshed. That fall she met former president Martin Van Buren, still a powerful New York politician. In 1845 the newly inaugurated president, the Democrat James Knox Polk, made an official visit to the Institution, where Crosby welcomed him with a stirring "poetical address" praising republican government.

Crosby's poetry frequently revealed her thorough familiarity with current events. She followed political news as well as the happenings that gripped the city. Sighted staff at the Institution devoted time daily to reading newspapers to the pupils, and Crosby's awareness of people, issues, and events demonstrated the success of this endeavor. For example, during a snow squall in April 1845, a Hudson River steamboat, the *Swallow*, struck a rock, broke in two, burst into flames, and sank. Quick action saved most passengers, but fifteen died, and Crosby's reaction captured not only the scene but also human emotion and divine providence:

> He pointed to a female form
> That floated senseless on the wave;
> "Leave me to perish! Fly to her!
> And snatch her from a threatened grave!"

And,

> Thanks to a Providence divine
> Two hundred passengers they save;

But, bitter thought! Full many sleep
Beneath the Hudson's rolling wave.

The 1845 Anniversary Week program featured Crosby giving an "expressive recitation" of an original poem:

Oh! 'tis a glorious morn, the golden sun
Just peeping from his orient chambers, calls
On Nature to rejoice, and banish sleep.
Up! Cast the drapery of thy couch aside
Nor waste in slumber precious hours like these;
To the blue skies above thee lift thine eyes,
Lovely as when its Maker's voice divine
Did first its birth proclaim, and the bright stars
In heavenly concert swelled their notes of praise.
Go forth where Nature's bounteous hand hath strewn
Her choicest beauties; her luxurian flowers,
West with the tears that night hath o'er them wept —
Woo'd by the sporting zephyr's mild caress,
They rear their blushing heads, and smiling greet
In silent eloquence the fair young morn.

Oh! Could we with the gloomy shades of night
Chase the dark clouds of sorrow from the brow;
Could pure affection feel no withering blight
And heart to heart in one sweet tie be linked;
How were the soul content to fold her wings,
And dwell forever 'mid such loveliness.

But earth is not our home; its fairest scenes
Entrance but with a momentary joy.
A few short months, and the green spot thou tend'st
Will smile no more, nor gentle flower be seen,
Nor carol sweet of the aerial choir
In that deserted spot will charm thine ear.
Thus the most sacred ties of human love
By death's cold hand are broken one by one:
Friend after friend departs; with mournful step

67

We bear them to the narrow house of clay
And to our hearts comes home the solemn truth,
"We are but dust, to dust we shall return."

In 1846 Crosby returned to Washington, D.C., where advocates of education for the blind from Boston, Philadelphia, and New York convened to support a bill offering federal support for education for the blind. Crosby recited original poems before congressmen, a House subcommittee, and in the White House, where she sang one of her poems for President Polk and accompanied herself on the piano: "Our President! We humbly turn to thee — Are not the blind the objects of thy care?"

Crosby enjoyed her visits to Washington and cherished lifelong the memories they left her, but the larger effort in which she took part ultimately failed. The bill, long promoted especially by the two-term Kentucky Democrat representative John Wooleston Tibbats, was buried in committee, and supporters of federal action on behalf of education for the blind gave up their fight.

The May Anniversary of 1846 scheduled a Wednesday afternoon focus on the Institution. The audience crowded the Broadway Tabernacle to hear one of the pupils play Handel's "Hallelujah Chorus" on the celebrated Tabernacle organ. Crosby had no poem (that was left to an eleven-year-old whose lines strikingly resembled Crosby's earlier offerings), but she examined a large class in grammar — "a very pleasing exhibition, especially in parsing," a writer for the New York Evangelist thought.

Listed as a student for the first time in the Institution's Tenth Annual Report, in 1846 (for the year 1845), was fifteen-year-old Alexander van Alstine from Oswego in upstate New York. He had enrolled as a result of the 1843 summer tour. The son of Alexander "Wells" van Alstine, listed in the 1825 Saint Catharines (Ontario) census as an engineer on Canada's Welland Canal (hence the "Wells"), and an Irish-born mother, Mary Dowd, van Alstine was legally blind although he had limited sight.

Young Alexander's family had moved to Oswego from Canada shortly after his father's death in the early 1830s. Van Alstine was a common name in New York, as in Upper Canada. It derived from the Dutch and referenced an old stone. According to the family historian, its preferred New World spelling used *i* instead of the *y* that some came to favor. The first van Alstines had arrived in New Amsterdam by the mid-1650s. During the Revolutionary War era one Peter van Alstine joined the British army. In 1783 he left the family's substantial holdings near Albany, New York, to lead nearly two hundred people on an arduous trip by flat-bottomed boat up the Hudson River and Lake Champlain to Canada. As United Empire Loyalists, this group received land grants along Lake Ontario in Adolphustown, Ontario. It is difficult to ascertain how or if Alexander related to this clan of people who shared his name, but Wells van Alstine, born in the old country, may have had ties to this proliferating New World connection.

He married Mary Dowd in Canada. She was a widow whose older children had been born in England before her first husband had brought the family to Upper Canada. Together Mary and Wells had two sons, Thomas (born in Canada in 1825) and Alexander (born in 1831 in Cayuga, New York). In 1831, shortly after Wells's death, his widow moved the family to Oswego, New York, a small village on the southeastern edge of Lake Ontario which became their home until Mary's death in June 1880. The page of the 1855 state census that bears some of the family's names reveals that a high percentage of Oswego's citizens, like the van Alstines, listed Canada, Newfoundland, England, or Ireland as their place of birth. There were also other van Alstine families in the city.

In 1845-46, van Alstine's first year at the Institution for the Blind, his studies focused in English, geography, and arithmetic, although instrumental music would soon become his concentration. For the next four years, Fanny Crosby and Alexander van Alstine knew each other casually at the school. A decade later, she would become his wife.

Pupils enrolled at the Institution at different ages, and there was no rule about precisely how quickly they needed to finish their educations. In fact, some who completed the available programs — and "mature men" who had lost eyesight through accidents — were indefinitely connected to the Institution's "industrial department." (For example, the superintendent estimated in 1855 that 100 men "derived support from the Institution while not living within it," earning between one and seven dollars per week by manufacturing goods for sale.) Like many others pupils, Crosby had nearly reached adulthood before enrolling. After ten years she had completed the course work the Institution offered. Much later her friend Robert Lowry summarized the transformation her student years had effected: "The darkness that was upon the face of the deep gave place to the form and symmetry of intellectual expansion. Her vivid imagination, which had been running for years with but little restraint, came under the control of her broadening intellect." She began helping with the younger children while continuing to develop her musical skills and her way with words. Her transition to greater independence came gradually and marked the next stage in her life.

Crosby's years as a pupil expanded her social and intellectual world and exposed her at least superficially to major trends, events, and personalities. Her mind observed and remembered, and her emotions found expression in rhyme, but she apparently did not engage in any deep way the great gulfstreams of contemporary history swirling around her. Sheltered in a community that filtered how pupils experienced the larger world, she was aware but not connected in meaningful ways to much of what occurred outside the Institution. Some events excited or enthused her; others summoned her to activities; still others directed her energies toward the problem of sustained support for education for the blind. Yet over time Crosby's exposure in New York City to conflicting public opinions especially on race, immigration, and temperance beckoned her to deeper reflection and conviction, and regular exposure to Protestant preaching helped her frame her moral responses.

3 Transition (1846-1858)

All the way my Saviour leads me,
What have I to ask beside?
Can I doubt His tender mercy,
Who through life has been my guide?

The Institution's 1846 Annual Report recorded a change in Fanny Crosby's status. She was now an instructor, with responsibility to teach rhetoric, grammar, and Roman and American history to the younger children. That change did not preclude the usual inclusion in the Annual Report of a Crosby poem (this time "Morning"). The managers now billed her as a "graduate pupil." A few years later they acknowledged her as a full-fledged teacher.

At the beginning of 1847, Crosby seemed unusually frail. Helen DeKroyft, a friend at the Institution, wrote in a letter: "The choir in the chapel are chanting at the organ their evening hymn, across the hall a little group with the piano and flute are turning the very atmosphere into melody; but Fanny, the poetess, is not there. Many weeks her harp and guitar have been unstrung, and we fear the hand of consumption is stealing her gentle spirit away." By spring Crosby had recovered enough to enjoy the energetic displays of patriotism that marked the final days of the Mexican War. The papers carried detailed accounts of engagements, and a succession of American victories under General Taylor prompted a holiday on 7 May, just before the festivities of the annual Anniversary Week. Visitors thronged the city, residents decked it with flags, and a "great military procession" accompanied by the booms of cannon and culminating in an enormous evening "general illumination" gave vent to patriotic fervor. As usual, Crosby thrilled to the excitement of the moment:

> Yes, let the trumpet tongue of fame
> Tell of the deeds by Taylor done;
> A nation's honors crown his name
> The honors he hath justly won.
> Let others seek — they cannot win
> One laurel from his brow away;
> We'll twine our wreaths alone for him
> Who fought so brave at Monterey.

Meanwhile, a handful of wealthy investors invited the crowds to the banks of the Hudson where steamboat races tested the newest transportation technology. Barely twenty years after Crosby's twenty-four-hour childhood journey to Manhattan, the *Oregon,* owned by George Law, in competition with Cornelius Vanderbilt's *Commodore Vanderbilt,* set a record for the trip to Crosby's upstate haunts and back, making the seventy-five-mile round-trip in just 3.25 hours.

Henry Clay pursued the Whig nomination in 1848, and on Thursday, 9 March, a whirlwind campaign tour brought him to New York. Tens of thousands "covered the Battery and adjacent piers," and a mass of humanity lined Broadway to do him honor. The celebrated Hutchinson Family Singers, renowned for their close harmony, offered a musical welcome. Clay wended his way to the New York Institution for the Blind, where he found an audience attuned to his theme of "Freedom, Temperance and brotherly love." Accompanied by the members of the city council and greeted with the strains of the pupils' orchestra playing "Hail to the Chief," he thrilled the scholars with "one of the most felicitous and beautiful speeches" they had ever heard. And Crosby was one of two Institution folk who responded with a "poetical address":

It comes, it swells, it breaks upon the ear;
Millions have caught the spirit-stirring sound.
And we with joy, with transport uncontrolled,
Would in the chorus of our city join:
Thou noblest of the noble, welcome here!
How have we longed to meet thee, thou whose voice
In eloquence resistless, like a spell,
Holds e'en a nation captive to its powers!
Well may Columbia of her son be proud.
Firm as a rock, amid conflicting storms,
Thou by her side hast ever fearless stood,
With truth thy motto, principle thy guide.
And thou canst feel as rich a gem is thine,
As ever graced the loftiest monarch's brow:
A nation's honor and a nation's love.

These festivities coincided with the sadness of the arrival in New York of the remains of another of Crosby's heroes, the aged John Quincy Adams. The nation paused to honor him as his funeral procession made its way from Washington, D.C., to the Adams family home in Quincy, Massachusetts. In deference to the former president, Clay — and the city — took a day from the campaign excitement to commemorate him.

May 1848 brought another Whig idol, Mexican War hero General Winfield Scott. After a morning "levee of this distinguished veteran" at City Hall on Friday, 26 May, Scott drove out to visit Manhattan's public institutions. Crosby still clung to her Democratic sympathies, but she revered the hero of the Mexican War, and when his carriage drew up to the Institution to the strains of the student band playing "Hail to the Chief," she was standing by. After a greeting from the superintendent and Scott's reply, Crosby came forward to recite a poem:

Hail, son of Columbia! The patriot flame
Burns bright in each breast while we tell of thy fame;
We have heard of the deeds thou so nobly hast done,
We have heard of thy battles so fearlessly won.

Yes, welcome, thrice welcome, again and again!
With transport unbounded we echo the strain;

Thy triumphs so glorious shall ne'er be forgot —
Hurrah for the patriot General Scott!

Each statesman or war hero reinforced Crosby's romantic notions about American history and destiny. She remembered less about what they said than she did about the aura of greatness they projected. They were great because they grappled with great issues that impacted the robustness of democratic institutions, or great because they extended democracy's sway, and great because they took time from national issues to interact with blind students. They represented the unfolding of American destiny. Her conception of their greatness resided as well in her convictions of a common moral commitment to liberty under God.

The May 1848 *Christian Register* carried a column on that month's anniversary program for the Institution, an event that took place on Wednesday afternoon, 10 May, in the commodious auditorium of the Broadway Tabernacle. Perhaps 90 percent of the thousands who taxed the facility's capacity were women whose "warmly sympathizing natures" presumably influenced their "deep interest in such acts of benevolence." The unnamed *Register* reporter gushed enthusiasm for "Miss Crosby": "She is perfectly familiar with the whole range of English poetry and produces herself the sweetest verse, retaining it in her memory without the necessity of committing it to paper. She is equally interested in, and conversant with, the affairs of practical life, familiar even with politics." The newspaper reported that Crosby led an exercise entitled "Conversations on Familiar Things" in which younger pupils discoursed intelligently on the motions of the planets and the causes of night and day. Crosby's principal contribution to that year's anniversary was an original poetic address on music — music in nature, in friendship, in the ocean, in twilight, and in heaven — "those mansions of light." The crowd eagerly purchased the large number of copies prepared for distribution, and the poem went up for sale at Dodd's Bookstore to raise funds for the Institution to purchase books in embossed type. Horace Greeley's *New York Tribune* carried the full poem. On 26 May Greeley offered another composition by Miss Frances Jane Crosby, "Lines to James R":

I marked a sadness on thy brow the morn when first we met;
The tale that from thy lips I heard I never can forget:

Disease hath swept forever a father from thy side,
And still within thy bosom flows sorrow's restless tide.

A brother and a sister devoted cling to thee,
As closely twines the ivy around the hawthorn tree;
A mother, too, beholds thee with pure affection now;
Then why, O! why, should sorrow leave one trace upon thy
  brow?

Each year the coming of summer left the Institution quiet and empty. In 1848 one of Manhattan's favorite attractions, Christy's Minstrels, arrived after dark on the date most pupils departed, to relieve the loneliness of the few left behind in the enormous buildings (among them Crosby). Awakened by the strains of the Minstrels' "Ethiopian songs," residents of the Institution were reminded of the goodwill of the people of their adopted city. Such treats did not come often, but they did occur occasionally, and over the years Institution pupils enjoyed the best entertainments the city had to offer.

The next year's anniversary program took place on Wednesday, 9 May 1849, again at the celebrated Broadway Tabernacle. Throngs of people crammed the building's seats, its aisles and its stairs, while many were turned away. They heard from the best of the Institution's 140 pupils, among them Master van Alstine, who performed at the piano a composition he had arranged himself.

That program fell amid a week destined to live on in American memory. On Monday (7 May) a long-simmering feud between two highly regarded actors spilled over into rowdy, unseemly conduct among the masses. For two days the city's well-to-do were on edge, fearing public chaos. Anniversary Week proceeded on schedule, but the tense atmosphere pervaded events. On Thursday night, 10 May, New York showed its ugly side in an incident that revealed deep hostility between the city's working and middle classes.

The trouble grew out of an old rivalry between William Charles Macready, a celebrated British Shakespearean actor, and Edwin Forrest, an acclaimed, self-made American-born actor (the first to be internationally known). Their personal distaste for one another had long been public knowledge. Macready's reputation as a fastidious man with little regard for either Americans or republicanism placed him in

75

sharp contrast to Forrest, a man of the people who, by his own hard work, had made good. The heirs to the cherished principles of Jacksonian democracy — the so-called rank and file — idolized Forrest, who basked in their adoration. Long before May 1849, then, class lines had been drawn.

That May, New York City's three principal theaters played to the simmering public tension by announcing the same fare on the same day — competing productions of *Macbeth*. The Astor Place Opera House, standing at the intersection of fashionable Broadway and plebeian Bowery, billed Macready. The so-called Bowery B'hoys (a street gang whose haunts stretched along the streets that intersected the Bowery) entered the theater and interrupted Macready with hoots and hisses. Next they hurled eggs, apples, and a few chairs toward the stage, and Macready called off his engagement. His irate fans objected, and against his better judgment Macready acceded to a petition signed by prominent New Yorkers (Washington Irving and Herman Melville among them) urging him to stay for another performance.

On 10 May, as Macready tried again, a crowd estimated at 15,000 strong massed outside the Astor Place Opera House. A few hundred turned violent, and 250 policemen could not subdue them. Two divisions of the Seventh Regiment succeeded only after firing three volleys, two of them directly into the crowd. In the end 23 New Yorkers died and over 100 were wounded. Macready fled the city in disguise in an enclosed carriage, leaving many New Yorkers shocked and outraged by the propensity for violence they had witnessed. The next night apprehensive well-to-do New Yorkers cleaned their guns and prepared for renewed attacks. The Bowery B'hoys had sworn vengeance. To everyone's relief, "the Unwashed" (as they were also known) disbanded when the cavalry threatened to "treat them with a little artillery practice." The incident ended, but its repercussions lingered.

The riot revealed simmering class tensions that grew more acute every year as the city's population mix changed. The Astor Place Opera House stood at the junction of two ways of life — the elegance of Broadway and the rough-and-tumble egalitarianism of the Bowery. The ruffians known as the Bowery B'hoys construed the elitism of the Opera House — where white kid gloves and silk vests were de rigueur and boxes rented for thousands of dollars a season — as a patrician affront to democratic equality and posted notices dubbing it the "English ARISTOCRATIC Opera House." Macready and Forrest (whose publics acted out a far larger drama than either actor ever attempted) represented a similar clash of cultures. Forrest was the sort of self-made success story that appealed to working-class Americans. He commanded the astonishing sum of $2,000 per week, but his adoring fans did not begrudge him wealth: in their minds it proved his democratic success story.

The riots did not deter the ritual of Anniversary Week, but they laid bare realities of urban life that introduced a discordant note into the self-congratulations that filled the air. Among the many results of the public soul-searching that followed 10 May 1849 was an increased effort by middle-class Protestants to alleviate the conditions that professionals believed were responsible for juvenile delinquency. For example, with the support of many who encouraged his work among the blind, John Denison Russ — principal founder of the Institution for the Blind — took a hand in creating in 1851 the New York Juvenile Asylum, providing services to thousands of needy children under twelve years of age.

Crosby and others at the Institution could not dismiss as irrelevant the simmering tensions the riots brought into the open. In 1849 their neighborhood was far enough from the violence to assure physical safety, but each year more immigrants poured in, and poverty and unemployment edged closer to their immediate environs. Memories of 1849 and experiences in the years immediately following shaped Crosby's comprehension of the urban problems exacerbated by immigration. She associated professionally with prosperous middle-class citizens, but she often chose to live among the poor and to expend her energies to aid the dispossessed. She lived for decades at the potentially explosive intersection of lower- and middle-class Manhattan life where a brief eruption in 1849 forced the city to take a hard look at itself.

Early June brought Institution residents a visit from the chief of the Ojibway Indian tribe. Poetry, tributes, and responses marked the occasion, and the students heard an impassioned, firsthand Indian perspective on American history. This visit especially captured Crosby's imagination, and Indian themes made their way into some of her prose and poetry.

A few weeks later life in New York took another somber turn as citizens anxiously charted the relentless progress of a new epidemic of the dreaded cholera. People still shuddered at the memories of its reach in 1832 and 1839, and now newspapers again carried front-page accounts of its relentless global march. Tens of thousands of people died abroad — some 70,000 in Britain alone — and Americans knew they were vulnerable, too. The first cases in the United States were reported in New Orleans, where a ship from France had brought the sickness. It quickly claimed 3,500 lives in the city. By May 1849 cholera had pushed north, leaving behind a trail of death. At last it struck New York. It appeared first in Orange Street in the notorious Five Points district, where conditions were "filthy in the extreme." The city responded immediately with whitewash, disinfectants, and street washing, but the epidemic refused to be contained. From mid-May through June, 805 New Yorkers died of cholera.

The epidemic ebbed slightly, but the summer heat renewed its intensity. After a particularly hot and dry spell in July, some 1,000 people died in Manhattan in one week, 484 from cholera. "Vegetation is burning up unregarded all around us," the *Daily Tribune* observed. "There is no mitigation of sickness and cannot well be until we have a soaking rain succeeded by cool weather." Cholera prompted another massive city cleanup. In one ward alone, street sweepers removed 5,277 loads of manure and 4,826 loads of dirt from the streets in a month. Fresh whitewash and disinfectants applied to all houses in which deaths occurred seemed futile as remedies but gave the people the satisfaction of doing something to try to stay the plague. By August much of the city had shut down waiting for the weather to change and the epidemic to abate.

The Institution's officers decided to send pupils home for vacation. Some had nowhere to go, however, and Crosby and several other teachers opted to stay. By late July six hundred to seven hundred people were dying each week in New York. A new cholera hospital near the Institution provided neighborhood care, but demand promptly exceeded space. The city converted a building on West Thirty-fifth Street into a second neighborhood cholera hospital, and there the sick from the Institution found treatment. Ten pupils were among the 5,072 New Yorkers who succumbed that summer to the dread illness. Remarkably, Crosby nursed the sick, especially those from the Institution, until she feared she, too, was coming down with the disease. She helped the Institution's physician, J. W. Clements, prepare the "cholera pills" on which people relied — two-thirds calomel, one-third opium, as Crosby recalled — and she took several herself when she felt sickness coming on. For the next few months, perhaps partly as a result of the horrors of the cholera epidemic and the haunting echoes of the wagon driver's call, "Bring your dead," Crosby seemed worn, languid, even depressed. When the Institution reopened in November, she taught an abbreviated schedule and sought solace in renewed religious commitment.

Commentators on the Institution's Anniversary Week in the spring of 1850 remarked as usual on the crowd of interested persons who filled every available seat at the Broadway Tabernacle long before the late-afternoon program was scheduled to begin. Music, recitations, and readings filled the hour, interspersed with examinations in arithmetic, history, and geography. Eighteen years after they had joined hands with John Russ, New York's benevolent Protestants could look with pride on the results of their investment in the state's blind citizens.

In July 1850 President Zachary Taylor's death of cholera elicited mournful lines from Crosby:

A wail is in the Capitol,
A wail of anguish deep,
That startles with a fearful sound
The night wind from its sleep.
The brave old oak hath bowed its head,
A victim to the blast;
Death holds within his conquering arm
The conqueror at last.

In the fall of 1850, the arrival of Jenny Lind, "the greatest singer and noblest woman of our times," courtesy of the indefatigable P. T. Barnum, provided New Yorkers another diversion. In September — before the singer arrived — Jenny Lind fever swept Manhattan. While the masses awaited a star and a cultural experience, Barnum, the city's irrepressible "master of humbug" and showman second to none, dubbed Lind "the Swedish Nightingale" and carefully calculated the business end of his "Lind enterprise." It began with an enormous staged display to welcome her to New York harbor. Barnum created an intense furor for Lind, the sensation of the moment in European music, whose reputation had preceded her.

79

Educated at the Royal Theater School in Stockholm in piano, voice, and dance, Lind had an unusual soprano voice. Critics raved about its unique qualities. The most popular soprano in Europe, she had enjoyed the friendship of Mendelssohn and was esteemed by some as "the greatest artistic performer in the world." She was simply too good for Barnum to ignore, and she had the added charm of decidedly Puritan personal tastes. (Her marked affinity for pietism had divided some of her Swedish public.) Barnum did not care on his own account, but he knew this reputation would endear her to the broadest possible American public. He negotiated a contract for a national tour that he was sure would amply line his pockets.

New Yorkers set an extravagant tone, as Barnum knew they would. Some 40,000 showed up to greet Lind's ship, the *Atlantic*, as it sailed into New York harbor. They crowded ships, piers, and rooftops when the streets could no longer hold them. Bands serenaded Lind with "Yankee Doodle" and "Hail Columbia" as her carriage made its way under floral arches to her lavishly appointed hotel suite at the massive Irving House. The public showered her with "little articles of luxury and use" and kept the hotel staff busy with "costly bouquets coming in rapid succession." With carefully staged publicity, Barnum auctioned off one ticket to Lind's opening concert at the famous Castle Garden, the commodious auditorium at the southernmost edge of Manhattan, just off Battery Park. Attached to the Battery by a wooden bridge ninety paces long, the Garden was lit by gas, and managers set its ticket prices high enough to keep the riffraff out. A local hatter won the bidding at Barnum's auction, paying $225 for his seat. The *Daily Tribune* suggested that gentlemen provide themselves with "opera hats or caps such as can be easily stowed away" and that "ladies should sit without bonnets during the performance." After all, everyone wanted to see as well as to hear the Nightingale.

Lind lived up to expectations. On Thursday, 12 September 1850, the *Daily Tribune* gave front-page coverage to her "great triumph." "All doubts are at an end," the paper enthused. "She is the greatest singer we have ever heard, and her success is all that was anticipated from her genius and her fame." For the next year she toured America's cities and villages. Critics extolled "the liquid purity of her voice." Unruly fans complained about ticket prices but still filled venues to capacity and beyond. The rich and famous — Millard Fillmore, Henry

Wadsworth Longfellow, Henry Clay, Daniel Webster — mingled with ordinary folk and marveled at Lind's voice. During one intermission in New York's Tripler Hall, the crowd transferred its enthusiasm to Daniel Webster. He stood in the dress circle, bowed his thanks, and waved his handkerchief to loud cheers for Webster and the Union. But as soon as Lind reappeared, Webster, forgotten, merged back into the spellbound crowd.

Lind's eager public renamed streets, schools, and other public places in her honor. People wore Jenny Lind gloves and shawls and drank their tea from Jenny Lind cups. Her likeness adorned alphabet plates for children, and her name described varieties of gooseberry and muskmelon as well as the Jenny Lind Cake, an item on respectable New York hotel menus for the next fifty years. Arkansas named a town after the prima donna. That December (1850), *Godey's Lady's Book* offered a hard look at the bold use of Lind's name: "It was a bare-faced shopkeeping ruse," the author declared, "but nevertheless it succeeded; and half the American public are now wiping their heated brows with Jenny Lind pocket handkerchiefs, or dressing their hair with Jenny Lind combs." And P. T. Barnum made over $700,000 before he and Lind parted ways.

Fanny Crosby heard Lind several times, but none of those thrilling concerts even approached the supreme moment when Lind climbed the steps of the Institution to give a special performance for the school. She arrived unexpectedly, but confusion soon gave way to a touching scene. For forty-five minutes her voice transfixed the students with Scandinavian folk tunes. Lind then allowed the pupils to crowd around her and "see" her face with their fingers. In old age Crosby, who tended to gush over celebrities she had met, insisted that she "never hope[d] to listen to such melodies again until I hear the choirs of the Eternal City." A few years after Lind's visit, Crosby turned much of her attention to music. Memories of Lind's artistry nurtured Crosby's convictions about the power of music for good and helped shape her approach to writing song lyrics.

Crosby's Manhattan environment changed dramatically between 1835 and 1850. In 1835 public transportation reached only as far north as Twenty-sixth Street; in 1850 it connected far-flung parts of the city. Broadway, "the most wonderful street in the world," remained the city's pride. Sixty feet wide, jammed with vehicles of all sorts (the police estimated it carried some 20,000 vehicles per day), Broadway was a magnet for dense foot and vehicular traffic that necessitated police assistance at pedestrian crossings. New Yorkers knew it as the headquarters of the new and expanding "express" businesses in the country. Such influential places as news offices, City Hall, and the city's premier emporium, Stewart's palatial Marble Drygoods Palace, could be found along Broadway.

At midcentury the causes that activists had brought to public notice when the teenaged Crosby arrived — like temperance and abolition — continued to agitate the city. The slavery issue seethed more furiously than ever. The Fugitive Slave Act, the Dred Scott decision, and the publication of Harriet Beecher Stowe's *Uncle Tom's Cabin* would soon fuel the flames even more. And immigration continued to change the complexion of the city. Just a week after its report of the Institution's 1850 Anniversary Week program, the *Evening Post* described as "a prodigious freight of humanity which has scarcely if ever been surpassed" the arrival in one week of some 10,000 immigrants into the Port of New York. One packet ship alone, the *Albert Gallatin*, deposited 849 steerage passengers, besides those in cabin class. Since tallies did not enumerate cabin passengers and since smaller ships from "unimportant ports" were also excluded from published counts, the *Post* estimated that an average of 2,000 immigrants per day typically arrived through New York harbor. The ships came primarily from Liverpool, Hamburg, Bremen, and Havre, ports to which people from all parts of Europe flocked to disembark.

By 1850 steamboats (with screw propellers rather than paddle wheels) had begun vying with packet boats as the choice for transatlantic voyages. One evening in April 1838, New Yorkers had thronged the Battery to watch the SS *Sirius* steam into New York harbor. This first steamship to make the Atlantic crossing came from Cork to New York in eighteen days, prompting a prophecy by one Philip Hone: "Steamers will continue to be the fashion until some more dashing adventurer of the go-ahead tribe shall demonstrate the practicability of balloon navigation, and gratify their impatience on a voyage over and not upon the blue waters in two days instead of as many weeks." In the meanwhile, steamships sparked new lines of business in New York and brought to prominence Cornelius Vanderbilt, a native of Staten Island.

If steamships revolutionized water travel, steam engines transformed transportation on land. The first New York City railroad ran 7.75 miles along Fourth Avenue from City Hall to a bridge over the Harlem River, and more miles of track crisscrossed the city — and the nation — every year. People marveled over the sight of a train rumbling down a track. "What an object of wonder! How marvelous it is in every particular!" was a typical remark at the sight of an approaching locomotive. Already in 1835, trains rattled along at unheard-of speeds — twenty miles per hour made them twice as fast as the stagecoach, and four times faster than canal boats. Entrepreneurs saw dollar signs and wasted no time laying track. Crosby arrived in Manhattan less than ten years after the opening of the first railroad in the United States. The entire country boasted a mere 700 miles of track. In 1860, just after she moved on, 30,000 miles connected a westward-expanding population and trains were fast becoming a mainstay of transportation and commerce. By the time Crosby reached middle age, these "brigades of cars" had revolutionized her world. Improved transportation made family and friends a more regular part of her life than had seemed possible when she sailed into New York harbor in 1835.

Other changes proceeded apace, sometimes with dizzying speed. The population more than doubled between 1840 and 1855. In 1820 fewer than 20,000 New Yorkers (a mere 11 percent of the total) were aliens. By 1860 some 384,000 (fully 48 percent of the population) were born outside the United States, over 200,000 of them in Ireland, with Germans numbering 120,000. A sense of the scope of change that penetrated all aspects of life in those heady decades may be gleaned from the following. When Crosby had arrived in the city in 1835, daguerreotypes were unknown, mutual life insurance companies such as those in England and France had no counterparts in New York, express services did not exist. These, with the railroad and countless other new things, had become customary by midcentury. The city itself was constantly in flux. By 1850 more than sixty hotels served visitors to New York. The most magnificent was undoubtedly still the aging Astor House on Broadway. Built on farmland owned by John Jacob Astor, America's richest man, this "model of architectural beauty and massive grandeur" at Broadway and Vesey Street boasted a grand interior garden with fountains and trees. Inns and small hotels catering especially to the city's ethnic population had sprouted with the population. As the city grew, real estate business boomed and justified the faith of those like Astor who had invested long before in apparently worthless acreage farther north on Manhattan Island.

More philanthropic institutions appeared every year, many geared toward young Americans. The same John Russ whose efforts shaped the Institution for the Blind figured largely in other humanitarian efforts. Russ estimated that some three thousand children "floated on the current, educated only in crime," and he made them his cause. While Russ tended the needs of the dispossessed, others worried that good citizens needed a strong public library (Astor's will bequeathed $400,000 to the city for that purpose), educators discussed the quality of public schools, and proliferating societies attended to "the relief of distressed persons."

The early 1850s were tumultuous as well as expansive years for the city and the nation. Debates over slavery and sectionalism sometimes turned violent. Tammany Hall, an association formed for benevolent purposes, now excelled at using its resources to influence the political behavior of masses of recent arrivals. More than fifty newspapers — monthly, weekly, and daily, most of the latter delivered to regular subscribers for six cents a day — kept New Yorkers abreast of the news. One of the most popular of these, James Gordon Bennett's *New York Herald*, flourished with its vocal opposition to Tammany Hall, headquarters of the local Democratic Party. The *Herald*'s chatty format offended the social elite for the same reason that it thrilled the masses: its spicy glimpses of fashionable events irked the city's social set that was accustomed to privacy. Bennett regularly violated the unwritten rule that women's names should appear in a newspaper only twice — at marriage and at death. Though husbands and fathers dreamed aloud of thrashing the editor, the *Herald* remained a "flourishing sheet." An array of recent foreign-language dailies and weeklies supplemented such sheets and manifested the astonishing variety within the larger ethnic populations.

The "uptown march" of the churches continued unabated. Observations in the January 1853 *Christian Advocate* about that march's most recent steps describe a typical scenario: "Last week we noticed the sale of the Protestant Episcopal church in Anthony Street, and now the Reformed Dutch church in Franklin Street has followed suit. Dr. Spring's church in Beckman Street and Dr. Mc Elroy's in Grant Street (both Presbyterian) are expected before long to remove from their present locations. The Methodists are the only religious denomination in the city which have never forsaken a spot in which they have ever had a church." Such Methodist boasting would not ring true much longer. The "uptown mania" eventually "seized" nearly all the downtown Protestant churches, one chronicler noted, "with fatal results."

All things considered, it was an exciting and troubling time to be an American, especially in the nation's bustling northeastern urban hub. Evangelical religion still animated democratic impulses and voluntary associations, but evangelical denominational bonds had been broken by slavery. Crosby apparently concentrated on her duties. In 1851 she managed to ready another collection of poems for publication. It appeared that year as *Monterey and Other Poems*. Crosby's preface alluded to her ill health and her declining years, words that brought a smile to her face when she recalled them more than fifty years later.

The early 1850s brought Crosby another musical delight with the visit of the colorful virtuoso violinist from Norway, the celebrated musician Ole Bull. In her old age Crosby still claimed she drew strength from her memories of his music and conversation. "He gave me a clearer vision of life and love," she mused. "And his music has made my own songs more sweet, more divine." She sat in rapt attention as he played his violin. The notes stirred her so deeply that she seemed literally to *see* the musician play. Bull had a promotional flair that rivaled P. T. Barnum's, and Americans — especially those of Scandinavian extraction — plastered his name on their schools and streets and erected statues of him in their public places. A virtuoso impatient with aspects of Norwegian society, Bull earned a fortune with his music and put it toward his dream of a Norwegian colony in Pennsylvania.

Her busy life did not diminish Crosby's family loyalties. Occasional visits to her mother's home in Bridgeport — sometimes with friends from the Institution — offered physical and emotional renewal. The irrepressibly cheerful Crosby that the public knew easily became emotionally exhausted and physically drained, and her mother's home was her sanctuary. The feelings she voiced in verse at her birthday in March 1852 suggest the strength of the sentimental ties that bound her to her nuclear family:

My birthday eve is gone, mother,
And didst thou think of me?
Each moment while I counted o'er
My thoughts were fixed on thee.

And oft I wished thee here, mother,
Our social group to join;
For I long to clasp thy hand, mother,
And in thy arms recline.

The spring of 1852 brought back to New York General Winfield Scott, hero of the Mexican War, who had won the Whig Party's presidential nomination. Crosby, now moving away from Jacksonian politics, again expressed in verse her deep admiration for the war exploits of this American hero. (But the irrepressible Crosby could not resist noting the Democrat Franklin Pierce's victory with the lines "The election's past and I'm pierced at last: the locos have gained the day." [New York Democrats were popularly known as locos.]) Her animated memories of visits like Scott's would refresh her old age and entertain her young admirers.

Also in 1852, Crosby accepted an invitation from her friend Alice Holmes to participate in a literary and musical entertainment in Jersey City. Holmes considered Crosby a "brilliant star." Crosby and Robert Elder, a contemporary of the women at the Institution and for forty-two years the organist at Manhattan's Sixteenth Street Baptist Church, helped establish what became a popular annual event across the Hudson River.

Crosby always cherished memories of 1853, for the fall of that year brought to the Institution the young Grover Cleveland. His older brother, William, had accepted a post as teacher and recommended his brother for employment. Their father, Presbyterian pastor Richard Cleveland, had recently died, leaving a large family in financial straits, and seventeen-year-old Grover temporarily relinquished his college plans for gainful employment in the metropolis. The Institution had grown to enroll 116 students, most of whom resided on the premises, and young Cleveland taught writing, arithmetic, and geography in addition to performing secretarial duties for the superintendent.

The outgoing Fanny Crosby, now listed in the register as preceptress (a sort of dean of students), immediately befriended Cleveland, whom she later remembered as a young man with a mature way that enabled him to mingle as an equal among the older teachers. Long conversations apparently cemented a bond between them. Cleveland proved ready to take dictation of Crosby's poetry, and the two spent hours together after the day's work was done. Both objected to the stern corporal punishments frequently administered to students by the austere new superintendent, T. Colden Cooper.

If the residents of the Institution found Cooper's administration distasteful, they preferred to keep the knowledge to themselves. In the summer of 1854 a visitor to the Institution offered the *New York Times* his "severe strictures" on Cooper's management, citing particularly "neglect, slovenliness and bad management" complicated by "petty jealousies and feuds" among the staff. The occasion for the comments was a Musical Festival offered by Institution scholars. Music, the visitor opined, "is a special gift to the blind; they excel in it. . . . How wonderful their delicacy of touch! How quick their perception of sound!" And how inexcusable the response of the hapless superintendent to a simple query about the performance. "I am not a musician," Cooper said. "I thank God I know nothing about music." This despite the tireless efforts of instructors George Root, "a vocal tutor and composer without superior in the City," and of Anthony Reiff, a gentleman under whom students played "with *ensemble* and effect." The visitor was thrilled by the pupils but appalled by the superintendent's crassness, and he thought the city needed to know.

The day after the paper carried these comments, it published a response signed by four Institution teachers, Frances Crosby leading the list. Whatever internal unhappiness disturbed the equanimity, the teachers lavished glowing public praise on their administrator: "The writer in yesterday's *Times* labors to prove [Cooper] destitute of the finer feelings of humanity. We feel bound to deny most absolutely the truth of these aspersions. We know too well that to us, at least, the benevolence of his nature has flown forth not merely in his friendly counsels, but in his direct solicitude for our welfare."

A united public front did not ameliorate the conditions that frustrated Grover Cleveland, and he found little to hold him at the Institution. Most of the teachers gave part-time service, leaving the Cleveland brothers to supervise the boys dormitory while the three full-time female teachers took charge of the girls. His complaints of meager pay, poor food, and general dissatisfaction may have expressed a deeper disinclination with the life of a clerk, and unhappiness with the superintendent proved the final straw. Grover Cleveland resigned in the fall of 1854. In later years Crosby professed to have recognized that the teenaged Cleveland would go on to bigger and better things. She heard from him on special occasions and met with him several times after he had risen to fame.

MUSIC

Since her arrival at the Institution, Fanny Crosby had made good use of its program of musical training. Instrumental music instructor Anthony Reiff had arrived in 1835, a few months after Crosby. He stayed for forty years and made music an integral part of daily life at the Institution. A founder and the first vice president of the New York Philharmonic, Reiff was a distinguished bassoonist and participant in the flourishing effort to establish classical music venues in the United States. His oversight of Institution music assured pupils unusual opportunities. Before long, Crosby learned to play the piano, organ, harp, and guitar. She also discovered she could sing solos with ease. Guided by Reiff and musicians who served under him, Crosby and several other students made commendable progress. Charles Rossiter Coe went from the Institution to a salaried post as a church organist. He also gave recitals and offered music lessons. Another student, Anna Smith, led the choir at Mission Church in Vandewater Street. One Mary Brush took voice lessons at the Institution and became a noted "blind vocalist." Another pupil, Charles Hazlet, son of a well-known Manhattan Baptist minister and temperance activist, found a career in vocal music, too. Crosby, then, was but one of several pupils and teachers whose musical training at the New York Institution for the Blind opened doors for wider "usefulness."

Crosby also took advantage of the vocal instruction the Institution's contract with George Root made available to its scholars. In the mid-1840s Root had accepted the challenge of teaching the blind to sing, and so followed his mentor, Lowell Mason, who had done the same with Samuel Gridley Howe in Boston. Without access to his usual aids — blackboard, books — Root had to rely on the ear alone. He found it difficult to divest himself of the notion that the sixty pupils in his first class could see him, but patience paid off. "Suffice it to say," he later recalled, "that never had teacher more attentive and eager pupils, and never had pupils a more interested and zealous teacher. They sang so soon and so well the ordinary four-part music, both sacred and secular, which I had been accustomed to use in teaching, that before the close of the first year I found myself compelled to give them the more difficult glees of Mendelssohn, with choruses from oratorios." To Root's amazement, his blind students in some ways manifested greater proficiency than the 500 vocal students in his choirs at the Abbotts Seminary and Rutgers Institute. "They know, by hearing a phrase or two, the key and the kind of time," Root explained. "The variety of time must be told them, and then they know the pitch and value of every note as they hear it." Root, and the larger public that formed appreciative audiences, was justly proud of the musical opportunities at the Institution.

Busy with her regular teaching load and her music practice, Crosby prepared another small volume of poems and prose for publication. Titled *A Wreath of Columbia's Flowers*, it appeared from the publisher H. Dayton in 1858. Unlike Crosby's earlier books, the *Wreath* opened with several short stories of multiple chapters. Among the poems Crosby included a tribute to Daniel Webster, who had died in the fall of 1852:

A casket is broken, a jewel has fled,
The mighty is fallen, the peerless is dead,
And the hearts of a nation are bleeding once more,
For the eagle lies low on our desolate shore.

Oh, statesman beloved! Thou wert faithful and true
To the country whose tears will thy ashes bedew,
Rest, rest where affection her tribute shall pay —
How soon hast thou followed the patriot CLAY!

She dedicated the book to Perley D. Whitmore, a Connecticut insurance actuary who had once delighted her by bringing a bit of bark from the fabled Charter Oak, the Hartford tree where legend held that

Connecticut patriots had in 1687 hidden the colony's charter. The preface deplored the current fashion of reading European writers and beckoned Americans to enjoy "native American genius," urging "those who love to encourage every well-directed effort of their countrywomen" to give Crosby's words their attention.

A few weeks later Crosby moved from the Institution to a new life just across the East River on Long Island. She left as the bride of Alexander van Alstine, her longtime acquaintance from the Institution. After finishing his studies in 1850, van Alstine had pursued further work in Greek, Latin, philosophy, and theology, perhaps at Union College in Schenectady, New York. (So Crosby claimed, although the college finds no record of his attendance. If he attended but did not graduate, there would be no record.) In 1855 (after teaching music briefly near Oswego, New York) he returned to Manhattan as an instructor in vocal music at the Institution. He stayed until 1857, when he moved to the small town of Maspeth on Long Island, a community just across the Queens County line from Brooklyn, to become a private music teacher (he enjoyed playing the piano and the cornet) and a church organist. Crosby resigned from the Institution on 2 March 1858, almost exactly twenty-three years from the day of her arrival. She married Van, as she called him, in Maspeth three days later.

Just as her arrival at the Institution opened a new world, so her departure closed a chapter of her life. Of her life at the institute she had written a few years earlier:

> Here many a rolling year has flown,
> The brightest joys I e'er have known
> Here have I felt, nor could my heart
> Endure from scenes like these to part.

This moment offers an appropriate time to reflect on her journey. She had arrived in Manhattan an eager but naive teenager. She departed a competent adult who easily navigated the busy streets of New York and participated in its cultural and political life. She left the distinct impression that she often did this alone, though that would have been uncommon in these days long before distinctive canes and Seeing Eye dogs offered independence. Crosby claimed she always found people willing to help her cross, conductors to find her a seat on public transport, or passersby to offer an arm. The Institution preserves no records that indicate precisely how it taught students to move about the city. It insists only that they would never have gone out alone. This diminutive woman — she stood a mere four feet nine inches and weighed less than one hundred pounds — had dined more than once at the White House, walked arm in arm for an hour conversing with General Winfield Scott, sat spellbound at the feet of Jenny Lind, and supervised the education of scores of sightless girls. She had three published books to her credit, as well as the lyrics of a handful of the era's popular songs and cantatas, prepared with the voice instructor, George Root. Such accomplishments must have exceeded whatever dreams she had brought with her in March of 1835.

She had participated in the rapid growth of the Institution for the Blind. Its physical plant and teaching resources had expanded exponentially, and it had found a permanent niche in the city. In the years when such demonstrations mattered most, Crosby had exhibited the ability of the blind to learn, lead, and teach. Though she moved on from the school, she did not leave the networks to which the school had introduced her. Crosby's life at the Institution enabled her accomplishments beyond its premises.

Still, leaving demanded courage. To follow her first acknowledged romance, she forsook the setting in which she had risen to leadership — its opportunities to teach others, to lead and to be promoted publicly for her varied abilities. The relative obscurity of Maspeth stood in stark contrast to the Manhattan in which she had prepared to face life on her own. She approached her thirty-eighth birthday embracing for the first time the challenge of a life independent of the supportive community in which, until then, she had thrived.

4 Faith

Jesus, Saviour, once betrayed,
Sacrifice for sinners made,
Wretched, lost, to thee I fly;
Save, O save me, or I die!

Blessed assurance, Jesus is mine!
Oh, what a foretaste of glory divine!
Heir of salvation, purchase of God,
Born of His spirit, washed in His blood.

When the van Alstines settled into their home in Maspeth, they shut the larger public out of their lives. Crosby's recollections refer briefly to her happiness with Van but offer no details about their relationship or where in Maspeth they lived and worked. One thing is clear: Van apparently insisted from the start that Crosby use her own name for her poetry and song lyrics.

The area to which they moved had been settled in colonial times, though the village of Maspeth remained small. Into the early nineteenth century, prominent families like former New York governor

DeWitt Clinton owned summer cottages nearby. Since Van taught music privately and played the organ in at least one church, it is worthwhile noting that in 1858 tiny Maspeth — population some 200 — boasted three churches. St. Savior's Episcopal Church had been consecrated in 1848. The Dutch Reformed church, built in 1832, traced its history back to 1642 and its specific organization to 1804, although the congregation had no church building until 1735 and no pews until 1740. The Methodists arrived in 1854, served in rotation with the congregation in Newtown, on circuit from the main area church in Middle Village. With Sunday school in the afternoons and preaching only in the evenings, the Methodists gathered weekly around two large potbellied stoves under the light of kerosene lamps. Their music came from "a rather throaty Mason & Hamlin reed organ" (made by the firm founded in Boston in 1854 by Lowell Mason's son Henry), which Van may well have played. What might Maspeth church musicians have earned? The only hint comes from records of the Dutch Reformed church showing that in 1858 its chorister received $150 per year.

In 1850 Mt. Olivet Cemetery had opened near Maspeth. The swelling of Manhattan's population had already necessitated the laying out of cemeteries beyond Manhattan Island's confines. Large, beautifully landscaped plots of land in Brooklyn and Queens served the purpose, and whole graveyards in Manhattan were dug up and moved. An expanse of land in rural Maspeth was laid out to receive Manhattan's dead and renamed Mt. Olivet. Though no record of the van Alstines' life in Maspeth survives, it is relevant to note that much later Van would be buried in Mt. Olivet Cemetery near the first home the couple shared.

Late in Crosby's life she revealed in a few interviews that she had once been a mother, but that "the angels came down and took our infant up to God and to His throne." She never spoke publicly of motherhood, and since she never elaborated on the experience, the death of a child (ordinary in those days) did not become part of the contemporary Crosby legend. Nor, apparently, did it prompt a poem, at least not a public one. It is likely that this sad chapter of Crosby's life occurred in 1859, a year over which she forever after preferred to draw a veil of silence. An 1859 city directory (Manhattan) reveals that the couple had already left Maspeth behind for the more familiar bustle of Manhattan. Their address was now Spruce Street, near the present entrance to the

Holland Tunnel. Their home was a brick building that bordered St. John's Park. The 1860 census reveals that they had moved again, this time to a private home near the Institution. The sighted proprietor rented rooms to eight blind men and women, of whom the van Alstines were the only married pair.

If little is known of her personal life immediately following her marriage, much is known of Crosby's sympathies during the tragic years that followed. The Civil War evoked from Crosby an outpouring of songs — some haunting, some mournful, some militaristic, a few even gory. Northern presses churned out reams of patriotic verse, and writers had little trouble finding publishers or tunesmiths. Crosby's erstwhile teacher and sometime collaborator George Root became one of the most successful Northern songwriters of the Civil War era, manifesting astonishing ability to churn out appealing melodies for the spate of poems that followed the onset of war. His brother's publishing company, Chicago-based Root and Cady, reaped enormous profits from his composition of such enduring favorites as "Tenting Tonight," "Tramp, Tramp, Tramp the Boys Are Marching," "Just before the Battle, Mother," and "The Battle Cry of Freedom," songs Hollywood still uses to evoke the Civil War era. While Root made money writing tunes for his own patriotic texts, Crosby vented patriotism in verse, often with popular folk tunes in mind. She produced no Northern "hits" comparable to Root's, but her texts testified to her clear moral sense about the issues that fomented in the war years as well as to her allegiance to the new Republican Party. She stood wholeheartedly against slavery and for temperance and public schools — over which heated debates pitted Catholics against Protestants in New York.

During the 1850s Crosby's youthful enthusiasm for the politics of Jacksonian Democrats had yielded to ardent support for the antislavery Whigs. (She mentions party allegiance, though not issues other than slavery that swayed her.) In the election of 1852, differences between Whigs and Democrats blurred as confrontations over slavery intensified, and during the decade political parties reorganized to meet the unavoidable challenge. In the mid-1850s nativism ran rampant, for the first time giving national political focus to anti-Catholicism in general and to the recent tide of immigrant arrivals in particular. The goal to curb the expansion of slavery brought the Re-

publican Party into existence. In 1858 Abraham Lincoln gave the famous speech in which he quoted the words "A house divided against
itself cannot stand." He insisted that moral indifference to slavery —
especially as manifested in recent compromises about its spread —
had seriously eroded the principles on which the United States had
been founded. In Chicago in May 1860, Lincoln won the Republican
nomination. By then, Crosby was his ardent well-wisher.

As war became reality, Crosby poured her Northern sympathies
into anti-Southern lyrics set to such popular tunes as "Wait for the
Wagon." Printed on inexpensive paper bordered with patriotic sym-
bols, her lines appeared without music. In this war, as in other conflicts
on American soil, Crosby had family on both sides. (Her mother's
brother, Joseph Crosby, had moved his family to Georgia, and the
cousins were still in close touch.) The war fundamentally changed the
fortunes of some of her Connecticut kin. Until the war Crosby's lyrics
more typically gushed with sentiment and republican pride. Now they
bristled with militarism, calling down God's wrath on Southern rebels
and urging Northern soldiers to the slaughter:

> Death to those whose impious hands
> Burst our Union's sacred bands,
> Vengeance thunders, right demands —
> Justice for the brave.

Her "Song to Jeff Davis" dared Southern forces to cross the Mason-
Dixon Line:

> Now, Jeff, when thou art ready,
> Lead on thy rebel crew,
> We'll give them all a welcome —
> With balls and powder too!
> We spurn thy constitution!
> We spurn thy southern laws!
> Our stars and stripes are waving,
> And Heav'n will speed our cause.

Crosby's Civil War lines also indulged the Victorian penchant for the
tender image of the praying mother:

I have fought for the Union and right, mother;
I have stood by the flag of the free.
That Banner so fair, with its colors so bright,
'Twas the pride of our nation and thee.

There's a chill on my forehead tonight, mother;
I am dying far distant from thee;
But the star of my faith is unclouded and bright,
For I know thou art praying for me.

In "Dixie for the Union," a song sung in the public schools, Crosby
urged Northern troops to retake the South:

Go, meet those Southern traitors
With iron will
And should your courage falter, Boys,
Remember Bunker Hill — Hurrah!

Unfurl our country's banner
In triumph there,
And let those rebels desecrate
That banner, if they dare — Hurrah!

Music publisher and vocalist Philip Phillips featured Crosby
texts in *Home Songs for Young Patriots,* a book he compiled with the inmates of homes for soldiers' orphans in mind. Phillips aimed to "promote a correct and elevated public sentiment in relation to the merit
and claims of these children" and the "refining lights of Religion, Generosity, and Patriotism" that sustained them. Crosby's "I'm a Soldier's
Orphan Boy" led off, followed by her heartrending "Who'll Protect My
Children Now," both set to music by the talented Hubert Main, a rising star at the music publisher Biglow and Main. With Phillips she
wrote a "pathetic song and chorus" suggested by an incident at an am-
putation table in a Nashville hospital: "It has been torn from my body
that not one State should be torn from this glorious Union":

Good-by old arm — that strong right arm
'Twas once my pride to wield;

'Twill never bear the sword again
My country's flag to shield.

Crosby's postwar interest in philanthropic work among the freedmen shone through in the lyrics for "Our Call":

Though no longer called to mingle
In the struggle for the right,
We can go among the freedmen
With the Bible as our light,
We can lead them out of darkness
With a brother's helping hand;
We can preach the blessed gospel
To the poorest in the land.

Such sentiments won the enduring gratitude of the Grand Army of the Republic, whose aged veterans often invited Crosby to ceremonies and, when she died in 1915, paid tribute at her funeral. Crosby's enthusiasm for their exploits lasted a lifetime, and she arranged her bombastic sentiments, tempered by time, into tributes for the annual memorials in which a nation paused to express its gratitude to fallen heroes:

Their work is done; and from year to year
We hallow their graves anew;
Their work is done, and our banner bright
Unfurled to the breeze we view;
And we look with pride on the Stars and Stripes
That were saved by the Boys in Blue.

Crosby's welling patriotism often took poetic form quite apart from the stimulus of Northern pride. The popular singer Phillips sang and published other Crosby text across the land, text that carried strong echoes of the Crosby family legacy:

Our country, the birthplace of freedom,
The land where our forefathers trod,
And sang in the aisles of the forest

Their hymns of thanksgiving to God.
Their bark they had moored in the harbor,
No more on the ocean to roam;
And there in the wilds of New England
They founded a country and home.

During these troubled years the van Alstines moved again, away from the familiar immediate environs of the Institution, first to 416 Ninth Avenue, and then farther south to the older part of the city, establishing a pattern that continued for the rest of their lives. Like many New Yorkers who depended on day-to-day earnings, they moved often, at first together and later individually, renting rooms or a modest apartment without leases, and they never purchased a home. The appearance of a To Let sign in a window that seemed more inviting than one's own might prompt a move the same day (and, in turn, the hanging of another To Let sign inviting someone else to move). The city's working citizens were always on the move, seeking a "better" block, lower rent, a brighter kitchen, better board, or proximity to loved ones, church, school, or work.

Crosby had left New York in 1858 just as a notable revival swept through its churches and beyond. She returned in 1860 to a city roused by the approaching drumbeats of war but still attuned to matters of the heart. Ever since a dramatic religious experience had helped lift her spirits toward the end of 1850, Crosby had felt her own heart strangely stirred, warmed by gospel fire. Her religious world had again been expanding, and in the fervor of her new apprehension of spiritual things she approached the threshold of life's next adventure.

CROSBY'S PROTESTANT NEW YORK

The urban religious setting that formed Crosby's adult Protestant sensibilities underwent rapid change between 1850 and 1865, the years most important for this part of Crosby's story. New York had a population approaching 900,000 at the time of the Civil War, of which some 500,000 were Roman Catholics and 350,000 were Protestants. The rapid increase in the Catholic fold was recent and testified to the influx of the Irish. When the first St. Patrick's Cathedral rose on Mott

Street in lower Manhattan in 1815, the church was only the third Catholic house of worship in the city. Another was erected in 1826, and six more followed in the 1830s. The explosion of the Catholic population in the 1840s brought fourteen new Catholic churches before 1850 and prompted as well the digging of the foundation in 1847 for a new St. Patrick's Cathedral among the fashionable dwellings that lined Fifth Avenue near Fiftieth Street. In 1850 the Vatican named the affable Irish immigrant John Hughes the first archbishop of New York. Pope Pius IX marked the importance of the occasion by personally bestowing on Hughes the pallium (a narrow circular band worn on special occasions only by archbishops, with permission from the Holy See) in Rome the next year. The change came too rapidly for Manhattan's Protestants to grasp its long-term significance. After all, in 1850 Methodists, Presbyterians, and Episcopalians each had far more houses of worship than did the Catholics.

To understand the Protestant New York of the mid–nineteenth century, one must reach behind caricatures and assumptions that often shape conceptions of the city's pre–Civil War religious landscape to try to grasp who Protestants took themselves to be. The lenses of historical inquiry through which later generations examined this world offered views colored by subsequent realities. Most pre–Civil War Manhattan Protestants described themselves as evangelicals, a label far more expansive in that era than its twenty-first-century usage implies. In the twenty-first century, coupling the words "evangelical" and "New York" seems oxymoronic; before the Civil War, "evangelical" encompassed a wide range of theological views and styles that described the vast majority of Manhattan's Protestants. The rapid influx of Catholics and Jews that toppled Protestant power bases, exacerbated by internal Protestant battles over theological modernism, later decisively shifted the balance of religious influence in Manhattan. But before the Civil War, Protestants enjoyed cultural ascendancy that they used to articulate a moral vision for society. Protestant similarities — intellectual and social — were at least as remarkable as Protestant differences. At midcentury Protestants were only becoming conscious of the immediate implications for themselves of the other worlds that jostled for space on Manhattan Island, worlds peopled mostly by masses of Catholics and Jews whose languages and social customs distinguished them as much as did their worship practices from the northern European

Protestants accustomed to leadership in New York affairs. In the vanished world of this North Atlantic Protestant New York, webs of relationships united Protestants, and a definite set of intellectual assumptions animated them. They tended to diagnose the same problems and to prescribe the same remedies for the perils and opportunities of their day. Evangelicals all (with the exception of a few Unitarian congregations), they routinely cooperated in scores of endeavors whose buildings and publishing houses dotted the city and whose influence reached the farthest corners of the globe.

During the 1860s Protestants produced a flurry of histories and descriptions of the city from their point of view. The books revealed both a degree of arrogance about "the superiority of our national character" and a solemn sense of the need to articulate "a moral principle, too elevated to be swayed by ridicule and too deeply seated to allow the first dereliction" so that democratic society could flourish. Their cultural authority made them confident, though it obscured the realities that would soon alter their power. They edited papers and built institutions like Bible House, the busy hub of the American Bible Society and related good works, in Manhattan's thriving commercial district. Supporters of the Bible Society and the host of interrelated agencies that promoted a Christian America were forward-looking and democratic, not backward-looking or conservative. Their leaders were not in retreat from modernity but eagerly endeavored to bend its promise to the cause of the gospel. Marked by republican sympathies and hard work, canny Protestant businessmen and their wives dreamed of a democratic society tempered by Christian virtue. United by an array of shared assumptions, ambitions, and instincts, thousands of nineteenth-century New York City Protestants were energized by the conviction that the transforming power of the gospel pointed unerringly to a wondrous and imminent millennial dawn. The same pulsating urgency that fueled Manhattan's relentless economic and cultural growth urged its Protestants to industry on behalf of Christianity.

Manhattan, observers generally noted, seemed a "paradise of preachers." Well supported, the Manhattan Protestant clergy, at least those in the city's influential pulpits, "seldom left till borne to their burial." While not all the clergy might have concurred that they enjoyed either affluence or job security, most would have agreed that Sunday quiet offered a decided contrast to the city's weekday bustle.

On Sunday mornings well-dressed people could be seen hurrying to church; only druggists, streetcar operators, and journalists headed out to work. Yet Protestants recognized, too, that Sunday pastimes in New York had recently taken a bewildering turn. Preachers worried about declining attendance at the traditional Sunday afternoon and evening services. Unless something radical happened, it seemed only a matter of time before the afternoon meetings would disappear altogether. Some already had. The recent introduction of Sunday afternoon concerts of classical and sacred music drew people elsewhere, as did walks and rides along the new Central Park's winding paths. More troubling, beyond the immediate sights of the well-to-do, other options beckoned youth. Socializing, dancing, bowling, and "carousing" in the lower Manhattan neighborhoods favored by recent immigrants distracted sons and daughters of the faithful from the sanctuary. It seemed only a matter of time before such activities moved north from the Bowery to trouble the righteous closer at hand. Some blamed the undeniable upset of the respectable Sabbath in the city's southern wards on the new and immense foreign population that attended no churches. Jews who opened their shops on Sunday were the bane of Protestant clerics. Every wave of immigrants, Protestant pessimists moaned, "lessened the dry land of religious observation" and strengthened a sentiment intent on "pushing out" both traditional Sabbath observance and attendance at public worship. But a Protestant wag deposited some of the blame squarely on the Protestants' own doorstep: one gospel sermon a day, he reminded them, was simply as much as they cared to hear, and more than they were willing inwardly to digest. Another pundit suggested in a jingle that preachers in popular churches had learned to "preach to please the sinners and fill the vacant pews," but, he ventured, cultured sinners could only tolerate small doses of sermonizing.

Still, most people agreed that "decency" required Protestants to attend church on Sunday morning, and those who frequented the fashionable churches dressed accordingly. In a city where ladies regularly "dressed for the street" with an elegance unmatched elsewhere, Sunday finery tended to be a costly and important social statement. The rich dressed as for a soiree or a matinee. One needed substantial means to look appropriate in such company, and strangers sometimes found that the warmth of the sexton's welcome depended on the quality of their apparel. Social climbers also required ample funds to cover the high annual fees for the "right" pew at the "right" church. An observer of the scene in the 1860s noticed "hosts of professing Christians" who opted not to belong anywhere but "drifted from church to church" to avoid these excessive pew rents. At midcentury Grace Church, at the corner of Broadway and Tenth Street, was considered "the height of fashion" with the most superb music of all Manhattan's elegant sanctuaries and a pew price that matched its reputation for excellence.

The most popular preachers addressed audiences that filled their sanctuaries long before the appointed hour. Edwin H. Chapin at the Fourth Universalist Church and Henry W. Bellows at the Unitarian All Souls Church vied with Brooklyn's Henry Ward Beecher for the biggest crowds. The best-known Presbyterian was the Reverend William Adams of the Madison Square Presbyterian Church. His congregation was reputedly the wealthiest in the United States, though Crosby's relation, the Reverend Howard Crosby, also preached to large and affluent crowds at the Fourth Avenue Presbyterian Church. Within the elegant white stone walls of St. Paul's Methodist Episcopal Church at Twenty-second Street and Fourth Avenue (the old Mulberry Street Methodist Church), H. B. Ridgeway (and given the Methodist three-year rule, a list of others) presided over the most fashionable and the wealthiest Methodist congregation in the country. While some of his cohorts received $10,000 salaries, Ridgeway had to be content with the $5,000 maximum the "Methodist rate" allowed. At Fifth Avenue Baptist, Thomas Armitage held sway, while Henry C. Potter served the Episcopal flock at the fashionable Grace Church. Stephen H. Tyng, like his rector-father an irrepressible Low Church Episcopalian, became something of a popular celebrity after his denomination put him on trial for violating ministerial courtesy. Tyng had preached at St. James Methodist Episcopal Church in New Brunswick, New Jersey, without the permission of local Episcopalians, and New Yorkers "read all about it" in their daily papers. Tyng took advantage of the publicity and began preaching on Manhattan streets, all the while working as very much a "hands-on" rector at the Church of the Holy Trinity on Madison Avenue and Forty-second Street where, true to his track record, he built a widely regarded Sunday school. Contemporaries generally described him as pale and emaciated, but this "uncompromising foe of the dram shop" was perhaps Manhattan's most colorful evangelical cleric. Hearing Tyng was "the thing" for visitors to Manhattan to do.

On the surface it seemed to some that New York, the self-styled "almshouse for the poor of all nations" and home to "the greatest scoundrels and the purest Christians," did not tend particularly assiduously to the religious welfare of those of modest means, nor did its fashionable Protestants always seem duly concerned about the city's abject poor. A few discharged their obligations to "the humbler class" or "the plain people" by sponsoring "auxiliary chapels." Most churches stood north of Bleecker Street, while the newly arrived huddled in the crowded streets to the south. Manhattan's five hundred or so Protestant churches did not have nearly enough seats for the masses, had the masses chosen to attend. In the oldest neighborhoods on the southern tip of the island, one curious inquirer found that only two old Episcopal churches, the famous Trinity Church, whose spire rose above the end of Wall Street, and St. Paul's (where Washington prayed after taking the oath as first president), together with "the Old Dutch Church" on Fulton Street opened their doors to the public, and only Trinity endeavored consistently to make the poor welcome.

Many of the poorest were immigrants, often Catholics or "infidels," and they took their Sunday leisure outside the churches. Everyone admitted the need for some relief for these people from the bleak living conditions in which they seemed trapped, conditions exacerbated by the staggering rate of population growth. Introducing a book describing their plight, pastor, editor, and activist Lyman Abbott later remarked of the city's impoverished neighborhoods: "There are wards in New York City in which the population is so dense that there are less square feet of the earth's surface for a person than is allowed therefore in the most crowded graveyard in the country." Scarce land, immigrant masses, and human greed drove the proliferation of tenement houses. The law defined a tenement house as a dwelling occupied by three or more families living independently and doing their cooking on the premises, or by more than two families on a floor living independently and having common rights to halls, stairways, yards, etc. By this definition all "flats" and apartment houses were tenement houses. Many landlords kept their property in good condition. But in popular imagination "tenement house" quickly became synonymous with filthy, crowded, stench-filled, dark, unsafe buildings, indifferently constructed, encroaching on courts and alleys or back-to-back with other buildings, planned by "selfish men who wanted to make money" without regard for adequate sanitation or ventilation. Conditions in such dwellings bred illness at alarming rates, and a rise in the city death rate prompted the city to act in 1856 to "reform" tenement houses.

The first sanitary inspections occurred early in 1864 and led to the immediate installation of 46,000 windows. An 1867 count enumerated 18,582 tenements and labeled just under 3,000 "in good condition." More than half of those "in bad condition" manifested "overflowing accumulation of filth" and/or failed to supply water. Twenty years and many efforts later, another inspection revealed little if any improvement in the most densely populated neighborhoods. Even England's notorious East London was much less crowded than Manhattan's Fourth Ward (175,815 persons per square mile versus 290,000). The vilest tenement house neighborhoods, Protestants knew, robbed people of their dignity and bred crime. The buildings constituted the city's slums, but those who lived there did not think themselves at the bottom of the heap. They reserved that distinction for the squatters who built shantytowns in the city's decreasing open spaces farther uptown.

At midcentury the poor were everywhere, but were most numerous along the East River, between Canal and Fourteenth Streets. Enormous beer gardens (some accommodating 1,200) and "dubious places of amusement" along the Bowery defied the Sunday law that elsewhere shut down the city's entertainments. Some called it Kleindeutschland in acknowledgment of the German-speaking craftsmen and shopkeepers whose businesses crowded its blocks, but the Irish packed its lodging houses, too. About one mile long, the Bowery was a wide, inviting street just east of Broadway, crowded with "cheap trade" and cheap lodgings. To be seen "in its glory," the Bowery had to be visited on Sunday. "Jews abound here," a contemporary explained, and these "Hebrews with no conscience in regard to the Christian Sabbath" did a brisk business on Sundays. Dance halls and cheap theaters catered to rowdy audiences, featuring "Negro minstrelsy of the lowest order, debasing theatricals, actresses too corrupt and dissolute to play elsewhere." Protestant horror was palpable. "On Sunday night," one wrote, "one would not believe that New York had any claim to be a

Christian city, or that the Sabbath had any friends." Those whose tastes did not run to such bawdiness knew that relief from the city's Sunday law could also be found a short ferry ride away across the Hudson River in New Jersey. The Hudson River ferry companies advertised gaslit boats accommodating 1,000 people per trip, and on Sundays they were generally crowded.

Thoughtful Protestants realized that Sunday laws — even if diligently enforced — could not in themselves remedy disregard for the Sabbath. After all, some of the morally saddest tales of New York life implicated those who abided by Sunday laws but enticed churchgoers the rest of the week to taste the thrills of the forbidden. Midcentury Protestants lamented most often the notorious Harry Hills's cavernous dance house on Houston Street, whose premises were "always jammed." Hills kept the letter of the law. He closed his bar at midnight on Saturdays, and no crimes occurred on his property; in fact, it was statistically one of the safest places in the city. But — like the police — Protestants could recite many tales of moral ruin that began at Hills's establishment but were acted out elsewhere. Theft and immorality of all kinds followed predictably in their minds the astonishing quantities of liquor consumed and the passions inflamed by dancing. If Hills was for them a type of manhood gone astray, Protestants easily identified Madame Restell, an abortionist with a "long and shuddering career," as "the wickedest woman in the city."

While earnest Protestants worried about their city — gambling, liquor, and vice were for them favorite symptoms of its spiritual need — they generally balanced their concerns with pride in their hard work to redeem New York and the world. "It is true that the Devil's work is done here on a gigantic scale," one of their spokesmen admitted, "but the will of the Lord is done on an equally great, if not a greater scale." A favorite example was the New York City Mission and Tract Society, an agency organized in the 1820s that by midcentury supported some 260 city missionaries who worked among the poor and whose efforts gave rise to missions, chapels, and occasionally new self-supporting churches. "Though much is said and written about the neglect of the masses in large cities," Protestants insisted, "it is nevertheless certain that few sections of Christendom are more thoroughly canvassed by the pious than the lanes and streets of Manhattan." Even the remote corners of the globe benefited from the good works of

Manhattan's faithful: "The lamp of religion, which burns in the dark islands of the sea, is fed by the hands of the bountiful in our city."

In her early years at the Institution, Crosby had begun exploring this bewildering Protestant New York. The array of Manhattan Protestant congregations she knew made amply plain that the much-touted fashionable congregations and their famous preachers represented only a small slice of the Protestant city. In addition to the famous, richly appointed sanctuaries that lined Fifth Avenue, Crosby knew and valued the modest neighborhood churches outside the limelight that tended the spiritual needs of the city's ordinary Protestants. The mid-nineteenth-century urban portraits that highlighted class, wealth, and social indifference were certainly accurate as far as they went, but taken alone, they distorted the true picture. There were always significant exceptions among wealthy churchgoers. And the public face simply did not tell the whole story. Just beneath the sights of Protestantism's boosters and critics was a second tier of congregations where image counted less than service and where pews were inexpensive or free. The earnest inhabitants of this domain did not blissfully ignore the poor, though they could not keep pace with population growth. Crosby nurtured her faith in this busy arena just beyond the sights of the popular depicters of New York's Protestant religious face. The New Yorkers in Crosby's circle (some of whom happened to be devout members of the city's wealthy congregations) were often concerned and active participants in faith-based attempts to right New York's (and the world's) ills. They cooperated readily in thriving transdenominational causes, showed concern for authentic religious experience, and vigorously embraced a practical Christianity that accepted as its middle-class responsibility the uplift and ennobling of the less fortunate.

Crosby remembered especially participating in class meetings at the Eighteenth Street Methodist Church, a congregation that never made a list of the city's top churches. Located at 305-313 West Eighteenth Street, this congregation traced its roots to 1828 and worshiped in an early American brown brick and sandstone building, dedicated in February 1836. Some of its members manifested concern for the spiritual welfare of scholars at the Institution and sponsored regular Thursday evening religious classes at the school. At these, Crosby accompanied the singing on the piano with the understanding that she

would not be asked to speak. Class meetings were all about participants' speech — testimonies to God's grace, requests for prayer, fervent supplication, exhortations to the gathered brothers and sisters.
Crosby cited timidity and spiritual indifference to Methodist warmth
as her excuse for silence.

In the end, however, Crosby's regular contact with Methodist
ways awakened her spiritual energies. She attributed a renewed concern for her own soul to a man from the Eighteenth Street church
named Theodore Camp, a teacher in the public schools who one
Thursday attended the Institution's class meeting. In 1845 Camp
joined the Institution's instructional staff, and he and Crosby developed a friendship. Crosby always said that an unusual dream about
Camp — rather than a direct conversation with him — roused her
soul. In the dream she was summoned to his sickbed, where Camp appeared to be dying. He asked, "Will you meet me in Heaven?" and she
responded, "Yes, I will, God helping me." As she awoke, she seemed
to hear him say, "Remember you promised a dying man." From that
waking moment she claimed the question of her personal assurance of
heaven haunted her.

Crosby found no peace until 1850 when the Thirtieth Street
Methodist Church offered its annual fall revival services. This church
(it later merged into Broadway Temple Methodist Episcopal Church)
stood near the Institution. It was there as the result of the Reverend Joseph Longking's farsighted decision in 1838 to plant a Methodist mission west of Eighth Avenue in what was then the sparsely populated
upper part of the city. By 1850 thousands of squatters thronged the
nearby riverfront, overwhelming even fiery Methodist evangelists and
presenting visionaries with a congregation-in-the-making. Nearby
Eighth Avenue had become the main west-side thoroughfare, drawing
even more people to the neighborhood. The church began humbly in a
basement, moved to a second-story hall over a carpenter shop, then to
a small frame building. In 1849 the congregation moved to its own
new brick church at Thirtieth Street and Ninth Avenue, just four blocks
from the Institution. By then, church membership approached 300 (not
counting probationers and a host of regular attenders), having more
than quadrupled in the previous five years. Here Crosby attended every evening of the 1850 fall revival and even ventured to the altar
when preachers invited troubled souls to "pray through" to an inner

"witness" of salvation. Her third walk down the aisle to kneel at the "anxious bench" came on 20 November 1850. Her rendering of her sense of urgency was typical of nineteenth-century female conversion narratives. As she knelt in front of the gathered crowd, sensing it was "now or never," Crosby heard the congregation break into Isaac Watts's famous words, "Alas, and did my Saviour bleed." Crosby knew the words, but something unusual happened when the congregation approached the end of the final stanza: "Here Lord, I give myself away, 'Tis all that I can do." She described it in the metaphor of light that so often expressed her deepest emotions: "My very soul was flooded with a celestial light." Among nineteenth-century Methodists assembled for revival, Crosby's next move was hardly surprising: "I sprang to my feet, shouting 'hallelujah.'" The respectable Presbyterian had, in a moment of wakened faith, become a shouting Methodist. And she was not alone. On behalf of the New York East Conference, the venerable Nathan Bangs reported of that winter's revivals: "The work of both sanctification and conversion, or justification, is going forward with encouraging success and most of the preachers and people seem to be deeply imbued with the spirit of revival and are entering into the work most heartily."

The next week Crosby broke form and testified at the Institution's regular Thursday class meeting. Within a few weeks she had overcome her timidity about public religious speech so entirely that she could declare toward the end of her busy life that once she began participating in class meeting, "I believe I have never refused to pray or speak in a public service, with the result that I have been richly blessed."

The world of New York Methodism in which Crosby now moved boasted some of the denomination's best-known figures. Phoebe Palmer, the devout advocate of Christian perfection, led the list. The venerable circuit-rider-turned-educator Nathan Bangs commanded enormous respect. The saintly Bishop Matthew Simpson often graced New York pulpits. And the young Stephen Merritt, a local preacher of note and soon-to-be proprietor of his father's mortuary, proved that Methodists could combine lucrative business enterprises with effective witness and otherworldly preoccupation. The Methodist Book Concern, billed as "the oldest publishing house in the United States" and "the largest religious publisher in the world," operated from premises in lower Manhattan, flooding the country with inexpensive religious literature.

To be sure, the denomination's Manhattan flock was not large, but it was growing steadily. As recently as 1830 Methodism claimed in Manhattan just 3,886 white and 69 colored members, and preachers rotated from church to church under the oversight of a preacher-in-charge of the circuit. In 1832 New York City divided into an East and a West Circuit, and each church set up its own board to manage internal affairs. A single Board of Trustees had responsibility for all Manhattan Methodist Episcopal Church property. By 1840 both circuits had abrogated the custom of separate seating for men and women. In 1840, 12 Methodist churches gathered Manhattan's faithful, some 8,776 strong. Membership grew slowly for the rest of the century, and in 1900, 31 churches counted 11,727 members. Statistics ignored thousands more regular attenders. Sunday schools, too, boasted large memberships, often four or five times the church membership. (Neighboring Brooklyn, by contrast, numbered over 275 Methodist churches with well over 100,000 members.)

At midcentury New York Methodists still smarted from recent notable secessions from their modest ranks. Wesleyan Methodists and Free Methodists had left to form their own circuits friendly to abolitionism and opposed to the ever-more-evident wealth and formalism of the Methodist Episcopal Church. To be sure, more of these secessionists lived in upstate New York than in the city, but the rancor coursed through the state's Methodist conferences. The denomination itself had divided in 1844 between north and south over the appointment of a slaveholding bishop. Within Manhattan congregations, those who urged Christian perfection — a subject not favored everywhere — held places of prominence. Their control of the monthly magazine, *Guide to Holiness,* extended their views well beyond their city haunts.

The peculiar Methodist teaching on Christian perfection — Wesley had once dubbed this emphasis "the grand depositum of Methodism" — kept the day-to-day focus on the state of one's soul. In the able hands of Phoebe Palmer, Wesley's sometimes inconsistent thoughts on the precise process of becoming perfect were transformed into a formula for an instantaneous "second blessing." New York Methodists heard directly and incessantly from Mrs. Palmer, either in person or in print, about the importance of entire consecration — "placing all on the altar (Christ)" — and of recognizing by faith that "the altar sanctified the gift." Her system borrowed freely from Old Testament practice to illustrate New Testament experience. By reducing the discipline of a life headed in the direction of Christian perfection to a crisis experience that effected instant holiness, she helped lay the foundation for the Holiness movement of later decades. Indefatigable and comfortably off, she and her sister, Sarah Lankford, welcomed New Yorkers on Tuesdays to their gracious double parlors for "social meetings" in which to pursue personal holiness. While they did not limit their guests to Methodists, they did especially yearn to keep their beloved denomination committed to this particular strain in its historic past.

Stephen Merritt, Crosby's first Methodist class meeting leader, identified early and zealously with the American gloss on this peculiarly Methodist tenet. An aspiring songwriter, Merritt set his "take" on Christian perfection to the tune for the popular "Old Oaken Bucket":

> The blessed Abider has come as my treasure,
> Has taken His home in my heart, and my soul,
> I find Him the source of such exquisite pleasure,
> The purest and brightest; He takes sweet control.

At the time of Crosby's conversion experience, Merritt was barely seventeen, but his wholehearted zeal made him (most likely at first with his father, another Stephen and a seasoned Methodist exhorter) a leader in the Methodist class at the Institution. From that association forward, he would be part of the religious culture that nurtured Crosby.

Born in Manhattan's Chelsea section in 1833 and associated first with the Eighteenth Street Methodist Episcopal Church (where the elder Stephen Merritt was sexton), Merritt found himself drawn to ministry, but he was destined rather to become perhaps the city's best-known undertaker, and probably the only one convinced that he was "placed in the business by the Holy Spirit." A brief stint at Amenia Seminary (a small precollege rather than a theological program) in Dutchess County, New York, provided the rudiments of higher education, but family circumstances soon necessitated his return to Manhattan to as-

Faith

sist his father. His family business supplied him with sufficient means to live in comfort, employ several house servants and a coachman, and travel. As his reputation grew, Merritt's business clientele expanded to include some New York notables. In 1885 he presided over the arrangements for the lavish funeral of President Grant, and marched alone behind the coffin in the procession that wound through Manhattan's streets to the general's tomb. But to Crosby he was better known as someone whose fascination for religious experience drove him to preach to humble congregations, to promote the unconventional Methodist Bishop William Taylor's scheme for independent missions (Merritt served as Taylor's secretary for Africa, and Crosby herself thrilled to Taylor's oratory and recalled receiving his benediction), and to pursue "deeper" Christian truths with other New York devotees of a "higher" Christian life. He also found time to run for state office on the temperance ballot and to issue a monthly paper called the *King's Messenger*, all the while supplying Methodist pulpits. Crosby's acquaintance with him exposed her to a range of grassroots causes that flamed urban Methodist souls in the second half of the century.

Direct contact between Crosby and Palmer is more difficult to ascertain. Certainly Crosby later came to know and collaborate with Palmer's independently minded namesake daughter, Phoebe Palmer Knapp, and in 1886, for the fiftieth anniversary of Palmer's hallowed Tuesday Meeting, celebrated in the richly appointed sanctuary of St. Paul's Methodist Episcopal Church, Crosby composed a hymn sung at the public commemoration and recited a poem, "What Hath God Wrought," at the evening service. But while she appreciated the tradition of the Tuesday Meetings and in other ways manifested support for Palmer's teaching, there is no direct record of her participation.

Her affinity for the perfectionist strain within Methodism drew her occasionally during the 1870s to the era's premier camp meeting specifically devoted to that cause, a summer-long affair at Ocean Grove on the sandy shores of New Jersey, and to another at Round Lake, near Saratoga in upstate New York. But Crosby did not limit herself to Methodist circles. She found in the city's richly varied Protestant community a menu for worship that fed her ever-eager soul.

In the 1850s Henry Ward Beecher reigned supreme as America's pulpiteer. The son of the redoubtable New England pastor and Ohio

Lane Seminary professor Lyman Beecher and brother to an array of siblings famous in their own right, Beecher had arrived at Brooklyn's Plymouth Church of the Pilgrims in 1847. Renowned for his forthright persuasive style, Beecher regularly addressed overflow audiences. His famous ten-minute rule governed access to Plymouth Church: no one except pewholders could enter until a bell rang exactly ten minutes before service time. Then the doors opened, and late pewholders lost their seats to the public who arrived "with a rush" to fill every seat, staircase, and standing space. The services in his plainly appointed amphitheater-style sanctuary generally ran at least two hours, and Beecher presided affably and alone. His energetic opposition to slavery resulted in his congregation's fund-raising to arm opponents of slavery in the disputed United States territories. Known as Beecher Bibles, the fund-raising effort purchased weapons, some of which found their way into the hands of the famous radical John Brown and his sons. During the Civil War Beecher's church raised and supported a regiment. His particular blend of Union patriotism and Christianity appealed to Fanny Crosby. She considered him a friend and numbered Plymouth Church among her favorites.

Plymouth Church attracted hundreds of regular attendees from Manhattan, and Crosby certainly never had to make the trip alone. At midcentury a growing number of ferry companies plied the East River, offering service on large paddle ships every five minutes between Manhattan and Brooklyn. On Sundays New Yorkers called them "Beecher Boats" because so many riders (some of the ferries carried 1,000 people plus horses and carriages) were making their way to Beecher's church on the high ground that rose sharply on the Brooklyn side of the river. Known as Brooklyn Heights, the church neighborhood was the most prestigious section of the bustling city of Brooklyn, also known as "the city of churches."

Beecher combined a moderate theology with decided views on church music, a subject in which the musically inclined Crosby already had considerable interest. Beecher's innovative music had as much of a following as did his skillful preaching style. Most people's commentary on the music ran something like the following: "The volume of melody is seldom in power and sweetness equaled this side of heaven." Beecher could not sing, but he knew what he wanted to hear, and he believed that music could work powerfully and hand in hand with preaching to produce the desired effects. During his youth his father, Lyman, had been among the first Boston pastors actively to support Lowell Mason's early attempts to reform church music. Mason had directed the choir in Lyman's two Boston churches and had worked to improve the choir and to make the congregation sing. His efforts won the elder Beecher's unstinting praise. At the same time, Mason was also earning a reputation as an arranger and composer of hymn tunes. Among his enduring favorites are Bethany, the common tune for "Nearer, My God, to Thee"; Azmon, his arrangement of the common tune for "O for a Thousand Tongues to Sing"; and Hamburg, the favored American setting for "When I Survey the Wondrous Cross." Mason had published his first hymn tune, Missionary Hymn, the common setting for Reginald Heber's "From Greenland's Icy Mountains," before he moved to Boston. Lyman Beecher (known by contemporaries as "earnest in the employment of sacred song"), meanwhile, drilled into his numerous progeny the importance of congregational song.

Henry Ward Beecher refused to rely on hired singers, announced the gathering of a volunteer choir from his congregation, and enlisted that choir to lead congregational song rather than to sing for the congregation. To facilitate his plans he hired a gifted Swiss-born organist, Johann Zundel, paid him the largest salary earned by any American Protestant organist, and collaborated with him on a hymnal specifically for the use of Plymouth Church. On his part, Zundel had already established himself as a valued member of Mason's expanding circle dedicated to improving church music.

Contemporaries marveled at the hearty singing that marked every service. A longtime usher remembered that when the singing languished, Beecher simply stopped the song and had the people start again. He used midweek services to acquaint his weeknight audience of 1,000 with a wide array of hymns. He never announced hymns: he simply called out a number. Plymouth Church became a model for those across the country who shared Beecher's conviction that mid-nineteenth-century American Protestants would be vastly enriched by invigorated communal song. Plymouth Church operated several missions for the less advantaged in Brooklyn and Manhattan, and Crosby later took pride in Beecher's adoption of one of her texts as a mission theme song.

Crosby warmed to Beecher's powerful oratory, but she did not confine herself to the gospel according to Plymouth Church. Her rounds of the churches also included the congregation of her famous distant cousin, the prominent Presbyterian pastor Dr. Howard Crosby. He was part of her own extended clan in the New York counties just north of the city where his grandfather, Ebenezer Crosby, had made the family home. Howard was born to William and Harriet Clarkson Crosby and was the youngest brother of William and John Crosby, men Fanny knew from their work at the Institution. Howard's great-grandfather, William Ford, had signed the Declaration of Independence. His father, William, inherited the real estate fortune of Henry Rutgers. When Howard arrived at Fourth Avenue Presbyterian Church in 1863, the congregation had 120 members. A few years later it boasted 1,564 members, and he had opened at least three missions in needy parts of Manhattan. Fanny thrilled to Howard's preaching and took pride in their kinship, though there is no evidence that the two enjoyed any social contact.

Like many other city pastors of his day, Howard Crosby made time to identify with the causes that galvanized his parishioners. His outspoken support for high license fees as a means toward temperance made him a popular subject for political cartoonists. The chancellor of New York University from 1870 to 1881, he enjoyed a reputation — remarkable in that era of such local pulpit orators as Beecher, DeWitt Talmage, George F. Pentecost, and Theodore Cuyler — as a powerful evangelical preacher. (His sermon "Preach the Word" would later be included in volume 3 of the famous series *The Fundamentals*.) From Howard Crosby, Fanny heard the familiar Calvinist Bible-centered preaching of her childhood. Even after she became famous, Fanny remained a sort of country cousin to these privileged kin, but their shared religious and social inclinations were reminders that they hailed from the same New England stock. Like Fanny, Howard Crosby gave vent to religious emotions in poetry:

> Before the great white throne on high
> With all its holy brilliancy,
> Known and belov'd of Heav'n am I
> *Because* the Saviour stands for me.
>
> Tis this, when fetter'd by my sin,
> Restores my soul and sets me free;

It's now no longer what I've been
But that the Saviour stands for me.

In old age Fanny remembered other churches that fed her soul. She attended vespers at an Episcopal church and sometimes worshiped at the Dutch Reformed church on Twenty-third Street where the saintly Peter Stryker preached. She sat enthralled under the oratory of DeWitt Talmage at the Brooklyn Tabernacle, a place where excellent music and congregational song always flourished. Late in life, when asked to recommend one among the many whose sermons she had heard, she chose Theodore Cuyler, another Presbyterian who moved from Manhattan to Brooklyn, where he served a congregation billed as "the largest Presbyterian church in the world."

Not until the spring of 1887 did Crosby formally join a church. She then lived on Fourth (Park) Avenue, on Manhattan's upper east side, and she opted to attend a fairly new congregation, Cornell Memorial Methodist Episcopal Church. Named in honor of William Cornell, a wealthy benefactor of Methodist causes (as well as of the university named in his honor) of whom it was said, "His munificence and unaffected piety have rarely if ever been excelled," the church stood on Seventy-sixth Street between Second and Third Avenues. Begun in 1868 as a project of the New York City Church Extension and Missionary Society with a Sunday school quartered above a neighborhood grocery, Cornell Memorial quickly transitioned from mission to church, building facilities in two stages, a chapel in 1872 and a sanctuary seating 1,500 in 1883. The congregation boasted a thriving Sunday school (1890 figures record 425 church members, 59 probationers, and 1,250 Sunday school scholars — the largest Methodist Sunday school in Manhattan) and several active class meetings. Crosby joined one with 70 members that met on Tuesday evenings under the direction of James H. Stokes (who was also an officer of the Sunday school). The church records indicate that she joined the church on confession of faith and was received by the Reverend S. Beason Hamilton. She occasionally gave a Sunday morning address. New York City Methodist records note as well her attendance on occasion at Park Avenue Methodist Episcopal Church on Eighty-sixth Street in the nearby neighborhood of Yorkville. One May evening Pastor F. C. Iglehart of that church welcomed 24 new members into "full fellowship." Crosby attended and recited "in her impressive way" stanzas she had composed for the occasion. Despite its length, we quote the work in full as perhaps the most revealing statement Crosby made on her understanding of church membership and on the Christian life:

There are angels bending o'er us
From their cloudless realms tonight;
They are smiling down upon us,
And their eyes with joy are bright;
For another reinforcement
To our royal army grand
Has received a benediction
At our faithful pastor's hand.

And we answer, "Welcome, soldiers,
Your commander is the Lord;
You have girded on your armor
In obedience to His word.
You have 'listed in a warfare
'Gainst the tyrant hosts of sin,
And through grace you are determined
Life's immortal crown to win.

You are marching to the conflict
With your banners wide unfurled;
Let your battle cry be ever,
'Free salvation to the world!'
Be ye steadfast, look to Jesus,
And though oft severely tried,
You will all be more than conquerors
If you still in Him abide."

Could the veil of time be lifted
While our evening song we raise;
Could our spirit eyes be opened,
What a scene would meet our gaze!
We should view our dear ones watching
At the portals of the blest,

And their palms would wave us onward
To the paradise of rest.

Faithful pastor, God is with thee;
He has heard and answered prayer;
Precious souls, thy toil rewarding,
Are committed to thy care.
O, the joy, the bliss, the rapture,
When a few more years are o'er —
Thou shalt stand among thy people,
Shouting victory evermore!

Crosby's immediate religious world expanded dramatically during her years in Manhattan, then, to embrace a range of Protestant styles. She frequented most regularly churches within walking distance of her apartments, and her regular attendance corresponded loosely to her place of residence. But she frequently spoke at churches and missions of different denominations around the city. On city streets and in her boarding places, she rubbed shoulders with immigrants, Catholics, Lutherans, and other newcomers whose religious practices stood worlds apart from Southeast, New York, or Ridgefield, Connecticut. Her direct religious exposure, whether by happenstance or whim, confined her to what her heritage had defined as respectable, familiar communities of faith, with one striking exception. Family circumstances exposed her to a hardy homespun religion that made peculiarly American claims: the Church of Jesus Christ of Latter-day Saints.

THE CROSBYS AND THE MORMONS

Crosby met Mormonism head-on through her mother. With Crosby settled at the Institution and her own parents buried in Southeast, Mercy Crosby had little to hold her in Putnam County. In 1835 her brother Joseph had moved to Bridgeport, Connecticut, a small but rapidly growing town on the Connecticut coast west of New Haven, just across Long Island Sound from New York's Long Island. After a stint as an apprentice in the Bridgeport saddle firm of Fairchild, Lyon and Company, Joseph and William Wade and William May incorporated their own business, Wade, Crosby and Company, Saddlers. Joseph managed their factory and opened branches in Columbus and Savannah, Georgia, and New York City. Practical mechanics (among them a Nathan Crosby, certainly a close relative, perhaps Joseph and Mercy's brother Paddock) who knew the business "from beginning to end" and were deemed "very expert" in their trade, these men hired hardworking artisans who made the company a stunning financial success. (Between 1850 and 1854 a short-lived California branch alone yielded a $200,000 profit. In the twenty-first century Crosby saddles remain popular — and expensive — items.) In 1836 Mercy joined Joseph in Bridgeport, living with his family — wife Maria, son Frank, and daughter Ida. She continued to support herself by doing housework. In 1838 she married (within a month of making his acquaintance) a recent immigrant named Thomas Morris. What followed drew Fanny into a chapter of the American religious story that otherwise might have passed her by.

A native of South Wales, Morris, like Mercy, was born in 1799. As a child he lived in poverty in Pembrokeshire, where he received meager schooling and earned a few pence tending sheep. In 1803 his parents divorced, and in 1811 his father married a "spirited" widow with children, a marriage Thomas recalled wryly as having "an effect much reverse from his [father's] anticipations." A serious accident soon forced the father to the workhouse, where he could receive parish charity, effectively ending his married life. Meanwhile, Thomas hired himself out as a farm laborer and often found himself among Methodists. In 1823 he became a member of the Methodist Connection. In 1827 he married Frances Hall and decided to pursue his fortune in Gloucestershire. There in 1829 his son William was born, followed two years later by Jemima. Something of Thomas's temperament may perhaps be deduced from his observation on William's birth: "This was an addition to my family wants, not so much for his consumption, as for his engaging his mother's attention and deterring her from being otherwise advantageously employed."

Despite his best efforts, Morris failed to keep "the monster" of poverty at bay. A severe economic downturn aggravated his family prospects and disposed him toward North America. A letter from one Isaac Priest, recently settled north of Manhattan in Dobbs Ferry, New York, circulated in the vicinity and convinced Morris that common laborers had far brighter prospects in New than in Old England. Priest's brother, William, and Morris now planned to go. Morris had by this time joined the local Baptists, and he bared his heart to one of his new brethren. One thing led to another until local Baptists began sending donations to help Morris realize his dream. He next determined to raise the balance from his native parish of Carew, some 200 miles away. The parish refused him aid, Morris left his wife and children with her family, and he sailed alone for New York courtesy of his Baptist friends.

His story of his voyage reveals the resolve that made the journey endurable to the poor. Morris had just one pound sterling with which to purchase his "sea stores" for a trip of uncertain duration. These consisted almost entirely of potatoes. He traveled with 385 others on the *Mary Catherine,* a sailing vessel that made the voyage in seven long weeks. An enterprising man, Morris bartered potatoes for other items and, all things considered, had a satisfactory time of it. A succession of jobs in New York and Connecticut earned him the money to return to England to get his wife and children. The return voyage took just three weeks, and readying his family required two weeks more. After seven more weeks at sea, they sailed into New York harbor early in April 1836. The Morris family settled in Bridgeport, where in the next six months their "united industry and economy" made them the proud possessors of nearly $500.

The next year dimmed their prospects. In October 1837 Frances gave birth to a healthy son, Daniel, but three days later she died. Morris confided to his journal that he had not appreciated her until she was gone. New expenses — a dollar per week for the baby's nurse, another dollar for a housekeeper, and fifty cents for the care of Jemima — depleted his means, and Morris began looking for a wife. Mercy Crosby was then cook for a Mr. Malapah. She possessed $800 and seemed entirely suitable. Morris later admitted that he was "spurred forward" by opposition from Mercy's well-to-do brothers, citizens of "some consequence" in Bridgeport.

Thomas and Mercy married in 1838, and each contributed $150 toward the $600 needed for the house and garden of their choice. They mortgaged the rest, the Morris children came home from their nurses, and Thomas and Mercy planted a garden and furnished the house. As Thomas later told it, after just a few weeks he decided that he and Mercy were incompatible. He accused her of neglecting his infant and later complained that the "union was rendered extremely irksome for a while." According to Thomas, Mercy "plundered his house and credit" of some $100 and mistreated him and his children. After separating for five months, the couple tried again. "I yielded to her importunities," Morris admitted, "because she was a female and had a claim on my pardon the same as I hope to obtain pardon from my offenses from my Father."

In the next few years Mercy and Thomas had three children of their own, Wilhelmina in 1839, Julia in 1840, and Caroline in 1843. Wilhelmina soon died, but Julia and Caroline thrived. Then Mormon missionaries arrived in Bridgeport, and Thomas "had the good fortune to hear the fullness of the gospel." The "wholesome truths" of Joseph Smith's revelations "fell as idle tales" on Mercy's ears, but from the outset seemed "plain and easy to understand" to Thomas. He at once prepared to join the main Mormon community on the banks of the Mississippi in Nauvoo, Illinois.

Mercy obstinately refused to have anything to do with this new gospel, and Morris's older son, William, supported her. The circumstances were not unlike those Thomas recalled from his own childhood when irreconcilable differences prompted his parents to separate. He must have recalled his father's unhappy remarriage and the abysmal failure of that attempt to blend two families. Now Thomas insisted that Mercy had "prejudiced [William's] mind" and "secreted him" from his father's influence. (William later confessed that he had run away until he could be sure his father had left.) Courting pity, the elderly Thomas complained that he had done nothing more than choose "to work out his own salvation in a way contrary to popular opinion," and that Mercy denied him that fundamental right. And so he took Jemima and Daniel, his two younger children by his first wife, and headed west. He told Mercy he would be back when he had carefully examined Mormon teaching and had found it irreconcilable with Scripture.

Morris and his children arrived in Nauvoo on 27 May 1844. A month later he stood over the lifeless body of his "beloved prophet," Joseph Smith, murdered with two others in the Carthage, Illinois, jail. Two years later he and his children trekked west to Utah. His life among the Mormons convinced Morris that Smith's teachings were true, and he never returned to Bridgeport, nor did Mercy ever seek him out in Utah. He married several more wives, traveled the Pacific as a Mormon missionary, and wrote a hymn for the Mormon Battalion (a famous troop with which he served as it protected the trail to California). His new apprehension of things assured him that eternity would bring him the opportunity for a loving reunion with his underappreciated first wife, Frances, whom he remembered with professed regret for his misuse of her: "I believe I shall be able to call her to my arms in the resurrection inasmuch as she relinquished this state of probation calling on the Lord to extend His mercy to me and her children." He neither imagined nor desired such a future with Mercy Crosby. But along the way before he died, the temple rites of the Church of Jesus Christ of Latter-day Saints were dutifully performed on behalf of Mercy and her children, including Frances Crosby.

Her mother's difficult relationship with Thomas Morris affected Fanny Crosby deeply. She came home for a long period of rest and recuperation in 1844, just after Morris abandoned the family. Caroline was not yet six months old, and Mercy Morris had her hands full. Crosby stayed until September, and the family bonds were strengthened in the meeting of mutual needs. During the years of the marriage, Crosby had spent several long periods at home. Baby Wilhelmina's death had elicited from her a poem that suggested that Mercy and Thomas may not always have been as unhappy as he later depicted them:

> Yet, mother, check that starting tear
> That trembles in thine eye;
> And thou, kind father, cease to mourn,
> Suppress that heaving sigh.
>
> She's gone, yet why should we repine?
> Our darling is at rest;
> Her cherub spirit now reclines
> On her Redeemer's breast.

The Crosbys' firsthand encounter with the Mormon excitement that mounted across the country in the early 1840s resembled that of other families scattered across the Northeast and Midwest. Ardent missionaries recruited for the church that had been founded in 1830. In fact, during the 1830s Mormon missionaries in Massachusetts convinced a direct descendant of the Puritan Thomas Crosby of the truth of the new gospel. Jonathan Crosby, who traced his lineage through the Crosbys' Rowley, Massachusetts, branch, cast in his lot with the Mormons in New England and soon joined the small community in Kirtland, Ohio. An avid musician, Jonathan conducted the second Mormon singing school. He journeyed to Utah with the main Mormon migration in 1848 and took his place on the Council of Seventy. At least two branches of the Crosby family thus divided over the claims of this hardy American faith, just as many other families did in the same years when William Miller, the Adventist, insisted on dating the end of the world. New York, Ohio, Missouri, and Illinois refused in succession this New Israel the hospitality its leaders coveted, but their following grew nonetheless. Polygamy rumors began to surface shortly before Smith's death, but as yet the revelation had not been publicly promulgated. When Brigham Young assumed Smith's mantle, Thomas Morris — like any number of other recent-and-never-settled faithful — swore allegiance and followed. In the Church of Jesus Christ of Latter-day Saints he found the sense of belonging that had eluded him elsewhere. Until 1844 no Christian group had gained his firm allegiance. Briefly Baptist and Methodist, occasionally Anglican, Morris had apparently used religious affiliation to his own ends rather than allowing Christianity to mold him. He was ripe for conversion, particularly when offered a creed that permitted him to justify his unhappiness with Mercy in religious terms. Mormonism came to be Morris's personal declaration of independence from Mercy as well as from other constraints.

The Morrises' stormy six-year relationship left Crosby three people who became the delights of her life and her caregivers in old age: her half sisters Julia and Caroline and her stepbrother William Morris. His father may have blamed William's rejection of Mormon teaching on Mercy, but fifteen-year-old William clearly thought he had made his own choice. These three siblings constituted Crosby's new family. She was, of course, enough older than the girls to have been their mother, and in old age she fondly recalled the good times they shared during her visits. Thanks to them, she held Bridgeport in her mind as her real "home," complete to the family hearth. Though she spent little time there at midlife, Crosby enshrined the place and loved ones in her memory, and the diminutive woman from Putnam County, New York, for the rest of her life went "home" to Bridgeport, Connecticut, a place where she did not live until she reached the age of eighty. Crosby shared a wedding year with her much younger sister Julia, who became the bride of an apprentice coach lamp maker, Byron Athington, in 1858. Twenty years later, despite her own nontraditional marriage, Crosby penned an anniversary tribute:

Tell me, sister, does your memory
Touch its lyre and murmur low
How your heart of joy was dreaming,
Dreaming twenty years ago?
And the lovely wing of fancy,
With your smile of beauty played,
While you stood before the altar
In your bridal robe arrayed?

And to him who stood beside you
All your fondest hopes were given,
Vows were breathed and words were spoken,
Read by seraph eyes in Heaven?
You have trod life's vale together,
You have shared its good and ill,
Is your promise yet unbroken —
Do you hold it sacred still?

Crosby and her Morris siblings cherished a Mercy Morris who bore no resemblance to the one Thomas Morris criticized to rationalize his own life's choices. Mercy lived long, loved by her children and grandchildren, and her birthdays occasioned annual family reunions. For her mother's eighty-ninth birthday in 1888, Crosby composed a tribute that seems sharply at odds with Thomas's mutterings about his wife:

Tender thoughts their spell are weaving,
Hallowed memories round us twine,
'Tis the birthday of our mother,
And her years are eighty-nine;
Mother's birthday, and her children

Three in number, all are here,
From the sunny past recalling
Words of love we still revere.
Mother's birthday! God reward her
For her gentle, patient care,
May He light the path before her
Is the burden of our prayer.

Mercy's daughters made her birthday a family holiday, a tradition they continued even after she died. They always gathered for a family dinner at which Fanny recited a new poem. The *Bridgeport Daily Standard* carried a notice of Mercy's ninety-first birthday and the lines Fanny delivered:

Our mother's brow is wreathed in smiles,
Her friends and children dear
With children's children celebrate
Her one and ninetieth year!

Her mental powers are unimpaired
Her evening's skies are clear,
While memory's star unclouded hails
Her one and ninetieth year!

Mercy died 1 September 1890, a respected Bridgeport citizen whose life in the fast-growing community harked back to simpler times. Her funeral took place in her home, with the Reverend E. K. Holden, pastor of the city's Olivet Congregational Church, officiating. Fanny (in her seventy-first year) paid tribute:

Her voyage of life is ended,
Her anchor firmly cast,
Her bark that many a storm has braved
Is safe in port at last.
Surrounded by her treasured ones
Our mother passed away
Beneath the golden sunset
Of summer's brightest day.

We loved our tender mother
Far more than words can tell,
And while with deep emotion
We breathe our fond farewell
We know her tranquil spirit
Has reached the long-sought shore
And now with joy 'tis greeting
The dear ones gone before.

Oh, mother, we are coming,
The time will not be long,
Till we shall clasp thy hand again
And join the blissful song.
The sheaf of wheat is garnered,
The sickle's work is done
And everlasting glory
Through Christ her soul has won.

Crosby's encounter with the teachings of Mormonism did not impact her mind in any substantial way. Rather, it apparently reinforced her evangelicalism. Her mother and stepsiblings had no use for the religion that disrupted their family, and Crosby — who drew most of her impressions of the encounter from a distance — stood squarely with her family. But the event highlighted for her both personal and doctrinal consequences of the new religion and both drew her family closer and made her sensitive to the contemporary personal impact of Mormon expansion.

If her encounters with Methodism, other streams of evangelicalism, and such sturdy, homegrown varieties of American religion as Mormonism formed the adult Crosby, they also prepared her for the still larger stage that awaited her. She was about to become a nationally acclaimed author of texts for secular tunes and an astounding success as a hymn text composer. To grasp the import of her work in these areas, it is necessary to turn back for a glimpse of the architects of the world Crosby stood poised to enter.

5 Music

Holy, holy, holy is the Lord!
Sing, O ye people, gladly adore Him;
Let the mountains tremble at His word,
Let the hills be joyful before Him!

At least since the 1820s, a movement intent on elevating the nation's musical taste, improving congregational singing, and introducing music into the public schools had captured the imagination of growing numbers of Americans. The acknowledged pioneer of this "grand epoch" for American music was Lowell Mason, the same indefatigable Bostonian whose *Handel and Haydn Collection* Crosby had used as a child in Ridgefield. Convinced that the study of music was "a means of human development of great powers" and that its "highest and best influence" was moral, Mason believed music "should be cultivated and taught, not as a means of mere sensual gratification, but as a sure means of improving the affections, and of ennobling, purifying and elevating the whole man." His convictions, demonstrations, and energy ignited in Boston a movement intent on proving music's beneficent place among an informed and cultured citizenry prepared for the responsibilities of democracy. Together and separately Mason and his two best-known protégés, George Root and William Bradbury, would shape the context that nurtured Crosby's fame. Each made an enormous contribution to American Protestantism as well as to music education, performance, and teacher training. Each also earned a fortune; these men created, sustained, and met a demand for printed music that helped expand music publishing and distribution in a growing nation. The enterprise owed its existence to the persistence and energy of Lowell Mason.

The details that follow turn briefly from the narrative of Crosby's life in order to provide an essential background for understanding her popularization. Her public was greatly expanded by her relationship with the movement associated with Mason and by the perception his cohorts had of her usefulness to their larger endeavor. Crosby took enormous pride and satisfaction in her association with famous people, and her ties to these men and the movement they represented gratified her and nurtured her bent toward usefulness.

Like Crosby, Mason traced his roots to colonial Massachusetts. Mason's family arrived from England in 1653 and settled to the southwest of Boston in the new (1651) town of Medfield. Six generations later, Lowell Mason was born 8 January 1792 to Johnson and Catherine Hartshorn Mason. The family lived comfortably. Johnson Mason was town clerk, member of the state legislature, businessman, inventor, and schoolmaster. He played several instruments and sang in the parish choir. As a child, Lowell manifested a similar love for music. In 1805 he attended a singing school conducted by a neighbor, Amos Albee. By 1808 he hired out as a singing master and band conductor. In the religious upheavals that divided New England into orthodox and Unitarian factions, the Mason family was staunchly orthodox, and the Medfield parish church provided the context for Mason's exposure to sacred song.

In 1812 he moved to Savannah, Georgia, where he took work as a bank clerk. He quickly found a post as choirmaster and organist at the Independent Presbyterian Church. He also helped establish the only Sunday school in Savannah, and the scholars gave him ample opportunity to experiment with his musical ideas. In Savannah he met Friedrich Abel, a recent German immigrant thoroughly grounded in music theory who taught him theory and composition. After diligently studying the German music Abel recommended, Mason began composing and reharmonizing in German style. Guided by the scientific rules employed by German masters from the baroque forward, he soon completed a large collection of psalm tunes as well as melodies from Handel, Mozart, and Beethoven that he had reharmonized for three and four voices. After numerous unsuccessful efforts to publish this collection, Mason traveled to Boston where the Handel and Haydn Society (established 1815) undertook to publish his work. It appeared in 1822 as *The Boston Handel and Haydn Society Collection of Church Music*. At Mason's request, his name appeared only in fine print, though the introduction noted his "taste and science" as well as his "zeal for the improvement of Church Music." (He was, he said, a bank officer without "the least thought of making music my profession.") Later editions revealed that Mason had shifted priorities, and the title page conspicuously billed him as sole editor. The *New York Times* reported in 1854 that the collection had gone through thirty-five editions and become a standard text in the nation's singing schools.

Meanwhile, visitors to Savannah's Independent Presbyterian Church — some from far-off Boston, in Savannah on business — spread the word of Mason's remarkable choir and musical excellence, and by the mid-1820s several Boston businessmen pressed on him the advantages of Boston as a base for furthering his musical ambitions. Mason visited the city in the fall of 1826 and accepted an invitation to give two public lectures summarizing his views on church music. His "Address on Church Music," given first in the vestry of Lyman Beecher's Hanover Street Church and two days later at Boston's Third Baptist Church, drew enthusiastic response and was promptly published and reviewed in journals. It sold so well that a second edition followed.

Since the Boston address listed principles on which Mason built his later work, the text warrants brief summary. Complaining that many felt that "one must sing or shout the words audibly, in order to feel the full force of the sentiment of the hymn," Mason argued that congregational singing could only serve its purpose of "enforcing upon the heart the sentiment that is sung" if people learned the principles of music. He offered six points for his audience to ponder:

1. Church music must be simple, "chaste," "correct" (meaning, to Mason, conforming to contemporary European scientific standards),

and adapted to the performance abilities of congregation or choir. "Let there be simple, easy, and solemn tunes selected for use in public worship," he urged.

2. Care must be given to text as well as to tune. Text should be heard clearly; text and tune should "fit" and convey the same mood or idea. Mason vented his annoyance at the singing school practice he thought used words as "mere accommodation" to music. Text "sung amidst unrestrained levity and folly" in singing schools did not prepare singers to assist in worship. Rather, it tended toward "making an exhibition of musical acquirements" and "drawing forth the applause of the people."

3. Congregational singing must be promoted. "Every member of a congregation ought to feel an interest in the singing," he insisted.

4. "Judicious accompaniment" was "indispensable to complete success." Good vocal music required instrumental support, especially organ accompaniment.

5. Music education for children was the cornerstone for better congregational singing. "A thorough and permanent reformation in church music . . . cannot be effected, but by a gradual process. Children must be taught music as they are taught to read. Until something of this kind is done, it is vain to expect any great and lasting improvement."

6. Congregational singing as a corporate act is composed of individual acts of devotion to God. "Mere musical talent" did not suffice for effective playing or singing of church music.

Beecher and the leaders of eight other Boston evangelical churches, Congregational, Baptist, and Methodist, listened and schemed to bring Mason to town.

In 1827 Mason and his family accepted a call to Boston, and he took charge of the music in three congregations. When this arrangement proved impractical, he concentrated his efforts at Beecher's Hanover Street (later Bowdoin Street) Church. He stayed fourteen years, and the congregation's music gained renown. Change did not come without hard work and rigorous training, but Mason's passion and personality gained him the good will of singers. Thanks to Mason and Beecher, "pilgrims from all parts of the land" thrilled to "wonderful singing" in Boston as they had in Savannah. American Protestants had long quibbled about *what* to sing. Mason made an issue of *how* they sang. The unwavering support of the intractable Beecher (and of his successor, Hubbard Winslow) assured the environment Mason required to test and adapt his theories.

Mason's move to Boston coincided with the religious upheaval caused by the apparent triumph of Unitarianism in the city's oldest pulpits. All but one historic Congregational church (Third Church, or Old South) had recently been swept into the Unitarian fold, and an orthodox comeback seemed unlikely anytime soon. Boston's cultural elite had no qualms about public quarrels with Calvinists. In 1826 the struggling orthodox Hanover Street Church called Lyman Beecher to its pulpit. An experienced Connecticut pastor, Beecher accepted, ready for a fight. Beecher's daughter, Harriet Beecher Stowe, described the state of affairs her father found. The Unitarians, she wrote, were "a whole generation in the process of reaction united only in the profession of not believing Calvinism as taught by the original founders of Massachusetts." Orthodoxy, on the other hand, was "the dethroned royal family wandering like a permitted mendicant in the city where once it had held court, and Unitarianism reigned in its stead."

A few weeks after the Beecher family settled into a Boston parsonage, Stowe continued, "every leisure hour was beset by people who came with earnest intention to express to him those various phases of weary, restless, wandering desire and aspiration proper to an earnest people whose traditional faith has been broken up, but who have not outlived the necessity of definite and settled belief." Beecher found himself the target of public abuse and his message the object of public distortion, but these seemed to nurture rather than to quell steady evidences of revival in his congregation.

Beecher had accepted Hanover Street Church in 1826, just a few months before Mason arrived to lecture on sacred music. He seized on the possibilities of music as part of his larger plan to retake the city. Disappointed in his choir, Beecher shared Mason's passion for using sacred song as a partner in promoting evangelical religion. As a young man he had attended singing schools conducted by Andrew Law, one of the most talented of the itinerant singing masters of the Revolutionary era. Law's *Collection of Hymns for Social Worship* and *Rudiments of Music* (both 1783) were Beecher's early texts. In some ways Law prefigured Mason. His vision for national musical excellence led him beyond New England to establish singing schools in New York, Philadelphia, and Charleston. His work in the South included the training of singing masters whose influence reached deep into the rural regions of Virginia. Beecher, then, brought to his relationship with Mason excellent informal preparation as well as familiarity with Law's dream to improve the sacred tunes and texts central to American Protestant identity. And more profoundly, Beecher and Mason shared a millennial vision in which American destiny held center stage. They worked in different ways to ennoble Americans and form moral citizens, convinced that music promised the personal discipline, cooperative opportunity, and emotional outlet essential to national well-being and the triumph of "the faith once delivered to the saints."

At Beecher's churches Mason replaced Samuel Worcester's *Christian Psalmody, in four parts: Comprising Dr. Watts' Psalms abridged: Select Hymns from other sources; and select Harmonies* with *Church Psalmody,* a collection he compiled with the Reverend David Greene, a secretary of the American Board of Commissioners for Foreign Missions. *Church Psalmody* revealed Mason's concern for the singability (by ordinary untrained voices) of tunes and the sentiments of texts. Popular enough to run through fourteen editions, this hymnal proved a welcome substitute for its "cumbrous" predecessor (commonly known as Worcester's *Watts and Select*), a book that allegedly "weigh[ed] down the psalmody of some antediluvian districts like a nightmare."

Beecher's personal love for music (he relaxed by playing an old violin) worked to Mason's advantage, for Beecher grasped the need and the promise: "His full belief that the millennium was coming, that the Church was just about to march with waving banners to final and universal dominion, imparted to music, as it had to theology, an entirely new spirit." Old mournful tunes would not do. "It was," Beecher opined, "the natural tendency of persecution and exile to tune the harp of the daughter of Zion in the minor key." But a new day of independence and democracy had dawned, changing the church's key and commanding "a bolder, livelier, more triumphant character" in its tunes and texts. Mason did the musical work, but Beecher provided space and encouragement. An incalculable influence on sacred song radiated from their friendship, and their style influenced Protestantism broadly. Beecher (who always rushed until the church bells rang to put the finishing touches on his Sunday morning sermon) relinquished the selection of hymns to Mason. Over time Mason developed the pattern of choosing for the first two hymns songs of worship without reference to the subject of the sermon. The hymn after the sermon always "followed exactly in its wake." For Mason's unstinting devotion to the gospel in song, Beecher gave him high praise: "He did good. His influence was not secular, but as efficacious as preaching. Almost all who went to his classes, instead of being decoyed by it and made frivolous, were converted."

Early in 1830 a fire destroyed the Hanover Street Church. (Beecher's autobiography suggests that Unitarian firefighters watched and sang as the blaze progressed.) Beecher's congregation worshiped temporarily at Salem Church while the new Bowdoin Street Church rose. It featured an organ "larger and grander" than any in Boston. Soon after he dedicated the new building, Beecher accepted a call to Cincinnati, then the largest city in the West and home to growing numbers of westward-moving New Englanders. His move made no change in Mason's arrangement with the church. While Beecher pursued his grand scheme of saving the nation by saving the West, Mason broadened his efforts and found new partners. In Cincinnati, meanwhile, Beecher hired Mason's brother, T. B. Mason (already established in Cincinnati as a musical leader and children's choir director), to provide to his new congregation the advantages Lowell Mason had offered his Boston flock.

In 1832 Lowell Mason released the *Juvenile Psalmist* for his newest venture — the first children's singing school of its kind in the United States. Mason firmly believed that all children could be taught to sing. His efforts among children can be seen as part of an emerging cultural awareness of childhood that yielded the first children's literature, nurtured support for public education, and promoted a musical style adapted for children's tastes, abilities, and moral training. Mason's "gratuitous juvenile choir" met first in the vestry of Park Street Church (where Lyman Beecher's son Edward was pastor) and moved later to weekday afternoon rehearsals in the vestry of the new Bowdoin Street Church.

Every Saturday afternoon in 1831 and 1832, hundreds of children wended their way to Park Street Church for instruction in the principles of music. At one crowded Saturday concert, this first children's choir in Boston premiered a song Mason's friend Samuel Smith had casually shown him. Mason adapted the tune that had suggested the words, and "My Country, 'Tis of Thee," first sung at the Boston Sunday

School Union's Fourth of July festival in 1831, was born. It quickly became an unofficial national anthem as children in public schools across the land, like millions of others, rendered "Our fathers' God, to Thee/ Author of liberty,/To Thee we sing" on ordinary and momentous occasions. The orderly celebration at Park Street Church, featuring at least 2,500 people, including hundreds of children dressed alike singing of God and country, contrasted sharply to the unruly noise of cannon and crowds on the Common across the street and offered a sampling of music and text that attempted education and uplift.

Mason's next children's book, *Sabbath-school Songs*, brimming with "simple and easy" music "of a lighter and more melodious character than is usual in common psalm tunes," spread Mason's views on children's music well beyond New England. Though at least one other — Nathaniel Gould — had tried with indifferent results to promote juvenile singing in the Boston area a few years before Mason's arrival, Mason elicited from the start unbounded enthusiasm from children and parents. His energetic advocacy, experience, and advantageous connections brought him acclaim as the founder of a movement.

In addition to his church responsibilities, from 1827 to 1832, Mason filled a term as head of the Handel and Haydn Society. In this capacity he conducted chorus rehearsals and concerts, but his biographers suggest that his disappointment with the society's failure to catch his vision for music education contributed to his resignation. Certainly by 1832 Mason had established himself in Boston and beyond.

During the 1830s Mason's work with children stimulated his growing fascination for educational theory and practice. While evangelical convictions sustained his enduring interest in sacred song, educational work claimed an ever larger share of his time. He modeled his approach to music education on the innovative new ideas of a Swiss-born educator, Johann Heinrich Pestalozzi (1746-1827), whose controversial theories he found appealing because they "valued the cultivation of the fullest range of human capacities, integrating head, hands and heart." Pestalozzi rejected learning by rote, urging instead that children should learn from activity rather than from "mere words." This stood in stark contrast to the way American singing masters taught. Mason enthusiastically championed the ideas that Pestalozzi's European admirers turned into textbooks on the inductive method. His advocacy of the inductive method put Mason among an influential cadre of contemporary reformers intent on re-vamping American education.

During his years in Boston, Mason's early devotion to European musical and educational theory grew. His friends helped him translate German instructional books and prepare musical text, and Mason publicly advertised the promise of German music education theory with his juvenile choir in a series of free concerts in 1832. His admirers next moved to create the Boston Academy of Music with Mason as its head and the talented English-born organist and composer, George James Webb, as his associate. An Englishman who spent forty years as organist at Boston's Old South Church (and composed Webb, the common tune for "The Morning Light Is Breaking" and "Stand Up, Stand Up for Jesus"), Webb built a national reputation as a voice instructor. Formed to give Americans "the advantages derived from vocal music in Switzerland and Germany," the academy in its first year taught some 1,500 people to sight-read music, and to sing, understand, and value choral music performance. Its first president was Jacob Abbott (pastor, educator, father of Lyman, and author of an enormously successful [first-ever American] series of children's novels about one Rollo Holliday), who was followed by Samuel Eliot, soon to be mayor of Boston.

The academy aspired to cultivate public musical taste and train music teachers. Webb devoted most of his time to private lessons, while Mason dedicated himself to music education and the choirs that illustrated the effectiveness of his methods. The first classes met at the Bowdoin Street Church and the Old South Church. In 1835 the academy's backers provided a facility by renovating the Odeon, a theater they equipped with a large organ, 1,500 seats, and smaller rooms for teaching. That year the academy's Third Annual Report noted that between 800 and 1,000 children and 400-500 adults enrolled in academy classes. Mason and Webb also taught music regularly in some of the city's largest private schools. The academy inaugurated a class for teachers of music, and Mason's textbook, *Manual of the Boston Academy of Music* (1834), premiered to positive reviews. Children who enrolled in the academy's Wednesday and Saturday afternoon classes typically "read music more readily and performed it with greater correctness and taste than the leaders of choirs, many of whom have held the highest places as performers in our churches," Mason's friends boasted.

134

Mason was in demand as a lecturer and had recently accepted invitations to Hartford and New York. Letters poured in from Georgia, South Carolina, Virginia, Illinois, Missouri, Tennessee, Ohio, Maryland, New York, Connecticut, Vermont, New Hampshire, and Maine requesting help and advice implementing the academy's methods. Already Portland, Maine, boasted its own academy enrolling 500 children and 200 adults, and in Cincinnati Mason's brother, T. B. Mason, had several hundred children and adults under instruction, including students at the new Lane Theological Seminary with which Lyman Beecher affiliated in 1833. Clearly the Boston Academy of Music justified the enthusiasm of Mason's admirers and vastly extended Mason's influence.

From 1833 until 1840 Mason also taught music at the Perkins Institute for the Blind, a school opened in Boston in 1832 by Samuel Howe and named for its benefactor, Thomas Perkins. Howe thought the country "owed the blind an education," his wife, Julia Ward Howe, recalled. He concluded as well that music would "brighten the lives of his wards," and Mason accepted the challenge to devise a system for teaching music to sightless people, an endeavor that doubtless influenced his young protégé in these years, George Root.

In 1837 (and again in 1851-53) Mason traveled to Europe to observe firsthand the people and methods he had long admired. He lectured, observed, visited musicians, mailed to the States (for publication) his commentary on performances, and helped generate a North Atlantic community of musical interest. In Europe he purchased rare scores and books and the entire library of German organist J. H. Rink. Though he had little formal education, Mason devoted himself to study and built one of the finest private libraries in the United States. Some 10,000 volumes from his collection are now the property of Yale University. On his return in 1838 Mason relinquished his responsibilities at the academy to promote Boston's new public school music education program. The academy closed in 1847.

In 1836 Mason's friends had addressed a memorial to the Boston school committee requesting the introduction of vocal music instruction into the public schools. City elections had recently brought to the school committee at least three of Mason's longtime coworkers, and in August and September 1837 the school committee approved the request, specifying that music instruction be entrusted to the professors at the Boston Academy of Music. The city council, however, failed to appropriate funds. Undaunted, Mason (recently returned from Europe) volunteered to teach without pay. He began late in the fall and provided instructional materials at his own expense. A public exhibition at the end of the school year won rave reviews, and in 1838 Mason became superintendent of music education in the Boston public schools, an event the Boston Academy of Music reported as "the magna carta of musical education." Mason taught and supervised, enlisting his cohorts and music pupils as teachers. Horace Mann's *Report for 1841* noted that "Mason's circle" offered "two lessons of half an hour each in each school every week to students in the two upper classes."

In the early 1840s Mason developed a warm friendship with Mann, whose influential work on behalf of public education prospered in the same years that Mason's reputation grew. Mann's support enhanced Mason's growing reputation as an excellent teacher. A Whig in politics, a Unitarian in religion, and a lawyer by profession, Mann was elected president of the Massachusetts Senate in 1837. Edward Everett, former Harvard professor and future Harvard president, was the commonwealth's new governor, and his consuming interest in education matched Mann's own passion to prepare informed citizens so that democracy could flourish. Mann found in Boston's most famous Unitarian pastor, William Ellery Channing, a congenial mentor and friend who shared his conviction of the centrality of education to a fulfilling and useful life.

Mann (like Fanny Crosby) yielded as well to the persuasive charm of the Scottish phrenologist George Combe, who toured the East Coast in 1838. Mann recommended Combe's *The Constitution of Man* as "the greatest book that has been written for centuries" and endorsed its twentieth American edition (it went through twenty editions in seven years): "I look upon phrenology as the guide of philosophy and the mark of Christianity. Whoever disseminates true phrenology is a public benefactor." Mann thought phrenology gave a "solid basis" for natural religion and warmed to Combe's confidence in the improvability of humanity.

Mason met Mann at a grammar school in Boston's North End where Mann attended an exercise in one of Mason's music classes. He later recalled their conversation and Mason's remark that "if early and proper measures were taken with children, in regard to vocal music, there would be as few who could not sing, as there are now who cannot speak." Mann's career and Mason's educational work thrived amid growing grassroots demand through the 1830s for improved public education in Massachusetts. The American Institute of Instruction, an organization of teachers before which Mason sometimes lectured, and the American Lyceum, created for the dual purpose of "mutual instruction in the sciences and other branches of useful knowledge" and raising the "moral and intellectual taste of our countrymen," pressured for action. In 1837, at the urging of Governor Everett, the Massachusetts legislature established the Massachusetts Board of Education. Horace Mann was appointed its first secretary, its only full-time officer.

Like Mason, Mann subscribed to Pestalozzi's theories, and again like Mason, he believed in music's place in the elementary school curriculum. He gave musical instruction his strong support, both in Boston and in other parts of the state. The Lowell Mason Papers preserves sixteen letters that Mann addressed to Mason, and Mann's *Eighth Annual Report* (1844) specifically commended Mason's abilities and vision.

In 1845 Mason resigned as superintendent of music education in the common schools, but he continued teaching until his departure in 1851 for a prolonged European visit. In 1846 he published a collection of letters commending his success as superintendent of music in Boston's schools. Those who wrote on his behalf included the city's educational elite: Horace Mann, Samuel Gridley Howe, Jacob Abbott.

Mason threw his support as well behind Mann's drive for state-sponsored teacher training. As early as 1832 Mason had experimented with a summer Normal Institute for Music. He had also used the Boston Academy to pioneer teacher training. In 1836 the academy reported that the summer teachers class included twenty-eight men who organized themselves into a convention to discuss "musical education, church music, and musical performance" during their free time. When the class ended, participants adopted resolutions endorsing music education in the public schools and committing themselves to "the application of the Pestalozzian System of teaching music." Mason's European trip precluded a teacher training class in 1837, but a ten-day class in 1838 drew "ninety-six gentlemen and forty-two ladies" from all New England states, New York, Ohio, Kentucky, and Washington,

D.C. Mason and Webb filled the days, from 8 A.M. until 9 P.M., with lectures on teaching and music and plenty of singing.

In this effort, too, Mason was part of a broader attempt to establish teacher training. The proposed teacher training schools came to be known as "normal schools" following the usage in Prussia where *Normale Schulen* provided systematic teacher training. Mann endorsed the usage in Massachusetts because, he said, "the name is short, descriptive from its etymology, and in no danger of being misunderstood or misapplied." On the anniversary of the Battle of Lexington and Concord, 19 April 1838, Governor Everett signed into law a bill that established normal institutes in Massachusetts. Mason accepted Mann's appointment to the staff of the teachers institutes conducted by the Massachusetts State Board of Education. In November 1845, for example, he addressed a teachers institute in Bridgewater, and his remarks prompted Mann to respond:

> I now see more clearly than I ever did before that a way may be opened, thro' teachers' institutes, to introduce music into our common schools — a consummation most devoutly to be wished. While witnessing your exercises . . . I resolved to avail myself of an early opportunity to express to you the great gratification I experienced from witnessing your mode of teaching. In your adaptation of the thing to be taught to the capacity of the learner; in your easy gradation from the known to the unknown — the latter always seeming to spring naturally from, and to be intimately connected with, the former; and in your reviews which seem to link together the facts which had been separately given before — In all these points, your lessons appeared to me to be models, worthy of the imitation of teachers in all other branches. I have never before seen any thing that came nearer to my *beau ideal* of teaching.

Regarded as one possessing "rare tact in developing the vital principles of instruction in the simplest and happiest manner," Mason enjoyed a decade-long relationship with the emerging normal institute movement in Massachusetts. Mann gave him high praise: "It is well worth any young teacher's while to walk ten miles to hear a lecture of Dr. Mason, for in it he will hear a most instructive exposition of the true principles of all teaching, as well as that of instruction in music."

As the state's program emerged, Mason's academy endeavors shifted in focus. As noted, in 1836 Mason and Webb's teacher training class took the unusual move of constituting itself into a music convention. This use of spare time came later to be regarded as the first National Musical Convention. A modification of the normal institute idea, the conventions expanded beyond teacher training. (Mason sometimes scheduled a brief normal institute for the days just before the convention.) From modest numbers, these annual meetings grew to include hundreds of men and women. Reorganized in 1842 as the American Musical Convention, the meeting separated formally in 1843 from the more specialized work of the teachers class. Over 1,000 people came in October 1849 to the convention and produced a "surpassingly impressive and overpowering effect" by performing choruses by Handel and Giovanni Pergolesi. "It is worth a trip from Minnesota to hear such music," one attendee ventured. These conventions had broad appeal and reach, promoting Mason's books and spreading his ideas. Mason took the basic elements of the Boston conventions to Rochester, Harrisburg, Cleveland, and elsewhere, and some participants attempted similar endeavors in smaller communities. It was said that conventions "after the model of the Boston meetings" sprang up "all through the east, west, and south." Since not all Mason enthusiasts shared his abilities as a teacher, the mushrooming musical conventions tended to feature the study and performance of choral music rather than teacher training. Later regarded as "the first national schools of music pedagogy," music conventions spread grassroots enthusiasm for the new musical resources produced in Boston.

A four-day convention in Syracuse in September 1850 offers a glimpse of Mason's reception on the road. The local paper reported that Presbyterians, Baptists, Episcopalians, Methodists, and Congregationalists from more than twenty townships gathered for the promotion of "the cause" of better singing with such enthusiasm that they refreshed Mason's conviction that he would succeed on a national scale. At such gatherings choral performances punctuated discussions of congregational singing and of the new music, tunes and text, issued by Mason and his circle.

Amid this ceaseless activity and expansion, some worried about the rapidity with which new materials poured from the presses, arguing that change should be introduced slowly. A handful of music advocates advanced more profound objections to Mason's whole enterprise and indulged in the bitter recriminations that historically marked each major shift in popular music. One G. W. Lucas of Northampton, Massachusetts (a onetime Mason supporter who became a lifelong detractor), whined in an 1844 pamphlet about "the arrogance of [convention attendees] who could endure nothing but the glorification of [Mason]"; accused Mason of "a kind of plagiarism" for translating freely from German works without attribution; charged him with doing "all this for the sake of money and the sale of books"; and mocked his use of "glee singing" (which Lucas thought unacceptably mixed the sacred and the secular). "Why not open their churches to the comedian?" he asked. "The effect would not be more pernicious to sacred association. Who ever felt his heart warmed and his affections moved while listening to the music of any choir under the direction of Mr. Mason?" Lucas, editor of the *American Journal of Music* (where he regularly castigated Mason and his circle), found himself distinctly in the minority.

Mason's popular tunes (usually arranged from or suggested by existing tunes) for such perennial nineteenth-century Protestant favorites as Reginald Heber's "From Greenland's Icy Mountains" (Missionary Hymn); Isaac Watts's "When I Survey the Wondrous Cross" (Hamburg); Ray Palmer's "My Faith Looks Up to Thee" (Olivet); Sarah Adams's "Nearer, My God, to Thee" (Bethany); and Samuel Smith's "America" had sung a Northeastern version of evangelical sentiments into the hearts of millions of a new generation of American Protestants, few of whom realized how much their traditions of sacred song owed to Mason and his circle.

Measured in sales, Mason's 1841 *Carmina Sacra* (which the *New York Times* reported had enjoyed "a larger sale than any other music book ever published") was his most successful single endeavor, but he kept producing new collections. "Every well organized choir, if kept up with interest, must have a constant succession of new music. Without this there will be no advancement. . . . The progress of things is ever onward," Mason drilled into his following. Mason both stimulated and responded to the incessant clamor for something new: it nicely blended conviction and financial gain. Before he left for Europe in 1851, Mason was listed among Boston's 2,000 wealthiest men, with a net worth in 2003 dollars of more than $2.45 million. When his sons dissolved their music publishing company in the 1860s, the plates for printing Mason's books alone brought $100,000, a sum equivalent to about $1.5 million in 2003 dollars. Mason's affluence came at the price of incessant work. Admirers marveled at the self-discipline that made his output possible. A newspaper reported that during his Boston years, Mason edited music and text during every meal and devoted mornings and afternoons to teaching, lecturing, and other business. After his evening meal he gave lessons or worked with his choir. His days seldom ended before midnight, and work often occupied him until 2 A.M. "It is said," one observer quipped when Mason was at the height of his fame, "that for twenty years he was never known to spend even half a day in mere amusement. . . . His work was his recreation."

When Mason returned from Europe in 1853, he settled in New York City. In 1855 the University of the City of New York (later NYU) awarded him the second honorary doctorate of music conferred by an American university (the first to be awarded "with distinction"). (The first had been awarded by Georgetown University in 1849 to the German immigrant violinist and composer Henry Dielman.)

In 1855 the Masons moved across the Hudson River to a scenic seventy-acre estate twelve miles from Manhattan near Orange, New Jersey. They retired there in easy proximity to many associates and most of their children and grandchildren. Mason devoted himself increasingly to sacred song, taking particular interest in the musical programs of his local congregation, Orange Valley Church (now Highland Avenue Congregational Church). In 1867 Lowell and Abigail Mason celebrated their golden wedding anniversary. Their whole bridal party (save one who had died) joined them for a gathering of the Northeast's distinguished musical artists and church leaders. Mason died 11 August 1872, barely three weeks short of the couple's fifty-fifth anniversary.

In the heady days of the early republic, Northeasterners of Mason's stamp dared to believe they could mold an American culture. Noah Webster urged an American language, benevolent societies envisioned a moral social order, Mason's Boston cohorts supplied an American literature, Horace Mann imagined an educated public, and Mason himself made the case for the ennobling national benefits of music. While later critics sometimes grumbled about the "simplistic ditties" and "easily digestible arrangements of themes from the classics" that Mason permitted to "vitiate the tastes of generations," his contemporaries hailed him widely as one who offered both the plan and the tools to give the enjoyment and practice of music to ordinary Americans.

Mason both anticipated and reflected the larger currents in the movement for public education. Ideally situated in Boston, the center of much of the agitation for improvements of all sorts, he seized and created opportunities. Many of his interests — children, the inductive method, normal institutes — coincided with those of thoughtful American activists in the larger culture. Mason turned them into profitable businesses, blending cultural vision with commercial acumen that made him prosperous. His dreams for the nation translated easily into emerging strategies for marketing and publishing and kept him in the center of the business of American music as it grew with the nation.

Mason acted on his convictions about the importance and promise of music in congregations and schools in many ways, none more important than the training he provided a privileged coterie that might be described as his protégés and partners-in-music. Two of these had prominent roles in Fanny Crosby's life. One, George Frederick Root, found in Mason's Boston circle the building blocks for a distinguished career. In time he brought vocal music education to the New York Institution for the Blind. The other, William Bradbury — composer, publisher, teacher, editor — became Crosby's publisher, booster, and friend. Mason molded Root and Bradbury. They, in turn, made Crosby a marketable commodity and so shaped the second half of her life.

Fanny Crosby's birthplace and childhood home, Southeast, Putnam County, New York

The New York Institution for the Blind

Fanny Crosby's mother, Mercy Crosby (1799-1890)

Valentine Mott, pioneer American surgeon, who in 1825 pronounced Crosby's blindness incurable

Phrenologist George Combe, whose examination of Crosby's head reportedly led him to conclude that she was a "born poetess"

Fanny Crosby as she appeared when a student at the New York Institution for the Blind, c. 1840

William J. Kirkpatrick ("Kirkie" to Fanny), a holiness Methodist who often provided tunes for Crosby texts

Manhattan's Broadway Tabernacle at mid-century, site of Crosby's
recitations and William Bradbury's musical triumphs

Courtesy of the Burke Library, Union Theological Seminary

Broadway Tabernacle sanctuary, where Crosby often addressed Anniversary Day crowds

Courtesy of the Burke Library, Union Theological Seminary

BRADBURY'S

FRESH LAURELS

FOR THE SABBATH SCHOOL.

A NEW AND EXTENSIVE COLLECTION OF

MUSIC AND HYMNS.

PREPARED EXPRESSLY FOR SABBATH SCHOOLS, ETC.

By WILLIAM B. BRADBURY,

AUTHOR OF "THE GOLDEN CHAIN," "GOLDEN SHOWER," "GOLDEN CENSER," "GOLDEN TRIO," ETC.

" Whoso offereth praise glorifieth me."—PSALM 50. 23.

NEW YORK:

PUBLISHED BY BIGLOW & MAIN, 425 BROOME STREET,

(SUCCESSORS TO WM. B. BRADBURY.)

IVISON. BLAKEMAN, TAYLOR & CO., 138 & 140 Grand Street,

The title page of a typical Sunday school hymnal

Courtesy of Wheaton College Archives and Special Collections

George Root, Crosby's music teacher
and first musical collaborator

John Sweney, professor of music at
the Pennsylvania Military Academy,
with whom Crosby prepared
both secular and sacred songs

Philip Phillips, the singing evangelist
who often ordered text from Crosby

William Howard Doane, the millionaire
businessman who composed tunes for
many of Crosby's best-known songs

Crosby's and Knapp's famous "Blessed Assurance" was first published on the back page of an 1873 *Guide to Holiness*

Courtesy of the Methodist Collection, Garrett Evangelical Divinity School

At the Cross!

Written By Fanny J Crosby   July 24/75

1.

At the cross I found my Saviour
Found him precious to my soul
By his grace through faith he saved me
In his blood he made me whole

Chorus:—

Still the healing tide is flowing
Oh, that all, its power might know
Though our sins may be like crimson
It will make them white as snow

2.

At the cross I lost my burden
Mercy rolled it all away
Oh, the joy and consolation
Jesus gives me every day   Cho:—

3.

At the cross he, now is waiting
Careless one he waits for thee
Throw thyself upon his mercy
He will save thee come and see   Cho:—

4

At the cross I love to linger
At the cross I love to rest
There I found a full salvation
There my longing soul was blest   Ch.

**Crosby dictated hymn texts to many people,
and she sometimes edited as she spoke**

Courtesy of the Billy Graham Center Archives

Crosby in her prime, 1870s

Crosby and Ira Sankey collaborating at Sankey's Brooklyn home

Fanny and Alexander Van Alstyne

MRS. VAN ALSTYNE,

better known as

FANNY CROSBY,

The gifted BLIND POETESS, who has composed
so many of the favorite hymns that are sung in
our prayer meetings and sabbath schools, will
give a

Concert and Recitations

in the

Chapel of the South Church,

Monday Evening, Jan. 15th.

She will be assisted by others, including her
husband,

MR. VAN ALSTYNE,

who is an accomplished musician, and who is
also blind

Mrs. Van Alstyne, desiring to do good and at
the same time support herself, will devote one-
half the proceeds to the poor of our city.
Tickets, 25 cents, at E. A. Lewis' Book Store.
Concert to commence at 8 o'clock.   1—10 5d°

This advertisement contains the only known photograph
of Crosby with her husband, Van

The interior of the McAuley mission, which was typical
of the rescue missions Crosby frequented

The tabernacle at the campground at Round Lake, New York, where Crosby
regularly attended annual camp meetings and a Ferris tracker organ
accompanied the stirring singing of her hymns

Crosby (left) with Onandaga Indian Chief Albert Cusick and hymn writer
Eliza Hewitt at the campground at Tully Lake, south of Syracuse, New York;
Cusick performed a ceremony making the two women members of his tribe

Crosby ready to address an audience

Crosby at home in Bridgeport; her mother's portrait hangs above the couch

The Fanny Crosby Memorial Home, Bridgeport, Connecticut

Crosby at the age of eighty-six; despite her blindness, she preferred
to be photographed — and to work — with a book in hand

6 Facilitators:
George Root and William Bradbury

There's music in the air
When the infant morn is nigh,
And faint its blush is seen
On the bright and laughing sky. . . .

There's music in the air
When the twilight's gentle sigh
Is lost on the evening's breast
As its pensive beauties die.
Then, oh! then, the loved ones gone
Make the pure celestial song;
Angel voices greet us there,
In the music of the air.

Thanks to their association with Lowell Mason, at midcentury George
Root and William Bradbury stood at the crossroads of American music
education and had the ability to promote talent. Fanny Crosby met
Root first at an early stage in his own career, and with him she first

gained public recognition for her lyrics, but she enjoyed a closer and more fulfilling relationship with Bradbury.

GEORGE FREDERICK ROOT

A native of Sheffield in far western Massachusetts where his father's forebears had settled in colonial times, George Root was born 30 August 1820 (a few months after Crosby) to Frederick and Sarah Flint Root. In 1826 the Roots moved across the state to Willow Farm near his mother's extended family in North Reading, just outside Boston. There, among a tight-knit clan known for their love of music, Root spent his formative years. His immediate relations were staunch Congregationalists, though the religious disruptions of his childhood years found some of his extended family taking the Unitarian side.

Root apparently inherited the Flint family's musical interests. His great-uncle, Dr. Flint of Salem, compiled for the use of his congregation a hymnal that included some of his own texts. Another great-uncle built a pipe organ, and Root's grandfather taught singing school and led the choir of North Reading's parish church. Root's mother and her five sisters sang exceptionally well, and each played the bass viol, an instrument New Englanders favored for choral accompaniment. Musical family gatherings regularly relieved the tedium of daily life. Students from Andover Seminary — a few miles away — often trekked over to join the singing.

Frederick Root discovered in his son an uncanny ability to play any instrument that came to hand. The boy dreamed of becoming a musician, and a bold move in 1836 brought him into the Boston music shop of the musician Artemis Nixon Johnson, who hired and boarded him and offered his piano for practice. Johnson also insisted that Root learn to sing. A performer, composer, editor, salesman, and pioneer music educator in Boston's public schools, Johnson modeled the all-encompassing musical life to which young Root aspired.

Root auditioned successfully for the Boston Academy of Music's chorus and won a place in the Bowdoin Street Church choir. Mason took very seriously the training of this choir, and participation involved a substantial commitment of time for both choral practice and theoretical instruction. Root enrolled for voice lessons with George

James Webb, Boston's most esteemed voice instructor. Webb was just one of the ambitious Root's private instructors. He took lessons as well from Benjamin Franklin Baker, music director at William Ellery Channing's famous Federal Street Church. Baker strove for "effective harmony" — "easy of execution" but not "commonplace or trivial" — and his ideas fired Root's imagination. These associations linked Root firmly to the core of Mason's movement to reform American popular music, with its determination to replace shape (or "patent") note singing with European-style "scientific" music. Root's attention was soon occupied with private pupils, a post as church organist, and in time, responsibilities with the choirs at Boston's Park Street Church, the Winter Street Church, and the Bowdoin Street Church. Root's demonstrated ability to teach voice (Mason, the "master teacher," considered him an unusually gifted instructor) brought an invitation to participate in Mason's growing teacher training classes. Mason had an eye for talent and made Root his protégé, sending him to fill invitations he could not accept, and giving him experience in conducting, performing, and teaching.

In 1845 Root married Mary Olive Woodman and moved to New York. He had an invitation from Jacob Abbott and his brother, Gorham (Congregationalist ministers and educators also networked into Mason's Boston circle), who had recently moved to Manhattan. The Abbotts offered Root generous terms to teach at their family's new young ladies academy and recommended Root as music director at the Mercer Street Presbyterian Church. They courted Root with the reminder that, whereas in Boston he had to defer to Mason and Webb, New York could become his own "field." With the enthusiastic support of Mason (who had recommended him to the Abbotts in the first place), Root acquiesced. During the summers he returned to Boston to work with Mason and Webb in their teacher education programs.

Coveting the widest possible public recognition in Manhattan, Root immediately enlisted family and began rehearsing a home quartet composed of himself, his wife, and his brother and sister. Six weeks of daily practice on a repertoire of five numbers yielded the musical sound Root wanted. He had found (or at least assumed) that New Yorkers disdained what they called "New England music" and doubted Mason's views on "scientific music." Root now countered with a demonstration of the "unscaled heights of difficult concerted singing" the

Boston method could produce. Theodore Eisfeld, conductor of the New York Philharmonic Orchestra, invited the quartet to sing at a concert of the New York Philharmonic Society, and Root obliged with Mendelssohn's "Hunting Song" and William Mason's (Lowell's son) "Serenade." The results were all that Root desired. He vindicated a method and won recognition for himself in New York. A press critic called the group "probably the best quartet ever heard in America."

Root fully shared Mason's entrepreneurial instinct, and he quickly built a network. He became organist at the Church of the Strangers (a nondenominational congregation whose members were mostly recent arrivals, or "strangers" in the city) and accepted invitations to teach music part-time at the Rutgers Institute (a school heavily indebted to the financial support of Fanny Crosby's distant relative, William Crosby), the Union Theological Seminary, and the New York Institution for the Blind in addition to his ongoing work with the Abbotts.

Like Mason, Root found teaching the blind an especially rewarding effort. Convinced of the Pestalozzian principle that music education begins with hearing rather than seeing, Root devised ways to teach music as an aural experience. He found Institution scholars a receptive group. They advanced quickly through Root's basic four-part music, and he introduced more difficult music as well as instruction in harmony. These responsibilities — and the scarcity of resources appropriate to his teaching method (he might have used Mason's, but he preferred to pocket his own royalties) — turned his thoughts toward composing and editing music suited to his young students. He prepared his first book, *The Young Ladies' Choir*, about 1847 in multiple copies for his own use. He then began working with his brother to produce music pamphlets. He collaborated with Joseph Sweetser (organist at Manhattan's Church of the Puritans) in 1849 on his first published book, *A Collection of Church Music*.

In 1850 Root traveled to Paris for additional study. He returned, one observer commended, with the "foreign finish" that assured his future, at least in the growing circle devoted to Lowell Mason's principles. Root resumed his teaching at the Institution. He had known Fanny Crosby there at least since 1845, but a casual conversation with her in 1851 afforded a new opportunity for Crosby and a lucrative partnership for Root. She agreed to provide words for ideas and tunes

Root proposed. Root valued her "great gift for rhyming" and her "delicate and poetic imagination," and she did not disappoint him.

Their earliest collaboration yielded an elaborate cantata, *The Flower Queen; or, The Coronation of the Rose,* a work about flowers choosing their queen. Suggested by the famous floral concerts that William Bradbury's children's choir offered occasionally at the Broadway Tabernacle, *The Flower Queen* was a moral tale that promoted humility and service:

> Tis not in beauty alone we may find
> Purity goodness and wisdom combined;
> Forms that are lightest are first to decay,
> Hues that are brightest fade soonest away;
> Gentle in manner, in temper serene,
> These are the beauties we ask for our queen.

Advertised first for use by singing classes in academies, female seminaries, and high schools, the cantata was suggested as well for concerts, anniversaries, and other festive occasions. The cover sheet acknowledged Crosby as lyricist, identifying her as "a Graduate of the New York Institution for the Blind." Root dedicated the ninety-three-page work to George James Webb. The *New York Times* commented that the cantata — performed at Manhattan's Knickerbocker Hall amid the profusion of evergreens, trees, and flowers that distinguished a floral concert — "spoke volumes in favor of musical culture." Crosby attended two of the first Manhattan performances — at Abbott's Spingler Institute, the boarding school for young ladies run by Gorham and Jacob Abbott, and at the Rutgers Female Institute. Enthusiastic critics attributed to the series of six performances at these schools "a greater sensation than anything of the kind that has come off in New York for a long time." At the end of the performances at each place, Crosby was led forward to receive a floral tribute from the lead singer. At Abbott's Spingler Institute (where she felt particularly at home because Gorham sometimes preached in the Institution's chapel) she responded spontaneously "with some hesitation, in a very neat poetic speech":

> Thanks, many thanks! These flowers to me are dear;
> Theirs is a language of affection deep,

For Innocence has left her impress here,
And Hope and Love within their petals sleep.
Flowers by our great Creator's hand were given
To teach mankind the poetry of Heaven.

Dear, youthful group! While music's sweetest lays
My raptured heart have captive held the while,
How I have yearned upon this scene to gaze,
To catch the beaming glance, the joyous smile,
The buoyant step of pure, unsullied glee!
But something whispers that it may not be.

Root's autobiography offers a glimpse of how he and Crosby
worked:

I used to tell her one day in prose what I wanted the Flowers or the
Recluse to say, and the next day the poem would be ready — sometimes two or three of them. I generally hummed enough of a melody to give her an idea of the meter and rhythmic swing wanted,
and sometimes played to her the entire music of a number before
she undertook her work. It was all the same. Like many blind people her memory was great, and she easily retained all I told her. After receiving her poems, which rarely needed any modification, I
thought out the music, perhaps while going from one lesson to another, and then I caught the first moment of freedom to write it out.
This went on until the cantata was finished.

In 1852 Root's growing fame — based to a large extent on the remarkable success of *The Flower Queen* — won him a three-year contract
with publisher William Hall and Son to write ballads and popular
songs exclusively for them. Root had noted the nation's enthusiasm
for Stephen Foster, and he coveted a share of that market. Contemporaries recognized his flair for the ballad style, and critics gushed about
the "excellent taste in the selection of words and sentiment" that made
him worthy of an exclusive agreement. Root's salutary influence, they
opined, tended toward both the "gratification" and the "improvement" of his generation. Shortly after signing with William Hall and
Son, Root accepted an invitation to "direct Sacred Music" at Manhat-

148

tan's Union Theological Seminary (then in lower Manhattan on University Place, in easy proximity to Root's other endeavors), where another Mason stalwart, Thomas Hastings, had influence.

Meanwhile, the popularity of *The Flower Queen* encouraged Root to work with Crosby on a second cantata. Published in 1855 as *The Pilgrim Fathers*, this work featured the contemporary evangelical reading of American history. The cover again identified the lyricist as Miss Frances J. Crosby, the Blind Poetess, though advertising and critics' reports routinely referred to "Mr. Root's cantata." Its first performance in New York City elicited a critic's praise for its choruses: "We do not remember to have heard better choral performances in our city." Crosby's lyrics read like parts of her own family saga. Persecuted Puritans anguished:

> How long, O how long shall oppression's dark night
> Enshroud like a pall to dismay and affright?
> In sadness we mourn, and in grief we complain;
> The tears we have shed, must we weep them in vain?
> O freedom, where art thou, say is there no rest?
> No refuge for those who are wronged and oppressed;
> No arm that can shield us from tyranny's sway —
> Or must we in silence and meekness obey?

Faith sustained them:

> Though hardships be our lot,
> Safe in this hallowed spot
> Will we abide.
> Here will we joyful sing
> Praise to our God and King
> While the glad echoes ring
> Far, far, and wide.

The Flower Queen and *The Pilgrim Fathers* quickly became staples of the normal institutes' repertoire. Mason and his circle used them to instruct teachers and to train choirs in the dozens of institutes they sponsored every year. The *New York Musical Review and Gazette* estimated in 1857 that *The Flower Queen* — with its wholesome plot built around the moral maxim "to fill well the station allotted by Providence is to be happy" — had been produced at least 1,000 times in the preceding four years. Since these performances were often the main musical event of the long winter in places like Lyon, New York, or Janesville, Wisconsin, they generally drew large audiences. Not infrequently, popular demand occasioned extra concerts. Issued from the movement working toward common school music education and better church music, the Crosby-Root cantatas featured music suitable for instruction as well as pleasing to the audience. Small choirs without the resources to produce the full work often opted to master a few cantata songs. Despite later criticism of Root's "static bass line and lack of rhythmic varieties," contemporaries uniformly hailed the pieces. Crosby received almost none of the acclaim in which Root basked, nor did she share the money he made.

Even as Root helped Crosby find her voice as an author of popular lyrics, he devoted his own formidable energy to enlisting Manhattan's musical Protestants in the larger cause of music education for the masses, endeavors that framed his collaboration with Crosby. In 1853 he organized with Lowell Mason the New York Normal Musical Institute, "to afford thorough Musical Instruction, and especially to qualify teachers of music, leaders of choirs, etc." In addition to the vocal training and teacher education long featured at Mason's Boston Normal Institutes, Root purposed to add the teaching of harmony and what he called "general musical culture." The school began 25 April and ran for three months and demanded the entire time of its pupils. Instructors included Hastings and Bradbury, both long identified with Mason's circle, each of whom had his own considerable local following. The school drew several hundred (predominantly male) students (one commented on his surprise at "the *minority* of ladies in the class"), and their progress was "beyond the most sanguine expectations" of the conveners. Various performances, among them the cantata *Daniel* (music by Root and Bradbury; words by Crosby and C. M. Cady), attracted appreciative audiences and gave the students the opportunity to apply their lessons. Manhattan's musical elite donated free concert tickets enabling students to hear such sensations of the moment as Madame Sontag and Dodsworth's Band. Like other such ventures, the New York Normal Institute of Music proved a lucrative dissemination venue for its organizers' books and sheet music.

Sheet music, typically piano music or a popular song with piano accompaniment, had enjoyed popularity in the United States since the federal period, and in the mid–nineteenth century the growing prevalence of home pianos greatly expanded the market. Religion, politics, social causes, reform movements, and popular culture offered limitless themes for "parlor music." Sheet music flourished through the Civil War, with each side making its case in the popular musical market. The promoters of the normal institute movement knew well this intertwined piano and music market. Its dimensions are suggested by statistics indicating that in 1866 American families purchased 25,000 new pianos at a cost of $15 million. Root, Bradbury, and their cohorts were quick to meet growing market demand. (An indication of the size of the market is suggested as well by the inventory of a major music publisher, Oliver Ditson, which immediately after the Civil War carried some 33,000 piano pieces. By the 1870s, American publishers offered about 200,000 titles.)

The four principal instructors at the New York Normal Institute of Music — Mason, Root, Hastings, Bradbury — were Congregationalists and Presbyterians who saw no conflict in the convergence of their secular and sacred ambitions. Each aspired to improve music in general, but each had a devout participant's concern for the state of music in America's Protestant churches. Animated by personal faith and confidence in the providence of God, they cared deeply about congregational song, the training of church choirs, the use of musical instruments in churches, and the preparation of tunes and texts to support the era's burgeoning moral reform efforts. They borrowed freely for use in the church the forms and methods that "worked" in their secular endeavors. They blended sacred and secular — glees (unaccompanied part singing), cantatas, hymns, choruses, oratorios, and other music — to their larger purposes. Their network of colaborers — of Northeastern (usually New England) birth, Puritan legacy, abiding Protestant faith, and fervent love for the Union — shared the interwoven sacred and secular ambitions. Together and separately these people had a hand in crafting or popularizing many of the best-known Northern popular songs, gospel hymns, and Sunday school music of the mid–nineteenth century. Evangelical religion shaped their hopes for the church and the nation and validated the choice of music as their instrument for change. In their minds, their sacred and cultural ambitions constituted a seamless whole.

These interests found expression during the 1850s in the *Choral Advocate and Singing-Class Journal*, a monthly magazine that premiered in June 1850 and quickly found a place nurturing the normal institutes network. The journal laid out principles for teaching vocal music, training the voice, playing the pianoforte (in an effort to help country residents who lacked teachers), and "showing the relation of secular music to a sound music education." The last addressed a popular Protestant tendency to "look upon secular music with holy horror." The *Advocate* reported on musical events, secular as well as sacred, in major American and European venues, making the names of the era's famous performers familiar in out-of-the-way places. It juxtaposed introductions to European composers with texts like "Cultivating the Voice" or "Sacred Music in Michigan." In their broad scheme of reforming a nation, Mason and his protégés recognized that they needed to enlist clergy in the cause, and so they sent the paper free to those who applied and invited submissions from the clergy on the subject of psalmody in the churches.

The publication met with positive response. Such geographically scattered papers as the *Vermont Chronicle*, the *Gem of the North* (New York), the *Western Christian Advocate* (Cincinnati), and the *Lancaster (Pa.) Gazette* commended the journal to their readers. The monthly provided as well several pages of new settings and compositions by Mason and his cohorts.

In her first encounters with this enterprising group, Crosby produced secular text built around moral themes. During the 1850s, in addition to cantatas for the growing normal institute movement, she and Root collaborated on a handful of popular hit songs, sentimental ballads in the best genteel tradition of the day, of which the following three are representative.

In their shows at Manhattan's Mechanics Hall, the famous troupe the Christy's Minstrels (who had exclusive rights to premier Stephen Foster's compositions) popularized "Hazel Dell," Root and Crosby's first popular hit:

In the Hazel Dell my Nelly's sleeping,
Nelly lov'd so long!
And my lonely lonely watch I'm keeping,
Nellie lost and gone;

Here in moonlight often we have wander'd
Thro' the silent shade,
Now where leafy branches drooping downward,
Little Nelly's laid.

Chorus:
All alone my watch I'm keeping
In the Hazel Dell,
For my darling Nelly's near me sleeping,
Nelly dear farewell.

Two years later (1855) Root and Crosby issued "Rosalie the Prairie Flower," a jocular song that remained popular for more than a generation:

On the distant prairie, where the heather wild,
In its quiet beauty liv'd and smiled,
Stands a little cottage, and a creeping vine
Loves around its porch to twine.
In that peaceful dwelling was a lovely child,
With her blue eyes beaming soft and mild,
And the wavy ringlets of her flaxen hair,
Floating in the summer air.

Fair as a lily, joyous and free
Light of that prairie home was she,
Ev'ryone who knew her felt the gentle pow'r
Of Rosalie, the Prairie Flower.

"There's Music in the Air" appeared in 1857, became an instant favorite with vocal quartets, and remained a staple of the high school choral repertoire well into the twentieth century:

There's music in the air
When the infant morn is nigh,
And faint its blush is seen
On the bright and laughing sky.
Many a harp's ecstatic sound,

153

With its thrill of joy profound,
While we list enchanted there
To the music in the air.

There's music in the air
When the noontide's sultry beam
Reflects a golden light
On the distant mountain stream.
When beneath some grateful shade
Sorrow's aching head is laid,
Sweetly to the spirit there
Comes the music in the air.

There's music in the air
When the twilight's gentle sigh
Is lost on the evening's breast,
As its pensive beauties die.
Then, oh! then, the loved ones gone
Make the pure celestial song;
Angel voices greet us there,
In the music of the air.

Root typically paid Crosby $1 or $2 for such text. She had no share of any royalties. He profited handsomely, especially on "Rosalie the Prairie Flower," for which he turned down $100 outright in favor of a contract that netted him some $3,000 in royalties. Published as sheet music, a popular medium since the 1830s, such songs found places in schools, clubs, and family parlors. The sheets generally did not acknowledge Crosby as text author; rather, Root received full credit. For these popular numbers Root often used the German form of his name — Wurzel — drawing speculation that he did not want to detract from his reputation as a serious musician.

During the 1850s Root and William Bradbury spent most of each fall and winter on the road running short normal institutes that offered basic introductions to subjects like harmony, vocal music, and sight reading, and prepared one or two concerts (generally featuring cantatas for which Crosby contributed text) that became highlights on the social calendars of entire regions. The two charged a $100 total fee for three- or four-day institutes within 300 miles of Manhattan, more for those farther away. In addition, they used their own books, published annually with the institutes in mind. Bradbury and Root collaborated on one of these, *The Shawm* (named for early double-reed instruments, forerunners of the oboe, and offering 967 pieces of music and twenty-nine pages of singing class instructions), but more often each issued his own. The *Musical Review* charted the spread of the institutes and the grassroots enthusiasm for Root and Bradbury that seemed manifest everywhere. Root drew rave reviews as a teacher of voice, while Bradbury's instructions on teaching method gained acclaim. The small towns and larger cities of Maine, Vermont, Massachusetts, Rhode Island, New York, Pennsylvania, Ohio, Illinois, Michigan, Iowa, and Wisconsin were well supplied in the 1850s with institutes that featured one or the other, and sometimes both. The men often left behind fledgling musical societies intent on carrying on their work by using their materials.

A brief sketch of the musical conventions in the fall of 1853 (these followed hard on the rousing success of the three-month New York Musical Institute in Manhattan) suggests the pace of activity that established an irrepressible movement. A four-day state musical convention in Maine drew some 400 musicians for lectures by Bradbury and Boston's B. F. Baker on choir and congregational singing and chanting, glee singing, chorus singing, style, and expression. Two concerts attracted large audiences. Root, meanwhile, had charge of a musical convention in Rutland, Vermont, where some 300 singers gathered for a week of instruction culminating in the production of Root's and Bradbury's *Daniel*. A few days later another convention featured Bradbury and Lowell Mason and drew between 300 and 400 singers to Rochester, New York. This time, after Mason reviewed the origin, purpose, and progress of the musical convention movement, lectures on teaching and the practice of congregational music by Mason and on anthem and glee singing by Bradbury filled the hours. Instruction and exercises came from Root's and Bradbury's *The Shawm*, and St. Peter's Church hosted the open public rehearsal that concluded the sessions.

Bradbury moved on to Ravenna, Ohio, for "the first gathering of the kind ever held in this part of the Western Reserve." Four days of meetings with clergy, singers, and interested citizens convinced participants of the importance of the work and yielded the following resolu-

155

tion: "There exists an urgent demand for Conventions of the friends of Sacred Music . . . to elevate the standard of musical taste and secure a greater uniformity of style; to furnish opportunities of instruction of a high order; to afford the facilities of more intimate acquaintance among musicians. . . . We recognize in the person and talents of Professor Wm. B. Bradbury of New York city, a man eminently qualified for this task; and we do respectfully and earnestly recommend him to undertake it." A three-day convention in Jefferson, Ashtabula County, Ohio, followed immediately, and then Bradbury moved on to Muscatine, Iowa, for the first musical convention "ever held so far West." The experiment proved "most successful," and participants promptly announced three conventions in Iowa for 1854.

The Coldwater, Michigan, singers who responded to the announcement of a musical convention for their northern town praised Bradbury's "kind and courteous demeanor" as well as his "sterling qualities as a sound and competent musician." Root, meanwhile, filled similar engagements in other towns in western Pennsylvania, Ohio, and Illinois. Both he and Bradbury found an especially warm welcome in Galesburg, Illinois, where the energetic Jonathan Blanchard, president of the local Knox College, enlisted the entire town to participate in one way or another in three days of music. A November convention in Jamestown, New York, featured both Root and Bradbury and a performance of part of *Daniel*. The instructors found in Jamestown "singers of the right stamp — singers who are desirous of improvement and willing to work for it." The two returned home for the holidays encouraged by the prospects of musical institutes for a grassroots movement that embraced high standards of musical excellence and convened teachers to think collectively about how to teach music in the common schools.

Amid their travels the two found time for occasional teaching during three winter terms of the normal musical institute in Manhattan orchestrated by Mason, Hastings, and others. The three-month summer institute had generated sufficient interest to suggest a year-round program. Classes cost $12.50 per term, while private lessons with such distinguished local musicians as Johann Zundel, organist at Henry Ward Beecher's Plymouth Church, arranger, and hymnal editor, could be had for $25.00.

The rapid proliferation of the institutes opened opportunities for others to join the effort. Already in 1853, Root's friend Chauncey Cady and New York musician I. B. Woodbury helped meet the demand, assisted by a handful of promising attendees at the three-month normal institutes that featured Root and Bradbury in Manhattan in 1853 and 1854 and moved to North Reading, Massachusetts, in 1856. In the mid-1850s Bradbury and Root might conduct as many as fifteen musical conventions during their separate fall trips, and as many more after the holidays.

By then the movement had spread to the South. In March 1855 Root traveled to Richmond, Virginia, where some 250 singers gathered for instruction at the first musical convention ever held in that part of the South. May 1857 brought tidings from Richmond that those who "had the infinite happiness" of being present at the 1 May operatic performance of *The Flower Queen* had heard "forcible writing worthy to be imitated by all critics." At about the same time, Augusta, Georgia, papers "spoke highly" of a performance of *The Flower Queen* in the city's theater, and citizens of Limestone Springs, South Carolina, sent word to New York that their production of the cantata had been "a decided hit." Letters from California assured Root and Bradbury that some in the Golden State supported their goals, and reports from Manchester, England (where Mason pleaded personally for attention to the content, quality, and style of church music), noted that "singing-classes and societies for the practice of *good* psalmody, anthems, and other choral music are prevailing here very much now." For those beyond the reach of regular institutes, the *Musical Review* serialized "The Singing School of Twenty Lessons" by Bradbury. The men seemed to be making measurable progress in their campaign against shape (patent) note use without even mentioning the subject. Bradbury instructed convention organizers to "invite patent-note singers to attend and leave their patent-note notions behind them," and assured them that "they will care but little about them on their return."

In 1859 Root joined a national trend by moving his family west. He had traveled throughout the region for years, commenting on its "wonderful growth." He settled in the elegant town of Hyde Park, just south of Chicago (where, he noticed, everyone going anywhere in the West passed through), and joined the firm of Root and Cady, music publishers. He set up shop at a desk in the busy concern his brother Towner owned with Chauncey Cady and worked as publications editor close by the supply of Steinway pianos, other musical instruments (the house specialized in those used by military bands), and printed music that made Root and Cady one of the best-stocked musical venues west of New York. His move did not interrupt his educational forays into outlying regions. As troops mustered for the long Civil War, Root opened the first musical convention ever convened in Iowa City, Iowa. Soon, however, the distractions of war and the popularity of his Civil War songs would turn his efforts to new venues and effectively end his regular collaboration with his northeastern colleagues. His career blossomed in the Midwest. In 1872 the University of Chicago awarded him an honorary doctorate of music.

Bradbury, on the other hand, stayed in New York, and grew closer to Fanny Crosby than she had been to Root.

WILLIAM BATCHELDER BRADBURY

Hymnal users whose eyes wander to the tune credits may recognize Bradbury as the composer of the common tunes for such Protestant standards as "Jesus Loves Me," "Just as I Am," "Sweet Hour of Prayer," and "My Hope Is Built on Nothing Less." But the heavily bearded, forbidding-looking, volatile Bradbury was much more than a composer of simple, singable, sometimes catchy melodies. He — like Mason and Root — was a man with a musical mission. By the time he met Crosby in 1864, Bradbury had a reputation as one of Manhattan's most enterprising music promoters. Teacher, publisher, piano maker, composer, and facilitator, he did as much as anyone to assure a steady stream of music designed for use in the new urban religious and secular settings of his day. By welcoming Crosby into his circle, he in effect offered her the potential for usefulness beyond the dreams of her Puritan forebears. As a member of the extended Bradbury network, Crosby both mirrored and helped craft a profound shift in popular religious tastes.

William Batchelder Bradbury was born 6 October 1816 in York, a historic southern Maine beachfront town just sixty miles north of Boston. In 1830 his family moved to Boston. For the first time the music-loving Bradbury heard piano and organ music, and he opted to study organ. Like Root, he attended Lowell Mason's singing classes at the Boston Academy of Music and gained admittance to Mason's

Bowdoin Street Church choir. There he observed the master's method of conducting singing classes. Bradbury kept busy as church organist and choir director for several congregations. Mason gave him his first teaching opportunity, sending him to Machias, Maine, to conduct singing schools and offer private lessons. Bradbury met Mason's expectations, returned to Boston to marry, and soon accepted a call to First Baptist Church of Brooklyn as its director of music. Mason provided a letter of introduction to Cyrus P. Smith, Brooklyn's mayor and a lover of music who helped Bradbury get established as a private teacher.

The Bradburys arrived in Brooklyn in 1840, just five years after Crosby settled in Manhattan. In 1841 they moved across the East River to Manhattan, where Bradbury eventually took charge of the choir and organ at the Broadway Tabernacle built for evangelist Charles Finney a decade earlier. The Tabernacle offered Bradbury an advantageous situation to advance Mason's agenda in New York. Citizens were accustomed to attending many kinds of programs in its spacious auditorium, and Bradbury agreed to provide music for some of the groups that rented the facility. Following Mason's example, he began offering children's singing classes in the church and collaborated with Hastings to edit *The Young Choir,* a resource for his own and other juvenile choirs. Bradbury's tunes, texts, arrangements, and compilations, then, were rooted in his own hands-on experience but shaped as well by the fundamentals he learned from his mentor, Lowell Mason. Church members agreed to support Bradbury's first children's choir by paying him a salary and offering the singing school free to the children. Revenue from the concert that ended the choir term repaid more than double the outlay. The first class set the tone for the others. The *New York Musical Gazette* described its appeal:

> This first class was visited by many superintendents and others interested in Sunday schools, who were uniformly delighted with what they saw and heard, and the originator of the movement (Bradbury) soon found himself engaged with many similar schools in various parts of the city. So popular did these become that children sometimes assembled before the door hours beforehand in order to secure a seat. In the Spring Street Church there was a class of over six hundred. From these schools sprang the celebrated "Juvenile Musical Festivals" held at the Broadway Tabernacle.

The sight itself was a thrilling one. A thousand children were seated on a gradually rising platform. . . . About two-thirds of the class were girls, dressed uniformly in white with a white wreath and blue sash. The boys were dressed in jackets with collars turned over, something in the Byron style. Until the time of commencement the chattering and buzzing of the little creatures produced rather an amusing effect, albeit at times nearly deafening. But at the first stroke of the pianoforte the noise and confusion instantly ceased, and were followed by a silence so perfect that the ticking of a clock could be heard by the whole assembly. At the second sound of the instrument all instantly arose, presenting a sight that can be far more easily imagined than described.

The reader of some of Bradbury's hymnal prefaces and singing school materials may glean a sense of his teaching method from the suggestions he offered to others. "Secure a good beginning," he advised, "and you have the key to a successful and satisfactory course." Encouraging teachers to take advantage of every opportunity for their own improvement, he insisted that they show organization and self-control. Bradbury disapproved of the introduction of "foolish jesting" and "trifling nonsense" to arouse interest. Rather, he urged lively, "merry" hard work. Keep the class busy, he admonished. "Talk little — sing much." In *The Key Note,* a collection of music for singing schools, he advised of students punctual attendance, cheerful obedience, close attention, "gentlemanly deportment," and above all, Christian charity.

In the summer of 1847 the Bradburys took a leave of absence to travel abroad, going first to England and then to the Continent. They settled for a time in Leipzig where he studied at the Gewandhaus, the music institute famous for its association with Mendelssohn. Among other studies, he took piano with Johann Wenzel, harmony with Moritz Hauptmann, and composition with the famed Bohemian, Ignaz Moscheles. His letters from Europe, published in the *New York Observer* and the *New York Evangelist,* kept his name and ideas before American readers and offered a digest of musical events in the large cities of northern Europe.

On his return to New York in 1849, Bradbury resumed his responsibilities at the Broadway Tabernacle, meanwhile building an influential and ever expanding career apart from church duties. Although he conducted the Tabernacle's adult choir, he became especially well known for his children's choirs, his musical compositions, and his collections of music, most of which related — in one way or another — to his Tabernacle endeavors and, later, to the normal institutes he led. Committed to exposing children systematically to music, he worked to make music a source of pleasure by teaching basic musical notation and principles. That ambition meant he cared about such different schemes as educating children both inside and outside the public schools, producing accessible tunes, publishing inexpensive books for music enjoyment, and crafting the instruments that accompanied singing.

Bradbury's most active years spanned an era of Sunday school expansion that substantially broadened the appeal of his children's choirs and the resources he produced for them. Since each concerned itself with children, the Sunday school and normal institute movement had considerable overlap. Sunday schools in many places used *The Young Choir*. Bradbury published a series of other books, one or two a year, targeting the Sunday school market. Reviews brimmed with praise. A Sunday school worker's response to his book *The Golden Chain* was typical: "No music book has done so much to create an interest among the children as the *Chain*. It was issued at just the right time; its want had long been felt. Sabbath schools had been surfeited with new music books, but almost all of them were filled with old melodies that had either been worn out, or used in connection with secular songs. Fresh original music and words were needed. These were supplied by *The Golden Chain*."

The same writer expressed the perceived need for a steady stream of new materials, a widely held conviction that kept Bradbury and his cohorts in business. "After we had sung with much satisfaction almost everything that the *Chain* contained, we began to feel the want of something *new*, and you may judge of the pleasure it afforded us to hear that you intended to send forth its brother, *The Golden Shower*." The sales figures for such hymnals are staggering, even allowing for exaggeration. The most conservative estimates admit that Bradbury sold an aggregate of two million hymnals and songbooks, the majority intended for Sunday schools. Others claim that his *Golden Chain* (1861) — "the most popular Sunday school singing book ever issued" — alone sold two million copies (at $15 per hundred), while *Fresh Laurels* (1868) sold well over one million. In his preface to *Bright Jewels* (1869), a Bradbury collection released the year after Bradbury's 1868 death, editor Robert Lowry stated: "Bradbury has already supplied the Sunday schools of our land with four million Music Books." It was widely believed that only Mason's *Carmina Sacra* had sold more copies than Bradbury's books. Bradbury's most successful book for adults, *The Jubilee,* appeared in 1858 and sold over 250,000 copies.

Beginning with his first tune book, *The Young Choir,* published in 1841 (and edited by the more experienced Hastings), Bradbury issued hugely successful compilations of choral music, collaborating on occasion with Root or Hastings. The author of some 600 hymns and composer of over 1,000 tunes, Hastings issued with Bradbury *The New York Choralist* in 1847, *The Mendelssohn Collection* in 1849, and *The Psalmist* in 1851. *The Shawm* came next, drawing as well on the talent of Root, Hastings, and Lowell Mason's brother, Thomas. The collection's long subtitle reveals as well as anything the comprehensive audience Bradbury targeted: *Library of Church Music; embracing about one thousand pieces, consisting of psalm and hymn tunes adapted to every meter in use, anthems, chants and set pieces; to which is added an original cantata, entitled Daniel: or, The captivity and restoration. Including, also, The singing class; an entirely new and practical arrangement of the elements of music, interspersed with social part-songs for practice.* (*The Shawm* first published Bradbury's well-known hymn tune Olive's Brow.) With 725 tunes, 128 exercises and "easy glees" for elementary singers, and 85 anthems, the compilation (including Root and Bradbury's cantata *Daniel*) immediately found a place in the rounds of normal musical institutes that filled each autumn and winter. In 1858 Bradbury brought out *The Jubilee: An extensive collection of church music: for the choir, the congregation, and the singing-school, containing additional anthems, opening and closing pieces, etc.* The next year he and a new collaborator, Sylvester Main, issued *Cottage Melodies: A hymn and tune book for prayer and social meetings and the home circle.* The impact of industrialization on printing helped make such books possible. By midcentury, transformations in publishing and marketing books made books cheap enough for more Americans to afford. Music books in turn prompted changes in American musical experience.

Impressive as they were, these large compilations represented only a small part of Bradbury's work in the 1840s and 1850s. With Mason, Root, and Hastings, he was an editor of the *New York Musical Review* and the East Coast agent for the products that flowed from the presses at Chicago-based Root and Cady, music publishers.

Bradbury's own music helped make popular the repetitive choruses long favored by camp meeting audiences. At midcentury, camp meeting spirituals seemed irrepressible, and Bradbury — unlike Mason — made a conscious decision to ride the trend, and choruses became one of his trademarks. He incorporated camp meeting spirituals into his hymn collections, and the more he wrote, the more he seemed to pattern new tunes after these spirituals.

During the 1850s Bradbury's singing schools enrolled children and adults by the hundreds. In the spring of 1850 his "thousand singing children" offered one of their celebrated programs at the Tabernacle, an event so popular that the *Evening Post* reminded readers to arrive early since hundreds had been turned away from the preceding concert. In the fall of 1850 the *Tribune* commended to its readers one of his choral singing classes:

> A public meeting will be held at the Broadway Tabernacle this evening for the purpose of organizing a Choral Singing Class, on a plan similar to the large Choral Classes of Europe. The enterprise is a novel one in New York, and if we should become universally musical, the credit of the work would be an appropriate tribute to the labors of Mr. Wm. B. Bradbury — whose improved course of instruction will be adopted in the proposed class, should a sufficient number of names be obtained tonight to warrant the undertaking. To those who favor congregational singing, this project for general and comprehensive instruction in the elements of Music will commend itself with especial force.

Severe weather did not deter the curious, who attended a free lecture intended to build enthusiasm for the "mammoth singing class," and they enrolled in sufficient numbers to get the venture off the ground. The *Evening Post* assured the city that Bradbury needed "no stronger recommendation than the wide spread reputation he has already acquired as a teacher of vocal music." Stores on Broadway and in the Bowery sold tickets for the course, and within a week it was clear that Bradbury had launched a solid endeavor. For the more advanced, Bradbury offered an "upper Music Class" which he organized as a Glee and Song Union. By December 1850 he had generated so much enthusiasm for music that he organized yet another new choral singing class on "moderate terms," having as its specific goal "the promotion of congregational singing in the churches." Meanwhile, his annual concerts featuring a thousand children dressed alike singing his recent compositions, among other numbers, did more than demonstrate his abilities as a teacher. They also popularized new music and gave notice that the next generation cared about singing and perhaps knew more about it than their parents did. The effects, Bradbury believed, were bound to become evident in the churches as well as in the cultural choices the next generation made.

Like Mason and Root, Bradbury maintained a relentless schedule. September 1851, for example, found Hastings and Bradbury conducting a musical convention in Detroit. Back in Manhattan, Bradbury organized a Wednesday evening music class for adults, a class that became an annual twelve-week winter event. He typically began with a free lecture entitled "Music Reading and Singing by Note." The series of classes cost $3 for gentlemen and $2 for ladies. (Bradbury fiddled with fees. The 1854 price was $2 for an individual but $4 for a gentleman and two ladies.) Meanwhile he made sure that events at the Broadway Tabernacle — a mission society anniversary, annual adult choir festival, or Sunday school program — included "appropriate original hymns" presented by his choirs under his direction. February 1852 found Bradbury, assisted by his musically inclined brother, Edward, producing *Flora's Festival,* an elaborate cantata he prepared for a choir of 1,000 children. Hundreds of trees, evergreens, and flowers transformed the stage and choir gallery into a miniature forest or "grove of the Fairies." Single tickets cost fifty cents, but three tickets could be had for just one dollar.

In 1854 the ever-enterprising Bradbury went into business with his brother, Edward Bradbury, to produce pianos. Bradbury pianos became the rage of the day, winning gold medals at state fairs (Bradbury once boasted that in one four-week stretch his pianoforte took seven gold medals and a certificate of honor). The nation's most renowned pianists promptly offered endorsements. Louis Moreau Gottschalk, New Orleans–born international piano sensation who boasted "the highest European credentials of genius and success," enthused: "It is my opinion they are very superior instruments. I have especially remarked their thorough workmanship and the power, purity, richness and quality of their tone." Theodore Thomas, German-born conductor of the Brooklyn Philharmonic; concert pianist William Mason; and Henry Ward Beecher's famous organist, Johann Zundel, echoed the sentiments. In the 1870s the Hayes White House boasted an ornate model and Bradbury ads carried endorsements from Mrs. U. S. Grant, Chief Justice Salmon P. Chase, the Reverend T. DeWitt Talmage, and novelist Edward Eggleston, assuring consumers that the "sweet tones" of Bradbury pianos were especially well suited to accompany religious song and deserved "the fullest confidence of the Christian public." The instruments cost between $500 and $800, and the Bradbury brothers could not keep pace with orders for their "new scale, overstrung bass, patent-insulated, full-iron-frame grand and square piano fortes." Manufacturing drew Bradbury into the larger circle of New York piano makers (like the Chickerings and Steinways) and brought him the unwelcome interruption in the 1850s and 1860s of negotiations with the Journeymen Piano-forte Makers' Union.

In December 1859 fire reduced the Bradburys' piano-making plant to ashes, consuming several hundred pianos plus ivory, rosewood, and other valuable materials used in their manufacture. The brothers took a huge loss — insured for $39,500, their property was valued at far more than twice that. They announced that their lumberyard had not been damaged and proceeded to rebuild. A few years later, declining health forced William to withdraw from the management of the piano business. The *New York Times* commented in 1867 on Bradbury's notice of its sale: "The numerous friends of Mr. Bradbury will regret to learn that his health, which has for some time past been precarious, has compelled him to take this step. . . . Mr. Bradbury will retain the copyright of his well-known singing-books, and he hopes hereafter, when his strength shall be sufficiently restored, to again devote his attention to musical composition, a branch of his profession in which he retains all his old popularity." In fact, the firm did not dissolve. Rather, it passed into the control of others until the William Knabe Piano Company absorbed it.

The fragile health that plagued Bradbury had concerned his colleagues at least since 1854 when it had forced his resignation from his music responsibilities at the Broadway Tabernacle. Bradbury had struggled for much of his life with a tendency to tuberculosis. He had moved his family out of Manhattan, settling first in Bloomfield, New Jersey, where they became active in the Bloomfield Presbyterian Church, a congregation whose history reached back to colonial times. Once the Third Presbyterian Church of Newark, the church was renamed after a local Revolutionary War hero and stood on the Bloomfield village green. The air may have been purer on the west side of the Hudson River, but the added commute for his Tabernacle responsibilities proved too demanding. In May 1854, at an emotional gathering, the Broadway Tabernacle reluctantly released Bradbury. He continued composing, editing, publishing, and compiling, and for the moment held on to his piano interests in part because his brother bore a large share of the day-to-day responsibility.

From 1859 Bradbury's responsibility as senior principal of the Annual Musical School at Geneseo, New York, took him upstate each summer for extended educational endeavors. Thirty miles south of Rochester, Geneseo was built on the banks of the Genesee River. Residents lobbied hard for the privilege of hosting the summer musical institutes that had begun in Manhattan (1853), moved to North Reading (1855), and sought a new location in 1859. This summer institute seems to have been the source of a bitter quarrel between Bradbury and Root. There is some evidence that the trouble may have stemmed from moving the institute in 1855 from Manhattan to Root's Massachusetts turf. Bradbury had apparently sent a hired agent to obtain signatures on a petition inviting him to establish an institute and committing signers to attend (and pay the tuition). He neglected to indicate that his proposed enterprise competed with Root's announced school. The ploy (Mason called it "trickery, guile, shameless fraud") turned friendship into bitter acrimony until a few years later each did an about-face. The acrimony offers a glimpse of the rivalry that often marred relationships among those who produced America's sacred songs.

Meanwhile, William Killip of Geneseo — for forty years music director at St. Michael's Episcopal Church — had made Mason's acquaintance at the North Reading institutes. He facilitated an invitation to move the North Reading Normal Institute to Geneseo. Bradbury seized the opportunity and announced an eight-week session with Theodore E. Perkins, a prominent young teacher of "voice culture."

Son of a Baptist pastor, Perkins had attended the 1856 summer normal institute run at North Reading by Mason and Root and had quickly become a protégé.

On 11 July 1859 Bradbury offered opening remarks that set the tone for the Geneseo Normal Institute. After dismissing as a "dying remnant" the "old fogy" school of teachers (presumably those who clung to shape notes), Bradbury looked ahead:

> A better day is dawning. A class of men and women of the right stamp are entering the profession of Music teaching. Persons of sound sense, of taste and judgment — of progressive views — are seeking to qualify themselves for the great work upon which they have entered. Such must soon take the place of the superficial, the egotistical, the low and ignorant. It is worthy of remark that the applications we now receive for teachers enumerate in almost all instances among *indispensable qualifications* those that belong to persons of good taste and culture.

Citizens of Geneseo thought Bradbury and Perkins did an admirable job of inculcating taste and culture. The school "progressed finely" with over 100 students, more than Root had accommodated the year before at North Reading. The *Livingston Republican* boasted that the numbers "pretty fully show the estimation in which the Principals are held," and citizens banded together to raise $20,000 to ready a building for a permanent musical normal institute. By August 1859 just $2,000 remained to be raised. Supporters of the project appreciated music and instruction, but they also had an eye to the economic benefits the town would reap from a regular summer institute. Although Bradbury did not return the next year (his precarious health again forced him to cut back), the popular Perkins presided, at least through the mid-1860s, joined in leadership by such other stalwarts of the "better music" movement as Johann Zundel and the popular Italian-born voice teacher Carlo Bassini.

Meanwhile, in New York as in Massachusetts, growing public demand for state-supported normal institutes yielded results. In 1867 the state responded to requests from Geneseo's public-spirited citizens and established at Geneseo a normal institute that later became a branch of the State University of New York (SUNY). Instruction began in 1871.

For an additional fee, two female faculty offered prospective teachers instruction in vocal and instrumental music. The school's monthly expenses included rent for musical instruments, paid to William Killip. The Geneseo Normal Institute of Music thus blended into a larger and more permanent commitment to teach the teaching of music.

In the meantime the ailing Bradbury made the acquaintance of Fanny Crosby. Their remarkable partnership began in 1864 as the result of an unremarkable event — Crosby's after-church conversation with the Reverend Peter Stryker.

As she told it, Crosby went one Sunday to the Old Dutch Church on Twenty-third Street to hear Stryker, a well-known pastor who used his pulpit to encourage the philanthropic and reform endeavors that claimed the energy and resources of many Manhattan Protestants. An ardent advocate of Sunday schools, a respected leader among the city's Reformed clergy, and an able preacher, Stryker had years earlier joined Mason's movement for better sacred music. He now referred Crosby to Bradbury, a man Stryker knew was always eager to make the acquaintance of people able to provide song lyrics. On 2 February 1864 Crosby brought a letter of introduction from Stryker to 425 Broome Street, Bradbury's office at the corner of Broome and Crosby Streets in lower Manhattan. Bradbury knew her by reputation and extended a cordial welcome. That day she met as well Sylvester P. Main, her onetime playmate on the Ridgefield village green. She promised them a sample of her work and returned in three days with the words written on 4 February that she would always remember as her first hymn:

> We are going, we are going
> To a home beyond the skies,
> Where the fields are robed in beauty,
> And the sunlight never dies;
> Where the fount of joy is flowing
> In the valley green and fair.
> We shall dwell in love together;
> There shall be no parting there.

As Americans reeled in the horrors of recent Civil War battles — Gettysburg, Vicksburg, Chattanooga — it was at once unremarkable and surprising that Crosby's first words for Bradbury were about heaven. Note the images: home, beauty, light, joy, love, no parting. This hymn did not first envision heaven with reference to Christ and redemption or to grand Christian moments like "the marriage supper of the Lamb." Instead, Crosby used heaven to promise what a strife-torn nation surely needed: tranquillity and togetherness at home. For Crosby the thought came naturally, and the words poured quickly, as always, from her lips.

As Crosby told it, Bradbury sent for her the next week with an urgent request for patriotic words for a difficult melody he had composed. Crosby's adept mind retained the meter, and the next day she brought her lyrics to Bradbury. Delighted and surprised, he promptly promised her work for as long as he had a publishing house.

Her association with Bradbury drew Crosby further into the center of the thriving nexus aimed at revamping American Protestant song. Her collaboration with Root had yielded materials for the normal institute market as well as a few popular numbers. With Bradbury she turned her focus to sacred text, some of which was for the same market but much of which targeted other audiences, too. Bradbury's enterprises both led and followed public tastes. He exploited his contacts but advanced his own theories, too, and devoted his wherewithal to music education. He had long since won the goodwill of Manhattan's leading citizens, who often commended his efforts in public venues.

Crosby's association with Bradbury from 1864, then, gave her a place among those intent on providing for "the English-speaking multitude" a direct, simple hymnody in the idiom of the day. For Crosby this enterprise was less a "cause" than a direction for her steady outpouring of verse. She proved unusually adept at generating the regular meter and rhymed text that "worked" with new hymn tunes by Bradbury and his cohorts. And she knew well the various audiences for her lyrics: they were the people among whom she lived, whose churches she frequented, and whose causes she espoused. A tribute from one of Crosby's friends suggests why Protestants of all affiliations and of none easily embraced her words as their own: "She engages in no doctrinal controversies, but speaks the language of Zion with saints of every name." Her texts were not "great" by traditional standards for hymns, but contemporaries found her "genius" in her "faculty of touching the human heart to a remarkable degree." On her part, Crosby simply did what came most naturally. She prayed before she composed any verse, and she dictated to any available amanuensis.

Most of Crosby's texts fit the general description of a gospel song — a sacred folk song, as E. S. Lorenz described it, "free in form, emotional in character, devout in attitude, evangelistic in purpose." With subjective texts often addressed to other people and a refrain after each stanza, gospel songs featured four-part settings composed specifically for the text, or text prepared for particular tunes. Gospel song antecedents lay in the camp meeting spirituals and other music born in revival settings, but they also had ties to the Sunday school movement. Several collections of such songs, words and music, were published in the 1850s and 1860s, at about the same time Bradbury launched his endeavors. Gospel songsters rendered the camp meeting spirituals in four-part harmony shorn of "ornamental quaverings," often preserving the choruses. Bradbury helped along the transition while energetically promoting new material.

Crosby's output soon reached such proportions that the Bradbury Company began assigning her pseudonyms. (She said in 1905 that she had written under about 80 names. By the end of her life, some claimed the number was nearer 200.) These ranged from her married name, Mrs. Fanny J. Van Alstine, to Mrs. N. de Plume. For the most part her work appeared under women's names — Victoria Frances, Lizzie Edwards, Grace Frances, Rose Atherton, Viola. Every so often her publishers opted for masculine aliases like Lyman Schuyler and James Apple, or for initials — W.H.D., F.J.V., A., C., V.A. — or they used ### or The Children's Friend. To the public she was best known as Fanny Crosby, while "to those who enjoy[ed] the privilege of her confidence and affection, she [was], simply and sweetly, Fanny."

For much of 1867 Bradbury's losing struggle with tuberculosis forced him to leave his work and seek health elsewhere. Prolonged stays in Minnesota and Florida brought partial restoration and a new hymnal later that year, *Bradbury's Fresh Laurels for the Sabbath School, a New and Extensive Collection of Music and Hymns.* The preface revealed Bradbury's heart, and the first song featured words by his most prolific collaborator, Fanny Crosby. Bradbury stated forthrightly his evangelistic intentions for his Sunday school hymnals. "Believing in the early conversion of Children to Christ," he explained, "we have tried to put such songs in their mouths (hoping to fasten them upon their hearts) as shall lead them directly to their loving Saviour." He offered music that featured new melodies but included as well many standard hymn tunes. But, he admonished, "in order to keep up the interest in the school, *new music,* and GOOD music, suited to the tastes and adapted to the capacities of the children, must be frequently introduced."

The book's first number, Crosby's "Laurels for the Sunday School," befitted a time when Sunday schools were coming into their own in and around New York and an age when wreath laying and laurel decking were regular parts of public occasions:

> Laurels, fresh laurels for the Sunday School we bring,
> They will bloom in fadeless verdure through a calm eternal
> spring;
> Then gladly hail with a pure delight,
> Oh, hail our beautiful wreath so bright;
> Laurels, fresh laurels for the Sunday School we bring.

The sectional divisions of *Fresh Laurels* (which sold over one million copies) suggest the agendas of nineteenth-century Sunday schools: general worship, anniversaries, Christmas festivals, picnics, temperance rallies, social gatherings, special celebrations, deaths, revivals.

The burst of strength that allowed Bradbury to complete *Fresh Laurels* proved temporary, and he died of consumption at age fifty-two at his Montclair, New Jersey, home on 7 January 1868, leaving a widow, four daughters, and a son. A few days later special carriages met trains at the Montclair depot to shuttle Bradbury's friends, Crosby among them, to the Presbyterian church in Montclair for his funeral. Adults filled the main floor and children crowded the galleries. Five clergymen, among them Thomas Hastings's son (later president of Union Theological Seminary), graced the platform. Hastings's reminiscences reduced the crowd to tears. The casket stood in the precise spot where Bradbury had sat at a melodeon and led the congregation's song. Positioned close by, Crosby (who had been led to the casket and grasped Bradbury's cold hand) was particularly moved by the service because the program included her first hymn with Bradbury:

We are going, we are going
When the day of life is o'er
To that pure and happy region
Where our friends have gone before;
They are singing with the angels
In that land so bright and fair,
We shall dwell with them forever,
There will be no parting there.

Bradbury was buried in the family plot in the graveyard of the First Presbyterian Church of Bloomfield, New Jersey. A few years later his friends, rallied by Freeborn G. Smith, his immediate successor in the piano business, opened in Brooklyn in his memory the Bradbury Mission and an adjacent hospital for women and children staffed by the female physicians of the King's County Medical Society. These enterprises stood just behind the Bradbury piano factory on Willoughby Street, near Fort Greene. William Bradbury left a remarkable legacy, including some fifty-nine books of sacred and secular music, much of which was of his own composition. With Mason, Root, and Hastings, he played a vital role in what his cohorts liked to call the democratization of American Protestant song, and his work on behalf of normal institutes of music helped plant music education and music teacher training in many places.

CONCLUSION

The beliefs about music and culture that animated Mason, Root, and Bradbury had a parallel in the immigrant associations that proliferated in the same years. These often featured similar musical emphases, including commitment to the musical instruction of children. For Germans, choral singing both built community among immigrants and nurtured culture memory, and Manhattan German social life gave prominence to singing societies, Sunday concerts, and *Sängerfeste* (sometimes held at the Broadway Tabernacle). These, in turn, provided incentive to composers, instrumentalists, and singers. In the 1850s alone, German immigrants established in Manhattan eighteen choral societies that paralleled or overlapped Bradbury's expanding work in the city. Welsh immigrants sponsored groups that nurtured their legendary choral music, and other European immigrants found as well that the popular songs of their homelands helped span the distance between their new and old worlds. For Protestants among the immigrants, parallels to Bradbury's efforts assumed long-term importance in the late nineteenth-century shaping of American religious song. Northeastern Anglo-American efforts, then, coincided with a much larger explosion of popular choral music.

Part of a much larger vision for the place of education in the making of Americans and the role of music in elevating the quality of life, the mid-nineteenth-century burst of popular Protestant song issued from camp meetings, revivals, social gatherings, Sunday schools, and sanctuaries. Mason, Root, Bradbury, and cohorts — people rich in vision though short on formal training — showed that self-made entrepreneurs who interwove the common good, sacred song, and patriotic devotion could both mirror and mold grassroots Protestant impulses without shortchanging a healthy bottom line. Protestant and patriotic to the core, Crosby offered Root and Bradbury an idiom that assured success.

7 Sunday School

Don't forget the Sabbath
The Lord our God hath blest,
Of all the week the brightest,
Of all the week the best;
It brings repose from labor,
It tells of joy divine,
Its beams of light descending
With heavenly beauty shine.

When William Bradbury's declining health forced him to give up his children's choirs, he compensated by devoting himself all the more assiduously to supplying resources to help others cultivate children's song. Like Mason, Bradbury regarded Sunday schools as ubiquitous choirs-in-the-making, and he embraced the task of editing hymnals for their use. Bradbury set out to convince superintendents that all children *could* sing, that songs would popularize Sunday school values, and that music could help scholars transition from the schools to the churches. This last was a matter of concern at a time when Sunday schools met on Sunday afternoons entirely apart from the regular schedules of congregations. Some were mission enterprises; others had church quarters and entrances separate from those parishioners used. Bradbury enlisted music in the cause of effective bridge building between Sunday schools and their sponsoring churches. He had a disarming personality, packaged and marketed his products strategically, and discovered a public willing to be persuaded. Mason's circle had laid a broad foundation for the melodies Bradbury crafted with children's voices in mind. He paired them with texts redolent with moral advice. In this enterprise, as in all his musical publications, Bradbury found Crosby a ready ally. She welcomed the chance to cultivate a younger public in which she already took particular delight. (One of her pseudonyms was "The Children's Friend.") Crosby's words had a prominent place in a massive enterprise in Protestant religious education, an endeavor replete with advice on application as well as doctrine.

The modes of moral instruction that shaped mid-nineteenth-century Sunday school hymns are long gone, and most of Crosby's Sunday school texts are forgotten, though a handful of Bradbury tunes endure ("Jesus Loves Me," "Just as I Am"). But in her day and in the next generation, Crosby's Sunday school hymns won her a place in one of the era's premier Protestant crusades. Taken together, her texts stand as reminders for modern readers of the values and priorities that once animated an army of Sunday school scholars (and their resolute teachers) across the country. Their inclusion in Bradbury's best-selling, inexpensive hymnals that sold out runs of hundreds of thousands of copies in two or three months suggests that millions of scholars were exposed to her words. Bradbury printed Sunday school texts by other women — Lydia Baxter, Mrs. E. M. Sangster, Mrs. M. A. Kidder, Mrs. Dr. Palmer (Phoebe Palmer) — but none of these approached the volume of texts he selected from Crosby. Her partnership with one of the era's premier Sunday school music entrepreneurs, then, brought Crosby fame.

Technological strides — from printing to railroads — as well as the era's devotion to efficiency facilitated the dissemination of Sunday school hymnals. The recent popularity of cheap pulp paper, economical binding, and improvements in printing meant that Sunday school hymnals, like Sunday school fiction, were part of the flourishing of mass culture in the United States. Small and easily carried, the hymnals were inexpensively printed using electrotype plates. In 1866

Bradbury used up two entire sets of plates to meet the calls for his *Golden Chain;* unabated demand despite the release the same year of three new hymnals forced him to re-electrotype the older work. In the meantime, railroads created an exploding market, for the first time making efficient national distribution a real possibility.

Crosby's long life spanned these enormous changes in transportation and technology as well as the heyday of the American Sunday school movement. By all accounts she loved children and young people and cared deeply about their Christian formation. During her years as a member of Manhattan's Cornell Memorial Methodist Episcopal Church, the congregation supported a rapidly growing Sunday school that in 1890 enrolled over 1,200 scholars. This school and those that claimed the energies of her friends provided natural venues for her energies and kept her in touch with the progress and interests of the scholars. Her work with Bradbury linked Crosby to a host of other musicians intent on promoting Sunday schools — William Doane, William J. Kirkpatrick, Robert Lowry. They all found in the schools a lucrative market and, more, an extension of children's music education (a discipline Bradbury also helped introduce into the New York City public schools). Crosby authored Sunday school text as it came to her mind as well as by request. Van apparently shared this passion, and the preparation of Sunday school hymns provided the couple rare moments of collaboration. Van generally preferred (in Crosby's words) "the worldless classics." In a move unusual for her, Crosby even ventured a few tunes for her own texts, though few, if any, of these enjoyed more than brief popularity.

The Sunday schools (or Sabbath schools as they then were often known) in which Crosby and her cohorts took a hearty interest flourished as part of a larger Anglo-Protestant scheme to assure the nation's democratic future. In 1841 the editor of the *New York Herald* reminded his readers of the "dignity, importance and responsibility" of Sabbath school teaching, since teachers "educated the future judges and counselors, senators and representatives, governors and ministers of the land." Patriotism and religion blended easily in the schools' music and rhetoric, just as they did in the ambitions of Mason's circle. Crosby and her coterie of colleagues often waxed eloquent about the purpose and possibilities of Sunday schools for keeping the nation on course. Like other enthusiasts, they attributed an astounding range of public benefit to the efforts of Sabbath school teachers. The celebrated Sunday school activist H. Clay Trumbull, in his 1888 Lyman Beecher Lectures at Yale Divinity School, made the bold claim: "America has been practically saved to Christianity and the religion of the Bible by the Sunday-school." Crosby's cohorts tended to agree that, in an era of bewildering social change, establishing the young in love for God and country promised national as well as personal benefits. While they acknowledged as a progenitor of sorts Robert Raikes, the Gloucester layman whose eighteenth-century British Sunday schools helped jumpstart a movement for the education of the poor, Crosby and her cohorts were animated by a different vision, one that adapted Sunday schools to the American context.

For one thing, Americans changed the focus of the Sunday school by turning an endeavor associated in Britain with the lower classes into what historian Robert Lynn called "a prep school for the whole of evangelical America." When the indomitable Lyman Beecher gave force to his plea for a broader purpose for the schools by enrolling his own progeny in Sunday school, he modeled the direction American Sunday schools would take. They would not be simply schools for the poor or otherwise unchurched, nor would they focus on rudimentary education; rather, they would be centers of religious instruction for all children, churched as well as not. Intent on safeguarding a democratic society on the move toward the millennium, nineteenth-century American Protestants exploited this concept of Sunday school to inculcate virtue, instill a common moral vocabulary, drill basic doctrines, and motivate youth to biblical literacy, responsible citizenship, and private morality. In the hands of able promoters, Sunday schools soon stood at the heart of a growing cluster of profitable enterprises — literary, musical, social, reformist — intent on assuring the realization of a Christian America by planting Sunday schools across the nation, enlisting an army of adult teachers, and converting American youth.

Enthusiasm for Sunday schools, then, was part of a larger fabric into which dispositions dear to Protestant hearts were tightly woven — regard for the Sabbath, concern for the future, temperance, reform of society, manners and morals appropriate for those who grounded their lives in the biblical text. It also coincided with early glimmerings of a rethinking of childhood and the emergence of a children's literature. (Not surprisingly, some of Mason's network, foremost among them the best-selling children's author Jacob Abbott, produced the cheaply bound moral tales Sunday school advocates favored.) At their best, American Sunday schools reinforced the efforts of Christian parents, complemented the work of churches, and Americanized the children of immigrants. They generated an extensive children's literature, providing a steady diet of fiction, poetry, and instructional tools that inculcated Protestant (also understood as "American") values. They promoted Bible memorization and family religion, and, evangelical Protestants insisted, they accomplished as much good for their vast army of volunteer teachers as they did for their young scholars. They assured the biblical literacy of millions of Americans who presumably imbibed from the Authorized Version the morals Sunday school promoters believed upheld civil society. In short, the convinced insisted that Sunday schools fueled the steady progress of nineteenth-century American evangelicalism.

Especially after 1824, when early promoters of Sunday schools consolidated local efforts through a national umbrella organization, the American Sunday School Union, the schools assumed a particularly prominent role in the grand eastern seaboard Protestant scheme for Christianizing (Protestantizing) the West. Beecher not only enrolled his children, he also urged on his generation the centrality of the entire enterprise to the perpetuation of civilization beyond the Appalachians. (Beecher gave force to this opinion by accepting a pastorate in Cincinnati [the gateway to the West], where he encouraged among other endeavors children's choirs and Sunday schools.) In response to such pleas, Sunday school missionaries traveled by foot and horseback from town to town to establish the tens of thousands of schools that dotted the nation by 1860. Missionaries had strict instructions to sell the inexpensive moralizing literature endorsed by the American Sunday School Union. Sometimes Sunday school libraries were the only public libraries in new settlements, just as Sunday school missionaries often purveyed the first organized religion in frontier towns. Sunday school agents, one remarked, faced the daunting challenge of "supply[ing] the whole youthful population of a country with rational and profitable books." One count of libraries revealed that by midcentury, Sunday schools supplied fully 60 percent of public libraries. Their size ranged considerably: the Sunday school library at Crosby's Cornell Memorial Church was stocked with over 1,300 volumes while frontier schools might offer a few dozen. In Brooklyn in 1855, eighty-seven Sunday schools together owned 31,301 books.

Sunday school promoters dreamed of large things and accomplished more than many expected. After its first fifty years, the American Sunday School Union boasted that fully one-fifth of the entire population of the United States held membership in evangelical Sunday schools. The vast majority of members were children and young people, but an increasing number of adults enrolled, too, and membership options soon included a "cradle roll" of infants too young to attend as well as home extension programs that kept interested shut-ins on the rolls. (In her old age, Crosby maintained her involvement through the extension option.) While the U.S. population grew tenfold between 1800 and 1880, evangelical church membership counted a thirtyfold increase, a circumstance Protestant pundits attributed largely to Sunday schools.

American Protestants were not alone in the conviction that Sunday schools filled a larger purpose than the religious indoctrination of youth. Just after the centennial celebrations in 1876, a French commission concluded a multiyear study of primary education in the United States and offered the following observation: "The Sunday-school is an absolute necessity for the complete instruction of the child. . . . All things unite to assign to this institution a grand part in the American life." A contemporary Belgian observer, Emile de Laveleye, concurred: "The Sunday-school is one of the strongest foundations of the republican institutions of the United States." Catholics and Jews, the largest non-Protestant groups in the population, paid Sunday schools the ultimate compliment by adapting them for their own ends.

Nineteenth-century American Sunday schools came in many varieties, from urban to rural, rich to poor, denominational to independent, large to small. They fed the demand for a hymnody attuned to their special place in the American Protestant dream of a Christian America. Scholars in a lone Sunday school in a remote western village ideally recognized a kinship with scholars enrolled in all other Sunday schools across the land. In theory, at least, all promoted the same goals, and common literature as well as music accented shared purpose. By the end of the century, uniform lessons offered Sunday schools everywhere tangible proof of their common aspirations. Uniform lessons

179

made possible an array of cross-denominational teacher training opportunities, too, ranging from newspaper helps for teachers, to weekly
citywide gatherings at which they studied the lesson together, to carefully planned extended summer programs for teachers at the Chautauqua Assembly, a Victorian summer learning resort on a picturesque
lake in far western upstate New York. Uniform lessons also enabled
Sunday school hymnal publishers to select and then suggest appropriate related hymns for each week.

By the last quarter of the century, Brooklyn — America's fourth-
largest city (dubbed "the city of churches") — hosted annual Sunday
school parades second to none. The anniversary of the Brooklyn
Sunday School Union became Anniversary Day, a citywide holiday
celebrated on the first Thursday in June. Thousands of Sunday school
scholars poured into the streets for perhaps the most massive regular
public ecumenical celebration of the role of the Sunday school in the
making of Americans. Everything featured biblical themes, of course,
but it was understood that those themes nurtured the core of what it
meant to be an American. Waving American flags, the throngs of
scholars marched through city streets singing Sunday school songs
and greeting the city and state dignitaries assembled in the grand-
stands along the parade route. Bands played Sunday school music,
and floats emblazoned with Sunday school slogans carried the youngest members. Such public occasions celebrated, and reminded non-
Protestants of, the vigor and intentions of evangelical youth, and enlisted nonparticipants in Sunday school activities.

Protestants in the greater New York area, hub for printing enterprises and reform movements of all kinds, played a particularly critical role in preparing the resources of all kinds that Sunday schools
used to enlist American youth in the grand crusade for evangelical
Christianity and democracy. Even in the disruptive Civil War years,
the market for their wares was stunning. When he issued the *Golden
Censer* in 1864, Bradbury sold more than 50,000 copies in three weeks.
Crosby's "Sabbath Scholars' Compact" thus gained wide circulation:
"Let us never do a wrong, howsoever tempted; but in deed and word
love and serve the Lord." "We thank you a thousand times for the
Golden Censer," a Sunday school superintendent from New London,
Connecticut, wrote. "We anticipated much, but our anticipations are
more than realized."

A strong preference for "something new" in text and tune ran through the commendations heaped on Bradbury's Sunday school hymnals. Enthusiasm for his latest book thus turned quickly into eager anticipation of his next in the hope of keeping interest lively. Bradbury had nurtured and counted on such demand in his past music convention work. His fame as a children's choir conductor lent weight to his opinions on the need for an expansive repertoire for effective work with children. Sales figures demonstrated that he had an economic incentive, too. His prefaces claimed that he kept an educational objective in view: more hymns or new hymns did not in themselves suffice. Quality musical and moral education mattered more, he claimed, than numbers of hymns. This combination of philosophy, need, and market savvy underlay his success.

Bradbury was not alone in professing such concern for more than the bottom line. The participation of the prime movers in the movement for children's music in congregations as music directors and in Sunday schools as superintendents added weight to their opinions. They did not merely compose, compile, and publish to fill a market niche; they knew the market firsthand because they helped generate and nurture it. Their business and benevolent instincts overlapped, and the Protestant "insider" viewpoint they brought to their businesses contributed to a healthy bottom line.

Sunday school promoters had allies as well in a growing number of public educational and philanthropic endeavors that nurtured the kinds of music Mason had long advocated. An outpouring of religious verse combined with the composition of simple tunes and catchy choruses to promote songs appropriate to secular as well as sacred endeavors. Editors of English-language children's hymnals had as a precedent the work of the venerable Isaac Watts, who had addressed one of his four hymnals to children, but his eighteenth-century diction — with its stern reminders of impending death and judgment — seemed out of touch with the optimistic nineteenth-century accent on nurture and education and the sweetness and light of the gospel. Simplified Sunday school music had early emerged as a goal of the Boston music reformers. From the early 1820s Mason had been working with the Massachusetts Sunday School Association, and his early *Sabbath School Songs* (published under its auspices) delivered on his promise of music "of a lighter or more melodious character than is usual in common psalm tunes." The marriage of "light" melodies and assuring words soon made music a feature of successful Sunday schools.

Central as she was to the mid-nineteenth-century explosion of Sunday school hymnals, Crosby had nothing whatsoever to do with "Jesus Loves Me," the most popular of all the Sunday school hymns, though its text (set to music by Crosby's publisher, Bradbury) has striking similarities to the tone Crosby adopted for her Sunday school work. The words appeared first in a novel, *Say and Seal*, published in 1860 by Anna and Susan Warner. The Warner sisters taught a Sunday school class of West Point cadets and spent the rest of their time producing best-selling novels brimming with moral advice. In *Say and Seal* the sisters featured both Sunday school scholars and a youthful death scene into which they inserted four stanzas of a new text, "Jesus Loves Me." The Warners' lines had no chorus, but the next year the enterprising Bradbury added one and provided a tune. He thus transformed lyrics which the novel "tinged with death" into a cheerful jingle that became the best-known Protestant Sunday school song and, some suggest, a "theme song" for the Sunday school movement:

> Jesus loves me, this I know
> For the Bible tells me so;
> Little ones to him belong,
> They are weak, but he is strong.
>
> Refrain:
> Yes, Jesus loves me!
> Yes, Jesus loves me!
> Yes, Jesus loves me!
> The Bible tells me so.
>
> Jesus loves me, he who died
> Heaven's gate to open wide;
> He will wash away my sin,
> Let his little child come in.
>
> Jesus loves me! Loves me still,
> Though I'm very weak and ill,

That I might from sin be free
Bled and died upon the tree.

In their classic study of American Sunday schools, historians Robert Lynn and Elliott Wright suggest that "Jesus Loves Me" symbolizes a profound mid-nineteenth-century transition in the message and music of Sunday schools. Its lyrics reached back to the grim and familiar reality of death and grief and stern morality that pervaded the earliest Sunday school songs, but its upbeat chorus and reassuring lines pointed toward an emerging message characterized by reassurance, love, and faith and equally rooted in the Bible — "The Bible tells me so." By the time Crosby began writing Sunday school lyrics in 1864, that transition, facilitated for several decades by Mason's circle, had taken over the lyrics of Sunday school songs.

If Sunday schools in their first American adaptations revolved around such stern orthodox realities as divine providence, original sin, and the brevity of life, the midcentury influence of new thinking, driven theologically by respected pastors like Horace Bushnell in Hartford, Connecticut, and Beecher and his sons, featured confidence in the love of God and in the moral educability of children. And the midcentury middle-class discovery of childhood as a period of life to be savored for its own sake coincided with the reform of common schools and a popular embracing of the accessible choral musical style advocated by Mason and his cohorts. Such convergences had huge import for the direction of Sunday schools and their role in American culture.

But by midcentury Protestants were demanding a great deal of their Sunday schools. Beecher believed they could "reconcile prosperity and purity" and promote "the intellectual and moral culture of the nation," and his Protestant cohorts in pulpits across the land worked to that end. Crosby was just one of thousands who enlisted in what amounted to a national Protestant crusade on behalf of the Sunday school. Influenced but not halted by the Civil War, that crusade retained its promise in spite of bewildering changes in American life. Postbellum Sunday schools proved particularly adept at effectively organizing religious impulses. The Baptist B. F. Jacobs introduced Rally Days and Decision Days as well as national Sunday school conventions, and the Methodists John Vincent and Lewis Miller promoted teacher training in creative ways that ultimately influenced the emergence of both religious and secular adult extension education and schemes for self-improvement.

The songs Crosby wrote especially for Sunday schools offer revealing glimpses into her hopes for America and her expectations for this world and the next. Her Sunday school lyrics also feature relationships with people dedicated particularly to Sunday school work, and they highlight some of the flourishing business ventures that prospered in the wake of the amazing growth of Sunday schools. Above all, they show the love for children that she professed lifelong. In response to the question, "Do you love children?" she once replied:

> Love the children? What a question!
> Cold indeed the heart must be
> That can turn without emotion
> From their laughter gushing free;
> Yes, with all my heart I love them;
> Bless the children, every one!
> I can be a child among them,
> And enjoy their freaks and fun.

Sources do not reveal much about Crosby's personal experience with Sunday schools, and the people with whom she worked directly were teachers and superintendents rather than scholars. In childhood she apparently had only slight exposure to Sunday schools, though she recalled in old age participating in Bible memorization contests for children. Such contests offered her a welcome opportunity to make a point she often emphasized: blind children could learn as well as anyone else. She proved it in Sunday school by taking prizes. In her productive years, her outpouring of lyrics celebrating the schools makes obvious her sympathy for their work, though her own regular enrollment in a school cannot be established until she passed middle age. When she turned eighty and moved to Bridgeport, she continued her affiliation, moving her membership to the school of the city's First Methodist Church. On the other hand, evidence assures us that she visited Sunday schools, attended Sunday school entertainments, provided special songs and poems for Sunday school anniversaries, and felt at home among the young people in whose interests Sunday schools professed to operate. She sent Sunday school scholars poetic greetings at Christmas through vehicles like the *Christian Advocate:*

> Children of the "great Republic"
> Which to us our fathers gave,
> Land of Sunday schools and Bibles,
> Land where rest the good and brave,
> Children of this "great Republic,"
> Fairest clime beneath the sun,
> In the heart of Fanny Crosby
> You are treasured, every one.

When Crosby agreed in 1864 to an ongoing relationship with Bradbury Publishing, much of her work focused in putting songs in the mouths of children. Bradbury's Sunday school hymnals looked much like his other hymnals — small and convenient to hold, featuring multiple stanzas of text, usually followed by a chorus, with music printed in four-part harmony. For the most part, words were printed between the musical lines, though some stanzas, especially of longer hymns, appeared below. Some of Crosby's best-known hymns first appeared in such Sunday school hymnals, and a significant number of the texts she first wrote with Sunday school scholars in mind found their way into other collections intended for use in social meetings or evangelistic services. (The Sunday school lyrics she wrote for her Methodist friend Phoebe Palmer Knapp, on the other hand, generally kept Knapp's "infant class" in mind, presenting simplified text and music.)

Crosby began working with Bradbury shortly before he published his *Golden Censer* (1864), and he incorporated a few of her texts into the book. Most of its contents had been written expressly for it. His preface clarified his perception of recent developments in Sunday school music, with unapologetic recognition of the importance of his own work to the movement:

> A great improvement has been made within a few years in the Music of our Sabbath Schools. This may be attributed in part at least to

the character of the music and hymns recently introduced. No longer resorting to low Negro melodies for their devotional hymns, our Schools have turned their attention to music of a higher order; music composed expressly for and adapted to the use of Sabbath Schools. It has perhaps been as much the privilege of the author of the *Golden Censer* as that of any one to contribute to this result. The hundreds of thousands of *Golden Chains, Showers,* and *Oriolas* [prior Bradbury hymnals] that have winged their way all over the land testify to the success of the enterprise.

In the *Golden Censer* Crosby's name appeared first over a hymn that conveyed the vision of America's hallowed history to which this circle of Sunday school promoters subscribed. Her words implied relationship between the intentions of the first English colonists and the objectives of Sunday schools. Praying children loved their country and prayed for the national welfare, thus standing center stage at mythical moments in the national past.

> When across the ocean wide where heaving waters flow
> Came the Mayflower o'er the tide with our fathers long ago,
> When they neared the rocky strand and their chorus rent the air,
> Children in that pilgrim band clasped their little hands in
>   prayer.

> When our country's banner bright told her deeds of noble
>   worth,
> Children hailed its radiant light, hailed the land that gave them
>   birth;
> Children now rejoice to hear all their youthful hearts can know
> And the precepts still revere of their fathers long ago.

Among her other compositions, Crosby offered a "dialogue song" that mimicked the call-and-response pattern beloved at camp meetings and made clear that Sunday school was no haphazard affair:

> What do you do at the Sabbath school, happy Sabbath school?
> First we sing a song of praise, then in prayer our voices raise;
> Then we each our lesson say, closing with another lay.

What do you learn at the Sabbath school, happy Sabbath school?
First we learn Commandments Ten, God's law sent by him to
  men,
Then what Christ did here below to redeem our souls from woe.

Why do you love the Sabbath school, happy Sabbath school?
There we with our Saviour meet, at the blood-bought mercy seat
Where he ever whispers, "Come to thy blissful heavenly home."

The characterization of Sunday school as a happy place punctu-ated Crosby's songs. She contrasted the Sunday school's stable, happy, peaceful environment to the troubles and challenges that text writers assumed beset scholars during the week. Happiness resulted from lov-ing, caring individuals and from the proclamation of a joyous gospel. It was a matter of disposition and choice: scholars could trade preoccu-pation with life's difficulties for a communal experience replete with assurance and purpose. Sunday school hymns played a central role in creating community and providing metaphors for grappling with fear, poverty, uncertainty, and hopelessness.

When Bradbury's health deteriorated rapidly in 1866, he gave up much of his work, though not the editing of several new Sunday school hymnals. *Golden Shower and Censer* combined two of his earlier successes and added songs appropriate for missionary, temperance, and anniversary meetings as well as special numbers for the Sunday school concerts he wanted to promote. By familiarizing children with hymns appropriate to a wider variety of gatherings, the collection aimed to ease children's way into the sanctuary and other religious gatherings. The assumption that familiarity with music enabled blend-ing into a community resulted in the inclusion of texts later genera-tions would associate with adult gatherings rather than with Sunday schools.

To this collection Crosby contributed several temperance num-bers, suggesting the schools' awareness of children's exposure to alco-hol. Her words urged ("Oh, be warned of your danger, nor slight the day of grace,/The wine cup leads to sin and woe"), rallied ("Friends of temperance, quick to arms!/We must struggle for the right"), mor-alized ("Sad is the drunkard's life,/wasting in crime,/far from the path of right,/reckless of time"), and instructed ("Go where he sits alone,/burdened with care;/tell him his sinful course,/plead with him there"). Mindful of high childhood mortality, she also composed a ballad suggested by a real incident at the deathbed of a Sunday school scholar. Its emotion-riddled text made plain the fragility of life and the sorrows that beset the working-class New Yorkers among whom she lived:

Mother, tell me, do not tremble, hold me in your dear embrace.
Must I leave you? Am I dying? I can read it in your face.
All is well. My soul is happy. I am not afraid to go.
I have made my peace with Jesus; that was settled long ago.

Here our kindred ties are broken. Here our fondest hopes decay;
In that land of sacred pleasure God will wipe all tears away.
Those we love will bid us welcome in the regions of the blest;
Sorrow there can never enter; there the weary will find rest.

Crosby imagined Sunday school as a happy haven, especially for the children of the poor: "All are happy, all are glad; not a single brow is sad." To make the point that scholars could take happiness from the schools to the world as a form of Christian service, Crosby reminded children that smiles cost nothing but yielded much: "Scatter smiles," she wrote. "Your heart may never know/what a joy they may carry to weary ones/who are pale with want and woe." She put into easily learned verse reminders of the basic elements of the Protestant evangelical message, often making a corporate, not an individual, appeal that urged assembled children to united resolve:

Let us all from day to day try to live like Jesus;
Hand in hand we'll go in our path below.
Let us one and all engage that like friends and brothers
We in peace will live and our foes forgive. . . .

As tens of thousands of his books spread such sentiments among the nation's youth, Bradbury was fighting a losing battle with tuberculosis. He spent much of 1867 in the South, and a partial restoration to health enabled him to complete work on a new Sunday school hymnal, *Bradbury's Fresh Laurels for the Sabbath School, a New and Extensive Col-*

lection of Music and Hymns Prepared Expressly for Sabbath Schools. Crosby had been working with him for barely three years, but she shared fully his view that the purpose of a Sunday school hymnal was to "lead [children] directly to their loving Saviour." Convinced that children could have a vibrant and lasting relationship with Christ, Bradbury intended his hymnals to offer the gospel in "direct, practical, pointed" words. He hoped for a marriage of text and tune that would fasten the message on children's minds. "Through the medium of the tune," he believed, "the hymn will be stereotyped upon the memory." What children might not apprehend immediately would be imprinted on the mind, ready to be recalled when needed. Bradbury offered text to some standard tunes, but again he made an emphatic case that "to keep up the interest in the school, *new music,* and GOOD music, suited to the tastes and adapted to the capacities of the children, must be frequently introduced." Together with simple tunes — as Bradbury put it, songs so simple "that he who runs may read" (Habakkuk 2:2) — he also offered challenging tunes that stretched children's abilities within an appropriate range. "Such pieces will gradually introduce them to the regular songs of the Church," he opined. His books, then, had a didactic as well as immediate purpose. Bradbury, the children's choir conductor and normal school teacher, intended to provide what Sunday schools needed as well as to use Sunday school music to introduce standard Christian hymns.

In her text for the first hymn in *Fresh Laurels,* Crosby elaborated on the book's title. In these years immediately following the Civil War when wreath laying and laurel decking were commonplace, Crosby summoned children to bring "laurels, fresh laurels for the Sunday School." A few pages into the hymnal Bradbury provided a jocular tune for Crosby's hymn "Away! Away":

> Away! Away! Not a moment to linger.
> Haste we now with footsteps free
> Where those who love in the vineyard to labor
> Wait for you and me.
> To the Sunday school rejoicing we will go;
> 'Tis a place where all are happy here below,
> Where the way of life we learn to know,
> And seek our home above.

Bradbury's death in January 1868 did not end the string of Sunday school hymnals that rolled off his presses. Two of Crosby's closest friends among Bradbury's cohorts, Baptists William Doane and Robert Lowry, took over the business of editing some of the most successful Sunday school hymnals that his successors, Lucius Biglow and Sylvester Main (once Crosby's playmate on the Ridgefield Common), published after 1868. Doane was a Cincinnati businessman and lay Baptist leader; Lowry was a Baptist pastor. Main, a prominent church musician, meanwhile, received from Bradbury's widow the rights to his catalogue of music. With the merchant Biglow, he made this catalogue (second in size only to Mason's) the lucrative basis of the new company's inventory. The new releases followed Bradbury's style and soon rivaled the phenomenal sales figures his own books had reached. In 1869, in a tribute to their influential friend a year after his death, Doane and Lowry compiled a large number of unpublished Bradbury tunes with other fresh material, much of it from Crosby, into a hymnal they called *Bright Jewels.* Two years later their next release, *Pure Gold,* achieved "unprecedented popularity." *Royal Diadem* followed in 1873. By 1875 sales figures for the three combined exceeded 1.7 million copies. Such "extraordinary success," the editors boasted, "indicates the unabated confidence of Sunday School workers in our efforts to furnish them with the best material for the Service of Praise." Biglow and Main's only major competitor was the John Church Company of Cincinnati.

Brightest and Best, Doane and Lowry's offering for 1875, took its title from Reginald Heber's Epiphany hymn addressed to the star that guided the wise men, "Brightest and Best of the Sons of the Morning." Crosby, then fifty-five years old, had been diligently churning out hymn texts for over a decade, and this 1875 hymnal premiered some of the era's enduring favorites from her pen, songs future generations did not relegate to Sunday school hymnals. They made useful Sunday school numbers, especially among those who argued that "It is a cruel wrong to any child to deprive him of the opportunity to become familiar with hymns." They include: "All the Way My Saviour Leads Me" ("All the way my Saviour leads me;/What have I to ask beside?/Can I doubt His tender mercy,/Who through life has been my guide?"), "Saviour, More Than Life to Me" ("Every day, every hour let me feel Thy cleansing power/May thy tender love to me/bind me closer, closer, Lord, to Thee"), and "To God Be the Glory":

To God be the glory, great things He hath done,
So loved He the world that He gave us His Son
Who yielded His life an atonement for sin
And opened the life-gate that all may go in.

Their inclusion (with tunes by the hymnal's editors Lowry and Doane) perhaps illustrates the effort to offer music useful to both Sunday schools and social meetings. The ploy had distinct marketing advantages as well as Christian educational intent. These Crosby texts might invoke Christian experience beyond the range of Sunday school scholars and stretch their conceptions of Christian living.

Crosby's many contributions to *Brightest and Best* suggest the basic advice she and two of her closest associates thought appropriate to the Sunday schools' purpose. Lowry and Doane intended their hymnals to sketch the broad framework of the Christian life, giving Sunday school scholars something to which to aspire — glimpses of spiritual realities beyond their present experience. The editors believed that hymns should provide language for the Christian life into which Sunday school pupils would grow, and so Crosby — now a much more experienced crafter of Sunday school text than she had been in her early attempts in 1864 — wrote out of her own heart as well as in a didactic voice.

She crafted for the nation's children the same message of hope for this life and the next that would mark the hymns she wrote for other purposes. Her stark contrasts between the pleasures of the hereafter — beauty, life, plenty, glory, sight — and the trials of day-to-day existence — the poverty of alcohol-blighted homes, the ravages of epidemics, the hopelessness of tenement house life, the frightening specter of unemployment, the uncertainty of life — were characteristic of the larger genre of Sunday school hymns. Crosby's lyrics especially breathed fervent aspirations to future bliss. She described heaven as the hope that spurred the pilgrim on, persuaded the sinner to repent, and consoled the suffering, a message her texts placed in the mouths of children as well as adults. In Crosby's view the thought of heaven, the place of eternal joy, filled the believer's soul with empowering delight here and now:

There's a city that looks o'er the valley of death,
And its glories may never be told.

There the sun never sets, and the leaves never fade
In that beautiful city of gold.

Crosby's images of heaven and the life journey that led there borrowed freely from John Bunyan's *Pilgrim's Progress*, a text well known
to Sunday school boosters of her day. Crosby assured America's youth
that they could embrace death as the way to life, sure in the knowledge
that Christ was with them. And the end she promised resembled a
grand Sunday school reunion:

We shall meet on the banks of the river,
Happy, happy there forever more;
We shall dwell with the angels and join with choral song
Our loved ones, loved ones gone before.

If heaven, the place of reunion, rest, and joy, defied description —
if no words could capture its lavish display — this life was another matter. Crosby knew firsthand the living experiences of many children in
urban Sunday schools, and if her words about a blissful hereafter
promised the plenty and beauty that eluded many scholars in the
world, her descriptions of this life resonated with their experience. She
urged "poor souls" to "fly to the Ark of refuge" to shelter themselves
from life's billows. One "fainted 'neath one's load" or "walked a rugged road." "Worn by care and sorrow," with eyes dimmed by tears,
children needed solace, strength, comfort, safety, someone beside them
to care about them, quicken resolve, and dispel fear. Crosby hymns assured children that Christ did just that by his presence with them on
life's journey. She promised no health and wealth, but she guaranteed
sustaining grace. She also assured them that God rewarded persistence
in Christian pilgrimage with ever richer experiences of grace:

Brighter and brighter the way is growing,
We will journey on;
Purer and clearer the streams are flowing,
We will journey on.

Brightest and Best continued Crosby's characteristic exaltation in
redemption with her Methodist-style emphasis on the blood of Christ:

We're saved by the blood that was drawn from the side
Of Jesus our Lord when he languished and died.

We're saved by the blood, we are sealed by its power;
'Tis life to the soul and its hope every hour.

That blood is a fount where the vilest may go
And wash till their souls shall be whiter than snow.

Crosby also put into the mouths of the youngest scholars simple echoes of the gospel call:

Our Saviour loves the children,
On them his hands he laid,
Within his arms he held them,
And blessed them while he prayed
And still his mercy calls them;
Just now we hear him say
"I want your hearts, dear children,
I want your love today."

Coming, yes, we're coming,
Dear Saviour to thy fold.

Invitations for older children and adults often took the form of questions and warnings: "Why unbelieving?" "Still undecided?" "Do not delay." "Saving faith in Jesus,/This is what we need," she insisted, and she followed invitations with assurances: "Yes, there is pardon for you./. . . For Jesus has died to redeem you/And offers full pardon to you." But Sunday school workers hoped for more than moments of decision: they endeavored to cultivate moral firmness to do what was right and unwavering purpose to Christianize the world, and Crosby came beside them in these tasks, too. She celebrated the burgeoning missionary movement of her day — "Across the blue waters the message of grace/O'er kingdom and empire is flying apace" — and reminded scholars that "for the heart and hands there is work to do." Closer by:

God has told us that the poor are always with us,
He confides them to our kindness and our care;

Love your neighbor is the second great commandment,
All around us we can find him everywhere.

Crosby's personal commitment to duty shone through in her words to children. Everyone had a place and a divinely designated task, and she admonished youth to take on responsibility in church and society. "Go on in the glorious cause of the right," she implored; or,

Jesus hath appointed work for every one
All the day we labor till the work be done;
Faith and grace will teach us how the work to do,
Faith will help us onward,
Grace will bear us through.

Perhaps recalling her early reluctance to speak publicly of her faith, Crosby advised scholars to give voice to their spiritual experiences: "Now just a word for Jesus," she coaxed, "Twill help us on our way." In her mind every member played a role in building and sustaining Christian community. Crosby provided prayers, words of comfort, text that probed and prodded, and hymns that entreated. She warned and admonished, but she did not invoke hellfire or damnation. Her most dire images featured lost, storm-tossed, fear-riddled people to whom she held forth promises of rest, sustenance, and guidance, all assured in Christ. In this she resembled her most famous evangelical contemporary, evangelist Dwight L. Moody.

Crosby contributed far more texts than anyone else to *Brightest and Best,* and if her lyrics had a single overarching theme, one answer to all life's woes, it was the all-sufficiency of Christ.

Jesus in our trials, Jesus in our cares,
Jesus in our praises, Jesus in our prayers,
Jesus in our sorrows, Jesus in our song,
O 'tis always Jesus all our way along.

In 1889 Lowry and Doane released *Bright Array: A New Collection of Sunday School Songs,* into a market that remained steady ("healthful," as they put it). Fresh material now seemed to them, as it had to Bradbury, "a moral necessity," since even excellent songs, repeated too often, lost effect. "Hence the need of providing a continuous supply to meet a constantly increasing demand," they explained. As editors of some of the most circulated Sunday school hymnals, Lowry and Doane felt an obligation to "lead young people through the safe grounds of gospel hymnody," but they insisted that they had never led without keeping in touch with those following. Their regular involvement in Sunday schools, they felt, fitted them to make suitable selections. Like its predecessors, *Bright Array* featured Crosby texts, this time adding encouragement for financial support of the schools ("Now our pennies bringing/all of us are singing/cheerful givers we will be/for the Sunday school") and prayers for school leaders ("Cheer our superintendent, Lord, O cheer him with thy word"; and "Bless our teachers; may they share Thy ever watchful care"). As always, Crosby's songs about conduct urged cheerfulness and unity:

Hearts and hands to Jesus gladly we will give,
In the path of duty walking while we live;
Cheering on the sad ones, lifting those that fall,
Shining like the sunbeams, doing good to all.

Her Sunday school hymns insisted on honesty, diligence, responsibility, and kindness.

In 1870 Doane edited for Biglow and Main a book envisioned for use in the proliferating "Christian Associations" of the era. *Songs of Devotion* showed especially well Crosby's full-blown devotion to temperance: "Onward! Onward! Temperance band/Fling your colors far and wide/Though oppressed on every hand/Bold and fearless stem the tide," or "Cold water army is our name/For volunteers we call/ We'll conquer! We'll conquer/Our banner floating in the breeze/The ensign of the free." "Song is a sentiment maker," Women's Christian Temperance Union President Frances Willard acknowledged in 1897, encouraging temperance hymns. Sunday school musicians worked diligently to end alcohol abuse by teaching children about its alarming effects.

The success of Bradbury Publishing and Biglow and Main amazed contemporaries. "In the days of our fathers it was a matter of astonishment if the demand for any musical production exceeded 10,000," one commentator in the late 1870s mused in *The Guide to Holiness*. "Now, one house alone has bound hundreds of thousands, and even millions. We refer to the world-renowned firm of Biglow & Main."

Crosby's arrangement with Bradbury and his successors required her to provide the publisher with two hymn texts every week. In return they paid her a small wage. She gave them more than they could use but was also free beyond her contract to work with anyone she chose. Since she had several friends who were Sunday school superintendents, most of the texts she prepared specifically for children passed through one of their hands. Doane and Crosby collaborated both privately in Doane's Northern Baptist endeavors and through Biglow and Main. Joseph and Phoebe Knapp sought her services as well for the hymnals Phoebe readied for the large Sunday school they supervised at St. John's Methodist Episcopal Church in Brooklyn. One of these, *Notes of Joy* (1869), was very much a family enterprise — edited by Phoebe, copyrighted by her millionaire husband Joseph, and published by Phoebe's brother, Walter Palmer. Phoebe "tested" most of the contents in her Sunday school before offering the songs to the world. "No empty rhymes, nor tunes which are mere jingles," she promised. "Nothing wearisome, nothing dull."

The well-connected Knapps offered a warm endorsement from the saintly Methodist bishop Matthew Simpson, who commended recent efforts to prepare texts and tunes suitable for children's worship. *Notes of Joy*, he observed, was prompted "by a mother's love as she sang to her own dear children," by the needs of her Sunday school infant department, and by Phoebe Knapp's larger circle of friends. The reader who turned to the first selection found the unusual occurrence of text by Crosby set to music by her husband, Alexander van Alstine (who provided several tunes for the collection):

> Notes of joy for the Sabbath home,
> The home where the children meet;
> Where buds that bloom for a purer clime
> Burst forth in that dear retreat.
>
> Notes of joy for the earnest hearts
> That work for the souls of youth;
> That guide their thoughts to the Lamb of God,
> Their steps to the fount of truth.

Crosby's enthusiasm for Sunday school brought her invitations to visit and address Sunday school scholars in the greater New York area. In October 1872, for example, she provided poems and hymns for the fourth anniversary of the Morning Star Sunday school, a mission endeavor at Seventh Avenue and Twenty-sixth Street. In the spring of 1894 — her seventy-fourth year — she took the ferry to Brooklyn to visit the 600 Sunday school members at the Ross Street Presbyterian Church, just across Bedford Avenue from the Knapps' mansion. She brought a hymn for the school to learn — "The Cross and Crown," used again in 1895 at the Sunday school's thirtieth anniversary.

In 1899, with Crosby's eightieth birthday approaching, her public attributed her fame in no small measure to her hymns sung for more than thirty years in the nation's Sunday schools.

8 Collaborators

My song shall be of Jesus,
His mercy crowns my days,
He fills my cup with blessings
And tunes my heart to praise.

Regular work with Bradbury and his successors brought Crosby into a network of tune and text writers with whom she worked for the rest of her life. She had not aimed specifically for a career in hymn writing. In fact, in her youth she expressed no goals beyond an education and general "usefulness." She seized opportunities as they came along, exploited some of them, and at midlife had reason to be pleased with her accomplishments. Few Americans could boast of conversations with political and cultural icons, much less tell of several dinners at the White House. Her poetry had brought modest literary fame, especially when set to music by George Root. Though she was the first to admit that it was not consistently "great," it often appealed to popular tastes, and that meant it was in demand. And she had the satisfaction of her own education multiplied by the opportunity to teach other blind students. She professed to be happily married. All told, she had come a long way from the rugged hills of Southeast.

When in old age she wrote her memoirs, Crosby seemed to discount all her accomplishments before hymn writing. In her view she had found her career at the age of forty-four. One of her autobiographies identified 1864 as the year she "commenced the real and most important work of my life." In old age she recalled her admiration for the grand hymns of Watts, Wesley, and Montgomery but confessed it had not occurred to her that she could "write hymns that people would care to sing." "Still," she continued in 1903, "as the sweetness and grandeur of the religion of our Saviour sank into my heart, I felt more and more like putting my feelings into rhythm." She later identified as her first attempt an evening hymn based on Psalm 4:8 ("I will both lay me down in peace and sleep; for thou, Lord, only, makest me to dwell in safety"), published in her first book, *The Blind Girl:*

Drawn is the curtain of the night,
Oh, 'tis the sacred hour of rest;
Sweet hour, I hail thee with delight,
Thrice welcome to my weary breast.

O God to Thee my fervent prayer
I offer, kneeling at Thy feet;
Tho' humbly breathed, O deign to hear —
Smile on me from the mercy seat!

While angels round their watches keep,
Whose harps Thy praise unceasing swell,
"I lay me down in peace and sleep,"
For Thou in safety mak'st me dwell.

Drawn is the curtain of the night,
Thou bid'st creation silent be,
And now, with holy calm delight,
Father, I would commune with Thee.

Shepherd of Israel, deign to keep
And guard my soul from every ill;

Thus will I lay me down and sleep
For Thou in safety mak'st me dwell.

From 1864 Crosby attributed her ongoing vigor and inspiration in the writing of hymns to the memory of a dream — "really more than a dream — more even than a vision: it was a kind of reality — with my senses all at their fullest, though the body was asleep." In this state she approached heaven, pausing at a river which her guide did not permit her to cross. For a moment, though, heaven's gates opened and she heard a burst of music. The impression lingered for the rest of her life: "chords of melody such as I never had supposed could exist anywhere," she recalled in 1903. "The very recollection of it thrills me."

Once she demonstrated her ability to deliver text that suited contemporary religious demand, Crosby had work that occupied her for the rest of her life. Yet in important ways her success as a hymn writer built on her earlier achievements that had produced self-confidence, honed her communications skills, and exposed her to the worlds of publishing and performance. She was a known quantity when she arrived on Bradbury's doorstep, already well connected to the larger musical enterprise of which he was part.

When Bradbury contracted with Crosby, he gave her a regular outlet for a mode of expression in which she was most adept and for which her exposure (through the Institution for the Blind and elsewhere) to an array of Protestant preaching had prepared her. Her work habits harked back many years and always began with prayer. Sometimes words came quickly to her in a form that satisfied her; at other times, getting them just right required effort. She liked to think through difficult texts (often "difficult" because a tune demanded an awkward meter) at night when Manhattan was quiet and she could sit undisturbed. Oddly enough she felt most comfortable holding a small notebook in her hand, although she never wrote down her own texts. (Despite her education, her handwriting was barely legible, and on legal documents she signed her name with an X witnessed by friends.) And so she composed text and filed it away in what she termed "the library" of her mind until someone came by to take her dictation. She edited her poems in her mind, too, working on some for several days before she dictated anything. Crosby envisioned her mind as a library, and she trained herself to wander among its shelves and recall stored information at will. When an affable scribe appeared, she was likely to dictate several separate poems at once, sometimes as many as seven a day. The manuscripts of her dictated poems show that she occasionally edited as she dictated.

But Crosby could summon her muse for hurried daytime jobs, too. "Her versatility is well-nigh incredible," a *New York Times* reporter later noted. "Her pious muse is always ready, and can work without meals or sleep or any of that spirit-moving sentiment supposed to govern the versemaker." "Hymns written while you wait" seemed to the reporter an apt trademark. Crosby's friend Robert Lowry offered a revealing comment and an "incident" of a hymn: "She does not seem to need a special inspiration in order to write. She has her moods, and therefore her verses are not of uniform grade. But she is very susceptible to a suggestion from without. One day, while [she] meditat[ed] on the leadings of Providence, a friend came into her room and gave her ten dollars. The unexpected gift awakened a train of thought that formulated itself in one of her best hymns, 'All the Way My Saviour Leads Me.'"

Although from 1864 Crosby wrote under contract with Bradbury and his successors, from the start their larger network provided an expanding market for her hymn texts. The globe-trotting Methodist singing evangelist Philip Phillips favored her lyrics when he did not use his own, and he featured them in his evangelistic services as well as in the hymnals he edited. Revered as one of the first "to sing the gospel," this "singing pilgrim" was not an educated musician, but he used to advantage his "voice of peculiar influence" to "impress earnestness" on his hearers. Abraham Lincoln himself jump-started Phillips's career when this relatively unknown singer rendered "Your Mission" at a mass anniversary meeting for the Christian Commission in Washington, D.C. Moved, Lincoln scribbled a note asking Phillips to repeat the song at the close of the meeting.

> Go and toil in any vineyard,
> Do not fear to do or dare,
> If you want a field of labor,
> You can find it anywhere.

Lincoln's request effectively transformed Phillips into the sensation of the moment, and Phillips followed his own admonition and seized the opportunities that followed.

Another son of New England, Phillips traced his ancestry to the Massachusetts Bay Colony where Nicholas Phillips and his wife Elizabeth Jewson settled in the 1630s. One branch of the family left Massachusetts in 1816 for Chautauqua County in western upstate New York. There Philip Phillips was born in 1834. After studies with Mason, Phillips began conducting singing schools in western New York. A Baptist from childhood, Phillips joined the Methodist church in 1860. In 1861 he moved his family to Cincinnati, where he opened a music store and published *Musical Leaves* (1861), a songbook that sold some 700,000 copies. His Civil War work with the Christian Commission brought him opportunities in other parts of the country, and in 1866 he moved to New York. In 1868 he toured England and also compiled for the British Sunday School Union *The American Sacred Songster,* a collection that sold over one million copies.

A leisurely Singing Tour around the World, 1873-75, brought him to Australia, New Zealand, India, Egypt, Palestine, and the great cities of Europe. Phillips developed a program in which "each song was a sermon and an inspiration toward the spiritual and heavenly." In aggregate, his song services — 972 in Britain alone — netted well over $100,000 for charities. He returned to the States with an enhanced reputation that translated into more invitations than he could accept. He often gave Crosby specific directions, as in this typical note: "I want you to write me a new temperance song . . . about four eight-line verses or eight four-line verses. I want it to describe an intemperate life, in high life, commencing with the description of a young man whose parents are noble and wealthy and they look to the son with great expectations when lo they first discover he shows signs of intemperance." The rest can be imagined. But Phillips specified more than just the topic and form. "I want a fine poem," he wrote. "Have it finished by April 20th when I will call. Don't disappoint me here."

Crosby took pride in later relating that she once composed forty poems for titles provided by Phillips without dictating any of them until all were complete. Phillips was so pleased that he sent an additional forty titles that Crosby treated in the same manner. Her explanation revealed the rigorous ordering of the life of her mind: "The mind appears to me like a great storehouse into which we place various articles for safe keeping and sometimes even forget that they are there, but, sooner or later, we find them; and so I lay aside my intellectual wares for some future day of need; and in the mean time often forget them, until the call comes for a hymn."

At Bradbury's office in June 1864, Crosby met another of Bradbury's friends with whom she soon collaborated, Theodore E. Perkins. The son of a Baptist pastor, Perkins was born in Poughkeepsie, New York, in 1831 but moved to Manhattan when his father accepted a call to Berean Baptist Church in 1839. In New York he pursued the unexpected opportunity to study music — both voice and piano. He and his wife (a capable musician in her own right) attended the Normal Academy of Music conducted by Mason and Root in North Reading in 1856, and by 1859 he was ready to assume the oversight with Bradbury of the Normal Academy of Music in Geneseo, New York, a school he led at least through 1863. Perkins's hymnals reached phenomenal sales figures and featured the topics familiar to Crosby through her work with Bradbury. Over a long and distinguished career, Perkins served several Brooklyn and Philadelphia churches as music director. Students at Princeton University, Lafayette College, Union Theological Seminary (New York), Crozier Seminary, and Madison (now Colgate) University knew him as voice instructor. He established and chaired the music department at Temple University. Perkins also edited a long list of hymnals, some designed especially for Sunday schools. They bore titles typical of the era: *Shining Star, Golden Promise, The Royal Standard, Sabbath Carols*. Perhaps his best-known tune was for "Jesus of Nazareth Passeth By," a song popularized by Ira Sankey in the Moody revivals of the 1870s. (Sankey called it his "banner song for eight years.")

A reluctant traveler, Perkins was best known through his writing, editing, and teaching. He enlisted Crosby's help in several projects, and she provided him with texts for hymns, Sunday school songs, Civil War ballads, and rousing temperance tunes geared to a generation emerging from the Civil War:

> All hail! Ye vet'ran soldiers,
> March onward to the field.
> Defend your rights, defend your cause
> With buckler, sword and shield;
> Before our glorious colors
> The traitor foe shall fall;

Cold water army is our name,
For volunteers we call.

Or,

In the battle strong unite,
Brave the tempter undismayed,
Though he revel with delight
O'er the ruin he has made.
Withered hopes and plaintive cries,
Feelings crushed in deepest woe,
Blighted hearts and broken ties
Call for vengeance on the foe.

These male tunesmiths — most of whom also occasionally crafted text — took advantage of Crosby's ability to provide rhymes on any topic they chose. Gender conventions did not seem to intrude on their relationships. Her blindness may have made it easier to break with custom and spend time working with one or another of them in one of Bradbury's offices in lower Manhattan. It made her exceptional and permitted her to do things other women of her generation might not. She was also a married woman, though through her most active years she lived only intermittently with her husband. By the time she entered this male circle, she was well into middle age. When the company published a new hymnal, contributors gathered to sing through it. Few, if any, other women graced these scenes, but Crosby easily held her own.

For the most part, the tune writers on whom Bradbury relied had reputations apart from their work with hymns. They were players in the tight network of teachers, vocalists, performers, evangelists, and activists who shared participation in the expanding world of music education as well as in such popular causes of the day as temperance and Sunday schools. Most (like Crosby) wrote secular as well as sacred tunes and texts and enjoyed established reputations for their part in the era's popular culture, normal institutes, and music conventions. The breadth of their endeavors beyond the church assured their music a hearing in religious circles (at least among the rank and file) and lent legitimacy to the new efforts in popular sacred music.

Crosby, too, had found a small role in the secular, popular side of these endeavors, especially in collaboration with Root. Through Bradbury she now came into regular contact with many established tunesmiths and musical innovators. Crosby brought to her work an uncanny ability to versify in any meter the new tunes and choruses required. She had her finger on the pulse of popular tastes, and she wrote out of her knowledge of Manhattan's Protestants as well as from the depths of her own experience. She had few distractions and could devote her time to the enterprise. The combination of Crosby and tunesmiths whose work was known by both the secular and the religious publics generated some of evangelicalism's most enduring favorites, plus thousands of now-dated but useful songs for Crosby's own generation.

At New Jersey's famous Ocean Grove camp meeting in the late summer of 1877, Crosby first met two prolific Methodist hymn crafters, John Sweney and William J. Kirkpatrick. The two had formed the habit of collaborating annually on a new gospel hymnal. They also (together and separately) offered collections favored by particular evangelists and opened new markets to Crosby's texts. The Ocean Grove Camp Meeting — especially devoted to holiness and graced by Walter and Phoebe Palmer themselves (Phoebe died in 1874, but her place was taken by her sister, Sarah Lankford, who married Walter) — was a thrilling event that occupied the hot days of August. In 1877 Crosby was part of the largest group assembled to date at the thriving Christian seaside resort. Organizers (like the hymn text writer Mary James ["All for Jesus"]) thought they sensed beforehand an "incoming tide of worldliness," but "mighty prayer" brought "a tidal wave of salvation sweeping over the camp — the very same power they had at Pentecost." Amid such "old-fashioned Methodism," Crosby met the venerable round-the-world evangelist Bishop William Taylor, and thrilled to the preaching of a roster of first-order Methodist orators. Some 30,000 people preserved the sanctity of the Sabbath on 19 August, the "great day of the feast," forgoing boating, bathing, trading, and revelry in favor of earnest sermons, thrilling testimonies, and rousing song. Diligent seekers after "heart purity" had all along enjoyed daily meetings at 5:30 A.M. dedicated to their chosen theme in the cavernous Tabernacle. That Sunday a preaching service at 10:30 A.M. was followed by a mass meeting that attracted 15,000 to the beach in midafternoon, and the day ended with a stirring evangelistic challenge by Taylor at the Tabernacle. Such scenes — and especially the flow of words that poured from platform orators — left their mark on Crosby's future texts. She summarized her impressions in a poem she called "Ocean Grove":

> To see those cottages and tents,
> Where praise ascended to the sky,
> Was bliss; ah more; 'twas heaven below;
> In such a scene how sweet to die!
> We heard the Word of Life proclaimed,
> We heard the deep and fervent prayer,
> We heard with hearts so filled with love
> They scarce another drop could bear.
> God bless the church that keeps alive
> From year to year that custom old
> Of tenting in some rural wood,
> And gathering wanderers to the fold.

After her visit to Ocean Grove in 1877, Crosby collaborated most often with the Methodist professor and tune writer Kirkpatrick. A Pennsylvanian by birth, Kirkpatrick was a talented violinist and cellist who devoted his life to choral and Sunday school music, especially in Methodist congregations and Holiness movement settings. A member of the Handel and Haydn Society, he cherished the choral works of the European masters, sharing the commitments that animated people like Mason and Bradbury. But unlike them, he was a Methodist with a bent toward holiness, and his hymns often reflected these populist impulses. Both he and Crosby had a ready wit, and they enjoyed a close personal relationship, often using pseudonyms when corresponding. But most often Kirkpatrick was "Kirkie" to her. Their easy relationship turned productive at unexpected moments. A conversation about growing weary of earthly pleasures once prompted Kirkpatrick to observe: "Well, we are never weary of the grand old song." Crosby responded with "Glory to God, hallelujah," and so was born a lively "shouting Methodist" song brimming with echoes of the Tabernacle at Ocean Grove:

We are never, never weary of the grand old song,
Glory to God, hallelujah!
We can sing it in the Spirit as we march along,
Glory to God, hallelujah!

Oh, the children of the Lord have a right to shout and sing,
For the way is growing bright, and our souls are on the wing;
We are going by and by to the palace of the King.
Glory to God, hallelujah!

A reporter for the *New York Times* found Crosby at the holiness meeting at Ocean Grove in 1892 and took the occasion to fill an entire column of fine print with a tribute:

> Among the cottagers at Ocean Grove each Summer can be seen a unique and interesting old lady whose name is known in Sunday school and church circles the world over and one can safely say that she has more hymns to her credit than any mortal living or dead. . . . No happier or merrier creature lives than this remarkable old lady. She loves her work, glories in the assurance that her life has not been barren of good results. . . . She laughs at the notion of growing old. During the Ocean Grove season she holds a continuous reception to oblige the hundreds of Christian visitors who clamor for a chance to meet and thank the venerable blind maker of verses that have echoed through every Sunday school in the land.

Crosby could still be found at Ocean Grove in 1899. That year she made a point of celebrating the organization of an Ocean Grove tradition, the Young People's Meeting, by writing original verses for costumed virtues — Faith, Hope, Charity — to chant.

One can hear echoes of Ocean Grove in many Crosby texts, especially those set to music by Kirkpatrick. Her outpouring of praise, "A Wonderful Savior Is Jesus My Lord," is set to Kirkpatrick, a tune named after its composer, and the text, though widely sung, hints again at Crosby's holiness sympathies:

With numberless blessings each moment He crowns,
And filled with His fullness divine,

I sing in my rapture, "O glory to God
For such a Redeemer as mine!"

Though Crosby wrote many texts on request, she sometimes composed lines that welled from her own life's circumstances. For many years her poem "Hold Thou My Hand, I Am So Weak and Helpless" enjoyed popularity in English and other languages. It arose from a time of despair that overtook the generally cheerful Crosby. At length she believed that her prayer, "Dear Lord, hold Thou my hand," brought renewed confidence, and her praise "sang itself" easily into the lines of a hymn for which Hubert Main provided solemn music. Crosby cherished a note from the widow of the famous English Baptist Charles Spurgeon thanking her for the comforting and uplifting words of this hymn-prayer. This hymn's language seemed particularly poignant to singers who remembered Crosby's blindness:

Hold Thou my hand; so weak I am, and helpless,
I dare not take one step without Thy aid;
Hold Thou my hand, for then, O loving Savior,
No dread of ill shall make my soul afraid.

Hold Thou my hand, and closer, closer draw me
To Thy dear self — my hope, my joy, my all;
Hold Thou my hand, lest haply I should wander,
And, missing Thee, my trembling feet should fall.

Hold Thou my hand; the way is dark before me
Without the sunlight of Thy face divine;
But when by faith I catch its radiant glory,
What heights of joy, what rapturous songs are mine!

Sometimes sermons inspired Crosby's hymn texts. She credited her distant cousin Howard Crosby's comments on grace with prompting one of the "tenderest" of her songs, the beloved "Saved by Grace":

Some day the silver cord will break,
And I no more as now shall sing.
But, O, the joy when I shall wake

Within the palace of the King!
And I shall see Him face to face,
And tell the story — saved by grace.

Some day my earthly house will fall,
I cannot tell how soon 'twill be,
But this I know — my all in all
Has now in heaven a place for me,
And I shall see Him face to face,
And tell the story — saved by grace.

Crosby said she composed those lines after mulling over a Howard Crosby sermon on grace, and she kept them for herself. Then one summer night in 1894, during the annual Northfield Conference in D. L. Moody's Massachusetts hometown of Northfield, she stood unexpectedly at the podium with no remarks prepared. She mused briefly on the fact that the first face she would ever see would be Jesus', then recited the poem. Someone took the words down in shorthand, and the text became public property rather than Crosby's personal solace.

A watch night sermon by Presbyterian pastor Theodore Cuyler inspired "Press toward the Mark." Singing evangelist Philip Phillips's farewell after an afternoon visit — "Good night until we meet in the morning" — birthed a hymn by that title. Brooklyn Tabernacle pastor DeWitt Talmage's famous illustrations often spurred Crosby on and prompted musings on the world of songwriting of which she was now part. Even "the humblest fellow ministers of song," she ventured, "take us to heights of which the soul often dreams, yet rarely attains, in fact to those mansions of the blest where there are always light and warmth and love; where the thirst of weary pilgrims is quenched by draughts of mountain springs; and where this mortal spirit puts on its immortality."

Each of these relationships (and many others) expanded Crosby's public in different ways and demanded different kinds of hymns. Her friend (and distant relation) Mary Currier had enjoyed popularity as a secular vocalist until she embraced Christian perfection and changed her mind about "worldly" music. Repeated requests for secular numbers prompted her to ask Crosby for a song explaining her new views. The result did more than meet the immediate need. It also captured a vital part of holiness piety that resonated with emerging proto-fundamentalist sensibilities.

> I cannot sing the old songs,
> For me their charm is o'er,
> My earthly harp is laid aside,
> I wake its chords no more.
> The precious blood of Christ my Lord
> Has cleansed and made me free;
> And taught my heart a new song
> Of His great love for me.

Currier's schedule also gave Crosby a chance to try her hand at an ecumenical hymn — one intended to promote "brotherly love" and greater cooperation among Jews, various Protestants, and "Roman-ists." The result was "Let Him Be All in All":

> Then let us in our Father's name
> With holy reverence call,
> Forgetting creed, forgetting self,
> Let Him be "All in all."

This "all in all" theme worked in an exclusivist direction, too, giving rise to some of Crosby's most "Methodist" lines, lines redolent with echoes of Ocean Grove camp meetings.

> Take the world, but give me Jesus,
> All its joys are but a name;
> But his love abideth ever,
> Through eternal years the same.

> Oh, the height and depth of mercy!
> Oh, the length and breadth of love!
> Oh, the fullness of redemption,
> Pledge of endless life above.

This text, one of the many Crosby wrote for Kirkpatrick's friend John Sweney (longtime professor of music at the Pennsylvania Military Academy in West Chester), pulsated with the passion of Crosby's cohort at Ocean Grove and Manhattan's holiness settings, Mary James, whose text "All for Jesus" also expressed the purpose of a warmed Methodist heart. With Sweney, Crosby also prepared in 1882 "Where Are the Old Folks," a popular song released as sheet music and dedicated to "her friend," Philadelphia merchant and Sunday school activist John Wanamaker:

> Take me back, take me back where the sweet magnolia trees
> Where the white snowy blossoms on the merry laughing breeze
> To the once happy home where I never knew a care
> Take me back, O I wonder if the old folks are there.

Most nineteenth-century evangelical Protestants had at least once "felt the thrill that always touched the heart" with the singing of Robert Lowry's "Shall We Gather at the River" or his rousing Easter hymn "Low in the Grave He Lay." Born in Philadelphia, Lowry graduated from Lewisburg (later Bucknell) University in 1854 and became a Baptist clergyman. He served congregations in Manhattan and Brooklyn and thus had ready access to the influential hymn tune and text writers of the day. His own musical inclinations and his editorial ability made him a natural addition to their circle. Lowry and Crosby first met in 1866. After that, they often conferred on the phrasing of a hymn or the phases of Christian experience. Lowry proved ever ready with encouragement, but he could be a stern critic, too. (Crosby saw no harm in introducing Santa Claus into Sunday school Christmas entertainments; she soon learned that she could depend annually on a "stern remonstrance" from Lowry.) On Bradbury's death in 1868, Lowry assumed a large role in carrying forward Bradbury's publishing plans, and so his relationship with Crosby deepened.

Especially during the 1860s and 1870s, Lowry compiled successful collections of hymns. On his death in 1899, the New York Times estimated their sales at over three million. An ardent supporter of the Sunday school movement, Lowry attended the Robert Raikes centennial in England where recognition of the presence of the author of "Shall We Gather at the River" occasioned "uncontrollable applause." Crosby valued her acquaintance with Lowry and her visits to the home where he retired in Plainfield, New Jersey. For an 1875 Sunday school hymnal, their collaboration produced one of Crosby's enduring hymns:

> All the way my Saviour leads me;
> What have I to ask beside?
> Can I doubt His tender mercy,
> Who through life has been my guide?
> Heavenly peace, divinest comfort,
> Here by faith in Him to dwell!
> For I know, whate'er befall me,
> Jesus doeth all things well.

Other occasional Crosby friends and partners included many of the influential people on the contemporary popular Christian music scene: Silas Vail, Horatio Palmer, George C. Stebbins, Eliza Hewitt (whose friendship meant much to Crosby, especially in her old age), James McGranahan, Josephine Pollard, Mary Kidder, and, briefly, the "giant among them all," Philip Paul Bliss.

In 1872 Crosby received a letter from the well-known British hymn writer Frances Ridley Havergal. Though they never collaborated, they corresponded until Havergal's death in 1879. Havergal's tribute to Crosby suggests British familiarity with Crosby's early hymns even before Moody and Sankey introduced their gospel hymns across the Atlantic:

> Sweet blind singer over the sea,
> Tuneful and jubilant, how can it be,
> That the songs of gladness, which float so far,
> As if they fell from an evening star,
> Are the notes of one who may never see
> "Visible music" of flower and tree.
> . . . .
> How can she sing in the dark like this?
> What is her fountain of light and bliss?
> . . . .
> Her heart can see, her heart can see!
> Well may she sing so joyously!
> For the King Himself, in His tender grace,
> Hath shown her the brightness of His face.

Dear blind sister over the sea!
An English heart goes forth to thee.
We are linked by a cable of faith and song,
Flashing bright sympathy swift along;
One in the East and one in the West,
Singing for Him whom our souls love best.
. . . .
Sister! What will our meeting be,
When our hearts shall sing and our eyes shall see?

Among Crosby's long list of musical acquaintances, none played larger roles in her life than two millionaires, William Howard Doane (who preferred Howard to William) and Phoebe Palmer Knapp. With them she wrote her most enduring hymns. They delighted in her for herself, saw to her personal comfort, and looked out for her interests. Worlds apart in some ways, Doane and Knapp formed fast friendships with Crosby, though disagreements marred their relationship with each other. Their stories complement Crosby's and provide insights into the contexts from which some of her best-known and most enduring gospel hymns emerged.

WILLIAM HOWARD DOANE

Like Crosby, Doane came of New England Puritan stock. His ancestors, too, had sailed into Boston harbor in the 1630s. He, too, traced his family back to the *Mayflower,* and his grandfather fought in the Revolutionary War. The Doanes settled in Connecticut, where Doane's father, Joseph H. Doane, was partner in the cotton manufacturing concern of Doane and Treat. Doane was born in Putnam, Connecticut, 3 February 1832. The family enjoyed a comfortable life and in 1846 sent Doane to the Woodstock Academy, a recently renovated residential school in the northeastern corner of the state, to complete his education.

Under the sponsorship of Henry C. Bowen, New York City merchant and publisher of the *Independent,* Woodstock Academy enrolled students for four seasonal terms of eleven weeks each and placed them under the instruction of male college graduates. The "SLOW, THOROUGH and SYSTEMATIC course of instruction" targeted moral character as well as intellectual ability, and intended to "fit the student for *active life.*" Doane graduated in 1848. He next worked for three years with his father in his offices in Norwich, a town just up the Thames River from the port of New London. In 1851 young Doane left the family business for the employ of J. A. Fay and Company, manufacturers of woodworking machinery. Essential to the nation's first industrial technology, wood was the major source of fuel, construction material, and chemicals. Small American manufacturers relied on wooden machinery, and Doane shared the widespread confidence in technology's promise for American economic development. Woodworking fascinated the young man, and he rose quickly in the company. In 1858 he moved to Chicago to superintend the firm's interests in that growing metropolis. That year the patent claims listed in *The Scientific American* included Doane's claim for a patent for an "improved sawing machine," the first of a flurry of patents he filed in the next six years. Doane returned to Norwich in 1857 to marry Frances Treat, daughter of his father's business partner. In 1861, Doane, not yet thirty years old, and several partners took over the J. A. Fay Company, moving to Cincinnati, where the firm's main offices had been established in 1852. In 1866 he became president.

Doane enjoyed spectacular success in his chosen career. In addition to managing a profitable company, he registered more than sixty patents of his own. His cohorts heaped honors on him, electing him a fellow of the American Society of Mechanical Engineers, the American Society of Mining Engineers, the American Geographical Society, the American Society for the Advancement of Science, and the American Archaeological Society. He sat on various national boards, managed a large investment portfolio, and bestowed princely gifts on an assortment of religious endeavors. His "large interests" included the Barney and Smith Car Company of Dayton and the John Church Music Publishers of Cincinnati. When he semi-retired in 1893, Doane arranged a merger of the Fay company with its chief rival, the Egan Company, creating an entity that produced half the woodworking machinery in the United States.

His profitable career supported his avocation, which he considered his "real life." This centered squarely in music for the church. Even before he was old enough to attend school, Doane begged his parents for music lessons. He tagged along when his older siblings went to singing school, and by age twelve he had a regular place as flutist for the village choir. At thirteen he turned his attention to strings and became proficient on the violin and double bass. At the Woodstock Academy in 1846, he directed the student choir. He professed conversion at a Baptist revival and so identified with the church of his mother's family rather than with the Congregationalism of his father's.

As Doane climbed the ladder of financial success, his passion for music drove him to seek instruction from the best musicians available. It was his good fortune that Benjamin Baker, the famous organist at William Ellery Channing's Federal Street Church in Boston (and part of Mason's Boston coterie), spent time near Doane's Connecticut home, and this "fine American harmonist" instilled in Doane a taste for classical music. His musical ambition found its immediate outlet in the conducting of singing schools. He took a post as a church organist and by 1854 was conductor of the Norwich Harmonic Society. He studied music under the best teachers in western Connecticut, all with the aim of making a modest mark in the world of classical music.

Doane published several choral arrangements, and followed them in 1856 with a cantata, *Festal Morn*. It was so well received, Doane proudly reported, that Boston musicians performed it at Brooklyn, Connecticut. He routinely refused requests for Sunday school hymns or arrangements, fearing — he later said — to "compromise" his chances in professional music. This changed in 1862 in a moment Doane always recounted as a turning point in his life. Ill and restless, Doane consulted physicians who advised him to leave Chicago and recuperate on the broad, shaded porch of the home he still owned in Plainfield, Connecticut. A few weeks later, though, Connecticut doctors sent him back to Chicago. En route he took desperately ill. When his wife opened the curtains to his berth, he later recalled, "there seemed to be a flash of a thousand electric lights and all I could see was these words, 'You refused.'" She saw no lights but told him: "You know I always told you I was afraid the Lord would bring some judgement upon you for refusing to write the music for that good Chicago man."

Doane concluded (in the best tradition of his Puritan forebears) that his refusal to cooperate with Chicago gospel songsters had constituted rebellion against God and merited judgment in the form of illness. On the spot he vowed to do "anything the Lord wanted" and consecrated "his time and talents to Jehovah" in the interests of musical evangelism, if his life should be spared. Within twenty-four hours his health began returning, and within a week he resumed his journey to Chicago. He promptly made good on his promise. "This vow I have sacredly kept," he testified near the end of his long life, "and every dollar received from this source has been given back to the Lord." Those dollars were more than most people's annual salary: his daughters later estimated them at an average of $20,000 to $25,000 per year.

Doane's musical work filled every spare minute. He hummed and whistled new tunes as he moved along the streets or rails, and he kept a notebook handy to jot down bars of music or a nicely turned phrase. He evangelized in traditional ways, too, devoting his wealth to the support of the Bethesda Mission, Molitor Street, Cincinnati, where he preached early on Sunday mornings. He worshiped at 11 A.M. at the Mt. Auburn Baptist Church. Sunday afternoons found him busily engaged as superintendent of the Sunday school at Mt. Auburn, a school he built into one of the largest in the city. The mission and Sunday school functioned for Doane as musical laboratories of sorts, and Doane wrote many tunes for these, his own congregations. He teamed with local evangelists whenever possible, and Ohio audiences became accustomed to his "pleasing tenor" leading the singing at revival meetings. The Ohio Baptist Convention benefited from his ardor, too. He served as its president, bestowed generous gifts on its Denison University, and found time to work in the interests of the denomination at large. Doane helped found the Baptist Home for Aged Ministers at Fenton, Michigan, and filled a term as president of the American Baptist Publication Society. He also edited some of its official hymnals. He cared about missions, too, and in 1909 established the Fannie Doane Home for missionary children in Granville, Ohio. Named for his wife, the home sheltered missionary children pursuing education at Denison University. Doane money later became the core funding for the Overseas Ministries Training Center in New Haven, Connecticut.

Amid the incessant demands of this myriad of interests, Doane's company prospered. In 1889, in recognition of his inventions, the government of France awarded him the Legion of Honor at the Paris Exposition (where his company took the Grand Prix for its exhibit). His family flourished, too. Their hilltop Cincinnati mansion, Sunny Side, stood a few doors from the Mt. Auburn Baptist Church and for fifty-four years offered hospitality to countless guests. It boasted a music room that displayed one of the largest private collections of musical instruments — ancient and modern — in the world, a collection augmented during the family's two-year world tour, 1889-91. The walls were frescoed with measures of the "Hallelujah Chorus," and the music library featured original manuscripts and autographs of most of the old masters and modern composers. (The Cincinnati Museum of Art now holds this collection as well as the family's paintings.) The music room included a pipe organ run by a water motor and a grand piano. When the summer made southern Ohio's weather oppressive, the Doane family moved east to savor the ocean breezes at their gracious summer home at Watch Hill, Rhode Island.

Doane's first songbook, *Sabbath School Gems*, appeared in 1862, followed by *Little Sunbeams* in 1864 and *Silver Spray* in 1867. The substantial sales of these books seemed to vindicate Doane's decision to offer children something to sing besides the "mournful lays" that were common fare in the Ohio Baptist schools of his acquaintance. *Silver Spray* alone sold 300,000 copies in just two months. Doane insisted that church and Sunday school music should praise God or approach him in prayer rather than "display vocal culture," and some admiring contemporaries believed his tunes evoked devotion of "peculiar charm." On his part, Doane refused to publish tunes that did not "move" his own heart.

Crosby knew Doane by reputation, and when she heard he was in New York in the spring of 1867, she took the initiative to become acquainted. She had a new poem ready, and she summoned a messenger to carry it to Doane. The messenger found Doane in conversation with the Reverend W. C. van Meter, the well-known indefatigable superintendent of the Howard Mission. The mission stood amid the moral desert of the Fourth Ward and served a motley population packed into its streets at a density of 290,000 people per square mile. Organized by van Meter, the Howard Mission was intentionally nondenominational and had as its object doing "all the good we can to the souls and bodies of all whom we can reach." Since it opened its doors in 1861, its programs had served well over 10,000 children, and it was precisely the sort of place to enlist Doane's sympathy and benevolence. It was also a place that featured music. Van Meter had taken a prominent place in the normal institute movement, first as a student in Mason's and associates' 1853 three-month summer institute in Manhattan, then as an enthusiastic supporter of the methods and activities of Mason, Root, Bradbury, and cohorts. He arranged concerts for "the moral Renovation of the 'Five Points'" to raise money for the mission, but more significantly, van Meter practiced his persuasion that music had its own transformative role to play in the lives of impoverished, hopeless children. Before taking up his work in Manhattan slums, he had been a successful Midwest music teacher, but by his own admission he gained deeper insights into the promise of music when he placed it at the center of his work among the poor. In 1854 he wrote, "I never before realized the blessedness of music. I have taught the children of many of the great of our country; I have been honored with their kind regard; but never have I felt so highly honored and blessed as since I have been permitted to visit the abodes of the wretched, rescue these poor outcast children, and teach them to sing."

The city's May Anniversary Week was fast approaching, and van Meter urged Doane to supply a new hymn for the Howard Mission's sixth anniversary. Doane's admirers liked to say that, "like James Whitcomb Riley, [Doane] thinks in poetry," but for the moment he had neither text nor tune to offer. Then Crosby's messenger arrived with Crosby's text, "More Like Jesus Would I Be," and a note: "Mr. Doane: I feel impressed to send you this hymn; may God bless it! Fanny Crosby." To van Meter's delight, Doane promptly composed a tune, and the hymn debuted at the mission anniversary.

> More like Jesus would I be,
> Let my Saviour dwell in me;
> Fill my soul with peace and love,
> Make me gentle as a dove.
>
> More like Jesus while I go,
> Pilgrim in this world below;
> Poor in spirit would I be;
> Let my Saviour dwell in me.

Doane, meanwhile, took the trouble to locate Crosby in her upper-story rooms in lower Manhattan. From the start, both believed their acquaintance part of a providential plan. He paid her generously for her words and began a friendship that lasted a lifetime. Doane's partisans liked to say that he had "found that jewel, Fanny Crosby," and "placed her where the world could be helped by her breathings," while hers thought Crosby "made" Doane. While both were undoubtedly over-statements, certainly the hymns Doane and Crosby produced together enjoyed astonishing immediate as well as enduring success. A list compiled by *The Christian Endeavor World* (both Doane and Crosby would later become popular Christian Endeavor Convention speakers) offers as good a glimpse as any of the fruit of Doane-Crosby collaboration. "Famous Hymns for Which Dr. Doane Has Written Equally Famous Tunes" reads the header. Of the fifteen hymns listed, Crosby authored the texts of eleven: "Jesus, Keep Me Near the Cross"; "Rescue the Perishing"; "To the Work! To the Work"; "Safe in the Arms of Jesus"; "Pass Me Not, O Gentle Saviour"; "Saviour, More Than Life to Me"; "I Am Thine, O Lord"; "Only a Step to Jesus"; "Now Just a Word for Jesus"; "When Jesus Comes to Reward His Servants"; "'Tis the Blessed Hour of Prayer." Staples of evangelical collections and hymnals for social occasions, some of these quickly made their way into the more selective denominational hymnals, too.

Those who sang such hymns thrilled to Crosby's accounts of their writing. The story associated with the composition of "Safe in the Arms of Jesus" was perhaps the most repeated "incident of a hymn" during Crosby's lifetime and beyond. Doane "thought, talked and acted with great rapidity" and could not abide an unredeemed moment. When he traveled for business, he composed tunes on the train, and he generally combined the travel required for business with his religious interests. Late in April 1868, as he often did, Doane wrote a melody on the train. When he reached New York, he hurried to Crosby's apartment to hum his new tune and beg her for appropriate lyrics. Crosby had been thinking about "the sweet sense of security felt by the soul that puts its whole trust in Jesus," and now her thoughts rapidly took metrical form. After twenty minutes of concentrated effort, Crosby recited the words known since as "Safe in the Arms of Jesus." She insisted: "I sat down with a melody in my heart. I didn't know what happened. The Spirit wrote it. I do not want to take the praise for it." Doane took the words down himself and hurried off. That night he introduced the song to a rapt audience at a religious gathering in the parlor of New York's fashionable St. Denis Hotel at Broadway and Eleventh Street:

Safe in the arms of Jesus, safe on His gentle breast;
There by His love o'ershaded, sweetly my soul shall rest.
Hark! Tis the voice of angels borne in a song to me
Over the fields of glory, over the jasper sea.

Refrain:
Safe in the arms of Jesus, safe on His gentle breast,
There by His love o'ershaded, sweetly my soul shall rest.

Jesus, my heart's dear refuge, Jesus has died for me!
Firm on the Rock of Ages ever my trust shall be.
Here let me wait with patience, wait 'til the night is o'er,
Wait 'til the blissful morning breaks on the golden shore.

By some accounts, "Safe in the Arms of Jesus" was the Crosby hymn her generation preferred to all her others. Certainly it enjoyed immense and immediate acclaim. In the 1890s the *New York Times* reported that "no modern hymn ha[d] circumnavigated the religious globe more thoroughly than this one or been translated into more modern tongues." Its use in 1881 and again in 1885 as part of the national mourning for Presidents Garfield and Grant signified its broad acceptance and popular recognition of both tune and text. The United States Marine Band played it on 25 September 1881 for the throngs gathered in Cleveland to honor the slain Garfield. While his remains were lying in state, the papers reported that a ten-year-old relative of Garfield's died with "Safe in the Arms of Jesus" on her lips. On 10 August 1885 Professor Frederick Widdows played the melody on the muffled bells of Grace Church on Broadway as Grant's funeral cortege passed. From farther afield, word filtered back in 1887 from the shores of Africa's Lake Victoria about the comfort the hymn had brought the martyred Anglican missionary bishop James Hannington. Set upon by men he described as "vicious ruffians," Hannington confided to his diary: "They violently threw me to the ground and proceeded to strip me of all valuables. I was dragged by the legs over the ground . . . and the exertion and struggling strained me in a most agonizing manner. In spite of all, I sang 'Safe in the Arms of Jesus,' and then laughed at the very agony of my situation." Hannington's autobiography went through multiple English and American editions. In 1879 New Yorkers followed the case of the murder of George Estey, a schoolboy killed in Jersey City. His funeral, crowded with Sunday school friends, featured a floral tribute in which the words "Safe in the arms of Jesus" were traced, and the choir rendered the hymn.

The database of the Hymn Society of the United States and Canada indicates that the hymn appeared regularly in American hymnals until World War II. By 1900, in addition to its inclusion in the books published by Biglow and Main, the YMCA, the Christian Endeavor Society, Northern Baptist, Congregationalist, Christian, Northern and Southern Presbyterian, Southern Methodist, Augustana Lutheran, Reformed Episcopal, Canadian Presbyterian, Disciples of Christ, and Seventh-Day Adventist hymnals all included it. It appeared in 1921 in the Jehovah's Witnesses collection.

In spite of its frequent association with funerals, Crosby and Doane — and many of their cohorts — considered the hymn to be about life rather than death. For Crosby its words described a present reality in which the believer found safety from temptation and care in Christ's embrace. Crosby produced many texts with the same emphasis, texts about hiding, resting, sheltering while life's storms beat around one's safe retreat. In her mind "the arms of Jesus" sustained the believer in this life. "Safe in the Arms of Jesus" expressed a particular evangelical "take" on Christian living in a hostile world, one that suffering Christians like Hannington apparently grasped. Their confidence of safety enabled them to laugh in the face of the foe; their strength was rooted in passivity. Crosby's cohorts understood: one who had been imprisoned for faith confided to Crosby that "she had been greatly helped by singing nightly as she lay down to rest in prison, 'Safe in the Arms of Jesus.'" But this hymn's poignant human image of loving embrace also offered a metaphor that made heaven seem reassuringly familiar and, at a time of high infant mortality, comforted grieving parents.

If "Safe in the Arms of Jesus" suggests Crosby's ability to compose on demand, "I am Thine, O Lord" may represent the many Doane-Crosby hymns that resulted from what she called "a deep, though intangible feeling, whose expression demanded the language of poetry." She sat one warm evening on the veranda of the Doanes' Cincinnati mansion, the family nearby, watching the sun go down. Crosby perceived light giving way to darkness. Overcome by a sense of divine presence, she went to her room and composed the poem that became the hymn:

> I am Thine, O Lord; I have heard Thy voice,
> And it told Thy love to me,
> But I long to rise in the arms of faith
> And be closer drawn to Thee.
>
> Consecrate me now to Thy service, Lord,
> By the power of grace divine.
> Let my soul look up with a steadfast hope
> And my will be lost in Thine.

The Doane-Crosby hymn that first won recognition from the fussy English editors of *Hymns Ancient and Modern* was "Rescue the Perishing." This text blurred the boundaries among evangelicals, social gospelers, and liberal Protestants by summoning the Christian public to action on behalf of the dispossessed. Crosby provided it in response to Doane's request for text on the subject of rescuing the perishing. She mulled the topic over for several days. One hot August evening she went to a Manhattan rescue mission service. As she listened, the line "rescue the perishing, care for the dying" came forcefully to her. Overtaken by the certainty that "some mother's boy" present stood in desperate need of salvation, she rose and invited "any boy who had wandered away from mother's teaching" to chat with her after the service. A young man obliged, prayed with Crosby, and professed conversion. She went home and composed the text before going to bed. She dictated it the next day and sent it to Doane, who promptly composed the tune. More than thirty-five years later, at a meeting in Lynn, Massachusetts, a man came forward to tell Crosby that he was "the boy" who had spoken to her that August night. "Rescue the Perishing" enjoyed steady popularity from its first two printings in 1870. Reprinted almost every year for a century, often in more than a dozen hymnals in a year, it became a staple of American Protestant hymnody:

> Rescue the perishing, care for the dying,
> Snatch them in pity from sin and the grave;

Weep o'er the erring one, lift up the fallen,
Tell them of Jesus, the Mighty to Save.

Refrain:
Rescue the perishing, care for the dying!
Jesus is merciful, Jesus will save.

Down in the human heart crushed by the tempter
Feelings lie buried that grace can restore;
Touched by a loving heart, wakened by kindness,
Cords that are broken will vibrate once more.

Meanwhile, Doane collaborated with another associate of Crosby's, the Baptist text and tune writer Robert Lowry. Together they issued a long list of popular hymnals with typical Victorian era titles: *Brightest and Best; Fountain of Song; Good as Gold; Joyful Lays.* All the books they edited featured Crosby's texts. *Brightest and Best* first carried "To God Be the Glory," copyrighted by Biglow and Main (successors to Bradbury) in 1875. Despite its popularity in Britain, Americans warmed slowly to this hymn. By 1896 Northern Presbyterians, Disciples of Christ, some Lutherans, and Northern Baptists embraced it in denominational hymnals, but its real popularity in American hymnals came only in the mid–twentieth century.

Before long Doane and Crosby tapped the Christmas market by producing a series of musical Christmas programs designed for the Sunday school with titles ranging from the predictable *Immanuel* and *Night of Glory* to the unexpected *Santa Claus and the Fairies.*

In 1875 Denison University bestowed on Doane an honorary doctorate of music. Crosby could not have been more pleased. She was practically a member of this close-knit family, all of whom seemed inclined to embrace her as one of themselves. The Doanes gave Crosby costly items — a sable collar or piece of jewelry — sent "crisp new bills" in payment for lyrics Doane requested, and tended to her financial and personal well-being in thoughtful, unobtrusive ways. "Your most generous gift received," she wrote to the Doanes one typical Christmas. Doane's two daughters knew her affectionately as "Aunt Fanny" while she called them her "little snowbirds." Doane's wife — another Fannie — became a close friend. Her letters capture the easy relationship she enjoyed with the whole family. "Cheer up and you will feel much better," she once advised the ailing Doane. "Have a pleasant Thanksgiving together with Mrs. Doane and family, whom I send lots of love, keeping a plenty for yourself." Crosby cherished weeks spent at the Doane homes in Ohio and Rhode Island. In "A Tribute to Cincinnati" she wrote:

What? Forget thee, Cincinnati,
Lovely city of the West?
Never till the pulse of feeling
Throbs its last within my breast.
I have spent such days of pleasure,
O, such months of joy in thee,
That the very thought of leaving
Brought unwelcome tears to me.

On the first page of the book the family prepared for William and Fannie Doane's golden wedding, 2 November 1907, stood a tribute from Fanny Crosby:

A mental telegram has reached
Your Cincinnati home
From one who oft has been a guest
Within its princely dome.
In Bridgeport City she resides
And still, though far away
She hears the chiming bells that ring
Your golden wedding day.

God bless you, friends, her message reads,
And spare your children, too;
Oh! May his richest gifts descend
Like Hermon's precious dew.
God bless your friends, our hearts reply
And keep all clouds away
Till sweeter bells ring out the dawn
Of heaven's eternal day.

Crosby often said of Doane: "I thank the dear Lord that I have not got to ask for anything. Yet if I did, I have a friend who would always give to me and help, and that is Mr. Doane."

PHOEBE PALMER KNAPP

If Crosby's relationship with the Doanes drew her into a warm and private family setting, her collaboration with Phoebe Palmer Knapp beckoned her into the hectic world of Brooklyn society and social activism. Knapp, daughter of the famous Methodist lay couple Phoebe Worrall Palmer and physician Walter Palmer, grew up in lower Manhattan surrounded by religious people and events. Phoebe Palmer's fascination for "theology and spiritual impressions" governed family life, and earnest seekers after Christian perfection shared the family's home and table, where the conversation often turned on the state of one's soul. Contemporaries gushed approvingly that this was "a METHODIST home," by which they presumably meant that it featured order and comfort rather than self-indulgence. Without fail, bells summoned family, guests, and servants to morning and evening prayers. Meals began and ended with sung graces, and "more than learning, riches honor or aught else," Phoebe Palmer coveted her children's "entire sanctification." Perhaps marriage offered the best escape. Just after her sixteenth birthday, young Phoebe left as the bride of Joseph Fairchild Knapp, a twenty-three-year-old businessman — and a devout Methodist. Even then, her mother wrote to urge the couple "to be deeply devoted to God," for "radiant holiness, usefulness and happiness" were inseparable. Phoebe and Joseph set up housekeeping in Brooklyn and threw their prodigious energy into the work of the Knapp family's church, South Second Street Methodist Episcopal. Phoebe had no quarrel with her mother's faith, but she preferred activity and society to what some commended as her mother's "spiritual abstraction."

Joseph Knapp prospered in business and became a familiar figure on Brooklyn's civic and religious scene. A lithographer by trade, he built his firm into a huge enterprise, Major, Knapp and Company, that made him a millionaire. He played a key role in the transformation of the National Union Life and Limb Insurance Company into the Metropolitan Life Insurance Company, which he served as president. Under Knapp's direction, this struggling insurance company adapted a model for "workingmen's" insurance that enjoyed spectacular success in England. He brought Englishmen to New York to train an army of insurance agents to sell policies door-to-door and to collect modest weekly premiums, making insurance affordable to the working-class families crowding Manhattan and Brooklyn neighborhoods. As his social standing grew, Knapp joined other white Protestant Brooklynites of means in the Union Club (Brooklyn's largest social club, staunchly Republican), the New England Club (membership open to Brooklyn citizens with New England family roots — Knapp's family hailed from Fairfield County, Connecticut), and the Oxford Club (a conservative male province devoted to literature and the arts). He and his family summered with other wealthy New Yorkers at the era's opulent resort hotels along the New Jersey and Long Island shores or in New England.

Joseph and Phoebe Knapp lost their first son, Francis, in infancy but saw two children, Joseph (1864-1951) and Antoinette (1862-1948), grow to adulthood. They reared them in a lavishly appointed house (known popularly as the Knapp Mansion) on the edge of Williamsburg at the corner of Bedford Avenue and Ross Street. Williamsburg, the neighborhood in which Joseph Fairchild Knapp was born, was one of Brooklyn's oldest towns. After his father's death in 1846, Joseph Fairchild Knapp and his brother, William, were unusually devoted to their mother, Antoinette, a devout Methodist. The adult Joseph expressed his enduring devotion in lavish bequests to the church of his boyhood, a small frame building that commanded a fine view of the East River. There his own family attended until they moved to their mansion.

At the corner of Bedford Avenue and Wilson Street, one block behind the Knapp Mansion (an enormous structure whose solid square brick exterior belied the elegance within), rose the tall spire of St. John's Methodist Episcopal Church. An imposing building, the church seated well over 1,000 and sponsored a Sunday school 1,000 strong, superintended for twenty-two years by Joseph F. Knapp. His energetic wife took charge of the infant class. It numbered 200. This Sunday school offered a convenient laboratory for such musical efforts as Sunday school hymnals and musical Christmas programs, and Phoebe Knapp kept them coming.

226

The art room at the Knapp Mansion displayed costly works of the great masters, while the "splendid" music room boasted a pipe organ reputed to be among the finest in the nation. A gift from Joseph to his wife, the music room and especially its organ gained renown in the city and beyond. The Knapps hosted "musicales" second to none. Despite its Democrat leanings, the *Brooklyn Eagle* heaped praise on the staunchly Republican Knapps, calling the house "the nearest approach to a salon of the Old World ever in Brooklyn" and commending the Knapps' devotion to the quality of Brooklyn life.

In the years following the Civil War, Brooklyn turned out in style several times each year to celebrate and to commemorate. Perhaps most impressive were the Memorial Day parades when hundreds of thousands lined the streets to cheer marching veterans of the Mexican and Civil Wars. Each year the grandstand stood just outside the Knapp Mansion, accessible only through the mansion's drawing room windows. Everyone who "mattered" socially and politically in New York moved at one time or another through the receiving lines in the mansion and mingled at the receptions before and after such public events. Presidents and generals stepped out the Knapps' windows onto the grandstand to the cheers of gathered throngs. For Memorial Day festivities, the Knapps welcomed Presidents U. S. Grant, Rutherford B. Hayes, James Garfield, Chester Arthur, and Grover Cleveland, Generals Sherman and Sheridan, every Methodist bishop (at least so it was claimed), and such upstanding New Yorkers as Henry Ward Beecher, DeWitt Talmage, Seth Low, and Anson Phelps. Religious and public figures of the day could count on first-rate hospitality at the Knapp Mansion. So could humbler friends like Crosby and Van.

Running a close second to Memorial Day parades by the last quarter of the century was the annual parade sponsored on the first Thursday in June (a school holiday) by the Brooklyn Sunday School Union. Among the most active Sunday school unions in the country, this Brooklyn agency lined up the city's thousands of Sunday school scholars, black and white, for public view. Brooklyn turned out en masse to celebrate the ubiquity and success of its Sunday schools of all denominations. Although the black Sunday schools were not located in the Brooklyn Heights District, their superintendents — in a display of their esteem for Beecher's prominent opposition to slavery — generally opted to march with the Heights schools. Parades were occasions to bring the Sunday school from the church to the street for all to see.

The Knapps' all-consuming commitment to Sunday school made these parades an important part of their annual calendars. Methodists deemed their St. John's Sunday school "of the very best grade" and opined that it had "no superior in the whole country." It did not hurt, of course, that the Knapps gave unstintingly to promote its interest, even providing a fine organ to help the music along. The *Christian Advocate* reported that the Knapps supplied the school "with every thing which ingenuity could suggest or money procure." And Crosby, Van, and Phoebe Knapp did their best with the music, too.

The Knapps used their music room for more than entertainment, for Phoebe was an untrained but gifted musician. She sang, played, and composed. Her pleasing "sweet" soprano (usually described by contemporaries with the qualifiers "though not great and full") assured her a place on programs dedicated to her favorite causes: Methodist good works of all kinds; temperance; home missions; rescue mission work. She sang often at evangelistic services and women's meetings. She offered tunes for sacred texts intended for use beyond the Sunday school. Her husband's ample resources were hers to command, and she put these to use on behalf of Methodism, temperance, the King's Daughters, the International Sunshine Society, and impoverished aspiring musicians.

She numbered among her inner circle Margaret Bottome, the saintly founder of the King's Daughters. Dedicated to a threefold program of religion, education, and philanthropy as training for useful Christian service, the King's Daughters devoted their energies to various good causes. Bottome and Phoebe Knapp participated as well in the larger circle dominated by Frances Willard and Lady Henry Somerset, the indefatigable temperance-minded generals of the formidable white ribbon army of women and men united "for God, home and country." And Bottome also wrote a column, "Heart to Heart," for the *Ladies' Home Journal*. But Bottome and Knapp had a musical as well as a benevolent friendship, for Margaret's husband, Francis (or Frank), an English-born Methodist Episcopal minister, gave the world such holiness favorites as "The Comforter Has Come" and "Sing of His Mighty Love." Knapp and Bottome enlisted Crosby's enthusiastic cooperation in the King's Daughters as well as in their musical pursuits.

Phoebe Knapp may have had a difficult relationship with her spiritual giant of a mother, Phoebe Palmer (certainly Palmer was more comfortable in the company of her other daughter, Sarah Foster), but the two Phoebes communicated easily around music. Phoebe Palmer tirelessly generated hymn texts, and Phoebe Knapp set them to music. When Walter and Phoebe Palmer took over the editorial responsibilities for the longtime monthly advocate of Christian perfection, the *Guide to Holiness,* they printed a hymn at the end of every issue under the heading "Our Hymnal." Knapp tunes abounded, often linked to Palmer texts. But Phoebe Knapp wrote Sunday school tunes, too, and edited hymnals designed especially for Sunday school use. Crosby often provided text for these, and in Knapp-edited Sunday school collections Van frequently composed the tunes to which his wife's words were set. Phoebe took an interest in Fanny and Van, and the two women enjoyed each other's company.

Joseph Fairchild Knapp saw his wife's musical efforts as business propositions. At a time when copyright law was still evolving, he copyrighted all her tunes as soon as she wrote them. The most enduring of these, known around the world almost from its composition, was published with text by Crosby and appeared in 1873 as "Blessed Assurance." The familiar story of its composition described how Knapp composed a melody, played it for Crosby, and asked her for text. Crosby responded that the music "said" "blessed assurance," and so a hymn was born. It appeared the same year in the *Guide to Holiness,* the first Crosby text of many to be featured in the next decade in the Palmers' influential holiness Methodist monthly, and it quickly spread around the world. Crosby and Knapp collaborated as well on the Palm Sunday hymn "Open the Gates of the Temple" ("Open the gates of the temple, strew palms on the conqueror's way"), and on songs popular at the time.

"Blessed Assurance" enjoyed immediate popularity in the United States. By 1875 it had found its way into Methodist publications. The Disciples of Christ published it in their 1888 hymnal, and the Methodist Churches of Canada added it in 1889. In 1898 nineteen more American hymnals added "Blessed Assurance," including that of the Church of the Brethren–Dunkers:

Blessed assurance, Jesus is mine!
Oh, what a foretaste of glory divine!

Heir of salvation, purchase of God,
Born of His spirit, washed in His blood.

Refrain:
This is my story, this is my song,
Praising my Saviour all the day long!
This is my story, this is my song,
Praising my Saviour all the day long!

Perfect submission, all is at rest;
I in my Saviour am happy and blest!
Watching and waiting, looking above,
Filled with His goodness, lost in His love.

Phoebe Palmer died of Bright's disease in 1874, twelve years before the fiftieth anniversary of her renowned Tuesday Meeting for the
Promotion of Holiness. The indefatigable Phoebe Knapp saw to it that
her mother's persistent efforts on behalf of Christian perfection were
duly celebrated. Though she did not always frequent the Tuesday
Meetings, she took a hand in organizing a daylong program that taxed
the ample facilities of St. Paul's Methodist Episcopal Church on Tuesday, 9 February 1886, and she enlisted Crosby's help with the music.
Crosby obliged with two new hymns for the momentous occasion.

Bright sunshine streamed into the sanctuary as Crosby's lyrics
consecrated the day:

O Thou Master of Assemblies
Consecrate this sacred hour;
To Thy children here before Thee
Grant a Pentecostal shower.
Since our meetings first were opened
Fifty years their course have run;
Now we come to give Thee glory
For the wonders Thou hast done.

When the busy proceedings ended that night, pleasant memories of
"the power of holy song" lingered. Crosby favored the assembled
throng with a recitation of another poem she prepared for the occa-

sion: "What Hath God Wrought?" Led by Phoebe Knapp at the organ, the people had sung "lustily" through hymns that reveled in the assurance and simplicity that were Phoebe Palmer's hallmarks:

> Precious souls that long have doubted
> Prayer has brought the light to see;
> In the way so plain and simple
> They are walking now with Thee.

Phoebe Knapp poured her energies into many benevolent causes suggested in her hymn texts and tunes, but toward the end of the 1880s her husband's declining health interrupted her good works. The couple went abroad on an unsuccessful quest for health. Joseph Knapp died at sea en route home in September 1891.

Despite the business savvy that made him a millionaire, Joseph gambled and lost when it came to anticipating Brooklyn neighborhoods. Once plans were laid for the Williamsburg Bridge, it quickly became evident that his family's mansions (he built a second in the 1880s, attached by a wide conservatory to his own, as a wedding gift for his daughter) would lose value. The completion of the bridge in 1903 made once-proud Williamsburg the most densely populated and poorest neighborhood in Brooklyn, a continuation of the desperate poverty on Manhattan's lower east side at the other end of the span. By then the widowed Phoebe Knapp and her daughter had traded their Brooklyn addresses for Manhattan homes. Knapp rented spacious apartments in the Savoy Hotel at the fashionable corner of Manhattan's Fifth Avenue and Fifty-ninth Street. There she installed a pipe organ and entertained royally, often using her wealth quietly to encourage young musicians. And there she continued to shower favors on Crosby, who occasionally spent time as her guest.

The Knapp children, meanwhile, went their own ways, manifesting little interest in their parents' and grandparents' faith but keeping alive the family tradition of benevolence. Antoinette first married Edward Copeland Wallace, a wealthy iron manufacturer, and moved with him to a fashionable neighborhood a few blocks from her mother's apartments. He died in 1915, and she married a Paul G. Brown. Joseph Palmer Knapp married three times, moved to Manhattan's west side and became a low-profile multimillionaire publisher, a director of the Metropolitan Life Insurance Company, founder in 1895 of the American Lithograph Company, and CEO of Crowell Enterprises, a group of magazines with a circulation of over 15 million worldwide. He developed baseball cards, a multicolor press, and in 1903 the first Sunday newspaper magazine supplement. He combined his father's hard-nosed business sense (a friend called the younger Joseph "a demon for work") with his grandmother Palmer's reputation as "a dreamer." But the religious fervor that fired their parents' benevolence took a secular turn with their offspring. Their grandmother's fiery holiness message, their mother's collaboration with Crosby, and the parade of Methodist bishops who had climbed the steps to the family's Brooklyn mansion became ever more distant memories.

Phoebe Knapp died of a stroke in July 1908 while on vacation at one of the Victorian era's premier resorts, the Grand Hotel at Poland Springs, Maine. Though nearly seventy, she had kept to the end "the face, figure and charm of a woman in her forties." Her wizened and much older friend Fanny Crosby (whom she could never convince to forsake unsightly neighborhoods or, later, the distant city of Bridgeport and come under her care) outlived her by nearly seven years.

Crosby's relationships with Doane and Knapp drew her into worlds of wealth and privilege. Both associations yielded rich personal enjoyment and elicited some of her best texts. Doane's Baptist interests promoted evangelism; Knapp's warmed Methodist heart cared deeply about social ills. Both shared Crosby's devotion to Sunday schools. Crosby's hymns, then, arose from varied sources, prompted by the wide variety of circumstances that filled her life. Thousands of Crosby texts languished unpublished in the offices of Biglow and Main. But many more filled the hymnals that poured from late nineteenth-century religious presses. Hymns were made by the marriage of texts and tunes; texts became known and useful when they were sung. And Crosby's soon were sung and promoted at a critical moment far beyond the useful arenas in which they already thrived.

Crosby's remarkable agility with lines of verse in anapestic meter — two short syllables followed by a long one — suited her lyrics to many gospel tunes. Rhyming lines had been her trademark from childhood. Her hymn lyrics tended to use "true rhymes" rather than "sight rhymes," a habit related, perhaps, to the fact that she heard rhymes rather than visualized words.

Shortly after Crosby and Knapp copyrighted "Blessed Assurance" and just as Crosby and Doane produced their enduring "Rescue the Perishing," the premier Protestant movers and shakers of the day, Dwight L. Moody and Ira D. Sankey, arrived in Brooklyn. Bradbury had once invited Crosby to assist with providing music for children, singing schools, social meetings, and congregations. The popularity of Bradbury music books assured Crosby a wide public. But Moody and Sankey took what Bradbury had started and multiplied it exponentially. The staying power of Crosby's texts — and the hallowing of a Crosby legend — was assured in the context of the Moody-Sankey revivals of the 1870s. Moody and Sankey accelerated a trend already under way and made Fanny Crosby (often as set to music by Doane and Knapp) a household name to Protestants around the world.

9 Gospel Hymns: Context

Oh the wondrous gospel story!
There is life in every word;
There is hope and consolation
Where the message sweet is heard;
Let us tell it to the weary,
And its beauties all unfold;
'Tis the only guide to heaven,
And the story *must* be told.

On Sunday, 25 October 1875, thousands of Brooklyn Protestants donned their Sunday best a few hours earlier than usual. At seven o'clock Brooklyn offered the "unwonted spectacle" of well-dressed men and women hurrying toward the downtown unaccountably early for an 8:30 A.M. meeting. Destination: an old skating rink with entrances on Clermont and Vanderbilt Avenues. The rink had a nearly square interior that measured about 120 feet on all sides. Recent renovations had hastily transformed open space into seating for more than 5,500. Galleries rose some 5 feet off the ground, enabling a few hundred more to squeeze in. A platform stretched 72 by 38 feet, with seating for 550. With no "architectural ornaments" in the way, those who arrived early enough to press in would have an unobstructed view of the makeshift platform. Those seated on the platform, in turn, would be completely surrounded by the audience, and thanks to careful planning, only a few hundred seats rose above the platform's height. The transformation of the rink had been a hurried effort in response to overwhelming popular demand, but commendable efficiency promised satisfactory results. By eight o'clock that Sunday morning, the last seat was long gone. Thousands stood on the stairs, in the aisles, in the doorways, and "in every nook and cranny" of the rink — in violation of the city's fire ordinance and contrary to the instructions received by the 100 volunteer ushers who were quite simply overwhelmed by the press of humanity. Masses more thronged the streets outside. Brooklyn divines mingled on the platform — the Reverend Drs. Cuyler, Talmage, Budington, Lyman, to name a few. Some 100 reporters sat at tables just below the platform.

At 8:30 on the dot, evangelist Dwight L. Moody strode across the platform, walked to the simple podium and announced a hymn. His song leader, Ira David Sankey — a "square-built, solid-looking man, dark moustache and side whiskers" — took his cue and slid onto the bench of a small organ. He instructed the congregation to stand and sing heartily. The rousing yet serious tones of "Sound His praises, tell the story of Him who was slain" echoed through the rink as the throng heartily followed Sankey's slow tempo. Written the year before by the Scotsman pastor and poet Horatius Bonar, the text was new in the United States, but its familiar melody, the common tune for "Revive Us Again," made the hymn seem an old friend. It excited the crowd and evoked shouts of "Amen," but Moody promptly took the emotion in hand and kept the program moving. He had neither time nor inclination for interruptions of any sort. "No man can imitate Mr. Moody," an admirer wrote soon after. "That is to say, no man who has not first acquired his soul of fire, and tongue of flame, which give such impetuous fury and vehemence to his winged words." Moody dismissed the meeting in time for people to make their way to their accustomed pews in Brooklyn's many churches. But he invited them back for more that afternoon.

Three o'clock found downtown Brooklyn again teeming with people pushing and shoving to enter the rink. Liveried carriages jostled the crowds that spilled into the streets trying to get through the press. Politicians, clergy, and distinguished professionals could be seen everywhere. "The jam was terrible," a newspaper reported, "and the confusion indescribable." Five minutes after the doors opened at 3:15, they closed because the auditorium was more than full. Police estimated that fully two-thirds of the would-be audience did not gain access. The nearby sanctuaries of Simpson Methodist Episcopal Church and the North Reformed Church were opened as overflow seating, and Theodore Cuyler and other pastors hastily prepared to preach to disappointed crowds. Before the afternoon was over, Sankey slipped out of the rink to ease their disappointment with a song.

Meanwhile, as confusion reigned outside, Sankey sized up the situation inside the rink and impulsively decided that music would calm the crowd and ready souls for the service, still an hour away. With "unusual effect" he led the assembled thousands in the three stanzas of Fanny Crosby's "Safe in the Arms of Jesus," a recent song they already knew well. Hymn after hymn echoed across the rink until Moody arrived, well in advance of the scheduled starting time. It seemed pointless to wait since the largest possible crowd already jammed the auditorium. And so the first day of Moody and Sankey's American adventure passed.

Brooklyn turned out in droves that October Sunday to welcome to America's "city of churches" the religious sensations of the hour — Dwight Moody and Ira Sankey — fresh from astonishing success in Great Britain (1873-75). They had returned home to a heroic welcome based largely on their accomplishments abroad, and Americans seemed eager to be taken by storm. Brooklyn claimed the right to start the stampede. The next evening, with the popular "Quakeress preacher" Sarah Smiley seated among such eminent Brooklyn divines as Theodore Cuyler and DeWitt Talmage, Moody entered the rink to the hearty rendering of Crosby's "Safe in the Arms of Jesus."

By the fall of 1875, most American Protestants had at least heard of Dwight Lyman Moody, a son of New England who found his calling on the streets of Chicago. During the 1850s and 1860s, amid the clamor and filth of that rapidly growing city, he manifested untiring evangelical zeal for the people he called "the unconverted." Focused and active, he took in hand unlikely people as well as unpromising projects and turned them around. His famous Sunday school evolved into a large, independent evangelical congregation. On his way to Washington in 1861, Abraham Lincoln stopped by to see the wonder Moody had created in one of Chicago's roughest areas. Moody's energy did not stop with children. He helped make the Chicago YMCA a model for the nation and showed Protestant America how the YMCA could serve the hope of a Christian America. During the Civil War his evangelistic zeal drove him to enlist for work among troops through the Christian Commission, and so he experienced the horrors of Shiloh and Chattanooga beside the wounded and dying. His cohorts could not easily predict what he might do next, but they could be certain that, whatever it was, it would play into Moody's larger scheme of promoting conversions. "Every man can do something," Moody urged cautious Christians. And he set the example, seeing every person and every moment as a gospel opportunity. Uneducated and unordained, he refused to apologize for imperfect grammar or undignified moments. His focus on ultimate questions made all else irrelevant. What mattered was one's soul. "No place is too bad, no class too hardened, to be despaired of," he assured his generation. Moody did not permit emotional outbursts to interrupt his rapid-fire evangelism on street corners or indoors; noisy "Amen's" or impulsive responses tended to call attention to oneself and distract other hearers from the all-important Word. He diligently adhered to a program that kept the pace of his meetings up and the time for interruptions down.

The young Moody did whatever it took to make things happen. He prepared meeting places, rounded up audiences, cajoled with candy or contests, and manifested practical interest in follow-up work. "He is a business man, and he means business," a contemporary critic wrote. "Every word he speaks is meant to lead to a definite business; if it does not do that, he regards it as thrown away." Such efficient focus played well to audiences familiar with canons of the industrial enterprises that drove the era's economy. Moody proved willing — even eager — to be different from the rank and file and to risk criticism in order to see results. Many considered his "pell-mell earnestness" a breath of fresh air in the staid, predictable world of middle-class Protestants. Tired of planning and discussing, he proposed instead to enlist them, get busy, and "take the land" for Christ. The press found his quips and strategy good copy.

Moody's spur-of-the-moment decisions generally paid off. His prompt acting on instinct served him particularly well during the YMCA convention in Indianapolis in 1870. Scheduled to lead an early-morning prayer meeting, he was disappointed when the singing languished. Tone-deaf and unable to help the situation along, Moody was relieved when a sure tenor voice rose from the audience. Ira Sankey, a delegate from Pennsylvania, gave his clear tenor to the familiar words "There is a fountain filled with blood," and set the congregation to singing. After the service Moody surprised Sankey with an impulsive demand: "You are the man I have been looking for, and I want you to come to Chicago and help me in my work." From Moody's point of view, Sankey could sing and had risen admirably and unprompted to the occasion. He was clearly a man after Moody's heart. Later that day a peremptory summons from Moody brought Sankey to a busy street corner for an impromptu street meeting directed especially to the workers pouring out of nearby factories. Sankey's singing drew an instant crowd, and Moody offered a "powerful address" and invited everyone into the Academy of Music for more. He stopped only when the YMCA convention resumed. Sankey was duly impressed with the results of their united efforts. Still, several months passed before he left his career and his home to partner full-time with Moody. He was in Chicago when the great fire of 1871 destroyed much of the city. Sankey made his own escape in a small boat that he rowed out onto Lake Michigan, and he sang eerily appropriate words by Crosby while he watched the city burn:

> Dark is the night, and cold the wind is blowing,
> Nearer and nearer comes the breakers' roar;
> Where shall I go, or whither fly for refuge?
> Hide me, my Father, till the storm is o'er.

Moody and Sankey set sail for England in June 1873. England was Emma Moody's homeland and the Moodys brought their children along, while the Sankeys left theirs with family. Moody looked forward to building relationships with English Christian workers from whom he was eager to learn. And from his point of view, England stood in desperate need of the gospel. Its churched population distrusted American revivalists, and certainly Great Britain boasted few preachers less conventional than Dwight L. Moody, but class differences and social customs did not trouble the intrepid Moody. If God sent him to England, then he would do his best in England for God.

In the end, despite small beginnings, Moody's directness and persistence won him a hearing that exceeded expectations, and Sankey's music captured the imagination of millions. Britons who worried about decorum were relieved to find "the devotional parts" of Moody's meetings "as calm and unexciting as the soberest parish church." No untoward emotionalism disrupted proceedings, but people warmed to the new music and soon whistled the tunes Sankey taught them as they went about their daily business. Some English evangelicals, Anglican and other, had heard Lowell Mason lecture and had already learned some of Root's and Bradbury's tunes, and some had attended Philip Phillips's evangelistic concerts, so the style of music was not completely new to everyone, but in Sankey's able hands and tied to Moody's energetic efforts, the gospel song assumed a larger life than before. Sankey made music indispensable to Moody's accomplishments. The songster tailored his texts and tunes to each occasion and manifested an uncanny ability to have at hand an appropriate song for every sermon Moody delivered — or, for that matter, for any other event, however unpredictable. Perhaps the best-known incident illustrating Sankey's prowess was his rendering in song of a poem he had clipped from a newspaper but not yet set to music. The poem seemed just the right clincher for Moody's sermon "The Lost Sheep," so Sankey — undaunted by assembled thousands (and employing a technique similar to the improvisation marking many contemporary African American worship services) — ventured to compose a melody on the spot and made his way unerringly through the four stanzas that people soon coupled with his name whenever the Moody-Sankey meetings were the topic of conversation:

There were ninety-and-nine that safely lay
In the shelter of the fold,
But one was out on the hills away,
Far off from the streets of gold,
Away on the mountains, wild and bare
Away from the tender Shepherd's care.

This song became the hallmark of the Moody-Sankey revivals and a symptom of the "Moody and Sankey fever" that followed the

239

evangelists. Each audience demanded that Sankey render it at least once during a crusade, and its sure popularity prompted Sankey and Fanny Crosby to collaborate on a hymn to give the parable a practical application. They put it to audiences as a musical question:

> Have you sought for the sheep that have wandered,
> Far away on the dark mountain cold?
> Have you gone, like the tender Shepherd,
> To bring them again to the fold?

Sankey's use of texts geared to the specific rhythms of an evangelistic crusade promised to be even more remarkable in Britain than in the United States. American Protestants had a generation of Mason, Root, and Bradbury behind them as well as memories of the 1858 revival and the social meetings that flourished in its wake. At home, too, Sankey's music drew mixed reviews both as *church fare* and as *music*, but Americans were accustomed to informal religious settings that occasioned their own musical style. Even critics were apt to admit — though grudgingly — "the use of whatever will bring the Gospel in music home to those to whom better music is as yet unintelligible," though an article in the *New Englander* in 1879 insisted that "namby-pamby songs" were *always* offensive, whatever their purpose.

British Christians, their press mouthpieces affirmed, associated revivalism with "mere fanaticism and excitement," and this skepticism made some reluctant to predict how Moody and Sankey would be received. British Protestant music had featured psalm singing for more years than anyone could recall. Only Nonconformists — Congregationalists, Baptists, and Methodists — regularly replaced psalms with hymns, and even they did not entirely forsake the Psalter. But England had also given the English-speaking world the majestic words of Isaac Watts, Philip Doddridge, Charles Wesley, John Newton, and William Cowper, and in the nineteenth century more and more Anglicans experimented with hymn singing. Hymnals prepared for the use of particular congregations, hymns for special occasions, or hymns at evening vespers offered opportunities to experiment with the medium. The Oxford movement, a nineteenth-century Anglican form of High Churchism, had yielded its own substantial hymnody, including John Keble's "Sun of My Soul" and the perennial English favorite,

John Newman's "Lead Kindly Light." Meanwhile, Anglicans John Mason Neale, Catherine Winkworth, Jane Borthwick, and others assiduously translated ancient hymns for modern people and introduced their compatriots to Continental texts, but the Church of England still quarreled over adopting a hymnal. When Sankey arrived in 1873, *Hymns Ancient and Modern*, a first attempt at an official church hymnary, was barely a decade old, and the whole project was mired in controversy. The editors altered texts and resolutely excluded anything that suggested American revivalism. As the Anglican Church inched toward a full embrace of hymns, the editors of *Hymns Ancient and Modern* saw themselves as arbiters of the new tradition, and they proved finicky gatekeepers.

The situation in Scotland — where noninstrumental psalm singing was the order of the day — seemed to some even more problematic for the Americans. Sankey sometimes sang texts written by Horatius Bonar, a well-known pastor in the Church of Scotland, but most Scots did not. Americans smiled when the Scots objected to Sankey's "kist-o-whistles," but Sankey and Moody were not amused. They believed they had a point to make, though Sankey used a small melodeon rather than an organ, and they refused to back down. Their persistence ultimately helped pave the way for generations of Scottish male gospel choir festivals as well as for hymn-singing Scottish congregations.

Moody and Sankey, then, relying on music to draw crowds, drive home the message, and popularize it everywhere, walked into a musical situation fraught with historic and contemporary controversy. They offered yet another option to those at hand, and they stood ready to stake their work on its effectiveness. Their way worked, and the pragmatic Moody thought it needed no higher recommendation. Neither Moody nor Sankey lacked the courage to try. Sankey adopted as a hymnal for the meetings *Hallowed Songs*, a collection first produced in 1865 by the American Methodist singing evangelist Philip Phillips in collaboration with Theodore Perkins and Sylvester Main. These editors, "fixtures" around the offices of Bradbury Publishing and its successor, Biglow and Main, had designed a collection of hymns they considered "more practical, more easily read and understood, better adapted to every shade of religious experience, and more singable" than the songs most American congregations used on Sunday mornings. The editors aimed for accessible music that was still *music*, choruses that had *capacity*, and melodies of *rich variety*. They offered an ample supply of the old staples of Watts, Wesley, Doddridge, and Newton, a sprinkling of texts by the Scotsman Horatius Bonar, and a fair sampling of their own work, including numerous early Fanny Crosby texts. A revised edition in 1871 removed duplicate tunes and added nearly 100 pages of new material. Phillips advertised it for use by those intent on avoiding "light and meaningless hymns," some of which circulated in the array of Sunday school and social hymnals popular since the 1850s. *Hallowed Songs* made amply evident that a small cadre of composers and editors controlled lucrative and effective venues for gospel hymnody. Their shared goals gave it form. And, as Sandra Sizer pointed out in *Gospel Hymns and Social Religion*, they formed a school of sorts — a network of mentors and pupils whose paths regularly crossed at music conventions, normal institutes, revival meetings, Sunday school conventions, and related endeavors.

Sankey supplemented *Hallowed Songs* with various texts he had found useful during his short time at Moody's side in Chicago. He had brought along to England what he called his "musical scrapbook" — a random collection from which he generally chose his solos. His growing British public — some of whom had first warmed to his style of music during Phillips's recent visit — swamped him with appeals for copies, and Sankey unsuccessfully lobbied the publisher for a new edition of *Hallowed Songs* with an appendix of his own choice of revival hymns. The British publisher Morgan and Scott came to his rescue and produced twenty-three of his most popular numbers in an inexpensive sixteen-page pamphlet called *Sacred Songs and Solos, sung by Ira D. Sankey at the meetings of Mr. Moody of Chicago*. The first 500 copies retailed for sixpence each and were sold in a single day. A second printing also immediately sold out, and Morgan and Scott began issuing larger printings. Shops of all descriptions sold the books — known as "Sankey's." Owners proudly carried their copies to revival services. Some purchased piles of penny editions and distributed them as tracts. Sankey liked to tell of a soul saved because an English traveler left several on a table in the lobby of the Grand Hotel in Paris. The princess of Wales favored the book, presented to her by Sankey himself. She told him she used it for devotions with her children. Morgan and Scott had unknowingly accessed what became the single most valuable musical property of the era.

At Newcastle upon Tyne, Sankey organized the first of the famous Moody-Sankey mass choirs that became hallmarks of all later meetings. In Edinburgh in the fall of 1873, Sankey first tried his hand at gospel tune writing, a facility he soon put to good use with Crosby and others to turn out the gospel songs that suited his needs. Appropriately Sankey's first effort set to music words by Bonar, a frequent platform guest during Moody's meetings in Scotland. With Moody, Bonar could sing the hymns, including his own, that he never would hear in his own Scottish congregation.

In 1873 and 1874, meanwhile, P. P. Bliss, a prominent singing evangelist in the United States, was working up a modest collection of gospel songs for use in his work with evangelist Daniel W. Whittle. Though based in Pennsylvania, Bliss, too, had participated in the influential gospel song circle around Bradbury, Root, and Perkins. After it fired his imagination, as a young man in 1858 and again in 1863 he spent six weeks at the Normal Academy of Music in Geneseo, New York, where he found incentive for his life's work. His first musical effort — a secular song he called "Lora Vale" — was refused by Bradbury but published by Root. He made his living conducting singing schools, publishing songs, and, later, working for the Root brothers' music publishing company, Root and Cady, in Chicago. Bliss shared as well the Puritan roots of his gospel songwriting cohorts. A few years younger than most of them, he nonetheless fit easily into their circle. His work compared favorably with the best of theirs. In 1875 Bliss already had many gospel hymns to his credit, and their use by Sankey had gone a long way toward building his reputation. His "Hallelujah, What a Saviour" (also known by its first line, "Man of Sorrows, What a Name") and "Wonderful Words of Life," for example, became instant evangelical favorites, but for Moody's generation no Bliss texts approached the popularity of "Dare to Be a Daniel," "Only an Armorbearer," and — the best-loved of them all — "Hold the Fort."

Bliss first made Moody's acquaintance in Chicago in 1869 and had helped him with music occasionally before accepting a post as choir director and Sabbath school superintendent at Chicago's First Congregational Church. He was, then, a known quantity to Moody. His songs had been tried out on Moody's home turf, and his cooperation with Moody and Sankey was a natural outflow of past circumstances. In response to Moody's urgent insistence, Bliss had recently relinquished his employment to devote himself entirely to "singing the Gospel." When Moody and Sankey finished their triumphal tour of Britain in 1875, Sankey and Bliss agreed to combine the *Sacred Songs and Solos* with songs Bliss found useful for evangelism (many of which he authored himself) and to issue a single hymnal called *Gospel Hymns and Sacred Songs* for use during Moody's upcoming meetings in the United States. This book — necessary in part because American copyright laws made it impossible for Sankey to proceed in the United States as he had in Britain — was a joint venture between the two largest sacred music publishers in the United States — Biglow and Main, and John Church and Company (a Cincinnati concern in which William Doane had an interest and with which Bliss published after the Chicago fire destroyed Root and Cady). The book debuted at the Brooklyn Rink in 1875 and circulated in enormous numbers. Although musical detractors grumbled that it "carried the more emotional and less cultivated element of religious people off its feet," even they recognized its unprecedented appeal to "vast numbers hitherto unacquainted with hymns and unused to public worship." Its words and tunes penetrated secular venues, where "Hold the Fort" ("Ho, my comrades, see the signal waving in the sky/Reinforcements now appearing, victory is nigh!") and "Dare to Be a Daniel" ("Dare to be a Daniel, dare to stand alone/Dare to have a purpose firm, dare to make it known") especially captured imaginations. Gospel hymn texts became household words and entered the popular vocabulary of Victorian America as they had already done in Britain.

As prepared for the New York meetings, *Gospel Hymns and Sacred Solos* was a compact book of 133 hymns, most printed with tunes. Bliss and Sankey offered them with the hope "that a like blessing will accompany the use of them in this land." If blessing can be measured in sales figures, the "like blessing" soon exceeded anything publishers and compilers of sacred song had ever before seen. An incessant demand for "more" resulted in a series of hymnals published on both sides of the Atlantic under Sankey's name, the last of which offered well over 1,200 gospel texts in a single volume. But for the moment, a modest effort sufficed. As soon as the pressure of the first round of meetings eased, Sankey and Bliss met in Chicago to spend a few weeks working closely to expand and improve their hymnal.

The first edition of their book opened with Bishop Ken's "Old

Hundredth" ("All creatures that on earth do dwell") and then moved quickly to the new songs of the day. Toward the back were a group of tried-and-true standards by Watts, Wesley, Cowper, Doddridge, and Newton, and of course, the hymn by Edward Perronet that was fast becoming an American revival theme text: "All Hail the Power of Jesus' Name." Bishop Keble's "Sun of My Soul, Thou Saviour Dear" found a place, as did Augustus Toplady's "Rock of Ages" (to Lowell Mason's tune). And, not surprisingly, words and music by P. P. Bliss were most numerous of all.

Fanny Crosby's name appeared first above hymn number 4, her already widely sung "Safe in the Arms of Jesus." Number 18 offered "Rescue the Perishing," then a new and unproven text, set to a tune by Doane, and destined to enjoy wide popularity. Paging through the hymnal reveals a sprinkling of other Crosby texts. "Pass Me Not, O Gentle Saviour," like "Rescue the Perishing," had been born in one of the New York City rescue missions that Crosby frequented. Sankey found Crosby's "Jesus, Keep Me Near the Cross" useful in the crowded weekday prayer gatherings that supported the mass evening preaching services. (During the Brooklyn meetings, these prayer meetings taxed the capacity of Talmage's enormous Brooklyn Tabernacle.) In this first American Moody-Sankey hymnal, it stood across the page from "Oh Sing of His Mighty Love," a song by Crosby's Britain-born holiness Methodist friend Frank Bottome, set to music by William Bradbury. The turn of a page brought another Crosby-Doane hymn, "Saviour, More Than Life to Me," a prayer for cleansing power, nearness to Christ, and comforting assurance. "All the Way My Saviour Leads Me," set to a tune by the ever popular Robert Lowry, was number 60. The final Crosby text in this first edition of Sankey's American book assured the penitent of pardon ("Yes, there is pardon for you") and urged people to "escape to the cross." The inclusion of these texts by Crosby in this first hastily assembled American version of the Sankey hymnal assured her verse exposure to the widest possible Protestant audiences. Of all the contemporary hymn writers Sankey used, only Bliss had more texts in this first hymnal than Crosby. The hymnal proved so popular — and the public purchased copies at such a pace (one million before the spring of 1876) — that newspaper reporters at the Moody-Sankey meetings saved space by referring to the songs by number, confident that their readers could easily discover the hymn title and text.

The indefatigable nonmusical Moody pushed these songs in every possible way. He recognized the appeal of Sankey's solos and choirs, but occasionally he snatched musical leadership from Sankey. In Brooklyn, for example, he had the congregation repeat a chorus so many times that Sankey finally stopped playing accompaniment, assuming Moody was ready to move on. "'Sing on,' shouted Mr. Moody. 'We are making Heaven ring with gladness this afternoon. We'll make all Brooklyn joyous.'" The audience obliged with three more renderings, and at last Moody pronounced the benediction. The incident revealed Moody's characteristic method of handling religious emotions: when they became irrepressible, he had people sing. He permitted emotional expression only as long as he channeled and controlled it, and sacred music offered the most orderly means to that end.

Moody and Sankey spent less than a month in Brooklyn in 1875 before hastening to Chicago for a few "welcome home" occasions and then hurrying on to Philadelphia. They crowded an evangelistic series in Philadelphia's recently renovated Old Railroad Depot into the hectic days before Christmas. When they had left the New York area in November, they had promised to return for a longer endeavor in a more commodious venue. Early in 1876 they kept their word with a series of meetings in the largest (though not the most appealing) auditorium in Manhattan — P. T. Barnum's Hippodrome, an 8,000-seat facility between Twenty-sixth and Twenty-seventh Streets.

New York had begun planning this second series of meetings even before Moody and Sankey returned from Britain, and the arrangements showed it. Prayer meetings, conferences, and cooperative endeavors enlisted members of all the city's Protestant churches and set the stage for a remarkable spectacle — two staid, portly Protestant evangelists commanding the attention of leading citizens of the nation's corporate headquarters. Anticipation had already "limbered up" the city's evangelicals, who for the most part made up the crowds of ushers, singers, and personal workers on whom an efficient result depended.

At one level the "Hippodrome work" was a business enterprise run by corporate giants with names like Dodge, Phelps, and Colgate for the purpose of saving souls, selling books, and filling empty pews in Protestant churches. Some regarded the stark setting itself an implicit rebuke of the city's fashionable Protestant sanctuaries. Their parishioners had become accustomed to bearing the brunt of the criticism leveled at Protestant Christianity in general. "Worshipping in the rude-walled Hippodrome, sitting on wooden chairs, led in song by a man with a melodeon, and preached to by a man without a pulpit," the attendees seemed to prove conclusively by their piety in this venue the superfluity of expensive appointments, costly pews, pipe organs, and professional (translate "pricey") musicians to the worship of God.

In the estimation of observers and participants, perhaps most remarkable of all — after Moody's commonsense direct style — was the music. Most people came prepared with their "Moody and Sankey Hymn-book," the same used in Brooklyn a few months before. A diligent *New York Times* reporter began his assignment by attending the choir rehearsal the night before the services began. Some 1,250 strong, the choir was reputed to be "the best Moody and Sankey have yet had." It prepared that night to introduce to New York a new song by Fanny Crosby, "Rescue the Perishing":

Rescue the perishing, care for the dying,
Snatch them in pity from sin and the grave;
Weep o'er the erring one, lift up the fallen,
Tell them of Jesus, the Mighty to Save.

Rescue the perishing, care for the dying!
Jesus is merciful, Jesus will save.

After a few trials, this Crosby-Doane piece was "sung in an excellent manner," the reporter noticed, and he predicted (correctly, as it turned out) that it would become a favorite. Recruited from area churches, this volunteer choir played an important role in setting the tone for services by singing with the thousands who arrived early, leading the singing throughout, and supporting with music the invitation to decision at the conclusion of every service.

As elsewhere, the Moody-Sankey hymnal sold briskly in Manhattan. It had the distinct appeal of being both inexpensive and small. Promoters urged its benefits over the typical bulky denominational hymnals containing songs "one-third unsingable and one-third padding." Sankey's was emphatically "the people's hymnal," combining what he deemed the most useful of the old with the appeal of the new. Ordinary people took it up, bought it, carried it to meetings, sang it and demanded more. Already in 1876, five million copies and twenty translations had carried *Gospel Hymns* beyond the North Atlantic to Asia and Africa. In short order the hymnal swept America and crossed from England to the Continent. "Even sedate Germany," one contemporary noticed, "has its own edition." With the book went the "new idea" of singing the gospel, "for many of these pieces are not hymns at all, but simply gospel songs, and they have been the means of converting many souls." Moody's many sympathizers quickly grasped the possibilities these songs offered for the task at hand, though a few detractors seized on musical innovations to focus their general distaste for revival, objecting to any hymnal that featured gospel songs in place of old standards. Despite such mutterings, though, *Gospel Hymns and Sacred Solos* did attempt to preserve a certain standard and dignity in the use of sacred song. And a growing number of critics acknowledged that it fulfilled its purpose if evaluated in the light of its own claims. A writer for the *Princeton Review* in 1879 admitted: "The popularity from Maine to India of music such as that of the Moody and Sankey hymns . . . justifies the use of whatever will bring the Gospel in music home to those to whom better music is as yet unintelligible."

Moody-Sankey crusades persisted through the rest of the century and nurtured a demand for multiple-purpose gospel hymns. When a train wreck took Bliss's life late in 1876, Sankey turned to George C. Stebbins and James McGranahan, musical evangelists of proven merit. Every one of their expanded collections featured more Crosby texts than the one it replaced, sometimes placing her words as the opening hymn. Over time their final summative compilation of all that had come before, *Gospel Hymns 1-6,* would be translated and reprinted for use around the world. Sankey, McGranahan, and Stebbins selected material for these expanded editions and enlarged the contents to include numbers for mass choirs as well as congregations. For a German edition Sankey enlisted the help of Walter Rauschenbusch, later to be the voice of the Social Gospel, who did much of the work himself but also recruited a cadre of capable assistants. Despite his own mounting impatience with evangelical individualism, Rauschenbusch's work on this project gave German evangelicals an enduring legacy of gospel hymnody. When Sankey died in 1908, the *New York Times* estimated that some 50 million of his variations on *Gospel Hymns 1-6* were in circulation; others claimed the number stood closer to 80 million. With 30 percent royalties coming their way, Moody and Sankey demonstrated the profitability of gospel hymn publishing. They simply followed the time-tested model of Mason, Bradbury, and Root, providing resources for use in venues they controlled. The first three had become wealthy men, but their success paled in comparison to Moody's and Sankey's.

A look at Crosby's hymns in these hymnals offers as convenient an entry point as any for exploring how her words served Sankey's ends. In the Sankey hymnals published on both sides of the Atlantic, Crosby produced an ever higher percentage of the total number of hymns, often writing under several pseudonyms (male and female) in a single collection. (She contributed about one-seventh of the songs in the last edition.) The success of the first hymnal established her right to a prominent place in the subsequent books, cemented her friendship with Moody and Sankey, and greatly expanded her public.

Taken together, the texts included in *Gospel Hymns and Sacred Solos* and the subsequent *Gospel Hymns* offer a window on evangelicalism as defined by Moody and Sankey, perhaps its ablest American popularizers in the last quarter of the nineteenth century. Their embrace of Crosby's lyrics moved her onto the larger stage from which the evangelists did all they could to address the world. When he had the floor, Sankey often described Crosby to the audiences that sang her words. His sentimental "incidents of hymns" and references to her pluck despite her blindness piqued enormous interest and an international correspondence. Her hymns, like others in his collection, had immediate impact as well as some enduring popularity in part because they captured the era's popular evangelical perception of the world and the Christian's place in it. The songs both shaped and expressed the evangelical impulse as it flowered in the urban revival crusades that became a hallmark of American revivalism. The act of singing them also molded the disparate individuals who flocked to revivals into a community by enabling them to express their deepest emotions with one voice. By the end of the century, an evangelist could stride to the pulpit in a revival crusade and unify the crowd simply by starting a gospel hymn.

The hymns in Sankey's hymnals were not arranged in thematic order as hymns were in denominational hymnals. These books offered only minimal apparatus: a brief preface and an index to first lines and common titles. The preface boldly commended the hymns as the most "useful and popular" pieces in the entire corpus of Christian song. "Popular" suggested a familiarity that all the songs had not yet achieved beyond the Moody revivals. Perhaps "useful" — claimed as it was in the heat of the compilers' battles for souls — was more to the point. And so the hymns seem simply strung together, with some logic to the selection of Old Hundredth as first and to the gathering of traditional hymns (mostly eighteenth-century British in origin) toward the end.

Crosby's songs are sprinkled among those of her peers — broadly speaking, the same cadre with which she often worked. Since Sankey wanted hymns appropriate to specific — but to some extent unpredictable — occasions, he included a mix of popular numbers (like Crosby's "Safe in the Arms of Jesus") while introducing new texts and tunes (like "Rescue the Perishing"). Later editions sifted new hymns based on their usefulness or audience appeal. Several themes of the era's popular evangelicalism immediately become evident in Crosby's contributions. Taken together with her other work, these offer revealing glimpses of her contribution to the evangelical idiom of her day.

10 Gospel Hymns:
Crosby's "Creed in Metre"

O wonderful words of the gospel!
O wonderful message they bring,
Proclaiming a blessed redemption
Through Jesus, our Saviour and King.

Believe, oh believe in His mercy
That flows like a fountain so free,
Believe and receive the redemption
He offers to you and to me.

While no one knows just how many gospel hymn texts Crosby wrote, no one disputes that she crafted thousands. Her older contemporary, Disciples of Christ founder Alexander Campbell, suggested that sacred songs constituted a "creed in metre" and "as good an index to the brains and to the hearts of a people as the creed book." Crosby's texts can be read as a lens on evangelical Protestantism. They achieved such popularity in her day that they offered defining metaphors of evangelical piety. If they were weak on carefully nuanced theology, her simple words had the virtue of indisputable clarity about religious experience and its practical outflow. Despite the unprecedented volume of text Crosby composed, her hymns cover only a few topics, often repeat metaphors, and lapse easily into sentiment — "Jesus, dear." In his recent monumental study *The English Hymn* (1997), literary critic J. R. Watson charged that they — like many other texts in Sankey's hymnals — "reduce[d] the complexities of human experience to an excitable repetition, an assertive sentiment." To her public, that was just the point. Many musical gatekeepers of nineteenth-century Protestant churches concurred with Watson, but they failed utterly to convince the millions of Crosby's contemporaries who attested the power of her texts (most often as set to music) to warm their hearts and spur them on toward the goals she held before them.

No one made a serious case for Crosby lyrics as "serious" hymns. Rather, her lyrics were "singable," "catchy in the best sense of the word," and their resonance with grassroots realities assured that they would be remembered and sung long after "more ambitious poems" had been forgotten. Her contemporaries did not expect to find her lines in books printed without notes and designed for devotional reading; few, they admitted, "will achieve poetic immortality." Instead, her words were emphatically for singing, and the simplicity, sentiment, "galloping," and repetitiveness that critics found offensive were the precise elements that charmed the masses. Since tunesmiths often approached Crosby for text for their new tunes, her options were limited by the wishes of the tune writer as well as by the occasions for which the text and tune were solicited. Her modest and limited education — begun formally when she was already fifteen — lacked the breadth and depth that breathed from the eighteenth-century hymn texts she loved. Literary critics and theologians might bestow careful analyses on the Wesleys or Watts but would find little to occupy them in the hymns of Fanny Crosby. While her lines revealed her beliefs, they made no claim to be (in John Wesley's famous words) "a little body of practical and experimental divinity." Rather, they were emblems of faith. In an era of mounting intellectual challenge to traditional Christianity, Crosby's words mirrored the views of a large percentage of rank-and-file evangelical Protestants who either failed to grasp the implications of modern thought or discounted its relevance to evangelical faith.

Crosby's gospel hymns fall easily under four general headings that reiterated the familiar claims of an older gospel to a generation beset by the theological challenges of modernity: salvation, consecration, service, heaven. Within these categories her texts touched on a handful of themes that shaped and mirrored what late nineteenth-century evangelicals emphasized about cleansing, rest, safety, intimacy with Christ, duty, readiness for Christ's return, and seeing Christ. Her sentimental Victorian phrases, infused with romantic sensibilities, stood in sharp contrast to the stark rejections of supernaturalism of the era's intellectual elite. She sang of faith in an age of doubt, and millions grasped for certainty by joining her song.

SALVATION

The largest single cluster of the Crosby texts in Sankey's gospel hymnals proclaimed God's gracious invitation to the sinner, often employing the image of a fountain of cleansing. This wording, familiar to contemporaries for its biblical associations as well as from William Cowper's famous text "There is a fountain filled with blood," urged all to "wash":

> Come with thy sins to the fountain,
> Come with thy burden of grief;
> Bury them deep in its waters,
> There thou wilt find sweet relief.
> Come as thou art to the fountain,
> Jesus is waiting for thee;
> What tho' thy sins are like crimson?
> White as the snow they shall be.

Or,

> He has led me to the fountain,
> I have plunged beneath its flood;
> There I felt the precious cleansing
> Of his all-atoning blood.

Here "plunge" echoed Phoebe Palmer's "Cleansing Stream," familiar text in Crosby's day: "I plunge, and oh, it cleanseth me." Crosby lyrics urged prompt acting on the gospel invitation, as these addressed to the

YMCA in 1867 and used in the men's meetings that each Moody campaign featured: "Oh, what are you going to do, brother? Say, what are you going to do?"

In her summons to salvation, Crosby, like many Victorian hymn writers, favored the parable of the prodigal son. She invited the erring to come home, employing the familiar domestic language used as readily by male as by female hymn writers in her day: "Jesus is tenderly calling thee home," waiting, pleading as a parent with a wayward child. Crosby made only limited application of such domestic imagery to the Christian life, however. More often her rhetoric of home pointed to heaven. Yet her hymns helped make evangelicals comfortable with a sentimentalized Christ, approachable on familiar familial terms — brother, friend, companion (often with adjectives like "dear," "precious," "lovely," "gentle," "kind"), and ever welcoming host. Functionally they tend to depict him more as a sympathetic, patient, helpful, dependable friend than as the second member of the Trinity. Crosby often adopted an earlier evangelical usage that took the slur of the New Testament Pharisees — Jesus the "friend of sinners" — to construct a relational model with Jesus, friend, companion, and confidant at its core. Her lines offered abundant testimony about the faithfulness of this friend — he did it for me (rescued, found, forgave, cleansed), he will do the same for you.

In her formative years Crosby sat under pastors who preached the limited atonement, but the adult Crosby stood squarely in the Methodist camp when it came to free will and free grace, and this made her hymns particularly useful to revivalists who proclaimed "Whosoever will may come." One of her best-loved songs — kept alive by generations of the Scottish male gospel choirs first formed in the enthusiasm of the Moody revivals — made this point:

> Behold, behold the wondrous love
> That ever flows from God above
> Through Christ His only Son who gave
> His precious blood our souls to save.
>
> The "Spirit and the Bride say, Come"
> And find in Him sweet rest and home;
> Let Him that heareth echo still,
> The blessed *"whosoever will."*

All praise and glory be unto Jesus,
For He hath purchased a full salvation;
Behold how wondrous the proclamation,
"Whosoever will may come."

Crosby's gospel proclamation was Arminian in tone and emphatically Christ-centered in emphasis. Yet saving work was entirely Christ's gracious act:

Not of myself, dear Lord, I cried,
The gift is all Thine own;
I must be saved, O Lamb of God,
By faith in Thee alone.
From this glad hour that faith be mine,
The praise of my salvation, Thine.

Or,

'Twas not my love to Thee, Oh Lord,
'Twas not my love to Thee
That opened wide salvation's tide
No — 'twas Thy love to me.

Crosby texts on salvation also voiced a growing evangelical tendency to refer to the spiritually needy as lost, wandering, wounded, or broken rather than as damned and utterly corrupt. These, of course, were also biblical metaphors, but they seemed less harsh than the adjectives older hymns often evoked — "vile," "guilty," or Isaac Watts's famous identification (in "Alas, and Did My Saviour Bleed") of the unregenerate self with a worm. Yet one can overstate the contrast, for Crosby's gospel hymns did also employ the traditional evangelical language of sin. Crosby sometimes used Scripture directly ("Though your sins be as scarlet they shall be as white as snow") or crafted her own expressions to invoke traditional images: "Ye souls that long in darkness/the path of sin have trod" or "To Jesus fly. Why will ye die?/ See pardon flowing from His side" or "O sinner, bid thy conscience wake/Hast thou of death no fear?" She stated clearly that sinners had no hope of heaven, but her hymns seldom if ever assigned them to hell. Rather, she left their eternal destiny unstated. Perhaps her hymns, often presented by Sankey among selected eighteenth-century texts from Watts, Charles Wesley, and Philip Doddridge, suggest not that evangelicals had replaced an older, sterner rhetoric but that they also found an alternative rendering effective. In some ways Crosby's gospel hymns — while wholly devoted to biblical metaphors — suggested that evangelicalism was becoming "seeker sensitive."

While Sandra Sizer did not focus her study of gospel hymns, *Gospel Hymns and Social Religion,* on Crosby's text, her observation that, taken together, such hymns reconceptualized Christ offers a helpful glimpse of the direction that the heavy use of testimony and of the first and second persons indicated: "If the scenario of the older hymns was that of a criminal pleading before God with Christ as his advocate, that of the gospel hymns is one of Jesus on trial before a huge, anonymous, and largely hostile jury, with happy Christians appearing in the witness stand in his behalf. They describe the character and actions of the accused in glowing detail, celebrate his great deeds, ask others to consider his suffering and extend their sympathies, and finally plead for his acceptance into their hearts."

Among Crosby's hymns, Sankey found "Pass Me Not, O Gentle Saviour" the most popular of the entire collection of songs with the crowds that thronged to Her Majesty's Theater for Moody's meetings in London in 1874. The hymn invoked a biblical scene — Christ walking down a road, stopping to heed the cries of needy people along the way. It pictured the individual in the crowd, the single voice crying out for salvation from among the throng, corresponding nicely to the reality of the crusades in which individuals in the gathered mass were moved to respond to Moody's invitation.

> Pass me not, o gentle Saviour,
> Hear my humble cry;
> While on others Thou art calling,
> Do not pass me by.
>
> Trusting only in Thy merit
> Would I seek Thy face;
> Heal my wounded, broken spirit;
> Save me by Thy grace.

Thou, the spring of all my comfort,
More than life to me!
Whom have I on earth beside Thee?
Whom in Heaven but Thee?

All who came, cried out, and washed in the fountain embarked on a relationship with Christ, the Savior, characterized at once by peace and yearning. To know him at once satisfied and made one long to know him better; being "saved," "rescued," or "found" led inevitably for Crosby to wanting to live one's saved life in intimate relationship to the one who had saved.

CONSECRATION

Another large cluster of Crosby's hymns described this longing and testified to its ever deepening satisfaction in Christ. This cluster offers revealing insights into the blending of historic strands of evangelicalism in the popular Protestant piety of the late nineteenth century. Crosby texts focus on dependence and trust as foundation of evangelical spirituality. She both tapped and shaped a brand of Christ-centered piety using the Authorized Version's metaphors for the Savior: "a spring of joy," the "bright and morning star," a "precious treasure" to be valued more than life itself. In the end, Crosby lyrics made a case for Christ as all that one required — guidance, cheer, grace, sustenance, spiritual healing, tender love, salvation itself. With this in mind, Crosby thought of Christ as "my portion," most prominently in "Thou my everlasting portion,/More than friend or life to me," but also in less known lines: "And yet no thought so precious, so full of joy to me/Than this, thou art my portion, and shalt forever be"; or, "Thou, Saviour, art my portion/What wealth untold is mine/What pure and priceless treasures/Not earthly but divine." What was more, one could *feel* Christ near: she idealized him as the core of life itself. In 1876 Crosby put it as follows:

Jesus, what is life without Thee?
What are friends without Thy love?
What are joys that do not center
On the better life above?

257

> I have sought and found Thee precious,
> And my soul delights in Thee;
> But I need Thy constant presence.
> Saviour, Lord, abide with me.

For Crosby the cross held special appeal as a place for centering proximity to Christ. Since something good happened to one there, what better place to "linger"? Her "Jesus, Keep Me Near the Cross" looked upon Calvary as a place for the believer's imagination and will to tarry. The cross was a place of safety, nurture, and remembrance. The text stands in striking contrast to Watts's majestic "When I Survey the Wondrous Cross." Whereas Watts's contemplation of the cross culminated in a profound sense of what the cross *demands* of self, Crosby reveled in what the cross *gave* self as in these personal testimonies:

> Near the cross a trembling soul,
> Love and mercy found me;
> There a bright and morning star
> Sheds its beams around me.

Or,

> At the cross I love to linger,
> At the cross I love to rest.
> There I found a full salvation,
> There my longing soul was blest.

The use of the first person seemed to make Crosby transparent and vulnerable — to bare her soul while also providing language to assist congregations to form and articulate corporate desire (and holding up for any who did not yet have the desire a description of spiritual hunger to which to aspire). Such personal language had the dual task of showing the errant what they lacked and helping the convinced to define a common goal and then measure experience by it. These interwoven prayers and testimonies, then, defined ideals for evangelical piety. As songs of the pilgrimage that *was* the Christian life, they were highly personal, with exhortation implied indirectly (in prayers and testimonies) as well as directly. Texts described emotions and sentiments appropriate to the evangelical experience; sung corporately, they enabled singers to share expressions of stirred feelings — what Sizer called a powerful "community of feeling." In mass revival meetings they helped avoid the chaos of rampant individualism by directing emotional response, all the while allowing individuals to share through song a first-person account of intensely emotional aspects of the spiritual journey.

Crosby hymns on aspects of the Christian life reveal evangelicals' attraction to what Sizer and others have called "passive spirituality." While they still sang Watts's hardy words "Sure I must fight if I would reign! Increase my courage, Lord," late nineteenth-century evangelicals also featured hymns stating a need to relinquish control to an all-loving and merciful Savior. Words like "rest," "peace," "abiding," and "repose" expressed for Crosby the ideal state of the soul:

Passive at Thy feet and yielding
Every power to Thy control;
Pleading nothing but Thy mercy
I would lay my inmost soul.

Passive at Thy feet, my Saviour,
Rescued by Thy grace divine,
I would be a chosen vessel
Consecrated only Thine.

Passive at Thy feet, my Saviour,
Hoping, trusting, still I rest,
Waiting till Thy voice shall call me
To the mansions of the blest.

Crosby reminded those who worried about "temptation's snares" of their privilege to sit quietly in Christ's embrace where sin could not reach them. He held his own, while they longed for more intimacy, reveled in his presence, and coveted his approval:

Safe in the arms of Jesus, safe from corroding care,
Safe from the world's temptations, sin cannot harm me there.

Or,

O sweetest hours when I can say
Thou Lord, my strength, art mine,
When I can yield my all to Thee
And have no will but Thine.

Or,

Take all, but let me trust in Thee;
Take all, but be Thou all to me.

In a similar vein, Crosby's words for a tune and hymn familiar to German Protestants, "So nimm denn meine Hände," began with the German first line but then moved to Crosby's own petition for surrender:

Take Thou my hand and lead me, choose Thou my way;
"Not as I will," O Father, teach me to say;
What though the storms may gather? Thou knowest best;
Safe in Thy holy keeping, there would I rest.

Or,

Hold Thou my hand; so weak I am and helpless,
I dare not take one step without Thy aid;
Hold Thou my hand; for then, O loving Saviour,
No dread of ill shall make my soul afraid.

Hold Thou my hand, and closer, closer draw me
To Thy dear self — my hope, my joy, my all;
Hold Thou my hand, lest haply I should wander,
And, missing Thee, my trembling feet should fall.

Hold Thou my hand; the way is dark before me
Without the sunlight of Thy face divine;
But when by faith I catch its radiant glory,
What heights of joy, what rapturous songs are mine!

This dependence emphasized one aspect of traditional Christian spirituality and found growing appeal in popular evangelicalism during an era of rapid cultural and theological change. Pre–Civil War cultural optimism yielded after the war to the social stresses of urbanization, industrialization, and new immigration. At the same time, scientists, theologians, and biblical scholars raised doubts about the basic assumptions that had traditionally nurtured evangelical faith. Hopefulness about American agency in ushering in the millennium yielded in influential places to pessimism about realizing the kingdom of God on earth, and the premillennialist impulse urged personal holiness and aggressive evangelism as the most appropriate Christian priorities. Amid competing voices, then, many evangelicals found compelling the twin notions of safe shelter from the uncertainties of the times and personal submission to divine sovereignty.

Crosby prayer songs often coveted "hiding," usually in the "shadow of the rock," a biblical allusion of which she made frequent use:

Hide me, O my Saviour, hide me in Thy holy place,
Resting there beneath Thy glory, O let me see Thy face.

Or,

In thy cleft, O Rock of Ages, hide thou me;
When the fitful tempest rages, hide thou me.

Or, in words less known, she rejoiced in the safety of the rock:

My hope is anchored on a rock, a rock no time can move;
My soul looks up with childlike faith to rest in Jesus' love.

Crosby texts sometimes directly invoked the Holy Spirit, revealing her sense of the centrality of the Spirit's role in the spirituality she coveted:

Thou proceedest from the Father,
And Thy office is divine;
Blessed Spirit, truth's great teacher,
O, instruct this heart of mine.

To the school of heavenly wisdom
Let me now admitted be
And that I may learn with meekness,
O, impart Thyself to me.

How to feel a deeper reverence
For my Saviour and my Lord,
How to lean with more devotion
On the comfort of His Word;
How to labor for His glory,
How my hope may stronger be,
How to walk with Him more closely,
Blessed Spirit, teach Thou me.

Teach me, when beset by evil,
How the tempter's wiles to shun;
Teach me, in the hour of trial,
How to say God's will be done.
Teach me how by patient striving
Light to others I may be;
Every Christian grace and virtue
Blessed Spirit, teach Thou me.

Did such preoccupations entice evangelicals of Crosby's ilk from
the field of conflict imagined by their eighteenth-century forebears? So
Princeton's Benjamin Warfield thought when he accused some among
them of wanting to be "carried to the skies on flowery beds of ease,"
leaving others to "fight to win the prize and sail on bloody seas." Yet
one must realize that Crosby's language of refuge, hiding, and fellowship was not new. Pietist hymns, Methodist hymns, and Anglican
hymns offered abundant precedents: "O Jesus, nothing may I see/
Nothing desire, or seek, but Thee!" (Paul Gerhardt, 1653); or, "My Jesus, as Thou wilt;/Oh, may Thy will be mine!/Into Thy hand of love/I
would my all resign" (Benjamin Schmolck, 1704); "A heart resigned,
submissive, meek/My dear Redeemer's throne/Where only Christ is
heard to speak/Where Jesus reigns alone" (Charles Wesley, 1742); "Is
there a thing beneath the sun/That strives with Thee my heart to
share?/Ah, tear it thence and reign alone/The Lord of every motion

there/Then shall my heart from earth be free/When it hath found repose in Thee" (Gerhard Tersteegen, 1729; translated, John Wesley, 1736). In theory, passivity was power, not weakness, because it made Christ the effective source of Christian service: one did what he directed in the power he provided.

Literary critic J. R. Watson suggests how Crosby's texts differed from these standards of English hymnody. Whereas Wesley made his text "reflect not only human experience but also a profound examination of relevant passages from the New Testament," Crosby relied on evocations of "superficial emotional states" (as in "Perfect submission, all is at rest/I in my Saviour am happy and blest"). But if she lacked the profundity from which to do more, she satisfied the requirements of the times and the settings for which she wrote.

Crosby's attraction to this form of evangelical piety suggested her leanings toward the nineteenth-century Holiness movement where "the rest of faith" described the sanctified state and the faithful longed to know "Christ enthroned within." But it also revealed her awareness of what had come before, and it indicated as well the extent of shared language between evangelicals in general and proponents of holiness in particular, for they tapped a common heritage, though all who sang the words did not endorse the same theological details. And, most basically, holiness language was often simply familiar Christian terminology invested with particular meaning. One could employ its general sense without intending its particular connotations. Since it had both universal and particular Christian appeal, it proved especially useful in revivals where some of its themes — cleansing, the blood of Christ, transforming experience — corresponded to the core of the message.

While she did not record a profession of a second blessing, Crosby took delight in the company of those who did and manifested affinities for their views by spending parts of most summers at their camp meetings. Phoebe Palmer, perhaps the most able distiller of Wesleyan holiness in Crosby's purview, held that "total submission" brought "perfect rest." She told thousands to "lay their all on the altar." In her logic the altar was Christ, and "the altar sanctified the gift." One could simply "take" sanctification by faith. Crosby once put it this way, suggesting her clear comprehension of the teaching and perhaps her personal experience:

My gift is on Thy altar laid;
'Tis all I have, my God, for Thee.
And while I ask Thy mercy now
I cling by simple faith to Thee.

My gift is on Thy altar laid;
Oh, let the fire consume its dross;
This broken, contrite heart of mine
Take Thou, and nail it to Thy cross.

'Tis done! The prayer of faith is heard;
My load of guilt is rolled away.
A pardoned soul, with joy I sing,
Oh love divine, oh glorious day.

Again, Crosby's references to a heart refined by fire echoed holiness vocabulary but resonated with broader evangelical spirituality, too:

As gold amid the furnace do Thou my heart refine,
O banish every idol, and make me wholly Thine.
In perfect trust confiding my way, O Lord, to Thee
I'll take without a murmur whate'er Thou sendest me.

Versed in the writings of the seventeenth-century French Quietist Madame Guyon, northern leaders of the Holiness movement especially endorsed a Christ-centered perfectionism that featured the individual's "being nothing" so that Christ could "be all." In 1894 Crosby put it this way (to a tune by William J. Kirkpatrick):

How tranquil my spirit, how perfectly blest,
While safe on the promise I peacefully rest;
Believing, abiding, and trusting in thee,
My loving Redeemer, so precious to me.

Few gospel hymn writers with broad appeal testified as enduringly as Crosby to such holiness themes as the cleansing blood and power to live a Christian life. "I washed my soul in Jesus' blood/I washed, and now I see/The wondrous condescending love/That stooped to ransom me"; or "We plunge beneath the crimson flood/We rise renewed, forgiven"; or "In the blood my soul is hiding/Precious blood he shed for me/Only there is my salvation/Only there my hope shall be." Perhaps her most famous text on the subject repeated the line "redeemed by the blood of the Lamb" and channeled ecstatic response into the "safe" vehicle of song: "Redeemed, and so happy in Jesus/No language my rapture can tell." She often yearned to "feel" cleansing or power, a concept rich in Methodist and holiness overtones, but one that held much wider appeal in the romantic era: "Every day, every hour let me feel Thy cleansing power." Or, "O what transport now to find Thee/Now Thy pardoning love to feel/How it lifts my spirit upward/Earth such joy could ne'er reveal."

Such Crosby lines — set to music by the Baptist Doane and chosen for a hymnal by the Congregationalist Ira Sankey — remind one that fascination for the blood of Christ was not confined to Methodists. In Crosby's hand, though, exultation in the blood often seemed to contemporaries to have distinctly joyous "shouting Methodist," even holiness, overtones:

> We're saved by the blood that was drawn from the side
> Of Jesus our Lord when He languished and died.
> We're saved by the blood, we are sealed by its power;
> Tis life to the soul and its hope every hour.
> Hallelujah to God for redemption so free,
> Hallelujah, hallelujah, dear Saviour to Thee.

Crosby used effusive language about other aspects of Christian experience, too: "Glory, glory, all is glory/On the mountaintop I stand/Lost in wonder, filled with rapture/I can clasp my Saviour's hand." (Here — as part of the ecstasy — she grasps Christ's hand. Elsewhere — when troubled or anxious — she thrills to the thought of his grasping hers.) In January 1875 the words of Psalm 23 prompted her to exult:

> My cup runneth over, O Saviour divine,
> How rich are Thy blessings! What comfort is mine!
> My cup runneth over, all glory to Thee,
> For great is Thy mercy, Thy mercy to me.

My faith is unclouded, my anchor is strong;
I love Thee my Saviour, and this is my song —
Thy blood has redeemed me! All glory to Thee,
For great is Thy mercy, Thy mercy to me.

This language of feeling fueled Crosby's appeal to leaders and laypersons. She poured emotions into verse, summoned words to expose her warmed heart, acknowledged feeling beyond description ("no language my rapture can tell"), and enabled a congregation to respond in song without the unseemly personal behavior that might otherwise have invited disorder. Such passion made some form of proximity or another to its source a valued ideal, and "closeness" to Christ seemed to follow naturally in Crosby's text: "Close to Thee, all along my pilgrim journey, Saviour, let me walk with Thee"; or "Saviour, more than life to me, I am clinging, clinging close to Thee." "Oh, how I pine for Thee," she wrote in "Jesus My All." Perhaps her best-known lines about closeness began with entire consecration — "I am Thine, O Lord, I have heard Thy voice" — pined for deeper consecration — "Consecrate me now to Thy service, Lord. . . . [Let] my will be lost in Thine" — and ended with the refrain "Draw me nearer, nearer, nearer, blessed Lord, to Thy precious bleeding side." If urban life magnified a sense of human isolation, Crosby countered with a promise of enduring, ever-deepening intimacy.

Such references to feeling divine presence harked back to eighteenth-century text, too. Crosby did little more than evoke Charles Wesley's characteristic themes in her own verse, as in his text below:

O what a blessed hope is ours
While here on earth we stay!
We more than taste the heavenly powers
And antedate that day;
We feel the resurrection power,
Our life in Christ concealed,
And with His glorious presence here
His life in us revealed.
)

For Crosby this spirituality was emphatically dynamic: she regarded "his life in us revealed" or "coming nearer" as continuous action. No matter how "near" one was, one could always be "coming nearer," and the nearer one came, the nearer one wanted to be. In collaboration with Phoebe Palmer Knapp, Crosby put it this way:

> "Nearer the cross!" my heart can say
> I am coming nearer;
> Nearer the cross from day to day,
> I am coming nearer;
> Stronger in faith, more clear I see
> Jesus who gave Himself for me;
> Nearer to Him I still would be;
> Still I'm coming nearer.

Or,

> There is constantly joy in abiding
> In Christ my Lord and King;
> Of His love that passeth knowledge,
> My heart and tongue shall sing.

Or,

> O for an earnest longing,
> Into His life to grow;
> O for a deeper yearning,
> More of its joy to know.

Or,

> Redeemed by Him, my Lord and King,
> Who saves me day by day;
> My life and all its ransomed powers
> Could ne'er his love repay.

Crosby invoked a vocabulary of joy to accompany her cries for companionship. One indicator of the communion with God that "perfect rest" assured, joy flowed naturally in Crosby's mind from one's repaired relationship with God. And joy, like peace, could deepen and grow: "O for a deeper yearning,/More of its joy to know." In her "Like a River Glorious," Frances Ridley Havergal offered enduring lines that captured the dynamic spirituality that Crosby intimated: "Perfect, yet it floweth fuller every day,/Perfect, yet it groweth deeper all the way."

Historians have noted the prevalence of joy and its relationship to cleansing and divine fellowship in the songs of the early Holiness and Pentecostal movements, but the vocabulary was not limited to those contexts. In Christian understanding, a repaired relationship with God yielded joy, and joy drove one to covet fellowship with the one who had set wrongs right. Joy was a fruit of the Spirit, a biblical characteristic of every Christian's life. Long before the Protestant Reformation, Christians had sung about the joy of relationship with God. By giving joy prominence in her texts, Crosby expressed not merely her personal testimony but her sense of Christian theology.

Any consideration of the role of joy in nineteenth-century evangelical hymnody must recognize as well that the movement's immediate forebears had made much of joy in relationship to forgiveness, proclamation, and "rest." Take, for example, Philip Doddridge's well-known lines (included alongside Crosby texts in Sankey's hymnals, and a favorite on the camp meeting circuit):

O happy day that fixed my choice
On Thee, my Saviour and my God;
Well may this glowing heart rejoice
And tell its raptures all abroad.

Now rest, my long divided heart,
Fixed on this blissful center, rest.
Nor ever from thy Lord depart,
By Him of every good possessed.

Wesley said much the same thing:

How happy every child of grace
Who knows his sins forgiven,
This earth, he cries, is not my place,
I seek a place in heaven.

Or,

> O how happy are they who the Saviour obey
> And have laid up their treasure above.

The same Wesley text offered another rich image of the present spiritual benefits of redemption: "Twas a heaven below/My Redeemer to know." Such eighteenth-century descriptors frequently found their way into gospel hymns. Crosby's language borrowed especially heavily from the King James Version and the Wesleyan corpus.

In Crosby's day actual joyous shouts like those she sometimes urged in her texts were far more likely in holiness camp meetings than in Moody revivals, but — even if expressed only in song — the emotion remained appropriate to a mended relationship with God. And so she beckoned owners of *Gospel Hymns* to "sing in [their] rapture, O glory to God/For such a Redeemer as mine," and to see their redeemed lives as "filled with his fullness divine."

Crosby's yearnings and proclamations frequently flowed into bursts of confidence. "Blessed Assurance" has been an evangelical favorite since its first publication on the back cover of *The Guide to Holiness* in 1873:

> Blessed assurance, Jesus is mine!
> Oh, what a foretaste of glory divine!
> Heir of salvation, purchase of God,
> Born of His Spirit, washed in His blood.
>
> This is my story, this is my song,
> Praising my Saviour all the day long!

Crosby wove into this text, too, echoes of the holiness language that attracted her:

> Perfect submission, perfect delight,
> Visions of rapture now burst on my sight;
> Angels descending, bring from above
> Echoes of mercy, whispers of love.

Perfect submission, all is at rest;
I in my Saviour am happy and blest!
Watching and waiting, looking above,
Filled with His goodness, lost in His love.

For Crosby this language at once declared a reality and held forth
an ideal. Lines of assurance leaped as well from Crosby's substantial
corpus of hymns in praise of God and Christ. While it was not the
Moody revivals apparently that popularized the Crosby hymn that
later became perhaps her most familiar text, "To God be the glory,
great things He hath done," the form of that song, moving through adoration of each member of the Trinity to anticipation of the joys of
heaven, nonetheless characterizes one large group of Crosby hymns of
praise in Sankey's *Gospel Hymns*. She also summoned congregations to
adoration especially of Christ:

We praise Thee, we bless Thee, Our Saviour divine,
All pow'r and dominion forever be Thine;
We sing of Thy mercy with joyful acclaim;
For Thou hast redeemed us; all praise to Thy name.

All honor and praise to Thine excellent name;
Thy love is unchanging, forever the same;
We bless and adore Thee, O Saviour and King;
With joy and thanksgiving Thy praises we sing.

SERVICE

Lest any confuse Crosby's preference for repose of soul with an excuse
for inaction or view her yearning for Christ's presence as self-absorbed,
she offered another image of the Christian life in her songs about service. Her most famous service text was "Rescue the Perishing." Who
were the perishing? Most simply, lost, sinning people, or those lacking
awareness of the purity of the image of God within. They had strayed,
and so, "Back to the narrow way, patiently win them." They stood in
danger of death, so "snatch them [away] in pity." If the notion of
"lostness" seemed uncomfortable, Crosby had another handy — that of

goodness incapable of release, held down by evil. Grace, she suggested, could restore the buried sensitive feelings long "crushed by the tempter," and the attitude of the human rescuer, she suggested, was central to the endeavor — care, pity, tears, love, kindness:

> Rescue the perishing, care for the dying,
> Snatch them in pity from sin and the grave;
> Weep o'er the erring one, lift up the fallen,
> Tell them of Jesus, the Mighty to Save.

> Down in the human heart crushed by the tempter
> Feelings lie buried that grace can restore;
> Touched by a loving heart, wakened by kindness,
> Cords that are broken will vibrate once more.

Here, too, her descriptions of those "outside the fold" echoed language long familiar to evangelicals: Augustus Toplady's "Rock of Ages" (1776) described the penitent as "naked" and "helpless"; Charles Wesley's "Jesus, Lover of My Soul" (1740) depicted one's "defenseless head," helplessness, and need for support and comfort. His "Jesus, the Sinner's Friend" held more of the same: "Lost and undone for aid I flee/Weary of earth, myself and sin/Open Thine arms, and take me in" (1739). Joseph Hart's well-known lines echoed these words: "Come, ye sinners, poor and needy, weak and wretched, sick and sore" (1759). Evangelicals had many images at hand to describe God's prodigal children.

Sankey-era hymnals highlighted another characteristic Crosby service theme — Christian duty making each responsible for the other, especially for those in need of "rescue." "Duty" corresponded with "usefulness" and offered Crosby an incentive to face each day. Even if she did not employ an older evangelical idiom of hellfire and brimstone, the wanderers — whatever vestige of the divine lay buried within — were still perishing. In an era when people who were literally perishing were increasingly evident in urban America, the summons to rescue and salvation could easily be sung with this-worldly implications. Crosby called on evangelicals to care about those for whom few others cared. Her intent was to address their temporal as well as their eternal needs. The language of rescue lent an aura of desperation for both wanderers and rescuers. Crosby expressed clearly an evangelical consensus in her repeated insistence that there was no sphere of usefulness greater than helping a weary, wandering soul to find rest in Christ.

Crosby's metaphors and the humanity and accessibility of the Christ she depicted in familiar human features went a long way toward reassuring the wanderers she invited to Christ. The motivations she urged on workers in theory made their efforts more palatable to the lost by engaging the would-be rescuer at an intensely personal level. Speech and rebuke were not enough: rescuers needed compassion — tears, pity, love. Attitude mattered: "Speak not harshly when reproving" was a Crosby line familiar to her contemporaries. Simple kindness, indiscriminate cheerfulness, irrepressible hopefulness — she urged these virtues on evangelicals as forms of Christian service.

Evangelicals resonated as well with Crosby's images of Christians as soldiers and as pilgrims. Many Crosby lyrics revealed her familiarity with John Bunyan's *Pilgrim's Progress:* "Press on, press on, O pilgrim"; "'Tis a good and pleasant land that we pilgrims journey through"; "The pilgrim is longing for home, sweet home"; "Then throughout my pilgrim journey light will cheer me all the while." One of Crosby's earliest collaborations with William Doane yielded "I would go the pilgrim's journey/Onward to the promised land/I would reach the golden city/There to join the angel band." Like Bunyan's pilgrim, Crosby's fared best when focused on Scripture. Writing under the pseudonym Ida Scott Taylor, she put it this way:

> Blessed Bible, book of gold
> Precious truths thy pages hold,
> Truths to lead me day by day
> All along my pilgrim way.

> Word of God, thy love impart,
> Fire my zeal, and cleanse my heart;
> Keep me earnest, keep me true,
> Every day my strength renew.

The pilgrim bound for the heavenly land had a counterpart in the Christian soldier. Crosby reminded her cohorts, "No cross, no crown."

And the soldier could be sure of battle, for "foes" abounded on every side:

> Onward! Upward! Christian soldier,
> Turn not back nor sheath thy sword,
> Let its blade be sharp for conquest
> In the battle for the Lord.
>
> Onward! Upward! Doing, daring,
> All for Him who died for thee;
> Face the foe and meet with boldness
> Danger whatsoe'er it be.

In 1890, writing as Sallie Martin, Crosby reminded Christian soldiers that Christ led their battle and that victory was sure:

> Conquering now and still to conquer, Jesus, Thou ruler of all,
> Thrones and their scepters all shall perish, crowns and their
>   splendor shall fall,
> Yet shall the armies Thou leadest, faithful and true to the last,
> Find in Thy mansions eternal rest when their warfare is past.
>
> Refrain:
> Not to the strong is the battle,
> Not to the swift is the race,
> But to the true and the faithful
> Vict'ry is promised through grace.

Meanwhile, the biblical metaphor of the watchman on the wall warned Protestants to be diligent about their responsibility to "sound the alarm" of "the wrath to come" (*Pilgrim's Progress* again): "Plead with the lost by the wayside now/Warn them to come and the truth embrace/Urge them to come and be saved by grace." Crosby gently prodded Christians to a related round of duties. "Only a word for Jesus" reminded those who used shyness as an excuse that a simple testimony might awaken a soul; "O brother, life's journey beginning" instructed the convert to make careful choices; "O child of God, wait patiently" urged those beset by trouble not to despair — but not to take situations into their own hands, either. She liked to remind her co-horts to "scatter sunshine" — her term for smiles — as part of the "bat-tle for souls."

Crosby lived through the flowering and fading of evangelical hopes for a Christian America. Before the Civil War their leaders urged American Protestants to take sure steps toward realizing the kingdom of God on earth. In contrast, during Crosby's hymn-writing years, Moody announced his mission to remove people adrift on a sinking wreck. Most Crosby texts avoided these larger questions by focusing on individuals and employing the first or second person, but she sometimes echoed the familiar sentiments of those who saw the king-dom coming, as in "Toiling On":

> To the work, to the work,
> There is labor for all
> For the kingdom of darkness and error shall fall;
> And the name of Jehovah
> Exalted shall be,
> In the loud swelling chorus,
> "Salvation is free."

Crosby envisioned as well the prophesied day when all nations would "know the Lord," and her urgings mirrored the times in which she lived when improved communications, transportation, and tech-nology made the global progress of Christianity seem irreversible. An infectious optimism about world evangelization marked many evan-gelicals of the era who imagined with Crosby (as set to music by Sankey) the grand and not-far-distant day when Christ's promised kingdom would be realized:

> From her night shall China wake,
> Afric's sons their chains shall break;
> Egypt, where Thy people trod,
> Shall adore and praise our God.

> India's groves of palm so fair
> Shall resound with praise and prayer,

Ceylon's isle with joy shall sing,
Glory be to Christ our King.

The growing ranks of foreign missionaries, male and female, embraced gospel songs in the contemporary crusade to Christianize the world, though there was considerable division as to just when or how the second coming might occur. People occasionally sent Crosby copies of her hymns translated for use in faraway parts of the world. And Crosby liked to recall her visit with the venerable Methodist missionary Bishop William Taylor at Ocean Grove camp meeting, and the benediction he had given her. Crosby's impressionable mind imagined how gladly she would have devoted her own life to missions, and she committed herself to facilitating the endeavor with hymns. Her friend Stephen Merritt was Taylor's secretary for Africa, and close familiarity with the problems and triumphs of particular missionary endeavors animated her lyrics about the urgency of gospel proclamation. She provided several texts that, in this heyday of enthusiasm for foreign missions, became staples of missionary hymnody. Sankey included the most enduring of these in *Gospel Hymns 1-6*:

Speed away, speed away on your mission of light
To the lands that are lying in darkness and night;
'Tis the Master's command; go ye forth in His name,
The wonderful Gospel of Jesus proclaim.
Take your lives in your hand,
To the work while 'tis day,
Speed away, speed away, speed away.

In September 1871 Crosby wrote an apt summary of her views of Christian life and service that her publishers set aside as "too didactic":

'Tis a life of constant labor,
'Tis a battle strife with sin;
Friends of grace must meet in conflict
Foes without and foes within.

'Tis a life of self-denial,
Here no time or place to rest.

Set to labor thus for Jesus,
Blessing others we are blest.
We must wear a cheerful spirit,
Learn to curb our stubborn way,
Gentle, patient and forgiving
We must be in good or ill.

'Tis a life of calm devotion
If by humble faith we live;
We shall know a lasting pleasure
Which the world can never give.
When our warfare is accomplished,
And we lay our armor down,
Called from earth, to Heaven exalted,
We shall wear a victor's crown.

HEAVEN

Almost every Crosby text — including those she contributed to
Sunday school hymnals — anticipated heaven. Her lyrics moved toward heaven as the pilgrim's true home filled with joy and rest,
heaven as the place where loved ones met again to part no more, and
heaven as the place where the believer would see Christ face-to-face.
No subject prompted Crosby to clearer language than this, expressed
frequently in words that intimate Bunyan's pilgrim:

Through the gates to the city in a robe of spotless white
He will lead me where no tears shall ever fall;
In the glad song of ages I shall mingle with delight,
But I long to see my Saviour first of all.
I shall know Him; I shall know Him
And redeemed by His side I shall stand.
I shall know Him; I shall know Him
By the print of the nails in His hand.

This anticipation of sight especially punctuated the blind Crosby's lyrics about heaven: "And I shall see Him face to face"; "Oh, the

soul thrilling rapture when I view His blessed face, and the luster of His kindly beaming eye"; "We shall see Him by and by, hallelujah to His name!"; "I know I shall see in His beauty the King in whose law I delight." Crosby's many songs about *seeing* Christ made this expectation a central part of the evangelical hope. (Another blind hymn writer, Helen Lemuel, authored another favorite evangelical hymn about sight — "Turn Your Eyes upon Jesus.")

Crosby had a vivid anticipation of the physical return of Christ, and her hymns sometimes intimated the premillennialism that captured the evangelical imagination toward the end of the nineteenth century. Crosby's references to being "changed in the twinkling of an eye" or "caught up in the clouds," however, simply arranged biblical phrases and should not be read as dispensationalist jargon. Like Moody's sermons, Crosby's hymns show no predilection for particular "takes" on the second coming, but they do resonate with joy at Christ's return. In a song with echoes of the familiar "When the roll is called up yonder," she described "that bright and golden morning when the Son of man shall come." In keeping with the evangelical trend toward muting language of judgment and damnation, she did not dwell on judgment but, rather, anticipated Christian transformation in an altogether joyous moment. Most of her hymns, whatever their primary theme, offered at least a glimpse of the glory, peace, and plenty to come. Some, though, held echoes of earlier somber warnings — heaven denied, but no mention of hell:

If God should call our souls away without our sins forgiven,
We could not hope to see His face or sing His praise in Heaven.

Crosby texts suggest that the hope of *seeing* Christ sustained, convicted, and thrilled her, and she liked to think that its comfort to her own heart spilled over into her texts. She invested the evangelical message of the hope of heaven with practical implications for Christian living, anticipating, for example, the believer's joy in reunion with "those gone before":

When He comes in the clouds descending
And they who love Him here
From their graves shall awake and praise Him

277

With joy and not with fear;
When the body and the soul are united
And clothed no more to die,
What a shouting there will be
When each other's face we see
Changed in the twinkling of an eye.

Crosby sometimes used her firm belief in Christ's physical return to prod her generation to faithful "watching," an active rather than a passive duty as illustrated by her intertwining the New Testament parables of the talents and the ten virgins. With an eye to the parable of the talents, she suggests that one could "watch" productively only if one had worked faithfully. She gently told her cohorts, too, of their accountability before God:

If, at the dawn of the early morning
He shall call us one by one,
When to the Lord we restore our talents
Will He answer thee "Well done"?
O can we say we are ready, brother?
Ready for the soul's bright home?
Say, will He find you and me still watching,
Waiting, waiting when the Lord shall come?

The notion of "watching and waiting" had a prominent place in Crosby's dynamic piety — "Watching and waiting, looking above." These were active dispositions of the soul that yielded spiritual benefits that would not otherwise be realized.

I'm waiting for Thy blessings, Lord,
I'm waiting at Thy throne
Where sweet communion through Thy grace
Hath made Thy presence known.

I'm waiting for Thy spirit, Lord,
Thy promised gift to me;
I'm waiting for its quickening power
To lift my soul to Thee.

I'm waiting for a deeper love
My longing heart to fill,
To consecrate my every thought
And bend me to Thy will.

Waiting for Christ's return, then, connoted spiritual growth in preparation for the event. Crosby's hope of heaven often featured as well anticipation of reunion with loved ones: "Longing to meet the dear ones/Safe on the golden strand."

Crosby saw no contradiction in her use of metaphors that mixed passivity and action. Nor did she condone a "deeper life" piety preoccupied with the state of one's own soul. Rather, her understanding of Christian faith, rooted in Puritanism, developed by Methodism, warmed by the Holiness movement, and nourished by her Congregationalist, Baptist, and Presbyterian associates, insisted that the believer could only be effective in action if "hidden" in the Rock of Ages. Secure there, one could move into any arena safely and effectively because covered — or clothed upon — by Christ. Christ was refuge and shelter, a balm for life's ills, but even while he gave rest to the troubled soul, he set that soul to working for him, and according to Crosby's gospel, to singing. Even as she "waited with patience," "safe in the arms of Jesus," Crosby liked to think she busily "toiled on" and "sounded the alarm" in a perishing world. Taken together, her hymns enjoined only a few specific tasks — spreading cheer, helping the needy, and rescuing the perishing. More generally, she often implored Christians to watch, fight, work, wait, in short, to take hold of life, seize its opportunities, and make each day count: "Do with your might what your hands find to do":

O let us seek in all we do to please this heavenly guide
To walk with Him by simple faith who once for sinners died.
All needful blessings here below His goodness will supply,
And grace, by which we learn to live, will give us strength to
    die.

For Crosby the story ended where it began — with grace, the source of this-worldly activism and the Christian's eternal hope, lifting the soul to adoration of the name of Jesus:

Oh, wondrous name exalted high,
To Him all power is given;
By Him we triumph over sin,
By Him we enter heaven.

Oh, glorious name by angels praised
And ransomed saints adored;
That name, above all other names,
Our refuge evermore.

The wonderful, the counselor, the great and mighty Lord,
The everlasting prince of peace, the king, the Son of God.

SINGING

Finally, Crosby often summoned people to sing about singing. As one who enjoyed music, she believed wholeheartedly in the capacity of song to channel emotions and enable heartfelt corporate as well as individual praise. She associated singing with joy and regarded salvation as the ultimate joyous experience. Over the years her words have invited millions of people in scores of languages to share her point of view: "I sing, for I cannot be silent" was her testimony in "Redeemed"; "His love is the theme of my song." "There is constantly joy in abiding/In Christ my Lord and King," she mused in 1896. "Of His love that passeth knowledge/My heart and tongue shall sing." She thought of congregational song as foreshadowing an eternal song of praise with Christ as its theme: "This my song through endless ages, Jesus led me all the way." Long before Crosby wrote a hymn, she professed to have had a dream in which she momentarily heard the "new song" of the redeemed before God's heavenly throne. She liked to think that echoes of that moment animated her texts and nurtured her soul.

Crosby frequently expressed satisfaction about the usefulness of "Safe in the Arms of Jesus," but she named as her personal choice among her own lyrics "Saved by Grace." As her own favorite hymn, she cited a British text written during her young adulthood — F. W. Faber's "Faith of Our Fathers." Faber, a graduate of Balliol College, Oxford University, and an ordained Anglican clergyman, converted to

Catholicism in the mid-1840s. He had an abiding love for hymnody and produced three hymnals for Catholic use. The first appeared in 1849 under the title *Jesus and Mary; or, Catholic Hymns for Singing and Reading*. It included "Faith of Our Fathers." The words, written during the heyday of Anglo-Catholic sentiment, recalled the persecution of Jesuits in the sixteenth century even as it spoke especially to the hopes for England of those Anglicans who went "all the way to Rome":

Faith of our fathers! Living still
In spite of dungeon, fire, and sword;
O how our hearts beat high with joy
Whene'er we hear that glorious word!
Faith of our fathers, holy faith!
We will be true to thee till death!

Our fathers, chained in prisons dark,
Were still in heart and conscience free;
How sweet would be their children's fate,
If they like them could die for thee!
Faith of our fathers, holy faith!
We will be true to thee till death.

Faith of our fathers! Mary's prayers
Shall win our country back to thee;
And through the truth that comes from God
England shall then indeed be free.
Faith of our fathers, holy faith!
We will be true to thee till death!

Faith of our fathers! We will love
Both friend and foe in all our strife;
And preach thee, too, as love knows how,
By kindly words and virtuous life;
Faith of our fathers, holy faith!
We will be true to thee till death!

Faber's hymn found its way into two American Catholic hymnals in 1851, and in 1853 Frederick Henry Hedge placed it in the Unitarian *Hymns for the Church of Christ*. During the 1860s other Protestant denominations incorporated it in their hymnals; American Methodists first published it in the 1878 *Hymnal of the Methodist Episcopal Church*. These early American printings omitted the third of Faber's four stanzas. Later American hymnal editors adapted Faber's words to create text that shifted his focus on the Catholic martyrs (or fathers) of the early English Reformation (and on the reconversion of England) to the Protestant martyrs of Mary Tudor's reign:

> Faith of our fathers! We will strive
> To win all nations unto thee,
> And through the truth that comes from God
> Mankind shall then be truly free.
> Faith of our fathers, holy faith!
> We will be true to thee till death.

Protestants associated the "dungeon, fire, and sword" as readily with Reformation-era Catholicism as with the persecution of the early church; they owned as their "fathers" stalwarts of the (invisible) church through the ages, including the Reformers and New England Puritans. Faber's musing on Mary's intercession for the return of England to the papal fold became, in American hands, Catholic and Protestant, a determination to "win all nations" to "the truth that comes from God" as the requisite to the discovery of true human freedom. Crosby's view of Christian outreach resonated especially well with Faber's concluding phrases about "kindly words" and a "virtuous life" as forms of preaching with love.

One can only speculate about why Crosby particularly cherished Faber's text. Its patriotic and apostolic gloss, its notion of loyalty to death, and its evocation of the ancient appeal of martyrdom ("How sweet would be their children's fate/If they like them could die for thee!") apparently stirred sentimental chords and grounded the contemporary Christian task for her in history and tradition. Crosby certainly valued its appeal to the past, its vision of Christian progress, and its coupling of freedom and faith. Faber inspired her sense of identity with a glorious Christian heritage (even if his words intended to hallow a different past), her devotion to duty, and her emotional fervor. But the repetition of intention to be faithful to death resonated especially with Crosby's long-evident maudlin side. Among American Protestants, this Faber text became a prime example of hymn lyrics that crossed boundaries — words that suggested quite different things when read by a Catholic or a Protestant.

POPULAR EVANGELICALISM

Crosby liked to think that her own lyrics captured the essence of historic Protestant faith viewed through an evangelical lens. Her texts voiced a popular understanding of evangelical Christianity that, there is reason to believe (from scattered newspaper accounts and later obituaries in the black press), rang true among many African Americans as well. Familiar biblical contrasts — light and darkness, lost and found, stormy seas and quiet harbor, wandering and homecoming — filled her texts, suggesting the sharp distinction evangelicals made between themselves and "the world." Those "without Christ" faced storms, shipwreck, and darkness while the faithful enjoyed safety, companionship, and sunlight. Brimming with the certainty of acceptance for all who allowed themselves to be persuaded, Crosby's lines drove home the invitation that was the capstone of the evangelical message, described the consecrated life, enjoined duty, and beckoned heavenward. The life of the mind was simply not in Crosby's sights. She had no real opportunity to pursue it herself, and those with whom she mingled most closely did not particularly value it. She also could not imagine as appropriate Christian vocation service to humanity without personal evangelism. To nurture her soul Crosby pressed close a sentimentalized Christ, while to fulfill the Great Commission she faced the world and "toiled on." The evangelicalism Crosby presented in her hymns flourished in the paradox of simultaneous rest of soul and work for souls.

Though the popular press generally hailed Crosby, the era's musical critics found gospel hymns wanting in both music and text. Those who remained aloof from the grassroots causes that nurtured gospel hymns easily dismissed Crosby and her closest cohorts. For example, in his pathbreaking *Dictionary of Hymnology* (1892), John Julian noted that millions of copies of Crosby texts circulated. Nonetheless, he opined that they were "with few exceptions, very weak and poor, their simplicity and earnestness being their redeeming features." He ventured that catchy melodies had more to do with their success than did Crosby's text. In her *Lady Hymn Writers* (also 1892), Mrs. E. R. Pitman buried Crosby (using the unfamiliar Mrs. Vanalstyne) in the middle of her second chapter entitled "Minor Hymn Writers: American." Crosby found no place among the women Pitnam presented under the headings "Hymn Writers for the Sanctuary" or "Hymn Writers Who Were Also Poetesses."

Thanks to popular demand, though, gospel hymns pressed at the doors of the sanctuaries, but there, too, they found strong resistance. Only a handful of Crosby's hymns gained acceptance in denominational hymnals before 1900, though thousands circulated in books intended for specific religious markets. Perhaps that reality revealed as much about the distance between grassroots Protestants and Protestant elites as it did about the quality of gospel hymn tunes or lyrics.

As resources especially for revival meetings, Crosby gospel hymns gave common voice to evangelicals across denominational traditions, providing defining metaphors for the beliefs and aspirations they shared. Crosby came to be claimed by most in part because her hymns took preeminent place in Sankey's various editions of *Gospel Hymns,* the collections that most fully articulated the convictions of the millions who regarded themselves as partners in the era's best-publicized evangelical endeavors. But beyond their usefulness to Moody and Sankey, Crosby's texts effectively expressed the evangelical "creed in metre" and offered "an index to the brains and hearts" of evangelicals in the late nineteenth century and beyond.

11 Out and About

Rescue the perishing, care for the dying!
Jesus is merciful, Jesus will save.

Despite the volume of text she produced, writing hymns absorbed only a small share of Crosby's time. (One of her collaborators, Hugh Main, described her remarkable habit of dictating two hymns simultaneously, alternating between two lines of each and keeping two secretaries occupied.) Between 1875 and 1900, Crosby kept busy as well among marginalized New Yorkers. Her sympathies for such efforts were well known, and for years she had been involved indirectly by providing hymns for special occasions in missions among the dispossessed. For example, when the New York Port Society (for the promotion of the gospel among seamen in the Port of New York) celebrated its fiftieth anniversary in the spring of 1868, she wrote an ode entitled "Fifty Years Ago," sung at the festivities by the choir of the Mariner's Church. But in the late 1870s she began to go herself rather than simply to send a hymn. A familiar sight in blighted neighborhoods, Crosby long supported by her presence, exhortations, and poems a cluster of rescue missions that dotted the city's blighted southern wards. She once traced her endeavors among "erring ones" to a YMCA worker who enlisted her help in winning an alcoholic friend "back to the narrow way." She visited, he heeded advice, and the successful venture (she reported that the man became a "minister of the gospel") marked the first time she attempted the "rescue" of downtrodden men that absorbed an increasing share of her energies from 1880 forward. Her exposure to rescue mission clientele made her a warm friend of the thriving Women's Christian Temperance Union, a "white ribbon army" energized by grand goals and the determination of its indefatigable president, Frances Willard.

In the 1880s Manhattan was home to at least 121 evangelical city missions featuring "gospel meetings" and "Sabbath schools." Some added shelter and food. Only 34 had denominational ties; the rest relied on benefactors and volunteers. The Bowery Mission (on the Bowery between Canal and Bayard Streets) held Crosby's particular interest. She first visited in 1881, two years after the mission opened its doors to the "human drift-wood" of Manhattan. Run by the Reverend A. J. Ruliffson and his wife with the assistance of J. Ward Childs, the mission thrived at "the very center of vice and crime and degradation" in the country's premier city. The Congregationalist activist Sarah J. Bird, fondly dubbed "the mother of the Bowery Mission," played a central role in the preaching and social outreaches that gave the mission a reputation as "a Christian Gibraltar amid the swelling tides of sin that dash it on all sides." In this setting open to female gospel work, Crosby often attended and spoke at evening services. These attracted significant numbers of young men, not all alcoholics, some of whom experienced the "sound conversions" for which workers labored. An 1888 eighth anniversary report indicated that 300,000 men had attended evening services at the Bowery Mission; in 1887 alone, 2,000 had been "induced to lead sober and honorable lives." Among the "inducers" was Crosby, who recalled in old age her one-on-one "dealing with the souls" of "her boys." Several of her hymn texts came to her mind after experiences at rescue missions. The best known was "Rescue the Perishing," but there were many others that appealed in the idiom of the day to drunkards, tramps, and waifs.

Each November the Bowery Mission held daylong, well-advertised anniversary services that featured exhortation and testimony. The magnitude of interest in rescue work necessitated moving the celebrations to other facilities. In 1901, for example, 6,000 people crowded the Academy of Music to hear DeWitt Talmage commend the mission for bringing "the bread of this world in one hand and the bread of life in the other." "The depth of degradation from which many were rescued was revealed by the claim that each set up to having been the vilest sinner that ever lived," a *New York Times* reporter observed at another celebration. Crosby addressed sixteen of these anniversary services, bringing with her each time a new hymn composed in honor of the day. Bowery Mission organist Victor Benke set some of these rescue texts to music.

Crosby's convictions about the brokenness of all humanity made her reject harsh reproofs and judgmental language in her dealings with those evangelicals denominated "lost." Harsh words, she thought, only hardened hearts. Rescue mission workers stood as much in need of grace as did any social outcast, and so mission hymnals offered her advice to workers to know their own hearts. Sung in mission settings, one of Crosby's earliest texts (written before 1851 and published first as a poem, not a hymn) cautioned the well-intentioned and reassured the broken:

> Speak not harshly when reproving
> Those from duty's path who stray;
> If you would reclaim the erring,
> Kindness must each action sway.
> Speak not harshly to the wayward;
> Win their confidence, their love,
> They will feel how pure the motive
> That has led them to reprove.

Crosby's words make evident that she expected to deal primarily with men of Protestant background, people from "good" homes who had been beaten down by life. Mission workers played on this assumption by weaving references to home, mother, innocence and religion lost into their exhortations, hoping to bend sentiment to the cause of redemption. Crosby wrote a hymn that illuminates this supposition:

> "Backward, turn backward, oh time, in your flight,"
> Bring me my sunny days, happy and bright,

287

Give me my home and the dear ones again,
Make me the innocent child I was then.
O, for a moment to kneel and to pray
Close to my mother, who taught me to say
"Father, forgive me the wrongs I have done,
Father, forgive me through Jesus, Thy Son."

Over my life hangs a cold chilly blight,
I am an outcast and homeless tonight;
Dreading the evil I cannot restrain,
Lured by the tempter to sorrow and pain.
Often she told me that Jesus would save,
O will He take me, a poor wretched slave?
Mother still whispers that if I believe
Pardon through Jesus I yet may receive.

Crosby offered more than forgiveness: she envisioned broken homes restored. The women in her ballads about drunkenness were generally wronged, gentle, and forgiving. Crosby spent far more time anguishing over erring men than over erring women. Unlikely as the subject might seem for a hymn, she once provided a text titled "She Is Coming Home Tomorrow" that was published in 1890:

She is coming home tomorrow, can the happy news be true?
She is coming home tomorrow, and she'll bring the baby too.
'Twas my fault that e'er she left me, O my gentle, patient wife,
It was I that crush'd the roses and the sunshine from her life.

She is coming home tomorrow, with her voice so sweet and low.
I have been a cruel husband, but 'twas drink that made me so.
But she's coming home tomorrow, and she'll love me as before;
All the past will be forgiven, and our lives begin once more.

The texts resonated with countless claims of such reconciliations, nurtured of course by answered prayer and self-discipline: "Help me keep the resolution that I'll never drink again."

Crosby also used hymn texts to instill a sense of self-worth in men attempting to turn their lives around. She was devoted to her friend Margaret Bottome's organization, the King's Daughters, and the popularity and usefulness of that organization, which was dedicated to Christian service for others, suggested to Crosby "The King's Son," a hymn she wrote for "her boys" and dedicated to Bottome:

> Oh I am a son through faith in the name
> Of Jesus my Saviour, a Brother who came
> To purchase salvation, the world to reclaim,
> And make me a son of the King.
>
> And this is the standard that I must pursue
> 'Til finished the work that is left me to do:
> Be kind and forgiving, be loyal and true
> And honor my Father, the King.
>
> Chorus:
> A son of the King, a wonderful King
> The heir to His glory, His praise I will sing!
> A son of the King, a wonderful King,
> Oh, I am adopted a son of the King!

The most useful rescue texts expressed their message clearly and simply and differed little from Sunday school songs. Crosby often couched the evangelical message in a prayer, as in this 1890 text set to music by William J. Kirkpatrick:

> Dear Jesus, canst Thou help me? My soul is full of woe;
> My heart is almost breaking, I've nowhere else to go.
> I feel I am a sinner, and this my only plea,
> The sweet and blest assurance that Thou hast died for me.
>
> I've heard there is a fountain where cleansing waters flow,
> My sins, though red like crimson, may now be white as snow.
> Thy blood doth fill that fountain, Thy blood so pure and free;
> That blood availed for others and now avails for me.
>
> Dear Jesus, loving Saviour, Thou precious dying Lamb,
> While here my faith is pleading, now take me as I am.

Songs contained the message, instructed singers on how to respond, described the anticipated results, and articulated prayers that
promised results:

> Lord, at Thy mercy seat humbly I fall,
> Pleading Thy promise sweet, Lord, hear my call;
> Now let the work begin; oh, make me pure within,
> Cleanse me from every sin, Jesus, my all.

In addition to her regular appearances at the Bowery Mission,
Crosby knew Jerry McAuley, the famous unconventional founder of
the Jerry McAuley Mission on Water Street. One of the most colorful
Protestant figures in Manhattan, McAuley commanded a huge following among the city's prosperous citizens. Perhaps their best-
known "trophy of grace," McAuley exuded pathos and drama that
made him good copy. His efforts showed results, and results assured
him notice. Born in Manhattan in 1839, McAuley embraced as a
young teenager the life of a rough-and-tumble urban thug. Convicted
as a "river thief," he served time in Sing Sing, the sprawling
Westchester County prison built by prisoners themselves of local
marble. Inmates, confined in 1,000 windowless cells and forbidden to
speak, served out their terms in this fortress thirty-three miles north
of Manhattan on the banks of the Hudson River. There McAuley
learned to read, and there in the chapel he first encountered Protestantism. Pardoned in 1864, he returned to Manhattan, where he
lapsed into his old ways. Late in the 1860s Protestant mission workers
helped him reembrace faith, break the cycle of drunkenness, and find
work. Much later he described his transformation: "The Lord picked
me up when I was a dirty tramp, without a friend or cent in the
world. The Roman Catholic folks who heard of my conversion called
me a 'turncoat'; but I had no coat to turn — nothing but an old red
shirt — when I came to Jesus." Even his friends admitted how unlikely a convert he seemed. One of them — banker, philanthropist,
and president of the New York Stock Exchange A. S. Hatch — put it
this way: "He was perhaps as hard and hopeless a looking case as one
would be likely to encounter in tramping the worst streets of New
York day and night for a month." Their persistence paid off.

Married in 1872, McAuley and his wife, Maria, immediately

raised money among their newfound evangelical middle-class friends for a mission on Water Street among "the waifs, strays, wrecks and derelicts of humanity" they knew best. They made the camp meeting circuit — Sea Cliff, Long Island; Sing Sing (famous for its Methodist encampment as well as for its prison); Ocean Grove — and, McAuley recorded, "the Lord opened the way for me to begin the work." They repaired an old building at 316 Water Street and opened the Helping Hand for Men, a place McAuley described as "a resort for the forlorn wayfarers, sailors and others who frequented the locality." Beginning with a Thanksgiving dinner for 150, the McAuleys offered daily meals to the needy followed by evangelistic services every night. Their efforts spilled out into the neighborhood when they opted to "strike at the fountainhead" — the "dives" and the rum sellers who ran them. Colorful confrontations made for interesting testimonies and good copy when the McAuleys opened the floor for participants to relate their experiences. Over the next twelve years the McAuleys became a sensation in sensation-sated Manhattan. McAuley's unrehearsed slang-filled street brogue could not disguise the sincerity of his purpose, nor did it diminish his effect among those he sought to reach. His own tears typically flowed freely as he urged the unfortunates who meandered in to mend their ways. His perseverance and results brought him the support of well-known pastors whose church members volunteered to help. His youthful dissipation and imprisonment had broken his health, though, and he died at the age of forty-five in September 1884. The city's most famous onetime river thief and drunken thug was honored by an overflow crowd of respectable Protestants at the Broadway Tabernacle (recently moved uptown to Thirty-fourth Street and Sixth Avenue). The irony was not lost on them. The Reverend Dr. Deems, pastor of the Church of the Strangers, put it this way: "Here are the clergy, men of means, women of culture, all come to pay a tribute of respect to whom? To a hunted river thief. It is the romance of grace and of Providence."

Crosby met McAuley in 1880 or 1881, shortly before he left the Water Street Mission in the hands of an associate to devote himself to opening a new rescue mission at 104 West Thirty-second Street. This "beachhead in a vast jungle of vice and debauchery known as Tenderloin" stood near Sixth Avenue, the district's main thoroughfare, just a few blocks from the fashionable Broadway Tabernacle. Next door was the Cremorne Garden, one of the dives whose customers McAuley intended to evangelize. McAuley called his hall the Cremorne Mission. Inspired to the work by a series of well-publicized sermons by DeWitt Talmage that had recently exposed the area's seamy side, the McAuleys faced disruptive crowds, flying objects, and other challenges as they geared up to begin again. With years of publicity and a strong track record, though, they easily enlisted volunteers and funds. John D. Rockefeller gave generously to both of McAuley's missions, as did the wealthy merchant and politician William E. Dodge.

Crosby ventured into this uninviting neighborhood to attend services, exhort, and mingle. The large billboard welcoming passersby promised nightly testimony and song services at 8:00, with Thursday evenings devoted entirely to song. Drawn from the new gospel hymns and Sunday school songs, the music implored, entreated, testified, and praised, often to Crosby's words and Doane's tunes. Ballads recalling mother's prayers, reciting the evils of intemperance, or envisioning agonizing deathbed scenes intended to arouse long-buried memories and strengthen resolves.

In McAuley's memory Crosby penned a prayer that made its way into rescue mission songbooks. She envisioned hopeless men shuffling down the mission's center aisle to ask for prayer, and she filled her supplication with indirect assurances and appeals to the penitent:

Lord, behold in Thy compassion
Those who kneel before Thee now;
They are in a sad condition
None can help them, Lord, but Thou.

They are lost, but do not leave them
In their dreary path to roam;
There is pardon, precious pardon
If to Thee by faith they come.

Thou doest know their every feeling;
Their temptations Thou canst see;
Here they are, O Lord, receive them
As they give themselves to Thee.

Chorus:
Speak to them in tender mercy;
Now their cruel fetters break;
Speak to them, we humbly pray Thee,
Do, O Lord, for Jesus' sake.

At the Cremorne Mission, Crosby met Sidney and Emma Whittemore, the well-to-do founders of the Door of Hope, rescue homes for prostitutes. Members of a fashionable church, the Whittemores had visited the McAuley mission at the urging of friends who hoped they might help support McAuley. Dressed for the theater, they stopped in intending to stay just a few minutes. The press of the unkempt crowd and their growing fascination with the proceedings held them, and the end of the service found them kneeling at a front bench among "drunkards, tramps, thieves, and prostitutes," sobbing "God be merciful to me, a sinner." By 1890 the Whittemores were responsible for their own rescue efforts, which quickly added an international arm. Their attention to "unprotected girls" gave the mounting national crusade against the vice trade a human face. The gregarious and ubiquitous Crosby maintained a warm interest in the ongoing outreaches sponsored by this overlapping network of mission operators.

Among the influential New Yorkers Crosby knew on the mission circuit, the lawyer and publisher Colonel Henry Harrison Hadley held a special place in her esteem. Hadley (on his mother's side a direct descendant of Jonathan Edwards) first made Crosby's acquaintance when he requested that she put a heartrending news story into verse. Perhaps her most unusual ballad, the resulting lines gave drunkenness a female face, following closely the story line of the episode that had riveted the city.

Within a courtroom's crowded walls where many a case was
   tried
A slender boy of graceful mien drew near the Judge's side
And looking up with pleading eyes he sang thro' tears of woe,
That fell like raindrops on his cheek, "Please let my mother go."

"Not now, not now," the Judge replied, "Oh! Would it were not
   true,

But mother is a slave to drink, she must not go with you";
"My mother?" sobbed the trembling boy, "I'm sure it cannot be!
She does so many, many things and works so hard for me."

A sigh escaped the Judge's breast, he felt his pity move,
"What does she do, my boy," he said, "Which thus inspires your
    love?"
"Why sir, she gives me food and clothes, and proud I am to say,
She never keeps me home from school, but sends me every day."

"Enough, enough," the Judge replied, "Your mother I forgive,
And from this lesson may she learn a better life to live";
But ere the boy could speak his thanks for what the Judge had
    done,
That mother in her arms had clasp'd, and weeping, held her son.

Oh! Cruel fate that one so young such bitter grief should know;
Who could resist that sweet appeal: "Please let my mother go."

Pleased with the poem (he published it as a hymn with music by
Theodore Perkins), Hadley invited Crosby to provide verse every
other week for publication in *Moderation*, the paper he produced as
the organ for his Business-Men's Society for the Encouragement of
Moderation. Dedicated to the promotion of controlled (moderate)
consumption of alcohol, the society had the strong support of
Crosby's prominent distant cousin, the Reverend Howard Crosby. It
encouraged men to sign a card — red, white, or blue to make different
promises: to imbibe no alcohol, not to drink during the workday, to
abstain from hard liquor. To encourage people to sign, Crosby composed five stanzas followed by the refrain: "Take the red, white, or
blue that we offer tonight/And believe what we tell you, 'It pays to
do right.'" In 1879 Crosby's occasional collaborator, Perkins, produced the organization's hymnal, *The Golden Means, a Variety of New
Music, New Songs, and Choice Selections, Designed for the Meetings of The
Business-Men's Society for the Encouragement of Moderation*. Crosby's
text found a prominent place alongside lyrics by Josephine Pollard, a
popular Manhattan author of the day. As she could, Crosby wove into
her text encouragement for total abstinence. In "The Red Pledge" she

combined Hadley's advocacy of moderation with her own stricter preference:

> Now let others learn by me, mod'rate drinkers you may be
> If to drinking you for years have been inclined;
> But 'tis better that forever you resign the festive bowl.

In 1879 she wrote a ballad from a woman's viewpoint, "I Ought to Be Married," that began:

> I know a young fellow, warm-hearted and clever,
> Just handsome as ever can be;
> But then he's too handy with champagne and brandy,
> And so I can't have him, you see.
> Oh, why will he do it? If only he knew it,
> Tho' now he has plenty of wealth,
> Such evil pursuing will be his undoing,
> And he'll make a fool of himself.
> Rum, whiskey and toddy will hurt anybody,
> And yet he drinks all, I am told;
> And sometimes he stumbles. Oh, then how he grumbles!
> He soon will begin to look old.

Such sentiments addressed both men and women, urging women to spurn drinking men while informing men how women regarded drinking. Here, as elsewhere, Crosby manifested her support for the view that sentiment had cultural power. Stirring up "right feelings" about a subject like intemperance could be an effective agent for change.

Hadley's worries about his alcoholic brother, Samuel Hopkins Hadley, gave a keen edge to his perceptions of alcohol as a social problem. Despite his brotherly anxiety and his role as promoter of the Society for the Encouragement of Moderation, Henry Hadley himself often drank to excess, and his brother's conversion at Jerry McAuley's Cremorne Mission in 1882 forced him to admit his own growing addiction to alcohol. On 26 July 1886 Henry visited his brother's apartment above the McAuley Water Street Mission (where Samuel had recently become superintendent) and agreed to stay for the evening service.

The night was unusually hot, and only thirty-six people wandered in. Familiar with Christian teaching from childhood, Henry found his memory stirred by the testimonies and songs, stood among the men to admit his addiction, and moved forward to the bench where the penitent knelt for prayer. A few weeks later, sure that he would "hold out," he rang Crosby's bell to tell her "I have found the Lord." Crosby turned his testimony into a hymn:

> I longed to be a child of God and do my Saviour's will,
> And yet the sin that most I feared I knew unconquered still.
> "Dear Lord," I said, for as I knelt I saw Him on the tree,
> "This heavy burden on my heart I'll gladly bear for Thee."
>
> The cloud was lifted from my soul, my burden rolled away,
> The light of joy around me shed a calm and heavenly ray.
> "Dear Lord," I said, "I praise Thy name for Thy rich grace to
>   me;
> My load is gone and now I rest in perfect peace with Thee."
>
> I heard a gentle voice within — a whisper soft and mild:
> "Thy sin was cancelled by His blood Who owns thee for His
>   child."
> "Dear Lord," I said, "the work is Thine and Thine the glory be!
> My life, my soul, my every power I consecrate to Thee."

The personable Henry Hadley now forsook his business and Tammany Hall connections for a wide sphere of influence on the rescue mission circuit. Supported by St. Bartholomew's Episcopal Church, he took charge of a mission on East Forty-second Street for which Cornelius Vanderbilt had recently constructed a large building, complete with a fine pipe organ, at a cost of $300,000. An early "institutional church" and the beginning of St. Bartholomew's vigorous social programs in the city, the facility included recreational and educational space as well as the mission hall. Hadley succeeded as well in bringing to the United States the Church Army, an agency for rescue and evangelistic work in the Anglican Church, of which Bishop Henry Codman Potter named him United States General for the Protestant Episcopal Church. The Church Army devoted its resources to "needy tenement house people," a timely purpose as that segment of the population increased exponentially. Hadley established Church Army posts in other cities as well as at least sixty rescue missions around the country. In his biography of Samuel Hadley, Presbyterian evangelist, pastor, and songwriter J. Wilbur Chapman paid Henry Hadley tribute as "one of the most remarkable rescue mission workers in the world." Hadley and his son, W. T. Hadley, wrote hymn texts and compiled *Rescue Songs* (1890) for use in their mission work, using many Crosby numbers that pleaded, cajoled, and assured.

Crosby's heart for "her boys" who frequented rescue missions did not diminish her interest in the young men who networked through the YMCA. She accepted speaking invitations — like one in the 1890s to address a "men only" gathering at the East Eighty-sixth Street YMCA — and she composed hymns with such association gatherings in mind.

Crosby had a special interest in one branch of YMCA work. In the 1880s she began attending and sometimes conducting services for railroad branches of the YMCA, which thrived in this era when railroads were the backbone of the nation's economy. Started in 1872 to provide for the recreational and spiritual needs of railroad workers, the railroad YMCA associations enjoyed the financial backing of railroad management. In 1876 Cornelius Vanderbilt enabled the founding of the Manhattan branch and helped provide its permanent home, a building at 361 Madison Avenue. By the 1890s, 125 railroad YMCA branches offered lounges, restaurants, sleeping accommodations, and first aid. Through the 1870s and 1880s, all parts of the railroad YMCA work reported progress, with an increase of 21 percent in recent attendance at Bible studies, a statistic that boded well for the religious work "to which all others are tributary." Annual conventions — attended by some magnates and greeted in writing by others — moved from devotional exercises to railroad issues to reflections on Christianity's potential for "elevating the characters and improving the efficiency of railroad employees."

Crosby recalled late in life that an encounter on a Manhattan streetcar had sparked her interest in the spiritual and emotional uplift of railroad employees. She had apologized to the conductor for stepping on his foot, and his response, "You didn't hurt me at all; and if you had, you made up for it by speaking a kind word," turned her attention to the rudeness transportation employees often encountered. A few weeks later at the New Jersey home of William Rock, superintendent of one of the city's streetcar lines, she learned that Rock conducted a Sunday morning prayer meeting for streetcar employees. The predecessor to more organized efforts, Rock's meeting proved there was interest. Crosby wished him well and encouraged the effort by attending some of the services. A few weeks later, at her photographer's shop, Crosby met members of a railroad branch of the YMCA that had recently been organized across the Hudson River at Hoboken. She accepted their invitation to visit, and that properly launched her into more than two decades of speaking and writing for railroad YMCAs. From 1882, associations in the Northeast could count on her presence whenever possible, and she proudly wore a gold membership pin. If she could not attend in person, she often sent a few lines, like these she mailed to a railroad YMCA chapter for Christmas in about 1895:

How I would like to shake your hands,
And greet you one by one;
But we are now too far apart,
And this cannot be done.
Yet I can hope, and wish, and pray
That Heaven's eternal joys
May fall like dew upon your heads,
My noble railroad boys.

Crosby's mission and YMCA work placed her almost exclusively among men. She made the acquaintance of Manhattan's most diligent female city missionaries, but she spent far less time among marginalized women than among men whose situations disrupted home and family life. In part this may be because the problem of male alcoholism seemed both obvious and compelling; certainly it dominated the mission circuit. Given the episodic nature of Crosby's autobiographical recall, it is also likely that she may have left no clue to other involvements. Her sympathy for the King's Daughters is evident, and this society engaged in a wide range of efforts to feed the hungry, tend the ill, and help the impoverished. Christian Endeavor and other youth movements, too, had Crosby's support though not her direct involvement. Endeavorers engaged in a range of social programs for men, women, and children, making the alleviation of suffering an integral part of their Christian service.

Crosby thrived in these opportunities to be useful in social settings. She did most of her work in solitude or among a handful of people in her publisher's office. Rescue missions and youth associations offered her the opportunity to mingle with the objects of her attention, to imbibe the despair of the needy or the enthusiasm of youth and weave it into future texts. By grounding her experience in the lives of real people, mission and outreach work lent authenticity to Crosby's hymns about service.

BUSINESS

The post–Civil War rush of music publishing was a small part of an exploding commercial enterprise. As Sunday school hymnals, rescue mission songbooks, and other popular music, secular and sacred, poured from the presses, publishers and authors found themselves involved in the increasingly complex realities of the marketplace. Already in the decade before the Civil War, fierce competition forced music publishers to protect their interests by organizing the Board of Music Trade. Meanwhile, text and tune writers shared publishers' dismay over brash violations of weak copyright law and found solidarity with other authors clamoring for change.

The Board of Music Trade was part of a larger trend based on the mid-nineteenth-century assumption that collectivity was the best means to benefit all. The architects of the New York Philharmonic Society (established in 1849) shared this instinct, as did the activists who envisioned the American Musical Fund Society (for which Crosby's instrumental teacher, Anthony Reiff, served as treasurer), and these offered models. Chartered in March 1849, this society collected dues and raised funds to assist the ill, bury poor musicians, aid their widows, or support their orphans. As performers crafted agencies to bring order and benefit to their ranks, publishers turned attention to the competition that jeopardized profits.

Established in 1855, the Board of Music Trade resulted directly from fractious deliberations at a music publishers convention that met at Manhattan's Astor House. Large music publishers seemed poised to drive smaller concerns out of business. The immediate problem was an action by the New York publisher Hall and Son, which early in 1855 unexpectedly cut in half its price on noncopyrighted foreign sheet music while holding its price on copyrighted American compositions. Only the holder of the copyright or one with the holder's permission could print copyrighted American music, whereas noncopyrighted European compositions could be reprinted by anyone. By the 1850s certain music publishers had laid claim to the music of particular European composers. Lowell Mason and his cohorts had long staked their reputations on the superiority of European music over American, and Americans reprinted freely the works of European masters. Long sections of introductory material in some of Mason's books had been translated from the German and reprinted without attribution. The assumption of the preeminence of European musical style meant that American publishers sold European music at higher prices than they charged for American music, and they published more (pirated) European music, too. Hall's move jeopardized the livelihoods of small publishers, but it also provided an opportunity to make the point that American music was coming into its own, thanks in part to the efforts of some of the most ardent advocates of European music.

The organizers of the Board of Music Trade made room for small publishers by admitting as eligible those who issued at least 1,000 sheets of music annually and invited these to join the deliberations, but it ostracized Hall and Son and bound all members to have no business dealings with this firm. The assembled publishers agreed to end their price war and to assure "mutual welfare and protection" by establishing uniform pricing (five cents per sheet) for sheet music and uniform discount rates (not to exceed 33 percent — some publishers had been granting 50 percent) for retailers, schools, and teachers. The board's second meeting drew thirty music publishers to Boston, and the press marveled at the capital represented — well over $1 million, with four or five publishers controlling 75 percent of the total. The *New York Times* estimated that investment in printed music in the United States exceeded $5 million.

By the time the third convention met, the minutes boasted, "all the publishing houses of consequence in the United States" had joined. Proudly declaring that the day of European supremacy had ended, the board undertook to publish a catalogue of all music published in the

United States, noting that American-produced serious music was beginning to find an audience abroad. Music publishers were encouraged to price their music using dollars and cents rather than the traditional fractioned shillings, a carryover from colonial days. During the economic downturn that drove many Americans into bankruptcy over the winter of 1857-58, no music publishers failed — a result, they opined, of the order the board had brought to the mushrooming industry. The 1858 meeting, held in Cincinnati, first tackled the broader issue that agitated at all levels within the music publishing business: copyright.

American copyright law, modeled on a statute adopted by Parliament in 1710, passed Congress 31 May 1790 with the hope of facilitating learning by protecting authors and proprietors. Early copyright claims were recorded by the clerks of U.S. district courts. The first copyrighted music publication, Andrew Adgate's *Rudiments of Music,* was registered in November 1790. When Adgate deposited a copy of the work with the government, paid the requisite sixty-cent registration fee, and advertised his copyright, he could expect that the book would not be reprinted without his permission for fourteen years. An author might renew copyright for another fourteen years, but if he died before the expiration of the first fourteen years his estate lost all rights.

Noah Webster's interest in extending the copyright on his *Blue-Backed Speller* (next to the Bible the best-selling American book of all time) prompted him to argue that literary compositions were personal property and should be handled as such by the courts. He failed to gain his point and was forced to revise his *Speller* to renew its copyright, but he and others kept agitating. Meanwhile, a handful of American authors like James Fenimore Cooper and Washington Irving filed for copyright in England (a privilege rescinded in 1854 for nonresident foreigners). Cooper joined Webster in approaching Congress for what they called "perpetual copyright." An 1831 revision of American copyright law first mentioned music and permitted one's estate to renew copyright for fourteen years. When Congress established the Smithsonian Institution in 1846, it required that copyright seekers provide both the Institution and the Congressional Library with copies.

A revision in 1856 extended the law by requiring payment to authors for performance of their dramatic works, a provision that could have made a difference to George Root's pocketbook a few years earlier when he and Crosby published *The Flower Queen*. Ineffectively enforced, though, it made little difference in the short run. Historian Russell Sanjek notes that — despite a publishing explosion — copyright legislation advanced very little before the Civil War. In 1859 Congress moved the copyright department from the Department of State to the Department of the Interior.

By the mid-1850s, 120 volumes on the shelves of the copyright department held copies of some 57,000 songs and instrumental pieces submitted by American musicians. The numbers swelled in the 1850s as sheet music became more common, making copyright vital to publishers' profits. Songs by Root (Wurzel), like those of Stephen Foster, sold hundreds of thousands of copies, and such songwriters could demand royalties of up to 10 percent. In the meantime, costs had gone up considerably, impacted as well by improved technology and sales savvy. The nation's relentless westward march raised distribution costs. In his survey of the history of the American music business, Sanjek notes the significance for music publishers of the growth of the postal service in opening new markets across the country. Before its disruption by the Civil War, the Board of Music Trade had welcomed Hall and Son back into its fold, and its meetings had come to resemble a trade show.

A related business in printed text for popular songs flourished alongside but not within the members' ranks of the Board of Music Trade. During the Civil War publishers in New York, Philadelphia, and Boston printed millions of copies of words to songs. People either learned the tunes elsewhere or followed printed suggestions of well-known tunes that fit the text. Crosby's Civil War songs appeared in this format, cheaply though attractively printed. Steam-driven presses — in use since the 1840s — enabled mass production of small "pocket-songsters" (the same publishers produced the cheap books known as "dime novels") and gave to a handful of new publishers outside the Board of Music Trade enormous influence over the musical exposure of the urban masses.

Agitators for adequate copyright legislation renewed their campaign at the end of the Civil War. On one side were publishers, printers, and others who profited from lax laws; on the other, composers and writers. In 1865 Congress imposed a $25 fee on anyone who failed to deposit a copy of his or her work with the Copyright Office. In 1870 Congress established a 50¢ recording fee and imposed a fine of $1 per sheet of copyrighted printed matter republished without the author's permission. The 1870 law centralized copyright in the Library of Congress and required that all authors deposit in the library two copies of every publication registered in the United States. During the 1880s the American Copyright League (established in 1843 by the poet William Cullen Bryant) orchestrated a final successful push for a comprehensive revision of the Copyright Act of 1790. The bill passed Congress in 1891 and was promptly signed by President Benjamin Harrison. It extended copyright to twenty-eight years and covered matter published or manufactured in the United States; forbade the importation of foreign-copyrighted materials for sale; and required the secretary of the treasury to provide customs collectors and postmasters with weekly updates of copyright entries. In 1897 the Copyright Office became a separate department of the Library of Congress, and the first register of copyrights, Thorvald Solberg, was appointed. The register was charged with advising Congress on matters pertaining to copyright as well as with devising guidelines that kept up with expanding need.

Throughout Crosby's hymn-writing years, her texts were copyrighted by either her publisher or her tunesmith. In the first decades after the Civil War, the copyright fee was 50¢, a copy was placed on file, and a copyright notice accompanied each printing of the text or tune. Hymnal publishers learned to their dismay that each selection in a hymnal needed a separate copyright, for copyrights over hymnals extended only to reprints of the same collection, not to the individual pieces that composed the book. To use copyrighted materials publishers paid fees requested by the copyright holder, or they traded rights to other materials. Copyright presented a serious challenge. An unknown amount of uncopyrighted music appeared with copyright notices, and some publishers found it simpler and less costly to flaunt the law.

Bradbury and his successors held the rights to what Crosby gave them under contract. William Doane copyrighted all their joint efforts as single units and handled all requests for permissions. He routinely refused permission to use text without tune, thus assuring the marriage of his tune and her text in Protestant memory. The enormous success of the Sunday school hymnals edited by Doane and Robert Lowry cemented a friendship and led to a formal agreement between the two for free use of the hymns to which the other held copyright in any hymnals either edited. Biglow and Main negotiated a fixed percentage for the use of materials to which either Doane or Lowry held the rights. Such agreements between friends or between publishers and their most prolific contributors simplified the cumbersome process of seeking permissions each time a hymnal was compiled.

Requests for permissions for Doane-Crosby hymns came from some unexpected places. In 1890 Doane granted the Watchtower Bible and Tract Society (Jehovah's Witnesses) permission to use "Near the Cross," "Safe in the Arms of Jesus," and a few other hymns for an $80 fee. Arrangements with John Sweney, Lowry's estate, Kirkpatrick, Ira Sankey, and Biglow and Main enabled the Reorganized Church of Jesus Christ of Latter-Day Saints to include numerous Crosby hymns in their 1903 *Zion's Praise*. Other Crosby texts also found their way into *Desert Sunday School Songs*, published in Salt Lake City in 1909. Sweney's widow gave permission for this Mormon collection to put Crosby's text "Behold! A Royal Army" to a tune by the well-known composer Adam Geibel. Mary Lowry allowed "Parting Hymn," by Crosby and her husband, to find a place in the same collection.

In the drive for expanded copyright protection, authors of religious texts and tunes were part of a much larger coalition. And during the same years, they also followed with interest the fate of the demand for international copyright. That demand had been articulated in 1837 when Henry Clay had stood in the Senate to present a petition signed by fifty-six British authors asking for redress for "deep and extensive injuries inflicted on the petitioners' reputations" by the absence of international copyright. A distinguished committee — including, among others, Clay, Daniel Webster, and James Buchanan — recommended the enactment of a *"uniform* law of literary property" to apply in "all civilized nations." Clay drafted a bill and presented it four times without obtaining action.

Negotiations in 1852 and 1853 resulted in the preparation of a treaty with Britain declaring that authors entitled to copyright in one country should be entitled to it in the other on the same terms. Strong interests mobilized against this treaty, and the Senate failed to ratify it.

Among the opponents was Henry C. Carey, author of several famous "Letters on International Copyright" in which he held copyright to be an indefensible concept since ideas are common property. In 1868 publishers and authors raised the issue again, and William Cullen Bryant accepted the presidency of the International Copyright Association. Over the next few years proposals and counterproposals jostled for popular attention as writers, composers, and performers took their case to the public in such venues as the *Century Magazine*. In one 1887 issue *Century* offered five consecutive pages of letters from musicians chiming in to the heated discussion. The February 1886 *Century* had already aired the views of literary figures. People of prominence like Lyman Abbott wrote in favoring "universal" rather than international copyright. George Root's letter complained that during an 1886 visit to the British Museum to look for British reprints of American music, he had discovered over twenty-three pages listing his songs, not including his contributions to compiled hymnals and singing class books. He had received no compensation for any of this, and he took no comfort in the fact that Europeans made the same complaint about American practice.

Opposition — like that expressed by Philadelphia publishers in an 1872 memorial insisting that thought, when given to the world, is, as light, free to all — only fueled the flames. Harper and Brothers entered the fray with the warning that international copyright would increase the price of printed matter "and thus interfere with the education of the people."

In 1880 Congress debated a memorial bearing the signatures of such eminent Americans as Henry Wadsworth Longfellow, Oliver Wendell Holmes, Ralph Waldo Emerson, and John Greenleaf Whittier and urging an agreement requiring registration in both countries before publication in the country of origin, this registration to be in the author's (not the publisher's) name; and providing that the author of any work published in one country was not entitled to copyright in the other unless the author's work was also published in the other country within three months of its original publication in the author's homeland. Once again, the memorial failed to move forward. Presidents Arthur and Cleveland each went on record in favor of international copyright, but no action followed. In 1886 James Russell Lowell and Mark Twain appeared before the Senate Committee on Patents to reiterate the case for international copyright. A quatrain by Lowell captured his perception of the wheeling and dealing that hindered action:

> In vain we call old notions fudge,
> And bend our conscience to our dealing;
> The Ten Commandments will not budge,
> And stealing will continue stealing.

Decades of wrangling came to an end when President Benjamin Harrison signed provisions for international copyright as part of the Chace Act of 1891. The act extended limited protection on a bilateral basis to authors in selected countries — first, Britain and France. The first copyright treaties were in place by 1897. Copyright kept growing, expanding with technology to embrace new categories. Crosby's life spanned the fierce debates over copyright law. In 1820, the year of her birth, music was not even a category in the existing law. (That law covered only literary works and prints.) Shortly before her death, the Copyright Office created a new category for motion pictures.

While many emphasized the advantages of cooperation and lobbied for effective legislative protection, others made no pretense of concern for others. Those associated with making a case for music and education, citizenship, and religion proved as susceptible to quarrels over profits as any others. A long and bitter dispute between George Root and William Bradbury brought the competitive edge of the music business into Crosby's awareness. She had not yet met Bradbury, but she was working closely with Root. Much to his mentor Lowell Mason's dismay, Root took a strong turn in the mid-1850s against Bradbury. Friction between his two best-known protégés dismayed Mason, and he maintained his friendship with each while seeking to heal the breach. In 1860 Mason wrote that he had pled to no avail for several years with Root for Bradbury. Their rivalry during the 1850s for prominence in normal institutes as well as for venues for their publications was obscured at first by the number of invitations that poured in. Each had plenty to do. Institutes demanded arduous travel, but the featured instructors reaped handsome rewards — at the very least the equivalent of over $2,000 (in 2003 dollars) for each. The longer institute that debuted in Manhattan in 1853 and moved to North Reading, Massachusetts, in 1855 brought the two on a collision course.

Bradbury was not featured when the institute moved, and his attempt to run a rival school collapsed. For several years, even Mason could do nothing about the festering animosity.

In 1858 Root unexpectedly had a change of heart. Though Root gave no reason, Mason suggested that anyone "near the Book-Sellers" would understand. In fact, a profit motive apparently induced Root and Bradbury to become publishing partners. They neglected to inform Mason. His sons, though, looked out for his interests, and Mason instructed them to negotiate for him a partnership with Root and Bradbury. "The result," Mason explained, "is that we are all three of us in another's publications. I am as much pecuniarially interested in Mr. Root's and Mr. Bradbury's Books as my own — I mean of those which are to come." This rapprochement had implications for the normal schools that sold such books, and the three agreed to conduct some schools together. "Root's deportment," Mason noted in 1861, had "improved much." This mending of the rift did not heal all the wounds: Bradbury declined an invitation to join Mason and Root at North Reading in the summer of 1861. "The prospect of making something was not a sufficient inducement," Mason sighed.

Such broken and healed relationships proved common in the rough-and-tumble competitive environs of music business. Correspondence at Biglow and Main revealed occasional unhappiness in the 1880s with perceived heavy-handed behavior by Ira Sankey, who insisted that the company issue no other gospel hymnals during a year that it published one of his. In the late 1890s, when Sankey's son, Ira Allen, graduated from Princeton and chose to become a partner at Biglow and Main, the coterie that had known Bradbury worried about a generational change at the top. The younger Sankey proved up to the task of honoring the old-timers whose work had built the company while attending to the changing market of the early twentieth century. Moody Bible Institute's Daniel Towner, like the singing evangelist Charles Alexander, was another matter, however. People at Biglow and Main thought them unwilling to cooperate, eager to keep profits to themselves. Such tensions long troubled the waters. In 1874 a misunderstanding over copyright prompted Biglow and Main to refuse P. P. Bliss permission to use their songs. Doane salvaged the situation, extending permission for Bliss to use Crosby lyrics he had personally copyrighted, and obtaining in return permission to use Bliss songs if,

Bliss noted, "I've anything that people will sing half as much as they do [Crosby's] 'Near the Cross.' Profit motives often intruded on the business side of gospel and Sunday school hymns, and they sometimes drove deep wedges among those who composed texts and tunes.

Crosby knew only some of this; her friends and publishers kept business troubles from her because she tended to be excitable and to worry to the point of taking ill. She, in turn, preferred to trust them, especially Doane, to handle the business of her hymns. She had no financial stake in the matter, and her blindness forced her to rely on others anyway.

12 Honor

List to the clanging bells of time,
Tolling, tolling a low, sad chime,
A requiem chant o'er the grand Old Year,
Hark! He is speaking, and bids us hear:

"Friends, I am dying, my hours are few,
This is the message I leave for you —
'Bought with a price, ye are not your own,'
Live for the Master and Him alone.

Gather the sheep from the mountains cold,
Gather them into the Shepherd's fold,
Work for His cause till your work is done,
Stand by the cross till your crown is won."

"Fanny J. Crosby is one of the grand old women of her time."

Buffalo Courier, 7 July 1904

Audiences responded eagerly to Crosby's winsomeness and spontaneity, and as her reputation grew, so did her range of venues. In February 1885 she was a featured Sunday evening speaker at a women's revival conference hosted by the Seventeenth Street Methodist Church. She shared the platform with the formidable Maggie van Cott, the first woman licensed to preach by the Methodist Episcopal Church, North, and the second Mrs. Dr. Palmer (Sarah Lankford Palmer) of Holiness movement fame. June 1887 found her assisting at a camp meeting at the Jane Street Methodist Episcopal Church, "temperance apostle" Stephen Merritt, pastor. On 13 June Sarah Palmer presided there over women's day, and "Sister Crosby" was one of three women who led the singing.

During these years neither Crosby's much-touted cheerfulness nor her growing public appeal could obscure the reality that her relationship with Van had been stressed for decades. Together and separately, they had moved frequently. In the 1870s they lived for a time on Varick Street in lower Manhattan, first in a two-story frame dwelling on the east side of the street between Grand and Watts Streets, then three doors down in a two-story brick residence. In the 1880s records show that "Frances Crosby, authoress" left the familiar streets of lower Manhattan — and, presumably, Van — for the "better" environs of Park Avenue on the upper east side. She lived first on the southwest corner of Park Avenue and 114th Street. During the 1890s she moved several times, always on Park Avenue between Eighty-eighth and Ninety-first Streets, with each apartment in a similar building — five-story brick with a stone front. It is uncertain how much she saw of Van. By the end of the 1890s he had moved in with friends on South Third Street in Brooklyn. She had moved to another Brooklyn neighborhood near the Sankeys. She had her public and a full life. The record is silent on Van. No one knows what caused the rift between them. She wrote some intensely personal verses that may have had him in mind:

> O come, if thou art true to me,
> If yet thou lov'st me well,
> And meet me at our trysting place
> Within the mossy dell;
> Yes, meet me as when first we met
> Beneath a summer sky,

Long, long before our lips had learned
That cruel word, good-bye.

There's not a rose on yonder bush,
Nor flower we used to twine;
The birds have left that rural spot;
Perhaps the fault is mine;
I know my looks were cold and stern,
A frown was on my brow;
But I regret that fatal hour;
Wilt thou forgive me now?

O come, and let us plight once more
The faith of other years,
And bathe each link of sacred love
In sweet repentant tears;
Yet not one shadow would I cast
Around thy peerless name;
Mine, mine the wrong; I'll bear it all
And I deserve the blame.

Crosby was at Doane's Watch Hill estate in July 1902 when a telegram from Biglow and Main brought the news that Van had succumbed on 18 July to a massive stroke. Asthma had plagued him for years (he may also have suffered from cancer), and he had been cared for at the home of the couple's friends David Harris Underhill and Caroline Underhill, who lived on South Third Street in the Williamsburg section of Brooklyn. On the staff of the prestigious Astor library, Harris Underhill shared Crosby's colonial New England roots and knew Joseph Knapp through Brooklyn's New England Club. The van Alstines had had a long relationship with the Underhills. In 1892 Underhill had organized the Underhill Society to connect the estimated 7,000 Underhills descended from those who migrated from England in the 1630s. At the family's 1895 reunion in Yonkers, New York, the van Alstines performed. Van played a piano solo and Crosby recited an original ode to Captain Underhill, the progenitor of the American branch of the family.

Van had turned seventy in 1901, and though his death was not unexpected, Doane at first did not want to inform Crosby until the weekend had passed. He knew the news would excite and confuse her since it would entail numerous decisions, but he concluded she had the right to know.

Immediately upon hearing of her husband's death, Crosby went into her bedroom and closed the door. She emerged several hours later, entirely composed, and dictated a new hymn to William Doane. She titled it "I Am Satisfied":

> If he, my Lord, is with me still,
> And I in him abide,
> If he but whisper to my heart,
> Then I am satisfied.

> Thro' pastures green, or shadows deep,
> With him my constant guide,
> If step by step he leads me on,
> Then I am satisfied.

> And tho' at times the things I ask
> In love are oft denied,
> I know he gives me what is best,
> And I am satisfied.

> From him my soul, in life or death,
> No power shall e'er divide,
> I read the promise in his word,
> And I am satisfied.

Both the absence of emotion and the topic are striking. Crosby had written many lines about heaven, lines that brimmed with comfort, assurance, sentiment, and confidence of reunion. Protestants everywhere found peace in her promise that their departed loved ones were "safe in the arms of Jesus." She wove that hymn and others into poems of comfort she sent to her bereaved friends. Yet the end of her disappointing relationship with Van elicited no anticipation of meeting, no hint of the glories that had become his, not even an impersonal longing for heaven. Rather, Crosby recalled for herself the Calvinist dictums of her childhood and found in them a rationale that enabled her to put the past behind her and move on. It was a matter of will, not emotion.

As a young woman, Crosby had longed for romantic love. At age thirty-eight, she thought she had found it with Van. The rift in their relationship had left this daughter of primitive Presbyterians the option to interpret her failure to realize a loving marriage as a discipline God sent for her good. Crosby's third stanza suggests both a literal and a spiritual application. Van had deprived her of the love she craved, and God had seen fit to deny her prayers for a loving relationship. Yet God gave what was best, and she determined to be satisfied. And she made the choice to allow God's sustaining presence to fill her emotional void.

Doane and other friends encouraged Crosby not to go to New York, thinking the excitement and fatigue of the journey would take a toll on her limited strength. Biglow and Main oversaw arrangements to place Van's body in a vault until Crosby had time to decide where to bury him. Her recent move to Bridgeport complicated her oft-expressed wish for them to be buried side by side. For unknown reasons her family did not want him buried in their plot. Doane reported that Fanny was "bearing up bravely under the sad news, and knows in whom she has believed and His promise of the comforter to come in times like these." In the end, she did not got to New York, and Van had no funeral.

A few weeks after Van's death, the indomitable Phoebe Knapp took matters into her own hands and had Van's body moved to a plot in Mt. Olivet Cemetery in Queens near the first home the van Alstines had shared forty-four years earlier. Though she saw to his burial, the wealthy Knapp did not mark Van's grave, and no gravestone has ever been placed. The Crosby life story Will Carleton released in 1903 suggested that she sometimes knelt beside Van's unmarked grave and mourned his loss: "Though I cannot see the mound under which he rests, I can touch the turf with my hands, and try to make his spirit feel that I am constantly lamenting his temporary loss." That cannot have happened often: in 1902 she was living in Bridgeport, and Mt. Olivet Cemetery was well off the usual circuit she traveled on her occasional visits to New York City.

In fact, Van and Crosby had had a most unusual married life. At first they had boarded rather than kept house, a choice that better suited their blindness but that offered little privacy. Neither Crosby's nor her friends' reminiscences mention Van's accompanying her on her prolonged out-of-town trips, and public records suggest that she and Van had separate addresses at least during the 1880s and 1890s. Nonetheless, they kept in touch, sometimes worked together — as at the 1895 Underhill Society reunion — and Crosby made a point of stating that they maintained an amicable relationship. Crosby's only recorded admission of any unhappiness came in the life story she worked on just after Van's death. "He had his faults — and so have I mine," she owned, "but notwithstanding these, we loved each other to the last."

As her independence from Van had increased, Crosby's work and growing public had kept her occupied. The importance of Crosby's hymns to the Moody-Sankey revivals had drawn her into the circle of those who summered in Moody's hometown of Northfield, Massachusetts. During the 1880s Moody presided over an expanding conference schedule that transformed this community into a hub of Christian activity. Ideally located along the scenic Connecticut River in the Berkshire Mountains of central Massachusetts, Northfield became the site for student meetings, Christian Workers' Conventions, and other conferences geared toward energizing a generation of leaders for the task of evangelism. Moody's closer colleagues (like Sankey and R. A. Torrey) purchased homes in Northfield and shared responsibility for the gatherings that filled most days. Moody's associates from England stopped by, too, and their efforts helped fire a generation of American college youth to dedicate their lives to missions through the Student Volunteer Movement. Moody and Sankey poured the generous royalties generated by their hymnals into developing two Christian schools nearby — the Northfield School for girls and the Mt. Hermon School for boys. The *New York Tribune* reported that Moody received 30 percent royalties from the publishers of *Gospel Hymns:* as of June 1894, the books had yielded over $1.25 million (some $30 million in 2003 dollars). The school facilities built with these dollars made ideal venues for Moody's burgeoning summer conferences.

In 1886 Crosby paid the first of her eight visits to Northfield. She lived in the Sankey home, where Ira Sankey's wife, another Fannie, made her comfortable. While such summer visits were not working vacations, Crosby often composed lyrics as they came to mind. Her many social contacts as well as daily meetings and her close contact with Sankey stimulated her muse. In Northfield in 1886, for example, she wrote words for a Sankey tune: "O child of God, wait patiently when dark thy path may be." Sankey sometimes had her beside him on the conference platform to address the assembled crowds. In 1894 he invited her (with only a few minutes' notice) to address the Christian Workers' Convention. The (Methodist) *Christian Advocate* recorded her impromptu words and the poem that no one knew she had ready — the soon-to-be-popular "Saved by Grace":

> Some day the silver cord will break,
> And I no more as now shall sing.
> But, O, the joy when I shall wake
> Within the palace of the King!
> And I shall see Him face to face
> And tell the story — saved by grace.

By all accounts Crosby enjoyed Northfield, where young and old paid her homage. By her first visit in 1886 she had written most of her enduring hymns, and although she kept producing, twenty years of hymn writing had already elicited her best lines. And so Northfield attendees, gathered from around the country, sang her best-loved texts and honored her presence among them. She went back as often as she could. In 1888 she gave the convention a closing hymn:

> Within these consecrated walls
> Convened from year to year,
> We all have said, like one of old,
> "'Tis good to linger here";
> Though from the mount we must descend,
> And toil amid the plain,
> Yet we can sing, with joyful hearts,
> Good night, we'll meet again.

When Crosby failed to appear at the 1897 Northfield convention, the *New York Daily Tribune* reported that Ira Sankey was besieged with inquiries about her well-being. Assuring the assembled thousands that she was well, he reminded them that she was among them in "her beautiful and soul-inspiring hymns heard at every service." The convention hymnal, *Sacred Songs No. 1* (used, according to the *Tribune*, "in all Mr. Moody's meetings), included Crosby's established popular numbers, while the congregation knew as well her more recent work.

Crosby and Sankey shared the Northfield platform in 1900, the year after Moody's death. One August morning Sankey announced Crosby's "Saved by Grace" as Moody's favorite and invited the audience to sing it as they had a few months earlier at Carnegie Hall. There Crosby's hymns had been on the program of the ecumenical missions conference that had gathered thousands of delegates from around the world. Now different sections of the audience took turns singing the chorus as Sankey rendered the stanzas, and Crosby "sparkled with new light." Will Moody gave her a proper introduction, and Crosby spoke to the mood of the assembly (who "missed the tones of a gentle voice and the clasp of a friendly hand") in lines that evoked "the green hills and stately mountains" that stood as "sentinels" around Moody's beloved home:

> Oh, the music rolling onward
> Through the boundless regions bright
> Where the King in all His beauty
> Is the glory and the light,
> Where the sunshine of His presence
> Every wave of sorrow stills,
> And the bells of joy are ringing
> On the everlasting hills.
>
> When I wake amid the splendor
> That I see but dimly now,
> And behold the crown of jewels
> That adorns my Saviour's brow,
> Where eternal spring abideth
> And the sky no darkness fills,
> How my grateful heart will praise Him
> On the everlasting hills.

Another favorite Crosby summer location was not too far away and also had strong musical associations — the Doane family's retreat at Watch Hill on the Rhode Island coast. As she grew older, Crosby found extended relief from hot, humid urban summers amid the music and family circles of the Sankeys and the Doanes. Attendees at the Round Lake camp meeting just south of the famous harness racecourse and spas of Saratoga, New York, like those at the campground at Ocean Grove, New Jersey, could generally count on a visit from Crosby, too. And at both places Crosby could depend on meeting the aged Palmers and other proponents of holiness. (One Round Lake announcement assured that Sarah Lankford Palmer made "a specialty of full salvation as a distinct and immediate blessing, and ha[d] a wonderful faculty of winning people to her views and experience.")

In an article on Crosby that he contributed to the *National Magazine* in 1899, G. H. Sandison offered an unusually vivid description of Crosby walking Manhattan streets:

> On bright sunshiny days anyone who happens to walk in the neighborhood of Broadway and Ninth street, New York, may observe a cheery-looking little old lady, sprightly even in her feebleness, and always smiling, as she clings with almost child-like trust to the hand of some friend who is her companion. This little old lady, who always wears a pair of dark-colored spectacles, is garbed after a very ancient fashion; indeed, the style of her gowns and her bonnet might have belonged to a period so remote as fifty years ago. She is, however, wholly oblivious to such matters, for as she trips along she chatters entertainingly to her escort, while the bright, interested face shows that she is in full touch with what is going on in the big active world around her.

Crosby lived a quiet life, Sandison noticed: her principal outing was to her publisher where she conversed, dictated hymns, and received callers. She confided to him her persuasion that the "best" hymn she had ever written, the one that had "done the most good," was "Safe in the Arms of Jesus."

A writer in the *New York Evangelist* caught Crosby in another typical pose: "When we saw her she was knitting an intricate piece of lace, which, on examination, was found not to have a misplaced stitch in it. Her fingers moved busily while she talked in a modest way of the talents God had given her, saying what a comfort it had been to her that she had been enabled to write words that had helped other souls on to heaven. . . . After a day's jostling through the city streets, guided by some loving hand, Miss Crosby returns to her quiet room and pours forth her soul in song."

Much to the disappointment of her friends who had planned a celebration, Crosby spent her eightieth birthday on a sickbed. She had been seriously ill for several weeks when the 24 March date passed, cared for at the Brooklyn home of her friends, the Will Carletons. Biglow and Main's annual birthday festivities had to wait until Monday, 23 April 1900, when her friends, including the Sankeys, gathered for a luncheon and presented her with an eight-day chiming clock. Though she regained her health, her family in Bridgeport worried about her well-being, and later that spring her sisters — with support from the Sankeys and Hubert Main — succeeded at last in convincing her to move permanently to Bridgeport. They promised to facilitate frequent visits to New York; still, the move seemed to Crosby an unwelcome departure from the center of the life she loved. Only her severe illness convinced her to acquiesce to the desires of her family and the urging of her publishers.

In some ways Crosby had pictured Bridgeport as home since her mother had moved there in 1835, and over the years she had made many trips to family occasions in the city. Though her uncle Joseph Crosby and his family had long since left, Mercy Morris's sister Polly (Mary) Decker had returned to New England to live out her life in Bridgeport. Joseph had died in Georgia in 1858; his son, Frank, succumbed to tuberculosis in 1860; and his wife, Maria, died in 1861. On his death, Joseph bequeathed $500 to each of his sisters (about $11,000 in 2003 dollars), Mercy, Theda, and Polly.

Theda had died in 1876. Never married, she had spent her life as domestic help on the farm operated by the well-to-do Kelly family near her birthplace in Southeast, New York. Polly Crosby Decker, Mercy's youngest sibling, had lived for much of her life in Pennsylvania. Widowed, she, too, did domestic work until the 1870s when she moved to Bridgeport to be near the Morris clan. She died of a heart attack in 1888. Just three years older than Crosby, Polly had been her childhood playmate. Her death accented the passing of the years. Crosby's mother, Mercy, lived until 1890, past her eldest daughter's seventieth birthday. She died 2 September, having reached the age of ninety-one. Each year on her birthday, even after Mercy's death, her surviving daughters gathered for a reunion and celebration. Crosby always had a poem, and sometimes her lines made their way into a Bridgeport newspaper. For her mother's eighty-ninth birthday, she described the family circle:

Mother's birthday, and her children
Three in number, all are here,
From the sunny past recalling
Words of love we still revere.
. . . .
Four grandchildren grace our circle,
Breathing wishes kind and true,
Mother's joy to make still brighter,
See! Her great-grandchildren, too.
But our hearts must pause a moment
O'er the missing ones to mourn;
Where are William, Lee and Byron,
Will those dear ones ne'er return?

William, the son Mercy's estranged husband Thomas Morris brought into the family, had died in 1880, and Byron Athington, Julia Morris's husband, as well as Joshua Lee Rider, husband of Caroline Morris, had followed soon after. (Athington had never recovered from wounds sustained in the Civil War.) Crosby's half sisters lived out their lives in the city of their birth. William had left the sisters two nieces — Laura Frances Tait and Florence Booth — and a nephew, Albert Morris. These with their families, and Athington's married daughter, Ida Leschon (and son James), brought energy and laughter to the family circle, but the extended family had its share of sorrows, too. Less than a year after Mercy's death, Albert and Clara Morris lost their infant daughter. In 1893 the Taits lost an infant son. Crosby generally offered comfort in poetry that might evoke her beloved hymns:

Oh I know you are sad and lonely,
Through tears I hear you say:
"From Papa, Mamma and Mary
Our boy has gone away:

Our boy like ivy clinging
Around each breaking heart,
Our dear little baby, Morris,
'Tis hard from him to part."

Oh, yes, but your precious darling
In yonder home of rest,
Is "safe in the arms of Jesus,"
"Safe on His gentle breast";
And, oh, could the veil be lifted,
That hides your babe so fair,
How soon you would lose forever
The cross that now you bear!

Julia Athington owned a home where Caroline (Carrie) Rider had lived since the death of their mother. Crosby briefly moved into this two-family house with her sisters. Next, Rider and Crosby rented a room, then a five-room apartment where they lived together for the next six years. Ira Sankey paid their rent and mailed Rider funds for Crosby's expenses. Rider, a shy woman who preferred the quiet family circle to the bustle of public life, undertook to care for Crosby and to maintain her correspondence. Later the family engaged Eva Cleaveland to provide Crosby with secretarial support.

In 1904 Crosby formally transferred her membership from Manhattan's Cornell Memorial Methodist Episcopal Church to First Methodist of Bridgeport. Her sister Julia worshiped there, and Crosby was active in the congregation even before she joined. In Manhattan she had known Margaret Bottome, founder of the King's Daughters, and at First Methodist she actively participated in the King's Daughters Circle. She promptly made her way to Bridgeport's Christian Union, a rescue mission like those she delighted to frequent in Manhattan, befriended Charles Simpson, its superintendent, and attended the nightly services whenever she could. Often the evening's main speaker, Crosby — always in black dress and a quaint bonnet — delivered in prose and poetry the gospel message her hymns had carried for a generation.

This "home of [her] adoption," a "treasured spot" where she had spent "many a summer's glad vacation," became her home for the rest of her life, and the outgoing Crosby soon had many friends. In 1908 she composed "The State We Honor," a song in honor of Connecticut. (A few years later her friends submitted it unsuccessfully to a contest for a new state song.)

As Crosby aged, Bradbury's successors continued to pay her a small weekly stipend whether or not she provided lyrics. Changes in what the firm published meant that she wrote fewer new texts, and especially after she moved to Bridgeport, frequent travels and speaking engagements occupied more of her time. Her long-standing friends like Doane, Knapp, and Sankey contributed to her material well-being, though Crosby, generous to a fault, gave much away and refused to adopt a standard of living some thought appropriate to her fame. Phoebe Knapp and a newer Crosby friend, poet Will Carleton, thought her publishers owed her more than they gave. As she approached her eighty-fifth birthday, they schemed to tap for her financial benefit the reservoir of public regard for the hymn writer. The only results of their plans were stress and fractured relationships.

Among the era's poets, few enjoyed a wider popular following than Will Carleton. An enthusiastic contemporary declared that "the name of this poet has long been a household word. In simple, homely phrase, in unambitious rhyme, he has touched American and English hearts for more than a generation." An obituary writer aptly called him "a poet not exactly of distinction but of worth and certainly of renown." His reputation blossomed after 1871 when the Toledo *Blade* published his poem "Betsey and I Are Out," an emotional ballad about humdrum home life and a failed marriage. Copied in papers across the country and illustrated and featured in *Harper's Weekly*, the poem catapulted Carleton to fame as "spokesman of the farmer and everyday citizen." Known for "superb pathos and dramatic effect," Carleton managed to make a very comfortable living by writing poems and prose. Published by Harper Brothers and featured regularly in such venues as *Harper's Weekly*, his work had wide circulation.

The Carletons lived in an affluent section of Brooklyn not far from Crosby's other Brooklyn friends, and the kindly and enterprising Will Carleton soon took an interest in Crosby. Prominent at authors' readings and receptions, Carleton also traveled the lecture circuit. He took pride in a series of addresses he offered on Crosby and compiled them into a book, *Fanny Crosby's Life-Story by Herself.* Published in 1903 by Carleton's Every Where Publishing Company (Carleton founded and edited the monthly *Every Where Magazine*), the book was part of a scheme to raise money for Crosby. "Every copy of the work that is sold adds substantially to a fund intended for the comfort of this grand old woman."

Carleton had served a term as president of the American Society of Authors (established 1891), one of three American associations dedicated to guarding the interests of authors from violation by their publishers. A mild-tempered man, Carleton associated in the society with people outspoken about their grievances with publishers. His ardor for authors' rights may have influenced his perception that Bradbury's successors were not caring adequately for Crosby, who by this time was, among evangelicals at least, regarded as something of a national treasure. He found an ally in the recently widowed Phoebe Knapp, and together the two launched several schemes to alert the public to Crosby's supposed lack of financial resources. They not only publicly regretted her poverty; they also openly criticized her longtime publishers.

Crosby proved easy to lead. She may not have grasped the full import of her friends' critique of her publisher, but the publisher understood a threat to its bottom line and reputation. The public was appalled and questioned the publisher's arrangements with Crosby (who earned no royalties on any song, but whose lyrics had played a large part in the company's success).

When Crosby granted Carleton permission to compile his articles into a book, Carleton offered her a 25 percent royalty on each copy (the royalty rate his own contract with Harper Brothers specified). Crosby did not seem particularly interested in the money but agreed to allow Carleton to compile a biography. (In the end Carleton gave her 10 percent.) No full biography had yet been attempted. A sketch Robert Lowry had prepared as a preface to *Bells at Evening,* a book of Crosby's poems whose profits had been promised entirely to Crosby, collected and summarized the best-known facts of her life. Crosby's cohorts at Biglow and Main thought Carleton's serialized life of Crosby jeopardized sales of *Bells at Evening.* They now disapproved of Crosby's decision to allow Carleton to issue a biography because they assumed he cared most about exploiting the huge interest they knew Crosby's life story would tap.

If Carleton disapproved of Crosby's financial arrangements with her publisher, Phoebe Knapp more than matched his censure of Biglow and Main. The two had sometimes tended to Crosby's needs and manifested their impatience with her choice to rent rooms in Manhattan apartment houses. Given her popularity — and the amount of money her lyrics had generated for Biglow and Main — Knapp thought Crosby should be provided her own home and the servants to run it. Knapp now threw her considerable energy into enlisting the support of powerful friends. She relied on Methodist bishop Charles McCabe to launch a campaign to provide for Crosby's financial needs.

McCabe asked Crosby's permission to raise for her "a testimonial" of American Protestantism's esteem and placed notices in religious publications inviting people to provide financial assistance to relieve Crosby's poverty. Knapp next arranged with Carleton to include in his *Fanny Crosby's Life-Story by Herself* a note that the sale of the book would "add substantially to a fund intended for the comfort of this grand woman, who has been singing in such far-reaching tones the praise of her God and her Christ for sixty years." He promised that profits would enable her "to have a house of her own in which to pass the remainder of her days."

In mid-1904 the religious press carried McCabe's request for money for Crosby under the heading "Fanny Crosby in Need." Noting that "her hymns have never been copyrighted in her own name," McCabe continued, "she has sold them for small sums to the publishers who hold the copyright themselves, and the gifted authoress has but little monetary reward for hymns that have been sung all over the world."

Crosby began receiving letters inquiring into her circumstances, and those close to her soon realized that both her publishers and her living arrangements had become subjects of vicious rumors. They contacted Bishop McCabe and requested him to place a notice informing the public that his earlier request for assistance for Crosby had been based on misinformation. He complied. Those who approached Crosby directly for clarification learned that she had "gladly assented to the proposition that her friends unite in making her a testimonial of their love and admiration," but she had not understood "that it was to be based on the plea of her poverty." Meanwhile, correspondence among those associated in Biglow and Main revealed their disgust with Carleton and Knapp. In Rhode Island, Doane explained matters to Crosby, urging legal action against Carleton to stop the sale of the book. While no such action was taken, Crosby did issue a statement of clarification through the religious press. The 12 January 1905 *Union Signal* (organ of the Women's Christian Temperance Union [WCTU]) printed it as follows:

> May I state that I am in my usual good health and have a comfortable home. Concerning a book that is being sold ostensibly to buy me a home, I wish to say that it was mainly not written by me, but was compiled from incidents of my life first for a magazine published about four years ago, and finally was issued in book form, with my toleration rather than my full consent. . . . The book is not an adequate biography, especially of my life for the last forty years when I have been writing hymns. I have never authorized anyone to advertise that this book is being sold to raise money to buy me a home, and personally, and through legal counsel, I have requested that it be not so advertised. My royalty has been ten percent, and has amounted to less than $325.
>
> Furthermore, I wish it known that the publishers of my hymns (The Biglow and Main Company of New York) have dealt with me in a manner wholly satisfactory to myself. I regard them highly as among my best and truest friends, and I have so considered them for almost forty years.

Biglow and Main placed notices in the religious press, too:

> We desire to state positively that Fanny Crosby does not need help nor is she the object of charity which the article implies. . . . She is receiving from us, and will continue to do so as long as she lives, a regular weekly salary amounting to the average amount which she received per week for hymns sold to us during her prime. In return for this we ask nothing of her except to be happy and live as long as she possibly can. . . . We wish Fanny Crosby all the riches of this world (she is sure of those in the next); but please do not make her out an object for charity, for she is not.

This tempest passed, but not before Knapp "went up to Bridgeport ostensibly to talk to [Crosby] about hymns and gave her a big blowing up and put Fanny on her back." Knapp followed her outburst with two letters threatening heavy damages if Crosby sued her or Carleton. "The fact is," Hubert Main wrote to William Doane, "Will Carleton wanted to ignore the Biglow & Main Company and all its writers as far as possible and set himself up as the one of her friends who was helping her." Crosby's publishers accused Knapp and Carleton of a "brutal attack on Fanny" and of plotting to "take over" Fanny Crosby. The publishers, meanwhile, sent her $8 per week, fumed among themselves, and awaited developments. Carleton soon realized Crosby's distaste for his plan of action. His wife died, and other concerns took over his life. The circle Crosby knew around her publishers remained distrustful of Carleton and Knapp ("Mrs. Knapp," they opined, "ought to be ashamed of herself"). Ira D. Sankey even suggested that Knapp and Carleton had been ploys of Satan. Crosby, though, preferred to believe they had sincerely wanted to do her good, and she remained on excellent terms with both. Her affection for her friends at Biglow and Main never wavered. "If you knew how much I think of you all and of you personally," she wrote to Main, "you would be sure that I love you just as well as ever and a good deal more so." They could count on frequent personal poetic greetings like the following Christmas carol "affectionately dedicated to my friends at the store with love":

Honored president, I hail thee,
And my loyal brother Hugh,
Round my heart you both are clinging
With affection firm and true.
Louie Glatz and dear Miss Dyer,
Happy greeting one and all
While I sing my yearly carol
And your treasured names recall.

In February 1904, in the midst of the tempest provoked by Carleton and Knapp, came Crosby's fortieth anniversary with Bradbury and his successors. Crosby traveled to Manhattan for a reception at Biglow and Main and a dinner overseen by Fannie Sankey and Louise Main where her friends did their best to give her a pleasant day amid the bickering. Conspicuous by their absence were Ira Sankey, whose declining health kept him home, and Phoebe Knapp, Crosby's hostess, who was persona non grata at Biglow and Main. Planning for the next year's milestone, Crosby's eighty-fifth birthday, proceeded under the leadership of Dr. S. Parkes Cadman, head of the committee to plan a national tribute in the form of a Fanny Crosby Sunday.

In March 1904 Crosby — billed as one of the WCTU's best speakers — conducted a Sunday afternoon WCTU meeting at the First Methodist Church in Meriden, Connecticut, where she charmed a crowd by giving incidents of her hymns. A few weeks later she returned to Brooklyn to celebrate her eighty-fourth birthday (24 March) with Ira and Fannie Sankey. A reporter for the *New York Daily Tribune* judged her to be in "excellent health and spirits" and to look "hardly more than sixty." She announced her intention of matching her paternal grandmother's 106 years. The *New York Times* informed Crosby's many New York friends that telegrams and gifts from all over the country poured into the Crosby home.

The fall 1904 program for the national WCTU convention listed Crosby among those invited to participate. Illness kept her away but the assembled crowd paid her tribute, sang "Rescue the Perishing," heard of her life from writer Ann Cobham, a longtime friend, and wired Crosby their sympathy and flowers.

Crosby's own autobiography, *Memories of Eighty Years*, appeared in 1906. Thanks to the assistance of her secretary, Eva Cleaveland, and a Yale graduate student, Adelbert White, Crosby's dictated reminiscences became an organized rendering of the memories she especially treasured. Published in Boston by James H. Earle and Company, the book's promotional blurb carried a recommendation from Grover Cleveland. Sold by subscription and door-to-door, the book earned Crosby $1,000. In addition, Doane traveled the lecture circuit to promote it and donated the proceeds to Crosby, just as Carleton had done years before. The book focused (as Carleton's had not) on her hymn-writing years, offered representative poems, and rendered "incidents of hymns" (stories associated with the usefulness of her texts). Much popular writing about hymns featured such "incidents," for which there seemed to be an insatiable demand.

The long-awaited day for the "Sunday bash" arrived on 26 March 1905, the Sunday closest to Crosby's eighty-fifth birthday. Hundreds of thousands of American Protestants — "Methodist, Lutheran, Presbyte-

rian, Congregational, and the rest," according to the *New York Times* —
sang her hymns in an organized recognition of her contributions to their
language of devotion. No one knew just how many hymn texts she had
composed in the past forty years (the *New York Times* announcement of
the event cited 8,000 while the *Union Signal* attributed to her closer to
6,000), but many Protestants found in her words expressions of their
own deepest intentions and hopes. And they honored the pluck and determination that her blindness had never repressed. At least for northern Anglo-Saxon Protestants, she epitomized the Protestant life.

The committee of New York clergymen who planned the occasion
with her publishers, Hubert Main and Allan Sankey, issued program
guidelines, and churches of many denominations interspersed vignettes from her life story among renderings of her best-loved hymns
— "Blessed Assurance," "Rescue the Perishing," "Saved by Grace,"
and "Safe in the Arms of Jesus" ("the titles which confirm Fanny
Crosby's place in the hearts of Christians everywhere," the *Christian
Advocate* explained). Louis Klopsch, distinguished philanthropist, creator of the first red-letter edition of the Bible, and head of the Bowery
Mission, used his magazine, the widely circulated *Christian Herald*, to
orchestrate national cooperation. The magazine had an enviable track
record for similar accomplishments, and Fanny Crosby Sunday proved
no exception. Klopsch's reach extended around the world, and Fanny
Crosby Sunday was celebrated in remote Tasmania and in other places
where missionaries had taken her hymns. Crosby cherished a service
program from far-off Honolulu as well as a congratulatory note accompanying a gift from former president Grover Cleveland (a note someone leaked to the press before the momentous day):

> It is more than fifty years ago that our acquaintance and friendship
> began, and ever since that time I have watched your continuous
> and disinterested labor in uplifting humanity and pointing at the
> way to and appreciation of God's goodness and mercy.
>
> As one proud to call you an old friend, I desire to be early in
> joining your other friends and admirers in congratulating you on
> your long life of usefulness, and wishing you in the years yet to be
> added to you the peace and comfort born of the love of God.

Crosby's publishers marked the milestone with a reception. The hymn writer Eliza Hewitt sent a tribute that began:

The friends are forming a garland,
Fragrant and lovely and sweet,
The roses and lilacs of friendship,
To lay at our loved one's feet;

This love-wreath is for our dear Fanny
Whose heart is so young and so true,
No wonder her songs, freely gushing,
Are as fresh as the morning dew!

Not to be outdone, Bridgeport's First Methodist Church celebrated Crosby's actual birthday, Friday, 24 March, with a special service that overflowed the sanctuary and Sunday school rooms. An American flag draped Crosby's seat, suggesting the role of heritage and patriotism in molding her worldview. The choir rendered "Blessed Assurance" as well as a hymn Crosby had composed for her birthday, "O Land of Joy Unseen." It interwove the familiar Crosby anticipation of heaven, sight, and light. The pastor of Bridgeport's First Presbyterian Church, H. A. Davenport, joined the Reverend Francis B. Upham, pastor of the First Methodist Episcopal Church, in paying tribute. A reception followed, and there Crosby responded: "Friends, I am shut out of the world and shut in with my Lord. I have served him as I could. As I have listened to the remarks tonight I have thought, 'Not unto me, O Lord, but unto Thee be all the glory.' The Lord is the sunshine of my soul."

On Fanny Crosby Sunday she visited Bridgeport's First Baptist, her half-sister Carrie Rider's church, where she presented the evening message and received eighty-five dollars — one for each year of her life. The *New York Times* reported that even John D. Rockefeller's Bible class had observed Fanny Crosby Sunday while awaiting the arrival of their speaker, Booker T. Washington. The wide publicity given Crosby's birthday elicited reflections on her life in numerous publications. "Probably no one since the days of Isaac Watts and the Wesleys has produced so many hymns that have been so generally accepted as expressive of the faith, hope, aspirations, and purpose of the Christian public," Henry Shumway ventured in the *New England Magazine.*

Allan Sutherland contributed a piece to the *Delineator* in which he mused: "More than ever, as the years go by, the popularity of Fanny Crosby's hymns increases. In every gathering where the salvation of souls is the chief concern one or more of her compositions are sung." The *Cleveland Journal*, a black newspaper, printed her photo with incidents from her life and the comment that her hymns were "known and loved by nearly everyone."

The years leading to national recognition on her eighty-fifth birthday had brought many changes to Crosby's life. Busy as ever, she basked in the esteem her hymns had won her. But she did not permit herself to rest on her laurels. Her later years were some of the busiest of her life, not just in preparing lyrics but in putting her injunctions to her public into practice in her own life.

As strength permitted, Crosby accepted invitations to visit church groups, Sunday schools, YMCAs, and the homes of her friends where she extended her wide circle of acquaintances. In early July 1904 an invitation to address a Christian Endeavor Convention in Buffalo became her excuse for a whirlwind tour of upstate New York. She and Ira Sankey had composed a "Marching Song" for the Endeavor movement. It appeared in one of several supplements available with one of Sankey's last hymnals, *Young People's Songs of Praise* (others were for Baptist Youth and the [Methodist] Epworth League):

> Christian soldiers all, hear our Leader's call
> Who will rally at the King's command?
> Firmly, steadily, on to victory,
> See advancing "Our Endeavor Band."

And,

> Storm the fort by Satan's host defended,
> Storm the fort, and set the prisoners free;
> Onward still, though legions rise against you,
> Follow Him who giveth victory.

Crosby spoke numerous times at the Buffalo Endeavor convention, sharing tidbits about hymn writing and rescue mission work as well as vignettes from her life. Local churches welcomed her as well to their pulpits. Her candor and simplicity endeared her to the Endeavor throngs, especially the night she rose spontaneously, joined arms with the soloist B. Jacobs, and joined his singing of her hymn "Saved by Grace." Deeply moved like the rest of the audience, a Buffalo reporter described how the soloist faded out as Crosby's voice increased in strength until it seemed to fill the convention center. Such spontaneous acts endeared Crosby to audiences throughout the Northeast.

The first half of March 1905 found her speaking in Massachusetts (the YMCA in Fitchburg), then in western New York where various YMCA branches hosted her. She returned home less than a week before her eighty-fifth birthday and the national recognition that evoked.

In 1906 her first visit to Cambridge, Massachusetts, brought her to a packed house at First Baptist Church on 26 October. A Salvation Army band playing her hymns accompanied her from her lodgings to the sanctuary. In this city where the first American Crosbys had lived, she took special pleasure in a reception that permitted extended conversation with some Harvard students and faculty. (She returned to Cambridge to speak at two services at First Baptist Church, 3 and 4 December 1911. More than 1,000 people crowded the sanctuary, and hundreds were turned away.)

Later in 1906 Crosby took sick. Bedridden for weeks, she — like her loved ones — assumed she was dying. As she recovered, she put the experience into a poem:

> Almost in sight of the harbor
> Surely my spirit has been;
> Yet to the dear ones I cherish
> Prayer has restored me again.

Crosby particularly enjoyed the company of young people and rejoiced in the promise of associations dedicated to their good. She sent a poem of welcome to students at Manhattan's Deaconess Training School. Among her Methodist cohorts she encouraged the Epworth League, the youth program the Methodists inaugurated in 1889 with the motto All for Christ. The Christian Endeavor movement embraced her as a sort of grandmother, and the attachment was mutual. The Endeavor hymnal featured Crosby favorites from the Moody revivals and the Sunday school movement, and she wrote others specifically for Endeavor meetings. Occasionally invited to Endeavor conventions, Crosby encouraged young people with the same admonitions that filled her hymns. Christian Endeavorers accorded William Doane similar honors for both his own sake and his work with Crosby. In Buffalo, Atlantic City, Manhattan, Crosby thrilled to the youthful energy of Christian Endeavor and the rapid growth of the movement. In 1906 the society boasted 4 million members, a constituency large enough to warrant telegraphed greetings from Theodore Roosevelt and Kaiser Wilhelm.

Already in the 1890s Crosby had added to her summers an annual trip to New York's picturesque Onondaga County to participate in the Chautauqua Assembly that met from 1891 on the shores of Tully Lake. A "Round Table" of Tully Lake regulars adopted the custom of opening its annual meeting with a poetic address by Crosby, their "poet laureate." Her greeting for 1906 evoked the scene:

In these classic wilds of beauty,
In our summer land so dear,
Crowned with blessings rich and boundless
We have gathered year by year.

From the village and the hamlet,
From the city's crowded streets,
In our summer home so tranquil,
We are spared again to meet.

Hail, Chautauquan sons and daughters,
Swell the chorus; let it break
O'er the forest and the mountain,
O'er the waves of Tully Lake.

Hours of conversation with the hymn writer Eliza Hewitt became a highlight of Crosby's stays at Tully Lake. Hewitt wrote because ill health precluded teaching, and she served several Philadelphia Sunday schools as superintendent. Her lyrics for "My Faith Has Found a Resting Place," "When We All Get to Heaven," or "There Is Sunshine in My Soul Today" bespoke the same confidence and joy that people associated with Crosby, while her holiness leanings seemed even more pronounced than Crosby's.

Crosby talked gladly to everyone, and so she made the acquaintance at Tully Lake of an Onondaga Indian named Albert Cusick. Resident of a nearby reservation that Crosby now visited annually and part of its Church of the Good Shepherd, Cusick was the first full-blooded Iroquois to be ordained an Episcopal priest. Bishop Frederick Dan Huntington, Harvard's first Plummer Professor of Christian Morals and the Protestant Episcopal Church's most famous convert from Unitarianism, had himself won Cusick to faith and presided in 1891 at Cusick's ordination. A fiery evangelist, Cusick spoke the dialects of all the Six Nations and was widely recognized as an authority on Indian lore. The two-person white ministry team at the Church of the Good Shepherd included Miss Julia Remington ("Sister Julia" to the tribe), and Cusick had no objections to Crosby's presentations from the pulpit. He was precisely the kind of person Crosby most enjoyed, and to her delight during her visit in 1904 he performed an adoption rite that he assured her (and Hewitt) made them members of the Eel Clan of the Onondagas.

In June 1907, at the age of sixty-three, Carrie Rider succumbed to cancer. She had suffered since the summer of 1906 until, unable to care for herself or her sister, she and Crosby moved to their niece's nearby home. Crosby lived the rest of her own life with Florence Booth, daughter of her stepbrother William. A few months later she lost her niece Ida Leschon (Julia Athington's daughter) to cancer. She missed the companionship of these women who had devoted themselves to her care, and friends worried about Crosby's ability to cope. She proved typically resilient.

March 1908 found her making the annual trek to Manhattan for her birthday open house at Biglow and Main. She traveled alone by train, stayed with Phoebe Knapp, and celebrated her birthday with her boosters at the office. She mingled the next week at the New York Conference of the Methodist Episcopal Church, paid her respects to Ira and Fannie Sankey, and went on to New Jersey for a visit with Grover Cleveland. On Good Friday she spoke at a sacred concert at a Princeton Presbyterian church, then returned to Bridgeport for Easter. Within a few months all three of the longtime friends Crosby visited that spring died, part of the long list of the promoters Crosby had lost in the past decade. In April 1909 she remembered Cleveland in an article for a dedicated issue of *McClure's Magazine*.

Besides Cleveland, the best known of the friends who had "gone before" was D. L. Moody, who died in December 1899, but the passing of others with closer ties to her day-to-day life impacted her more directly. Robert Lowry, her editor, collaborator, and critic since 1866, died at his Plainfield, New Jersey, home in November 1899 at the age of seventy-three. Plainfield had been the site of his last pastorate, and he had taken an active interest in local events (including the establishing of an indoor musical bicycle club of which he and his wife were charter members). His eulogizers estimated that he had sold some 3 million copies of his books and sheet music. A frequent collaborator with Crosby, he had also been her conscientious adviser and a friend who had welcomed her into his family circle.

Crosby's Brooklyn connections had changed significantly already in 1891 with the death of Joseph Knapp, who succumbed at sea while returning from an unsuccessful quest for health at European spas. Soon after, the Knapp Mansion — where Crosby had often enjoyed hospitality — went up for sale. Phoebe Palmer Knapp lived until July 1908 and remained Crosby's friend, though her occasional interference in Crosby's affairs frustrated others who tended to Crosby's well-being. Sixteen years of wealthy widowhood provided Knapp abundant time to establish herself in Manhattan as a supporter of emerging musical talent and an indefatigable worker for good causes. Her apartments at the Savoy Hotel on the corner of Fifty-ninth Street and Fifth Avenue held a pipe organ larger than those in most churches, and her luncheon musicales drew fashionable audiences. Crosby stayed with Knapp whenever she visited New York. Knapp's sudden death 10 July 1908 from a stroke a few days after she arrived at the swank summer resort at Poland Springs, Maine, broke another tie that reached back to Crosby's emergence as a hymn writer.

In her later years Crosby saw much of Ira and Fannie Sankey. Age could not dispel ingrained habits, and when declining health and the loss of his singing voice slowed Sankey's schedule, he and Crosby still sat and composed together at his harmonium. A famous photo shows Sankey at the organ and Crosby seated nearby, as they arranged texts and tunes. Crosby's summer visits to the Sankey home in Northfield had been one of her delights, and her visits to the family's stately Brooklyn home continued the tradition. Years earlier she had met the famous preacher Theodore Cuyler, of Brooklyn, pastor of the country's largest Presbyterian church, in Sankey's parlor. Sankey's Brooklyn neighbors became Crosby's friends, and the tradition continued in old age. In his *Recollections of a Long Life,* Cuyler said of Crosby: "The venerable and devout blind songstress, Fanny Crosby (whom I often meet at the house of my beloved neighbor, Mr. Ira D. Sankey), has produced very many hundreds of [hymns] — none of very high poetic merit, but many of them of such rich spiritual savour, and set to such stirring airs, that they are sung by millions around the globe."

In 1903 glaucoma completely destroyed Sankey's sight. Some 50 million copies of his hymnals circulated and the public showered him with kindness, but only Crosby seemed able to lift his spirits. His blindness deepened their bond, and his father's condition turned Sankey's publisher son, Ira Allan (Princeton, 1897), to writing hymns in his father's place. For Christmas 1902 Ira Allan Sankey presented his father with his first two hymns, one of which set a Crosby text to music. Ira Allan Sankey's best-known collaboration with Crosby was a hymn written with Ira D. Sankey's discouragement in mind. It brimmed with characteristic Crosby tenacity, "Never Give Up":

Never be sad or desponding,
If thou hast faith to believe,
Grace for the duties before thee
Ask of thy God and receive.

Ira D. Sankey died in the summer of 1908. As he sank into unconsciousness his family heard him softly singing the first stanza of his favorite hymn — Crosby's "Saved by Grace":

Some day the silver cord will break
And I no more as now shall sing.
But, O, the joy when I awake
Within the palace of the King!

Though many of her younger collaborators survived and some — like William J. Kirkpatrick, "Kirkie" to Crosby — kept up a lively correspondence with her, ever fewer of her original circle remained. William Doane was a staunch friend. He now spent his time at Watch Hill, and the guest book in the foyer of his Rhode Island mansion con-

334

tained Crosby's occasional lyrics of greeting and thanks in the hand of anyone available as she came and went.

In August 1910 a Bridgeport newspaper assembled four residents — three women and one man it described as "a very remarkable group" — for a photo it published under the heading "Four Nonagenarians." Crosby sat in the front on the right and was described as "a wonderful personality, retaining her intellectual powers unabated, notwithstanding her advanced age."

In 1911 (at the age of ninety-one) Crosby made her final trip to Manhattan. On 3 May she appeared at the opening rally of the Evangelistic Committee's seventh annual Tent, Open Air, and Shop Campaign. The year before, the committee's summer Christian outreach had attracted over 250,000 New Yorkers to 1,900 meetings in tents and shops and on street corners. The committee prepared for a new thrust by hiring Carnegie Hall (the *New York Times* reported that 5,000 people filled the hall while a massed choir of 200 sat on raised seats at the rear of the stage) for an inspirational kickoff and fund-raiser. "The feature of the exercises was the presence of Fanny Crosby, the venerable evangelist and hymn writer," the *Times* noted. When she entered, the choir and audience burst into "We're Traveling On," a Crosby favorite of long standing. When Crosby rose to speak, her frail body came alive and her voice was "well-pitched" and firm. "Oh, men of the Empire City, you are dear to my heart," she declared. "This scene takes me back to my twenty-five years of mission work. When I came in and when you greeted me so warmly, I wanted to weep tears of joy. This is the first time I have been in this mission (the annual tent campaign), but it is not the first time I have prayed for it. Until every soul has been gathered into Mercy, I shall continue to pray for it." The special hymnal prepared for the tent campaign carried many Crosby texts.

In the fall of 1911 Crosby took ill with pneumonia. She recovered but seemed more frail. She nonetheless honored her commitment to speak in Cambridge, Massachusetts, in December.

After 1911 Crosby appeared less frequently beyond Bridgeport. Her public came to her, and her correspondence kept her secretary Eva Cleaveland busy. Since moving to Bridgeport she had welcomed visitors on Thursday afternoons, but especially as she aged, they came anytime. George Stebbins, one of Moody's song leaders and a hymnal editor at Biglow and Main, came from New York for Crosby's ninety-third birthday. On 31 May 1913 Crosby and her surviving sister, Julia Athington, kept the custom of celebrating their mother's birthday. They placed flowers beneath her picture, set a place for her at the table, and Crosby recited a poem. With heaven even more on her mind than usual, Crosby addressed Julia:

> Once again, oh sister mine,
> Hearts and hands around us twine,
> While together you and I
> Look on yonder radiant sky,
> Where our friends and kindred dwell,
> Never more to say farewell.

On 2 April 1914, on a page devoted to "Modern Womanhood," the *Christian Century* published a tribute to Crosby. Two columns offered an overview of her life, much of it taken from the *Baptist Standard*. The third column (in a report that proved to be greatly exaggerated) announced her death: "Mr. Sankey went to heaven first; he it was who waited for Fanny Crosby. At ninety-two years of age, she followed him into the presence of the King who led her by strange paths to see His glory and do His work."

Crosby was, in fact, ninety-four, and though declining strength confined her more than ever to the environs of Bridgeport, she still kept her secretary busy and laughed at the thought of dying.

In the summer of 1914 (in what proved to be her last trip beyond Bridgeport), Crosby visited her longtime friends Mary and Reuben Currier at their Massachusetts home. An open house on the large lawn gave Crosby the chance to recite poems and address well-wishers, but she did not accept any speaking engagements. In the fall she had a mild heart attack, and seemed to be dying. Once again she believed the prayers of her friends held her back from death:

> Almost in sight of the harbor,
> Almost at home on the shore,
> Only the signal to enter,
> Only a stroke of the oar.

In Crosby's honor the King's Daughters Circle at First Methodist Church (of which Crosby was proud to be a member) took her name and became the Fanny Crosby Circle of the King's Daughters. Crosby maintained a lively interest in their activities, and their attentiveness eased her transition to a slower lifestyle. The Crosby Circle did significant outreach in Bridgeport, from running a Traveler's Aid desk at the Bridgeport Station to aiding the needy and brightening the lives of patients at a local hospital.

Despite Crosby's physical weakness, she made plans for the future. She wrote a dozen hymns for Biglow and Main and others on request for special occasions, and she frequently welcomed visitors. To accommodate the many who requested her autograph, she concentrated on learning to write her name. Father James Nihill, pastor of St. Patrick's Church and activist in Bridgeport's Catholic affairs, dropped by occasionally, as did would-be poets, neighbors, and tourists.

Just after the beginning of World War I, Crosby penned lines that expressed her hope for the world:

Warriors, sheathe the flaming sword,
The right shall rule through Christ the Lord.
'Twill not be long, 'twill not be long,
O praise His name, 'twill not be long!

Thou great supreme and judge of all,
While at Thy feet we humbly fall,
O, grant our prayer, our earnest plea,
That all the world at peace may be.

Evangelist Billy Sunday wrote about stopping in Bridgeport to see her, and she looked forward to a visit that was not to be. In February 1915 Crosby and Doane collaborated for the last time. Bedridden and feeble himself, Doane asked Crosby for text. She responded with the following, suggesting her sense of her own approaching mortality:

At evening time it shall be light,
When fades the day of toil away,
No shadows deep, no weary night,
At evening time it shall be light.

She spoke to her family about her funeral and her memorial, asking for a fund in her name to help the ill and aging in Bridgeport. She summoned a lawyer and drew up a will leaving half of her modest estate to her niece, Florence Booth, who had given her a home for many years. Booth held the remainder in trust for Crosby's remaining sister, Julia Athington. Crosby manifested no qualms about her own future. The anticipation of heaven so common in her hymns had woven itself into the fabric of her being. Every few days she remained in bed, but on Wednesday, 10 February 1915, she was up and about, entertained company, revised her will, and joined the family for dinner.

The next day, 11 February 1915, Crosby did not feel well. She declared her intention to stay in bed, though her niece reported that she got up several times to stand in the doorway and talk ("a habit she loved"). She refused food, but in the evening she summoned her secretary to take a letter to a bereaved family. She then dictated a poem:

> In the morn of Zion's glory,
> When the clouds have rolled away,
> And my hope has dropped its anchor
> In the vale of perfect day,
> When with all the pure and holy
> I shall strike my harp anew,
> With a power no arm can sever,
> Love will hold me fast and true.

Early the next morning Crosby suffered a massive stroke and died. The date was 12 February, the federal holiday (since 1909) marking the anniversary of Abraham Lincoln's birth. "I am lonesome, for she was both my care and my comfort," her niece confided. "But I know she is safely home. What a meeting she must have had with all gone before when — as she said so many times — the first her eyes would behold would be her Jesus."

Four days later Crosby's friends crowded First Methodist Church for her funeral, the largest ever held in Bridgeport. Ira Allan Sankey, Hubert P. Main, and George Stebbins represented Biglow and Main. Eliza Hewitt sent a poem:

> Away to the country of sunshine and song,

Our song bird has taken her flight;
And she who had sung in the darkness so long,
Now sings in the beautiful light;
The harp-strings here broken are sweetly restrung
To ring in a chorus sublime,
The hymns that on earth she so trustfully sung
Keep tune with eternity's chime!

Good-bye, dearest Fanny, good-bye for awhile;
You walk in the shadows no more;
Around you the sunbeams of glory will smile;
The Lamb is the light of that shore!
Some day we will meet in the city above;
Together we'll look on His face;
Safe, "Safe in the Arms" of the Jesus we love;
Together we'll sing, "Saved by Grace."

The headquarters of the King's Daughters sent representatives, as did Connecticut chapters of the Daughters of the American Revolution and Civil War veterans. The music included Crosby's favorite hymn, Frederick Faber's "Faith of Our Fathers," as well as two of her own best-loved texts, "Safe in the Arms of Jesus" and Moody's and Sankey's favorite, "Saved by Grace." A profusion of Crosby's favorite flower, the violet, greeted mourners at the door, and each took one to drop into Crosby's casket as they passed. Crosby's hands clasped the small silk American flag she had always carried with her. She was buried in the Morris family plot at Mountain Grove Cemetery. A small stone marked her grave: "Aunt Fanny, 'She hath done what she could.'"

Crosby's death prompted an outpouring of text in the secular and religious press. Pages crowded with World War I news made space for a paragraph or two about "America's sweet singer in Israel." Quoting the Philadelphia *Record,* the obituary writer for the *Literary Digest* eulogized her as follows: "Miss Crosby expressed universal religious emotion in fluent and rhythmic verse that found an echo in millions of hearts, and while no person can rise to poetic heights as often as she wrote a hymn, she had taste and a sense of melody, as well as piety, and many of her spiritual songs are permanent and valuable additions to religious literature."

The Chicago *News* invited comments from one Lucky Baldwin, head of a rescue mission. "It's the sorriest news I've heard in many a day," he shared. Of one reclaimed soul Baldwin remarked: "By the grace of God and Fanny Crosby's hymn ('Safe in the Arms of Jesus') [he] was led to Christ." The Boston *Transcript* remembered that once Crosby's popular songs had been "whistled all over the country." The paper referenced a recent interview with Crosby to offer samples of her homespun wisdom: "As for my age, it doesn't seem to me that I am in the nineties, and I attribute my good health and long life to the fact that I never let anything trouble me, and to my implicit faith, my implicit trust, in my Heavenly Father's goodness. If I didn't get the thing I wanted today, well, I'd get it tomorrow. If not then, I realized that it wasn't good for me to have it."

The *New York Times* noted the reach of her hymns "into every country of the world where the Christian religion has reached." The hymn writer and musical evangelist George Stebbins summarized her publishers' view: "Fanny wrote for the hearts of the people, and she wrote even better than she knew. She imbued all she ever did with a befitting spirit — the spirit of sweetness." In the rush of the moment, Protestants heaped praise on Crosby's life and work. "What a sublime record she has made in the world," the *Christian Advocate* observed. "If she could be so eloquent in a world of darkness, how much more divinely will she sing when the prophecy in the refrain of one of her own songs is fulfilled, 'I shall see Him face to face.'" Sixty years later (1975) another generation of admirers paid her tribute at the Dove Awards at the Grand Ole Opry House in Nashville when they inducted her into the Gospel Hall of Fame.

Before 1900 Robert Lowry had offered his own measured assessment, one that echoed Crosby's own intuitions:

> Songs and hymns in great numbers are thrown before the public and kept afloat for a time by a mellifluous or "catchy" tune. They have their brief day, and then disappear. Evidently there is something more needed than a mere jingle of words in order to give a hymn an abiding life. . . . There must be in a hymn something which is readily apprehended by the Christian consciousness, coming forth from the experience of the writer, and clothed in strong and inspiring words, if it would hold its place as a perma-

nent factor in Christian worship. The time has not yet come when Fanny Crosby's place among the hymn writers of Christendom may be determined; but it is safe to say that, of the many hymns which have come up from the throbbings of her warm heart, there will be found in the ultimate sifting no inconsiderable number which the world will not willingly let die.

Lowry was right. Generations have sifted the Crosby corpus, but some of it endures. And Crosby always resonated with intimations of the "warm heart" as source of her best and most enduring lines, for this child of the Puritans, pillar of the Sunday school, and gospel troubadour extraordinaire was, after all, a Methodist.

Afterword

When Fanny Crosby's friends approached her about how they might memorialize her, she expressed a strong preference for a venue that carried on her concern for needy humanity. She wanted no grand marble monument like the one P. T. Barnum had erected near the Morris family graves in Bridgeport's Mountain Grove Cemetery. Her friends obliged in the 1920s with the Fanny Crosby Home, a commodious dwelling on Bridgeport's Fairfield Avenue dedicated to offering a congenial atmosphere and caring environment in which, at modest cost, the elderly could live out their days. The home fulfilled this purpose for nearly eighty years until it amalgamated in the 1990s with the Bridgeport Rescue Mission and the property lost its tax-exempt status, jeopardizing the future of both endeavors.

Even as Crosby admirers raised money for the home, Crosby's surviving sister, Julia Athington, challenged Crosby's will. The will had been revised just two days before Crosby's death. It revealed a meager estate — a few cherished pieces of jewelry (of largely sentimental value) and $2,000 cash. Crosby had left $1,000 to Florence Booth (daughter of William Morris whom Crosby called her niece), who had cared for her for eight years. The other half she left in a fund in Booth's care to benefit Athington. Incensed that the $1,000 had not been granted her outright (as it had been in Crosby's first will [1907]), Athington hired a lawyer and went to court. She had no real case, but her action exposed some of the tension in this blended family. Athington attacked Crosby's designation of Booth as her niece, pointing out that no blood relationship existed. She was technically right: the Booth, Tait, and Morris families that had warmly welcomed Crosby among them were the children of William Morris and had no blood ties to the Crosby clan. They were not Mercy Morris's grandchildren, though she had embraced them as such. (Only Athington's grandson, James Leschon, and his daughters, Margery and Dorothy, carried Mercy Crosby's direct lineage forward.) In addition to her bequest from Crosby, Athington inherited on Crosby's death the full value of her sister Carrie Rider's estate, a sum that had been equally divided between Athington and Crosby since Rider's death in 1907. The Bridgeport public had little patience with Athington's unsuccessful challenge. "It seems too bad," one reporter wrote, "that any controversy should have arisen over the small amount which Miss Crosby was able to save out of the little income she had." Athington died in Bridgeport in 1922.

A generation after Crosby's death, a motley crew of self-described "friends of Fanny Crosby to whom her life was an inspiration" dedicated a marker at Crosby's grave in Bridgeport's Mountain Grove Cemetery. On 1 May 1955 an honor guard of Boy Scouts, a choir singing Crosby hymns, clergy from several Protestant churches, and assembled friends marched two-by-two from the cemetery chapel to the grave site for the unveiling. The new marker dwarfed the original gravestone. It bore the first stanza of "Blessed Assurance"; the dates of her birth, marriage (inscribed as 1855 rather than 1858), and death; and the words "Fanny J. Crosby who inspired and edified Christians all over the world by the writing of more than 3,000 hymns and poems."

The number 3,000 represents the low end. Most contemporary and later estimates attribute 8,000. The most recent Crosby movie (released by Gateway Films in 2003) asserts 10,000. The exact number is impossible to establish, and it makes no difference to Crosby's role in molding and expressing nineteenth-century evangelical sentiments. Her ubiquity in several generations of evangelical hymnals is striking and probably greater than is generally realized if one takes into account the number of pseudonyms she used and the vast venues supplied by the hymnals in which her collaborators published her lyrics. Contemporary journalists had an inkling of her reach. They imagined Crosby as "a preacher of righteousness to tens of thousands in every land." "It is a great thing to have such a gift as she possessed," one eulogizer ventured. "It is a greater thing to use it as she used it," writing hymns that sang a gospel "of love and hope, of salvation and faith, and of light beyond the tomb" in an idiom that "brought courage and strength of soul" to countless millions. Contemporaries always noticed that she managed this despite physical frailty, but they seldom acknowledged the context of relational disappointments in which she wrote her hope-filled lines. Despite the varying settings in which she lived out her evangelical faith, despite her Methodism, Crosby remained firmly anchored to the most basic tenets of the Calvinism of her childhood: God has a purpose, and disposition is a matter of choice.

In the Vietnam era, some of a new generation of better-educated and more discriminating evangelicals found Crosby musically and lyrically wanting. "Fanny Crosby has had her day," they insisted. They had a point: many evangelicals proved ready to relinquish the gospel hymnody that had sustained the movement for a century. But eliminating Crosby entirely was another matter, for a handful of her hymns have stood the test of time and made their way into the larger corpus of Protestant hymnody that still nurtures congregations in the evangelical tradition.

Crosby was formed by the values of New England orthodoxy and lived through the democratization of American Christianity. The Institution for the Blind trained her intellect, exposed her to culture, and facilitated the networking that made her achievements possible. As a blind woman, she faced challenges different in important ways from those that made feminists of some of her contemporaries. She had ample opportunities to speak, dictate her thoughts, and find public voice. She lived a nontraditional married life that encouraged her bent toward independence. Her blindness restricted her more than did her gender, yet her blindness also opened vast opportunities. She had nothing to say about contemporary gender matters, though it is tantalizing to note that in 1853 the Women's Rights Convention met on Crosby's turf — at the Broadway Tabernacle — and featured among others her acquaintance William Lloyd Garrison. She must have been exposed to the agenda such conventions promoted, but she left no record of her thoughts.

344

Shortly after Crosby's death World War I and the fundamentalist-modernist controversy (among other things) obliterated the evangelical ethos in which Crosby had thrived. The setting that had responded to her warm, fluid, nondogmatic style yielded to a rigidity driven by harsh conflict. More than most, Crosby encapsulated and popularized a nineteenth-century white northern evangelical ethos. Her evangelicalism, formed among people proud of their Puritan heritage, came alive in Methodism, thrived under gospel preachers of many denominations, and expanded in the world of Manhattan evangelical do-gooders. This blend, and Crosby's situation in Manhattan when Manhattan was a strategic hub for evangelical good works, enlarged her capacity to speak to and for all sorts of evangelicals and their endeavors.

The evangelical community to and for which Crosby spoke had remarkable reach, since from the outset her hymns readily crossed the considerable racial divide to be embraced by African Americans. Crosby, then, provides a wide and populist lens on American evangelical Christianity in the last quarter of the nineteenth century and beyond. Translated, exported, and embraced anew, her voice found a niche in world Christianity. Crosby thus deserves a place among those whose lives have both represented and formed modern evangelicalism.

A Note on the Sources

The dearth of scholarly literature on Fanny J. Crosby is at once surprising and expected — surprising because, for more than a generation, Crosby was one of the best-known North American religious figures. Journalists hailed her as a Protestant saint and portrayed her as an American archetype — a sort of Horatio Alger who by dint of character and hard work cheerfully overcame physical and economic hardship to wield vast positive influence in Victorian America. The frequent telling — by Crosby and a host of admirers — of bits and pieces of her life story created in time a Crosby myth that became embedded in evangelical lore. In this inspirational rendering of her life story, Crosby, the inimitably cheerful blind songwriter, found a place in thousands of Sunday school libraries. In recent years a bevy of Crosby impersonators travel church and religious convention circuits keeping the story alive. Meanwhile, for more than a century most American evangelicals have sung her lyrics, and their missionaries have translated Crosby into scores of languages. On the one hand, one might expect someone so prominently placed in evangelical memory to have commanded serious study. On the other, one must recognize that her blindness and the related lack of private papers frustrate the would-be researcher. Despite her prolific pen and her much-touted exemplary

346

life, few scholars have attempted to assess her place in the context of the history of American Christianity. There has, however, been a steady stream of inspirational accounts of Crosby's life, all based on her autobiographies.

Crosby's several autobiographies are the logical starting point for anyone seeking to place her in the larger story of American Christianity. The most important is *Memories of Eighty Years,* recollections Crosby dictated in 1904 and 1905 and published in 1906. Before attempting to organize her memories, Crosby sent letters requesting help in recalling the details of her life. The surviving responses indicate that her friends considered her memory better than their own. Her memoirs feature descriptions of her childhood, her education, her contacts with well-known people, and stories of her hymns. The book's publication followed that of another book compiled by her friend, poet Will Carleton, entitled *Fanny Crosby's Life-Story, by Herself.* Carleton's Every Where Publishing Company released this book in 1903. It included several photographs and represented a compilation of lectures Carleton had given on Crosby's life. Carleton wrote it in Crosby's voice. It did not feature Crosby's work with her longtime publisher, Biglow and Main, and that omission became part of a running feud between her publishers and Carleton. Both of these books existed in part to provide funds for Crosby's last years. Each also met the demand of her public for her life story.

Until these books appeared, the best available printed sketch of her life was by her longtime friend, the hymn writer Robert Lowry. It appeared in 1897 (with annual reprintings until 1905) as the introduction to a collection of Crosby poems, *Bells at Evening.* In 1915 Samuel Trevena Jackson compiled the other book that came to pass for an autobiography. A New Jersey pastor who spent considerable time with Crosby during the last decade of her life, Jackson presented his notes of their conversations (with "Aunt Fanny" speaking in the first person) as *Fanny Crosby's Story of Ninety-four Years, Retold by S. Trevena Jackson.*

In each of these contemporary accounts of her life, Crosby focused on slightly different aspects of her story. They became the primary sources for much of the inspirational Crosby literature that still enjoys wide evangelical appeal. The earliest of these life sketches (Lowry's) appeared when Crosby was seventy-seven, while the last was published in 1915, the year she died. They relied on her proverbial memory, and they bring to the selective events she narrated the perspective of a long life. While they are invaluable sources, they are limited in significant ways.

In addition to her memoirs, Crosby also published several books of poems: *The Blind Girl and Other Poems* (1844); *Monterey and Other Poems* (1851); *A Wreath of Columbia's Flowers* (1858); *Bells at Evening* (1897).

Another important primary source resides in the rare books section of the Fine Arts Library of the New York Public Library at Lincoln Center. A scrapbook including a random assortment of notes, clippings, invitations, letters, and other ephemera has been styled by some "Fanny Crosby Papers." The scrapbook relates almost entirely to her life after her eightieth birthday. Adelbert White, a young poet and Yale student who acted for a time as her secretary, compiled much of it. Of particular interest is a long list of Crosby pseudonyms that someone wrote on its first pages and notes from some of Crosby's longtime collaborators. The diary of Crosby's stepfather, Thomas Morris, is at the Utah State Archives in Salt Lake City. Librarians in St. Catharines, Ontario, helped me locate the van Alstine family there. The Oswego County historian provided invaluable assistance in tracking the van Alstine family in Oswego. She also copied newspaper accounts of the visit in Oswego of students from the New York Institution for the Blind. Published Crosby family histories help establish Fanny Crosby's lineage. See Nathan Crosby, *A Crosby Family*; and Eleanor Davis Crosby, *Simon Crosby, the Emigrant*. On Enoch Crosby see James H. Pickering, "Enoch Crosby, Secret Agent of the Neutral Ground: His Own Story," *New York History*, January 1966, 61-73; H. L. Barnum, *The Spy Unmasked, or Memoirs of Enoch Crosby*; Guy Hatfield, "Harvey Birch and the Myth of Enoch Crosby," *Magazine of American History* 17 (May 1887): 431-33; James Dean, "Enoch Crosby Not a Myth," *Magazine of American History* 18 (1887): 73-75.

The Billy Graham Center Archives at Wheaton College houses an extensive collection of original manuscripts of Crosby hymns. The property of Hope Publishing Company (successor to Biglow and Main), this collection represents a significant number of the lyrics Crosby prepared under contract with Biglow and Main. Hope Publishing Company also owns an extensive hymnal collection that is housed in the Archives and Special Collections of Wheaton College Library. Of related interest is the private hymnal collection of Hubert P. Main, one of the partners at Biglow and Main who often wrote tunes for Crosby lyrics. Main donated his large library to the Newberry Library in Chicago. The Newberry Library chose not to retain the hymnals as a collection but rather to catalogue them among its general holdings. The Newberry Archives holds the donation record, and this list makes it possible to find the books that once constituted Main's library. These hymnal collections at Wheaton College and the Newberry Library greatly expand possibilities for studying the gospel hymnody of the late nineteenth century. The Billy Graham Center Archives holds several other collections that include materials pertaining to Fanny Crosby. The database of the Hymn Society in the United States and Canada (housed at Oberlin College) includes the publication histories of hymns and makes it possible to track when and where different constituencies embraced Crosby's lyrics.

Of the many popular biographies of Fanny Crosby, the most useful and most widely available is Bernard Ruffin, *Fanny Crosby* (1976). Ruffin, a candidate for Lutheran ordination, stumbled on Crosby while studying at Yale Divinity School and had the opportunity to pursue his interest under the expert guidance of Don Saliers. Ruffin took advantage of proximity to Crosby's last home in Bridgeport, Connecticut, to interview surviving relatives and others who carried dim recollections of an elderly Crosby as well as to use local sources. His book is a delightful mix of anecdotes drawn from Crosby's memoirs and the results of his research and interviews. Other recent biographies have more of a devotional flavor and rely heavily on Crosby's autobiographies. The gist of some is evident in their titles: *Heroines of the Faith; Ten Girls Who Became Famous; Christians You Should Know.* The most worthwhile are Donald P. Hustad, ed., *Fanny Crosby Speaks Again* (1977), which presents 120 little-known Crosby lyrics from Hope Publishing Company's collection; Basil Miller, *Fanny Crosby: Singing I Go;* John Loveland, *Blessed Assurance: The Life and Hymns of Fanny J. Crosby* (1978); and Bonnie C. Harvey, *Fanny Crosby* (1999).

In addition to Bridgeport — where the public library and Golden United Methodist Church offer limited Crosby materials and much Crosby lore — are primary source collections in the Putnam County Historian's Office in Brewster, New York; holdings in the New York

State Library in Albany; and photos in the New York State Archives. The New York Historical Society (Manhattan) preserves, among many other sources useful to the Crosby researcher, city directories, newspapers, church records, and the early records of the New York Institution for the Blind; the New York Genealogical and Biographical Society holds genealogical records pertaining to the Crosby family as well as county and local histories that bear on the story; the Brooklyn Historical Society has rich print and photo collections that enable the researcher to recover the Brooklyn pieces of Crosby's story; the Rare Books Collection at the New York Public Library holds Manhattan's early Methodist records. The Queens Collection in the main branch of the Queensborough Public Library has a wealth of information on the area and churches in which Crosby and her husband made their first home. The Brooklyn Room at the Brooklyn Public Library has a variety of sources valuable to this project. The Methodist Collection at Garrett-Evangelical Divinity School, Northwestern University, holds many relevant nineteenth-century books and Methodist periodicals, including biographies and photos relating to Phoebe Palmer Knapp and her extended family. The Union Theological Seminary Library in Manhattan holds a valuable hymnal collection as well as an extensive collection pertaining to nineteenth-century Manhattan Protestantism. Of special interest are materials relating to Howard Crosby and John Crosby, for example Howard Crosby, *Memorial Papers and Reminiscences.*

Crosby primary sources are scattered far and wide and vary considerably in type. New England colonial sources — town histories, church registers, ships logs, marriage registers, vital records files — offer considerable detail on the early Crosby clan. Manhattan's Bowery Mission has a Steinway piano marked by a plaque that says it was Crosby's. Tradition has it — and living people insist — that with some regularity she attended Manhattan's John Street Methodist Church. There is no written proof: like much in the Crosby story, it is a cherished oral tradition, something "everybody" knows. Crosby's name appeared often in religious and secular periodicals and newspapers, some of which (like the *New York Times*) are now searchable, but most of which are not. The *New England Magazine, Harper's Weekly,* the *Century,* the *Delineator,* the *Union Signal,* the *Christian Herald, Record of Christian Work,* and the *North American Review* are a few of the nineteenth-century magazines useful to a glimpse of aspects of

Crosby's life. A display case in the Methodist museum in Nashville displays doilies Crosby crocheted. Inhabitants of Round Lake, New York, are attempting to prove their hunch that Crosby's "Blessed Assurance" premiered in 1873 at the Round Lake camp meeting. Making that connection still matters deeply. In their minds it would put Round Lake, a fading relic of Victorian America, "back on the map." The oral tradition is deeply embedded and impossible to ignore. Sites like the campgrounds at Ocean Grove, New Jersey, and Round Lake permit glimpses of settings Crosby especially cherished. Her childhood home as well as her childhood church still stand in Southeast, New York.

Internet sources bring nineteenth-century sheet music to any computer screen. The Library of Congress's American Memory Collection allows the researcher to view some of Crosby's Civil War ballads as well as music by Bradbury, Root, and other Crosby cohorts. See http://memory.loc.gov/ammem/amhome.html. Cornell University's "Making of America" offers access to full-text nineteenth-century periodicals and other resources. See http://cdl.library.cornell.edu/moa/. The Cyber Hymnal, www.cyberhymnal.org, posts video and audio versions of many Crosby hymns.

Collections of the papers of Crosby's peers contain information important to Crosby's biography. Most significant are the William Howard Doane Papers at the American Baptist History Center at Rochester Divinity School, Rochester, New York. This large collection includes correspondence with and about Crosby as well as information on copyright and on how Doane and Crosby created hymns. It is unindexed and seldom used. The Lowell Mason Collection at Yale University is a rich source for the emergence of the group of music educators with which Crosby worked most closely. Yale also holds a small collection of William Bradbury Papers. The Southern Historical Collection in the Wilson Library at the University of North Carolina at Chapel Hill holds the papers of Joseph P. Knapp, son of Crosby's collaborator Phoebe Palmer Knapp. Brooklyn newspapers mention the Knapps frequently. I found valuable some of the materials in the Frances Willard Collection at the headquarters of the Women's Christian Temperance Union, Evanston, Illinois. Such collections are supplemented by memoirs like George F. Root's *The Story of a Musical Life* (1891) and Ira Sankey's classic *My Life and the Story of the Gospel Hymns* (1907); William Mason, *Memories of a Musical Life* (1901); Theodore

Cuyler, *Recollections of a Long Life*. The *New York Musical Review* (published under a variety of titles) offers an invaluable window on the activities of Crosby's peers during the 1850s and 1860s as well as on the ideas that undergirded Mason's push for popular music education. Carol Pemberton's 1971 University of Minnesota Ph.D. dissertation, "Lowell Mason: His Life and Work," assesses Mason's associations, as does Arthur L. Rich, *Lowell Mason: "The Father of Singing among the Children"* (1946). Alan Burl Wingard, "The Life and Works of William Batchelder Bradbury" (Southern Baptist Theological Seminary, 1973), presents extensive work in the primary sources.

Students of hymnology have written dissertations (like the two noted above) that explore aspects of the lives of Crosby and her cohorts. While their interests are not primarily large questions pertaining to the story of American Christianity, their research contributes to a growing body of data on which historians can draw. For a century John Julian's pioneering *Dictionary of Hymnology* (1892) has been a logical starting point for an overview of church music. (Julian did not approve of Crosby's style and found it difficult to acknowledge her appeal.) The *New Grove Dictionary of Music and Musicians* (like its on-line counterpart, www.grovemusic.com) is an accessible starting point for understanding nineteenth-century music terms, movements, and leaders.

Also of interest are studies dealing with music education and education for the blind. Horace Mann championed both, and his biographers, like those of Samuel Gridley Howe, offer instructive insights into the larger story. For Howe see www.Perkins.org and *Letters and Journals of Samuel Gridley Howe* (1906); for Mann, Jonathan Messerli, *Horace Mann: A Biography* (1972); Raymond B. Culver, *Horace Mann and Religion in the Massachusetts Public Schools* (1929); E. I. F. Williams, *Horace Mann, Educational Statesman* (1937); Joy E. Morgan, *Horace Mann* (1936). Mann's *Annual Reports on Education,* prepared for the Massachusetts legislature, chronicle his thinking on music education and aspects of his relationship to Mason. These, plus various Mann lectures and pamphlets, are part of the Library of American Civilization microfiche collection. The Lowell Mason Papers at Yale University include correspondence between Mason and Mann. For the New York Institution for the Blind, see www.nyise.org. For an overview see www .disabilitymuseum.org. This site carries numerous relevant manuscripts in full text, including Crosby's *Memories of Eighty Years*. It also posts a large library of images. Two of Crosby's cohorts at the Institution left written reminiscences — S. H. DeKroyft, *A Place in Thy Memory* (1867), and Alice Holmes, *Lost Vision* (1888). The Institution published the program for the "Exhibition by Sixteen Pupils from the New-York Institution for the Blind, in the Presence of the Senate and the House of Representatives, Washington, Wednesday evening, January 24th, 1844" and Crosby, "To The Honorable Senate of New York," an address she gave in 1843. The Institution's history is chronicled in William Bell Wait, *A Manhattan Landmark: The New York Institution for the Blind at Thirty-fourth Street and Ninth Avenue* (1944). For an overview of attitudes toward blindness and education for the blind, see Gabriel Farrell, *The Story of Blindness*; Elizabeth M. Harris, *In Touch: Printing and Writing for the Blind in the Nineteenth Century*; Berthold Lowenfeld, *The Changing Status of the Blind*. Samuel Ward Francis, *Memoir of the Life and Character of Professor Valentine Mott*, introduces the physician the Crosbys consulted about Fanny's blindness. Mrs. C. M. Sawyer, *The History of the Blind Vocalists* (1853), includes contributions by Crosby as well as information on blind musicians.

For Crosby's childhood home in Ridgefield, town and county histories provide much information including evidence of the larger family's involvement in the community: William Blake, *The History of Putnam County, New York*; William Pelletreau, *The History of Putnam County, New York*; Frederic Shonnard, *History of Westchester County New York*; Silvio A. Bedini, *Ridgefield in Review* (1958); George L. Rockwell, *The History of Ridgefield, Connecticut* (1927); Daniel W. Teller, *The History of Ridgefield, Connecticut* (1878). George C. Baker wrote about the introduction of Methodism into Connecticut in *An Introduction to the History of Early New England Methodism, 1789-1839*. Henry Graham, *History of the Troy Conference of the Methodist Episcopal Church*, documents the history of the Round Lake camp meeting, one of Crosby's regular destinations. For Crosby's last home city see Elsie Danenberg, *The Story of Bridgeport*; Samuel Orcutt, *A History of the City of Bridgeport, Connecticut*.

A few dissertations wrestle with Crosby in a theological context — John Howard Danner, "The Hymns of Fanny Crosby and the Search for Assurance: Theology in a Different Key" (Boston University, 1989), and Wayne Frederick Albertson, "Narcissism and Destiny: A Study of the Life and Work of Fanny J. Crosby" (Princeton Theological Seminary, 1992). Also of interest are Patricia A. Tomasetti, "Deep, Wide, and Personal: The Legacy of Fanny Crosby and Her Hymns" (2000); Robyn L. Edwards, "'They Also Serve Who Only Stand and Wait': Resignation in the Lives of Charlotte Elliott, Frances Havergal and Fanny Crosby" (2001).

Historians of copyright and of American business provide valuable insights, too. See, for example, Aubert J. Clark, *The Movement for International Copyright in Nineteenth-Century America* (1960); Ronald V. Bettig, "Critical Perspectives on the History and Philosophy of Copyright," *Critical Studies in Mass Communication* 9 (June 1992): 131-55; Lyman Patterson, *Copyright in Historical Perspective*; Richard Bowker, *Copyright: Its History and Its Law*. On the business side of American music, Russell Sanjek's pathbreaking three-volume *American Popular Music and Its Business* (Oxford University Press) provides rich detail. Sanjek's second volume covers from 1790 to 1909, the period most relevant to Crosby's life. Gilbert Chase's classic text, *America's Music: From the Pilgrims to the Present* (1955), also gives context for the larger circle in which Crosby operated.

A vast literature details the lives of D. L. Moody and, to a lesser extent, Ira Sankey. Perhaps most relevant of the recent studies is Bruce J. Evenson, *God's Man for the Gilded Age*. Contemporary newspapers offer details important to understanding the use and selection of music in Moody's meetings. The most valuable — and almost the only — historical assessment of gospel hymnody is Sandra Sizer's *Gospel Hymns and Social Religion*, a revision of her University of Chicago dissertation. More recently, in *"I Sing for I Cannot Be Silent": The Feminization of American Hymnody, 1870-1920,* June Hadden Hobbs offers a literary assessment of gospel hymns grounded in personal observations and feminist methodology. More popular writing on related subjects appears regularly in the *Hymn*, the organ of the Hymn Society in the United States and Canada. Contemporary responses to gospel hymns and trends in church music surfaced in such magazines as the *Nation, Dial, Leisure Hour, Church Review, Congregational Quarterly, Christian Observer, Christian Examiner, Overland Monthly, Fraser's Monthy, Methodist Quarterly, American Methodist Magazine, Harper's, Outlook,* the *Atlantic,* the *Living Age,* the *Advance, Saturday Review, Guide to Holiness.*

An outpouring of scholarship marked the 1998 centennial of the joining of the five boroughs that compose modern New York City. I found most useful *Gotham: A History of New York City to 1898*, the Pulitzer Prize–winning volume coauthored by Edwin G. Burrows and Mike Wallace. This treasure explores all aspects of Manhattan life, includes a bibliography, and is comprehensively indexed. Nineteenth-century histories of Manhattan provide perspectives from Crosby's time. Many of these can be found in the microfiche Library of American Civilization. Especially helpful are Junius Henri Browne, *The Great Metropolis: A Mirror of New York* (1869); Edward Winslow Martin, *The Secrets of the Great City: A Work Descriptive of the Virtues and the Vices, the Mysteries, Miseries, and Crimes of New York City* (1868); Matthew Hale Smith, *Sunshine and Shadow in New York* (1868); Ezekiel Belden, *New-York: Past, Present, and Future* (1850); J. F. Richmond, *New York and Its Institutions, 1609-1872: A Library of Information* (1872); Charles Haswell, *Reminiscences of New York by an Octogenarian, 1816 to 1860* (1860).

Sources that provide context for Crosby's work in urban missions include Samuel Hadley, *Down in Water Street*; R. M. Offord, ed., *Jerry McAuley: His Life and Work*; Arthur Bonner, *Jerry McAuley and His Mission*; Jerry McAuley, *Transformed; or, The History of a River Thief, briefly told*; J. Wilbur Chapman, *S. H. Hadley of Water Street: A Miracle of Grace*; Emma Whittemore, *Mother Whittemore's Record of Modern Miracles* (1931); Delores Burger, *Women Who Changed the Heart of the City: The Untold Story of the City Rescue Mission Movement* (1997). These are all inspirational in intent. An excellent scholarly treatment of the railroad YMCA in the context of YMCA efforts among workingmen is Thomas Winter, *Making Men, Making Class: The YMCA and Workingmen, 1877-1920* (2002).

Anne M. Boylan's *Sunday School: The Formation of an American Institution, 1790-1880* and Robert Lynn and Elliott Wright, *Big Little School: Two Hundred Years of the Sunday School*, describe the ethos in which much of Crosby's work flourished. Other studies of Victorian America also provide context: Anne C. Rose, *Victorian America and the Civil War; Voices of the Marketplace: American Thought and Culture, 1830-1860*; Andrew Burstein, *Sentimental Democracy: The Evolution of America's Romantic Self-Image*; Mary Lenard, *Preaching Pity: Dickens, Gaskell, and Sentimentalism in Victorian Culture*; George H. Moss, *Victorian Summers*; a WPA Writers' Project pamphlet, *Entertaining a Nation: The Career of Long Branch*.

Crosby was one of the millions who thrilled to Jenny Lind's performances. On Lind see Gladys Denny Shultz, *Jenny Lind, the Swedish Nightingale*; Edward Wagenknecht, *Seven Daughters of the Theater*. For Barnum, Bluford Adams, *E Pluribus Barnum: The Great Showman and the Making of U.S. Popular Culture*; Irving Wallce, *The Fabulous Showman: The Life and Times of P. T. Barnum*. Crosby remembered as well the visit of the phrenologist George Combe. For Combe's American tour, see Charles Gibbon, *The Life of George Combe*, 2 vols. (1878).

I relied on these and many other sources, including a trove of local newspapers, local church histories, and correspondence and conversation with local church secretaries, pastors, and town historians. My forays into the "nearby history" of Northeastern localities proved informative and worthwhile. In pursuit of a sense of the landscape she negotiated, I visited the places in which Crosby spent time, and in each place I expanded my perspective on her life and times. The book is based, then, on varieties of local history plus the traditional local and general sources on which historians rely.

Appendix A: Family Tree

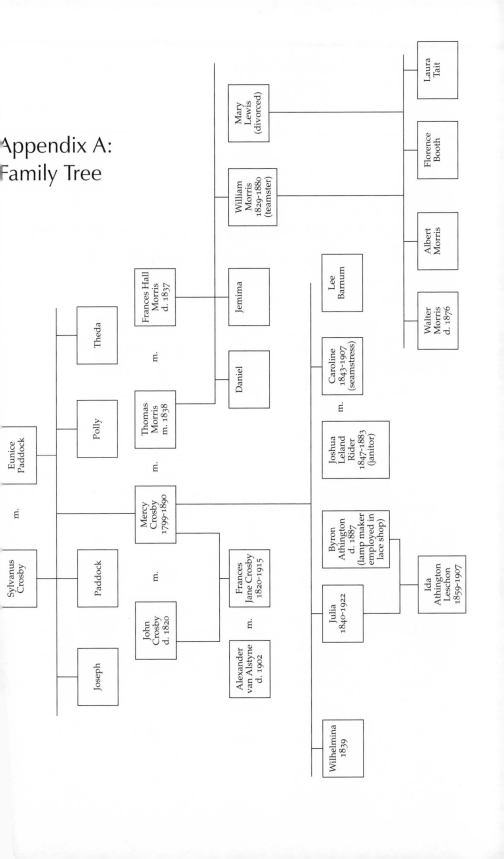

Appendix B:
A Partial List of Fanny Crosby Pseudonyms

##
###
*
Alice Armstrong
Alice Monteith
A. Monteith
Annie L. James
Arthur J. Langdon
Bertha Mason
C.
Carrie Bell
Carrie Hawthorne
Carrie M. Wilson
Catherine Bethune
Charles Bruce
"Children's Friend"
Clara M. Wilson
C. L. Clifford
Cora Adrienne
Cora Linden

D.D.
D.D.A.
D.H.W.
E. D. Jones
Edna L. Park
Eleanor Craddock
Ella Dale
Emily S. Prentiss
F.
F.A.N.
Fannie
Fanny
Fanny Crosby
Fanny J. Crosby
Fanny J. Van Alstyne
Fanny Van Alstyne
F. A. Stowell
F.C.
F.C.D.
F. C. Van Alstyne

F.J.A.
F.J.C.
(F.J.C.)
F. J. Crosby
F.J.V.A.
F. J. Van Alstyne
Flora Dayton
F.O.
Frances J. Van Alstyne
Frank Gould
George Sampson
Grace Frances
Grace Freeman
Grace J. Francis
Grace Lindsey
G.W.W.
Henrietta Blair
Henrietta E. Blair
H. N. Lincoln
(J)
James Apple
James Black
James Elliott
J.C.E.
Jennie Johnson
(Jenny V)
Jessie Clyde
J.F.O.
J. L. Sterling
Julia Sterling
J.W.W.
Kate Marion
Kate Marvin
Laura Miller
Leah Carleton
Lillian G. Frances
Lizzie Edmunds
Lizzie Edwards

L.L.A.
Louise W. Tilden
Louis N. Tilden
Lyman Cuyler
Lyman I. Cuyler
Lyman Schuyler
Martha C. Oliver
Mary J. Cappel
Mary J. Elliott
Maud Marion
Minnie B. Lowry
Miss Grace Elliot
Miss V.
Mrs. A. E. Andrews
Mrs. Alexander Van Alstyne
Mrs. A. Van Alstyne
Mrs. Clara M. Wilson
Mrs. C. L. Clifford
Mrs. Cora Linen
Mrs. E. C. Andrews
Mrs. E. Dale
Mrs. Edna Forest
Mrs. E. L. Andrews
Mrs. Ella Dale
Mrs. Ellen Douglass
Mrs. Ellen K. Chase
Mrs. E. L. Park
Mrs. Fanny J. Van Alstyne
Mrs. Fanny Van Alstyne
Mrs. F. J. Van Alstyne
Mrs. F. V. Alstyne
Mrs. F. Van Alstyne
Mrs. Helen Wells
Mrs. Jennie Glenn
Mrs. Kate Grinley
Mrs. Kate Smiling
Mrs. L. C. Prentice
Mrs. Leah Carleton

Mrs. Lizzie Wilson
Mrs. Louise W. Tilden
Mrs. M. L. Tilden
Mrs. N. D. Plume
Mrs. Rose Matthews
Mrs. V.
Mrs. V.A.
Mrs. Van A.
Mrs. Van Alstyne
Myra Judson
P.E.T.
Rian A. Dykes
Rian J. Sterling
Robert Bruce
Robert Lindsay
Roland Gray
Rose Atherton
Rose Matthews

Ruth Harmon
Ryan A. Dykes
S.
Sallie Martin
Sallie Smith
Sam Martin
S. M. Smith
V.A.
Victoria Francis
Victoria Sterling
Victoria Stuart
Viola
Walter S. Jones
W.H.D.
Wisen Meade
W Tidings
W.W.

Index